The Welsh
at War

The Welsh
at War

THE GRINDING WAR:
THE SOMME AND ARRAS

Steven John

Pen & Sword
MILITARY

First published in Great Britain in 2018 by
PEN & SWORD MILITARY
an imprint of
Pen and Sword Books Ltd
47 Church Street
Barnsley
South Yorkshire S70 2AS

ISBN 978 1 52670 031 5

A CIP record for this book is available from the British Library.

Printed and bound in England by
TJ International Ltd. Padstow, PL28 8RW

Typeset in Times New Roman
by CHIC GRAPHICS

Pen & Sword Books Ltd incorporates the imprints of
Pen & Sword Archaeology, Atlas, Aviation, Battleground, Discovery, Family
History, History, Maritime, Military, Naval, Politics, Railways, Select, Social
History, Transport, True Crime, Claymore Press, Frontline Books, Leo Cooper,
Praetorian Press, Remember When, Seaforth Publishing and Wharncliffe.

For a complete list of Pen and Sword titles please contact
Pen and Sword Books Limited
47 Church Street, Barnsley, South Yorkshire, S70 2AS, England
E-mail: enquiries@pen-and-sword.co.uk
Website: www.pen-and-sword.co.uk

Contents

Acknowledgements

Much of the material within these pages comes from a wide-ranging variety of sources, while details of the casualties themselves come from over a decade of research by the author into Welsh casualties and award-winners. The author is grateful for all the help he has received while carrying out his research into war memorials in west Wales over the past twelve years but is especially grateful to all at Pen & Sword Books, especially Roni Wilkinson, for showing continued support in publishing my work and to Nigel Cave for having the patience to proof-read and correct my last two works; to Pamela Covey for editing this latest series; to John Dart, former curator of the Welsh Regiment Museum at Cardiff for allowing the author to copy several of their excellent photographs; to Les Nixon, of Clynderwen, for his assistance and advice over the last ten years; and also to Bob Pike who, over the last decade, has supplied the author with countless photographs of war graves in France, Italy, Gallipoli and Israel.

The author did originally start out with the intention of writing a chapter on touring battlefield sites that are of interest to anyone following Welsh troops during the war but, as work on the book continued, it became obvious that there were too many stories to try to fit into the confines of this book and also that almost every part of every battlefield of the Great War was visited by Welsh troops at one time or another.

It is therefore recommended that anyone with the idea of visiting the battlefields, especially those of France and Belgium which the author knows well, should gain confidence in the fact that if he can make the trip in his usual disorganized manner then anyone can, but that good maps and guide books, particularly the ones written by Major and Mrs Holt and the more specialized books in the fantastic Battleground Europe series, all of which are available from Pen & Sword, are invaluable and packed with interesting facts. These books also contain tips on travelling, places to stay and must-see places to visit that may otherwise be missed. A list of publications particularly recommended for battlefield touring from the author's personal experience can be found below in the Bibliography section.

While the CWGC publishes a very useful pocket-sized book with maps of France and Belgium overlaid with locations of cemeteries and memorials, it should also be noted that for anyone with a Sat-Nav a free download is available from http:// www.poigraves.uk that contains the locations of almost every war grave in Britain, Belgium and France and makes life for the battlefield tourist so much easier. The download is also available through the Tom Tom updater itself. This excellent resource has proved to be a massive time-saver for the author on his last few trips to France and is highly recommended as preventing domestic disputes!

Introduction

Following the outbreak of the Great War on 4 August 1914, the allies had massively increased the size of their armed forces. By the time the New Year of 1916 dawned, the Canadians and Indians were well-established on the Western Front, the Australians and New Zealanders were in the process of being evacuated to Egypt prior to their move to the Western Front, the South Africans were preparing for their move to the Western Front, and the British army had expanded beyond all recognition.

Lord Kitchener, as Secretary of State for War, had overseen the expansion of the army by the creation of dozens of new divisions. In order to fill these divisions, each regiment had formed extra battalions and Britain was now a sea of khaki, with army camps set up along the length and breadth of these isles.

The Welsh contribution to the war effort thus far had been exemplary. Welsh units had helped stop the German advance on Paris during the early weeks of the war and had then done the same at Ypres by stopping the German drive towards the Channel ports through Flanders during the First Battle of Ypres. Welsh units had fought with some distinction during the Second Battle of Ypres and at Loos during 1915; but the conflict was still in the stalemate of trench warfare.

Recruitment at home had seen the formation of many extra battalions for the regular Welsh regiments – the Royal Welsh Fusiliers, South Wales Borderers and Welsh Regiment – while two wholly new regiments had been formed: the Welsh Horse Yeomanry and Welsh Guards. The Welsh Yeomanry regiments were in Norfolk readying for a move to the Middle East, while a reserve Welsh Division, the 68th (2nd Welsh) had been formed and was training in the area of Northampton and Bedford.

The New Year of 1916 saw Welsh infantry units either in action, ready for action or in training consisted of the following:

The Royal Welsh Fusiliers: thirty Regular, Territorial, Service, Reserve and Garrison battalions.

The South Wales Borderers: seventeen Regular, Territorial, Service, Reserve and Garrison battalions.

The Welsh Regiment: thirty-one Regular, Territorial, Service, Reserve and Garrison battalions.

The Welsh Guards: two battalions; one Regular, one Reserve.

The Montgomery Yeomanry: three battalions, all Territorial; two reserve.

The Pembroke Yeomanry: three battalions, all Territorial; two reserve.

The Glamorgan Yeomanry: three battalions, all Territorial; two reserve.

The Denbighshire Hussars: three battalions, all Territorial; two reserve.

The Welsh Horse Yeomanry: three battalions, all Territorial; two reserve.

This made up a total of ninety-five Welsh infantry battalions, comprising around 95,000 officers and men, plus the Welsh engineer, medical and artillery units attached to the two front-line Welsh divisions and countless other Welshmen and women in uniform serving with other services, regiments and Dominions.

Although Welsh units had taken part in some notable actions during the first sixteen months of the war, the forthcoming campaigns on the Somme, Arras, Messines and the build-up to the Third Battle of Ypres would see blood spilt more thickly than ever before, while new theatres of war would be opened or developed in Egypt, Salonika and Mesopotamia.

This book, the second in a series of three, is not intended to be an encyclopaedic record of all the Welsh units and is not intended to claim that the Welsh were the finest fighting race or that Wales won the Great War, but only to outline the heroic efforts of some of our Welsh forefathers during the epic conflict, to commemorate the actions fought by Welsh units and formations, and to highlight the major battlefields soaked with Welsh blood and sweat.

Each volume of the *Welsh at War* complements the others and details the story of overall Welsh involvement during the Great War.

Chapter 1

1916
The New Year Dawns

As the New Year dawned, as well as carrying out their trench initiation alongside the battalions of the 19th Division, many training schemes took place behind the lines for the newly-arrived men of the 38th (Welsh) Division. Following the introduction of gas warfare in 1915 it became necessary for the men to be instructed in the wearing and use of gas masks, so new recruits were put through gas school, while the battalion specialists received training in their allotted new professions. Bombers, machine-gunners and stretcher-bearers were all put through their paces by battle-seasoned instructors, readying the men for their first spell in the trenches without the guidance of their more experienced comrades.

Daily route marches took place, in almost continual rain, and the men were introduced to the new Mills bomb, a hand grenade designed and produced by William Mills, which replaced the previously amateur jam tins stuffed with nails and explosives. These new grenades in fact turned out to be almost as dangerous for the handler as they were for the intended victim, with many reported incidents of casualties among the men of the 38th (Welsh) Division. Private Shanahan of the 15th Welsh spoke of the dangers surrounding the handling of the Mills bomb:

We were busy fusing Mills bombs, whilst older servicemen were never capable of fusing bombs. Others had not fused a bomb before and to even handle the fuse one had to be extra careful, especially in how you treated the fuse, which was a copper tube containing detonating powder. We were warned that this needed careful handling and was liable to explode merely by handling it

A sectioned Mills hand grenade, a weapon that was to prove invaluable in trench warfare.

too long before inserting it into the centre of the bomb. The bombing, when demonstrated, seemed straight forward, but when you were standing in the trench, the pin holding the lever in one position, the arm poised to throw, a sort of paralysis seemed to affect the hand which became unwilling to leave the bomb go. You were sometimes so nervous that you would be liable either to drop it at your feet or throw it only as far as the trench top. I suppose that's why the instructors got into the next bay of the trench, to be out of danger.

The standard aimed for was that every man should throw 2 live bombs and that 128 men per battalion should be expert bombers, while 384 men should have thrown at least 10 live bombs. Due mainly to mechanical defects and sometimes to mishandling, several accidents occurred, one such killing an officer. On 12 January 1916 Lieutenant David Lyndsey Stranack Gaskell of the 16th Welsh died after being wounded during grenade practice the previous day. Gaskell was a solicitor and had worked for Thomas Mears of Great George Street, Westminster, prior to joining the Honourable Artillery Company on 10 August 1914 and was commissioned in the 16th Welsh on 20 May 1915. He is buried in St. Venant Communal Cemetery.

Lieutenant David Lyndsey Stranack Gaskell of the 16th Welsh died on 12 January 1916 after being wounded during grenade-practice the previous day.

Accidents with grenades led to the rare award of the Albert Medal to an officer of the 15th Royal Welsh Fusiliers (RWF). Second Lieutenant William Marychurch Morgan was attending a grenade instruction school at Locon when a man dropped a primed grenade. Morgan groped around in the mud for the bomb before throwing it safely away, saving several lives. Obviously a very brave man, Morgan was awarded the Military Cross later in the year. He was the son of the Reverend William Morgan, Congregational Minister at Saundersfoot and Sardis.

While grenade practice was dangerous, the troops were also finding out how dangerous the front line was as a steady stream of casualties began to be suffered. During January 1916 seventy-eight men from the division were killed while they were still in the so-called 'Nursery Sector', a quiet sector selected for training fresh divisions.

Breastworks in Flanders, similar to positions in which the 38th (Welsh) Division would have first served.

*Rifleman James Henry John (S/1027), 11th Rifle Brigade. John was the son of James and Mary Ann John of 1 Prospect Place, Haverfordwest. He enlisted at Barry on 4 September 1914 in the Rifle Brigade and after training at Winchester was posted to the 11/Rifle Brigade, which was attached to 59 Brigade, 20th (Light) Division. On 26 July 1915 the division completed concentration in the Saint Omer area, all units having crossed to France during the preceding few days. Early trench familiarization and training took place in the Fleurbaix area. When the Battle of Loos was launched on 25 September 1915 the division fought a diversionary attack towards Fromelles. Over the winter of 1915/16, the division remained in positions south of Ypres and fought at the Battle of Mount Sorrel in June alongside the Canadian Corps. They then fought through the Somme Offensive, at the Battles of Delville Wood and Guillemont. John was killed during this period on 27 August 1916. He was 25 years old and is buried at Péronne Road Cemetery, Maricourt. (*Courtesy of Philip Slade*)*

Meanwhile, in a letter sent home to his parents in Haverfordwest, which was published in the *Western Telegraph* at the beginning of 1916, James Henry John (S/1027) of 12 Church Gardens, Prendergast, who was serving in another sector with the Rifle Brigade, wrote:

The weather the last few weeks has been very miserable and the trenches are in a very bad state. It's impossible to walk without getting knee deep in mud and water, and it is also very cold, while to make things worse our dug-out is leaking so that we find it difficult to get a dry place to rest in. Well, never mind, we're not downhearted, and what is more we don't intend to be. It is some consolation to know that Fritz has to put up with the same. We are working one week in the trenches with four days rest and so on. We have been served out with fur coats now, and they are also going to give us jack boots, and the sooner these come the better, as we shall then enjoy dry feet. Last week we were billeted in some empty houses in the ruins of a town about a mile behind the firing line. It was rather draughty and a bit hard, but all the same quite a luxury after the dug-outs.

Jim had been eager to get involved in the war at its outbreak and enlisted in the 11th Rifle Brigade. However, his regret at his impulsive enlistment into a non-Welsh unit can be noted further into the letter:

Our battalion has been specially mentioned in dispatches, so we really should be proud to belong to such a good old corps, though I sometimes wish that I had joined one of the Welsh regiments. But as we are out for the same thing it really does not matter much. I remember well when the recruiting officer asked me what I wished to join, I replied: 'Anything, so long as it is the Army.'

He was, for the time being, fortunate that he had not joined the Welsh as the new army battalions were having a torrid time. The 14th Welsh 'Swansea Pals' had lost Lieutenant Donald Henry Devenish, a South African farmer, killed during a grenade training accident on 17 January, and then on 27 January a platoon of men from the battalion was sheltering in a dugout when a German shell crashed into the

The Gilchrist brothers, Levi and Tom, who enlisted together in the 14th Welsh. Levi was killed in his dugout on 27 January 1916 and is buried in St. Vaast Post Military Cemetery, Richebourg-l'Avoué.

mouth of it, killing five men and injuring two. The dead men were all from the town: Private Levi Gilchrist (17753) of Morriston; Private James Lumsdaine (17756) of Port Tennant Road; Private William Edward Paddison (17741) of Swansea; Private George William Sloper (17789) of Swansea; and Private Thomas Smitham (17758) of Dyfatty Terrace.

Privates James Lumsdaine (17756) of Port Tennant Road and William Edward Paddison (17741) of the 14th Welsh, killed together on 27 January 1916 and are buried in St. Vaast Post Military Cemetery, Richebourg-l'Avoué.

The two North Wales battalions, the 13th and 17th RWF, were also having a hard time of it. Over two days, 19 and 20 January, the battalions lost four men apiece killed, one of whom was a student at the University of Bangor prior to enlisting. Private Robert Jervis (17869) was the son of Thomas and Eliza Jervis of Gerlan Schoolhouse, Bethesda. His father was a personal friend of Brigadier General Owen Thomas, commander of 113 Brigade, and received the following letter about his son's death:

Private Robert Jervis (17869) of the 13th RWF, son of Thomas and Eliza Jervis of Gerlan Schoolhouse, Bethesda, Bangor.

It is with very great regret that I have to inform you of the death by accident of your son Robert, who was killed owing to the premature explosion of a bomb (hand grenade). Your son and another died shortly afterwards from serious wounds in the head. They were buried with due ceremony in the little British Cemetery nearby. I deeply regret the loss of your son, who has always been a good and steady lad, and I understand that he had just been gazetted as a second-lieutenant, and would have proceeded home in a few days to take up his new duties: this makes it all the more sad. I tender to you and your family my sincere sympathy. Your consolation is to know that your son died at his post doing his duty for his King and country just as much as though he had been killed in action.

Jervis and Private Frank Piper (33476), who had died alongside him, are buried side-by-side in Le Touret Military Cemetery, Richebourg-l'Avoué.

While the 38th (Welsh) Division was settling into trench warfare, the 2nd RWF were having a torrid time in the line at Cambrin, a sector the 38th (Welsh) Division would soon move into. The battalion had already begun suffering a stream of casualties through the Germans blowing underground mines in the sector, mostly through the attempts to consolidate the mine craters, and on 5 February the battalion was ordered to sap out to three freshly-blown craters and consolidate them by the digging of a new trench, linking them together and into the front line held by the battalion. Captain Stanway, a fierce soldier, led the party out and the work was completed by daybreak with the loss of eight men killed, Lieutenants J.M. Owen and C.R.J.R. Dolling and twenty-eight other ranks wounded. The dead men were Private Philip Davies (17014) of Hyde, Cheshire; Corporal William Grainger (8380) of Burslem, Stoke-on-Trent; Private Timothy Morris (23076) of Llansantffraid, Montgomery; Corporal John Mountford (9041) of Birmingham; Private David Nekrews (17367) of Port Tennant, Swansea; Private Joseph William Parry (5287) of Rhuddlan; and Private Walter Sargant (9882) of Birmingham, all of whom are buried in Cambrin Churchyard Extension. Private William Hopkins (6410) of Pengam has no known grave, and is commemorated on the Loos Memorial.

While many men were brave and willing to fight, on 7 February 1916 Private James Grist Carr (10874) of the 2nd Welsh became the eighth Welshman of the Great War to be executed in France. Carr had been detained after deserting from the battalion, but was caught and escaped detention before being recaptured. He had no previous convictions, but because of his escape attempt he was sentenced to death and executed at Auchel on 7 February. Carr was just 21 years old and is buried in Auchel Communal Cemetery.

The grave of Private James Grist Carr (10874) of the 2nd Welsh. Carr was shot for desertion on 7 February 1916 and is buried in Auchel Communal Cemetery.

During January the 1st SWB (South Wales Borderers) moved into reserve at the village of Ferfay, about 8 miles west of Béthune. Training regimes were carried out over the coming weeks, while drafts of reinforcements joined the battalion and on 14 February they marched to Maroc in readiness to re-enter the line. The men provided working parties behind the line for two days before moving into the frontline trenches on 17 February, relieving the 2nd Munsters at Loos.

The morning of 19 February was wet and miserable, and the men were on alert after noticing a flurry of activity in the German lines. This activity was thought to have been caused by a mining party, so during the night a party of men was sent out to investigate, capturing the edge of a position known as Harrison's Crater. Second Lieutenant Victor Charles Moore Mayne and four men were killed in the engagement and three officers were wounded. Mayne was born on 22 January 1896, the son of Colonel Charles Blair Mayne and Victoria Amelia Mayne of Camberley, Surrey. He was educated at the United Services College and the Imperial Service College before attending the Royal Military College, Sandhurst and was commissioned in the 1st SWB on 11 November 1914. He is buried in Canadian Cemetery No. 2, Neuville-St. Vaast. On the following day five more men from the battalion were killed while holding on to the newly-captured position at Harrison's Crater.

The two other Welsh battalions in the 1st Division, the 2nd Welsh and 6th Welsh, had in the meantime been kept busy constructing new trenches and defences. During one night in January 1916 the 6th Welsh dug a new support trench almost 300 metres long. The 2nd Welsh were put to work on the defences of Loos village.

Meanwhile at Ypres, following German phosgene attacks near Frezenberg on 19 December 1915, a defensive plan had been drawn up to make the line more resilient to any further attacks. On 4 February the 10th RWF had moved into a rest camp at Poperinghe, some miles behind the lines, where it received a number of reinforcements from Litherland Camp. Major Steuart Scott Binny assumed command of the battalion on the following day.

Facing the British near the village of Hollebeke on the left was Hill 60 and Zwarteleen and on the right St. Eloi. On the northern embankment of the canal, a spoil heap created when the canal was excavated and known as the Bluff gave the British front a viewpoint over the enemy. The retention of the Bluff was imperative to the British, who were determined to hold the position at all costs.

The German front line lay some 200 metres in front of the Bluff and the ground was scattered with small mine craters that had been blown at regular intervals between October 1915 and January 1916. Communication trenches ran back over the Bluff itself, while the canal cutting was steep-sided and over 100 metres wide, with the trenches on either side connected by a plank bridge.

The Germans began shelling Hooge and the Bluff on the morning of 14 February and at 5.45 pm the Germans blew three more mines, one under the Bluff, which buried a platoon of the 10th Lancashire Fusiliers, and two slightly further north underneath positions held by the 10th Sherwood Foresters. Shortly afterwards, German infantry attacked between the canal bank and the cutting. They entered and captured the frontline trenches but after fierce fighting were driven out of the support lines behind the front. However, the Bluff was now in their hands.

Lieutenant General Hew Dalrymple Fanshawe, commanding V Corps, ordered the 17th Division to recapture the Bluff and the German position known as the Bean and placed 76 Brigade, 3rd Division under their command for the operation. In response to this, the 10th RWF began moving up to the front line, reaching the trenches on 16 February. On the following day the battalion was caught up in some heavy fighting, losing two officers – Captain Bernard Digby Johns and Second Lieutenant Adrian Victor Cree – and twenty men killed. Three officers and thirty-five men were wounded.

Captain Bernard Digby Johns, 10th RWF, was the only son of Mr A.C. Johns of Carrickfergus. He was educated at Hatfield Grange, Repton and Oriel College, Oxford. In September 1914 he was commissioned in the 10th RWF. He had only just returned to the battalion after a week's leave when he was killed on 17 February 1916.

Heavy fighting continued here for the 10th RWF over the coming days, with six men killed and six wounded on the following day. On 19 February Captain John Arthur Walker was killed along with nine of his men while moving to trenches at Gordon Terrace, near St. Eloi. Captain Walker was the only son of John and Margaret Walker of Osborne House, Llandudno. He was educated at Shrewsbury, and at the outbreak of war was at Trinity Hall, Cambridge. He joined the Officer Training Corps (OTC) and was commissioned on 13 November 1914. He is buried in Reninghelst New Military Cemetery. There is a three-light stained-glass window memorial to him in St George's Church, Llandudno and he is commemorated on the Llandudno War Memorial.

The area between the Bluff and St. Eloi had become a hotspot, with the Royal Engineers tunnelling companies busy digging beneath the German front lines in order to lay a series of explosive charges or mines in order to attempt to break the stalemate. Six of these mines would be detonated in a little over twelve months' time.

On 2 March 76 Brigade attacked the area around the Bluff in a further attempt to recapture the position. The 10th RWF was in support of the 2nd Suffolks and suffered the loss of fourteen men killed, four officers and sixty-seven men wounded. A stretch of lost trenches was recaptured but the Bluff remained in German hands. As testimony to the state of the ground here at the time, all the men killed have no known graves and are commemorated on the Menin Gate Memorial. On the following day the battalion suffered even greater casualties after a shell fell on the HQ dugout and the battalion was immediately hit by a German raid. Four officers – Lieutenant Colonel Steuart Scott Binny, Major Edward Freeman, Captain (and Adjutant) William Thomas Lyons and Second Lieutenant

Captain John Arthur Walker of Osborne House, Llandudno, killed at Gordon Terrace near Ypres on 19 February 1916.

The Peace Pool at Spanbroekmolen, blown during the Battle of Messines in 1917 but very similar to the craters blown at St. Eloi, several of which still survive and provide fishing facilities for the locals.

Lieutenant Colonel Steuart Scott Binny of the 10th RWF. Born in Sydney on 1 July 1871, Binny was given command of the battalion in February 1916, after a long and distinguished military career. He was killed by a shell while in his dugout on 3 March 1916 and is buried in Spoilbank Cemetery.

Major Edward Freeman, second-in-command of the 10th RWF. The son of Harold and Alice Freeman of Malvern Wells and the husband of Katherine Freeman of Gallt-Y-Beran, Pwllheli, he was killed alongside Lieutenant Colonel Binny in their dugout on 3 March 1916 and is buried in Spoilbank Cemetery.

The grave of Major Edward Freeman at Spoilbank Cemetery.

William Hughes – and twelve men were killed. Unusually for a battalion war diary, every man killed, wounded or missing during the action was named in the diary entry.

The loss of its CO and second-in-command was a major blow to the battalion; Major G.R. Crosfield of the South Lancs assumed command.

At the end of February the 38th (Welsh) Division began to march south to take over a new section of the line near the La Bassée Canal. The ground was very similar to

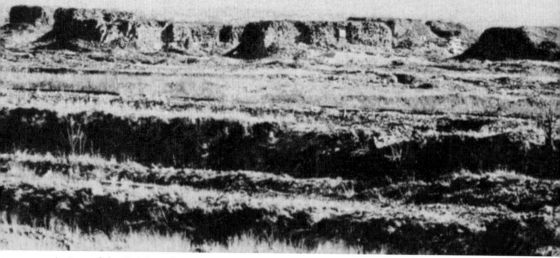

A view of the Brickstacks at Cuinchy, a notorious hotspot that had given the British terrible trouble during the Battle of Loos the previous year. Now it was the turn of the 38th (Welsh) Division to hold the line here.

that which the division was already accustomed to, flat and marshy; but here, below ground, lay a new terror as the Germans had been excavating tunnels beneath the British lines for several months in order to lay mines. They were also a lot more active in this sector, as the Welshmen would discover.

On 1 March 1916 the 15th Welsh of 114 Brigade began its move to this new sector, with companies spaced at regular intervals as laid down by Field Service Regulations, via a route through La Couture, Locon and La Pannerie. Battalion headquarters was set up on the La Bassée Canal. By this time Brigadier General Thomas Owen Marden, CB, CMG, DSO had become commander of 114 Brigade. Marden was a seasoned warrior who had commanded the 1st Welsh since its arrival in France and his experience was vital for this New Army division. All the Welsh units in France spent the second St David's Day of the war celebrating in the usual fashion once again: leeks, where available, were worn on their hats and units lucky enough to be out of the line sat down for celebratory dinners. Sergeant Hughes from Chirk wrote home to his parents:

> We celebrated Taffy's Day with all due ceremony. Leeks were plentiful, as all gardens in France seem to have very little else left. I think the Frenchmen thought us all mad. Where I stay there are about six or seven people living, all women, and I tried to explain to them what it was all about. They are, like most French people, very religious and were fairly shocked when I told them in my best Sunday French that it was 'the feast of the sacred leek'! I don't think that saint is in their calendar of saints, though it seems a fairly long one.

On the following day the 14th RWF, which was already in positions on the new section of the front, were in a position known as Gunner's Siding, which they had taken up on the previous afternoon. German working parties out in no man's land had been fired upon in the early morning, and a patrol from the 14th RWF had gone out under cover of darkness to leave propaganda letters near the German wire. Some intermittent machine-gun fire from the RWF broke the peace at dawn, but this prompted an angry response from the Germans who fired a trench mortar shell, making a direct hit on the entrance to Coventry Street trench opposite D Company HQ, killing five men and wounding another. All five men are buried in what is essentially a mass grave in Guards Cemetery, Windy Corner, Cuinchy. Also killed and buried in the mass grave were two men of the 15th Cheshires who had been attached to the battalion for instruction. The 14th RWF casualties were Private Robert Dale (20847) of Bagillt; Private Thomas Burton Hughes (20765) of Cilfynydd; Corporal Thomas Robert James (21070) of Widnes; Private George Henry King (21081) of Abertridwr; and Private Gilbert Roberts (19676) of Chirk.

On 5 March 1916 a number of officers from the 38th (Welsh) Division attended a demonstration of the use of the new flame-throwers and rockets. Flame-throwers had been used by the Germans at Ypres, where they devastated the British defenders at Hooge on 30 July 1915 and caused terror among the troops. Luckily for the Welsh, they were never fated to come across this awful weapon.

At 9 pm on 8 March 1916, the 15th Welsh relieved the 16th RWF in the trenches at Grenadier Street. After a successful relief, the men of the 15th Welsh settled down for a deserved night's sleep while designated sentries kept watch. They were rudely awoken by a terrifying noise on the following morning when a German mine was

The 'Mass Grave' at Guards Cemetery, Windy Corner, Cuinchy which contains the four men of the 14th RWF who were killed by a trench mortar shell on 2 March 1916, along with two men of the 15th Cheshire Regiment who were attached to them at the time.

blown opposite I Sap and the Germans launched a heavy trench mortar and artillery attack on the Welsh positions. This incurred the battalion's heaviest losses in a single day so far, with seven men killed and fifteen wounded and evacuated for treatment. The seven fatalities were all buried at Guards Cemetery, Windy Corner, Cuinchy.

Among the dead was 22-year-old Private Arnold Cecil Ewart Lewis (35027). Lewis was the son of Benjamin and Elizabeth Lewis of Pontycymmer, a mining town in the Garw Valley. His parents were from Saundersfoot but had moved to Pontycymmer looking for work. They both died of tuberculosis when Lewis was just 6 years old and he and his sister went to live with Bill and Ann Frost at Stammers in Saundersfoot. Bill was a carpenter and something of a local celebrity, having built his own wooden and canvas aeroplane in 1894, at least seven years before the Wright Brothers flew their own aircraft. According to an article in the *Tenby and County News* of 9 October 1895, it was reported that: 'Mr William Frost, Saundersfoot, has obtained provisional protection for a new flying machine, invented by him, and is supplying designs to secure a patent.' Local legend has it that Bill did indeed fly his invention for at least ten seconds at some time in 1894,

Private Arnold Cecil Ewart Lewis (35027), 15th Welsh, of Saundersfoot, killed by the firing of a German mine on 9 March 1916. (David Harries)

and so today Bill Frost is regarded in many circles as the first man to have ever flown an aeroplane. Lewis is buried alongside his fallen colleagues at Guards Cemetery, Windy Corner, Cuinchy and is commemorated on the Saundersfoot War Memorial outside St. Issell's Church.

That was not the last action of the day, however, as at 7.30 am another mine was blown between K and T Sap, and a larger mine was blown at 2.30 pm at the Duck's Bill, north of Neuve Chapelle. Fortunately no further casualties were inflicted on the battalion with these explosions, and the rest of the day passed quietly after the solemn burial of their seven comrades. However, the Duck's Bill would see further action before too long.

Mining was proving to be a real problem. On 14 March a party of men from the 5th SWB were at work in an underground pump house near the Duck's Bill when the Germans detonated another mine, destroying half the Duck's Bill Salient and bringing the roof of the mine down on the two men inside, burying them underground: Private Thomas Jones (14141) of Cynwyl Elfed, and Private Francis Charles Bennett (18098) of Pontardawe. Captain Croft quickly assembled a party of men to fill the gap left in their defences and five more men fell during the dash across no man's land under heavy fire. The two men killed in the mine gallery still lie underneath the now peaceful fields and are commemorated on the Loos Memorial. The other five men were Lance Sergeant John Bowen (18302) of Bryncoch, Sergeant Owen Connolly (13293), Private Harry John Hall (17986) of Stroud, Sergeant Charles Howe (18284) of Grangetown and Private William Skelton (14773) of Newport, all of whom are buried in Pont-du-Hem Military Cemetery, La Gorgue.

On the same day, the fourth of thirteen Welsh international rugby players to fall during the war was killed. Sergeant Louis Augustus Phillips (PS/5457) was born at Newport on 24 February 1878, the son of Charles and Rose Phillips. He played at scrum half for Newport and played throughout the Triple Crown-winning year of 1900, winning his fourth and last cap the following season before suffering a serious knee injury. In 1907 and 1912 he was Welsh Amateur Golfing Champion. Phillips enlisted in the 10th Royal Fusiliers at the outbreak of war. He was killed in action at Cambrin on 14 March 1916 and is buried in Cambrin Churchyard Extension.

Cambrin Churchyard Extension.

Back on the home front, London was twelve months into suffering its first blitz at the hands of the dreaded Zeppelins. These lighter-than-air craft flew at such great altitudes that existing designs of aircraft could not reach them and anti-aircraft batteries sited around the capital seemed unable to cause them any damage. However, all that changed late in the evening of 31 March 1916 when the first Zeppelin, L15, was shot down over London by crews of the Royal Artillery. The aircraft sustained damage to two gas cells and lost height before coming down in the sea, some 15 miles off Margate. Several crews claimed this first victory over the skies of London so the Lord Mayor, Sir Charles Wakefield, had a number of gold medals struck and awarded to the crews involved. Among them was a young gunner from Roath, Cardiff: James Henry Thompson (104).

Thompson had worked as a machinist for John Bland & Co. in Cardiff prior to enlisting into the Glamorgan Battery of the Royal Garrison Artillery on 11 June 1912. On 5 August 1914 he was embodied and was posted to Woolwich before joining No. 10 AA Battery. Following his part in the downing of L15, Thompson suffered several spells in hospital before being posted to France with the 221st Anti-Aircraft Section, RGA. He survived the war but died of influenza at No. 35 General Hospital, Calais on 29 November 1918 aged 24. He is buried in Les Baraques Military Cemetery, Sangatte. There was a joint claim for his medals from his widow Alice, who he had married on 28 February 1917, and his parents after his death but his war gratuity and medals were eventually sent to Alice.

In the Middle East, another theatre of war had erupted into action. This time it was in Mesopotamia, which had long been held by Ottoman troops, whilst other Welsh troops were settling into the line in Salonika.

Chapter 2

Mesopotamia:
The Siege of Kut

The 13th (Western) Division (8th RWF, 4th SWB and 8th Welsh) was ordered to Mesopotamia in February 1916 after its evacuation to Egypt from Gallipoli. Mesopotamia is an ancient Greek word which means '[land] between rivers' and accurately describes its position between the great Biblical rivers of the Tigris and Euphrates. The modern name of Mesopotamia is Iraq and its capital is Baghdad. The country is bare and dry and is well encapsulated by an old Arab saying: 'When Allah had made Hell he found it was not bad enough. So he made Iraq and added flies.' The campaign here would be dominated by terrible conditions and high rates of sickness and disease.

Baghdad.

After Turkey had come out as an active ally of Germany, Britain realized the need to force this once mighty empire out of the war. The failed Gallipoli campaign was originally thought to have been the solution to accomplish this quickly, but with the peninsula evacuated and the chance to bombard Constantinople gone it was realized that the only way to beat Turkey was to take her lands from her.

Britain controlled large swathes of land in Mesopotamia, including the vitally-important Anglo-Persian oilfields, but these were under threat from the Turks so Britain began sending troops to the Persian Gulf on 16 October 1914. Turkey committed an act of war against the allies on 30 October, and on 5 November the allies declared war on Turkey. On 6 November the Indian Brigade captured Fao, a fort protecting the mouth of the Shatt al-Arab, and on the following day landed at Abadan. On 13 November General Barrett arrived with the remainder of the 6th Indian Division and advanced on Basra, defeating the Turks.

The Turks had not expected an offensive in Mesopotamia and had removed much of its garrison to fight the Russians in the Caucasus and to reinforce their positions in Egypt. However, by early 1915 they had amassed enough troops there to launch a counter-offensive, so the 12th Indian Division was sent to reinforce the 6th Division and together with a cavalry regiment formed the II Indian Army Corps under the command of Lieutenant General Sir John Nixon.

Before the 12th Division had arrived, the Turks had attacked Basra from the desert route leading from Nasiriya. However, Barrett's 6th Indian Division beat off the Turkish attack and had retained Basra. The 12th Indian Division, under General Gorringe, arrived and advanced up the Karun River, pushing back the Turks and securing the oilfields. On 31 May the 6th Division, under Major General Townshend, defeated the Turks at Qurna and pursued them to the city of Amara which was occupied on 4 June 1915.

After more fighting the British gained control of almost all Lower Mesopotamia and decided to seize the town of Kut, the only place south of Baghdad that could serve the Turks as a strategic centre. British and Indian troops assembled on the Tigris at Ali Al-Gharbi and on 27 and 28 September General Townshend gained another victory, pursuing the Turks back 60 miles beyond Kut, where the pursuit came to an end on 5 October.

On 21 November Townshend advanced again but, after suffering heavy casualties and with many men weakened by sickness, the allies were forced to retire to the town of Kut. The town stands within a loop of the River Tigris and was well stocked with supplies of ammunition and food. The Turks had advanced to within 5 miles of Kut and Townshend was forced to decide whether to hold the city or to retire further. With a lack of available boats with which to evacuate the men and supplies he decided to hold fast, but evacuated all the sick and wounded and the 1,300 prisoners taken at Ctesiphon. By 7 December some 11,600 allied troops were in Kut, which began to be subjected to Turkish artillery fire. This marked the beginning of the Siege of Kut, where Townshend's gallant force was surrounded by the Turks; and it would last until 29 April 1916.

As a result of the disaster that had befallen Townshend's force, the British responded by sending more troops to Mesopotamia and it was for this reason that the 13th (Western) Division was moved from Egypt.

The first relief expedition comprised some 19,000 men already in Mesopotamia under the command of Lieutenant General Aylmer VC and moved up the river from

Ali Al-Gharbi in January 1916. On 6 January Aylmer's advance force, under Major General George Younghusband, moved forward from Ali Al-Gharbi towards Sheikh Sa'ad along both banks of the Tigris and came into contact with the Turks.

On the following day, 7 January, Aylmer arrived with the main forces and attacked; however, despite some success, the Turks held firm. Another attack on 9 January forced the Turks to withdraw but heavy rains fell, making the advance hard going for the British. After retreating for 10 miles the Turks dug in behind a wadi and on the other side of the Tigris. Aylmer's forces attacked again on 13 January, forcing the Turks into another retreat of 5 miles. Here they made a stand at the Hanna Defile, a narrow strip of dry land between the Tigris and the Suwaikiya Marshes, and the British suffered heavy losses.

By now over 20,000 reinforcements had joined the Turks and with Aylmer's advance ending in defeat at the Dujaila Redoubt on 8 March, he was replaced by Lieutenant General George Gorringe on 12 March. By then the 13th Division had arrived and Wales now had three battalions in Mesopotamia.

The 8th RWF had embarked at Suez on 14 February and reached Basra on 28 February. The 4th SWB embarked at Suez on 15 February, just 400 strong, and arrived at Basra on 4 March. On 18 February the 8th Welsh, comprising 22 officers and 862 other ranks, embarked for Mesopotamia under Captain Davidson DSO, Royal Scots Fusiliers and arrived at Basra on 6 March. The Tigris had flooded and conditions underfoot were terrible. The route taken by the 8th RWF upstream was recorded in the personal diary of Captain Powell, which was published at some length over several pages of the *History of the Royal Welsh Fusiliers*:

We started up the river about midday, being kept owing to the tide. Two hospital ships passed us to-day. The river is about a mile wide here, the banks being very green with cactus plants and palms. The country is very flat. We passed a large town with an unpronounceable name, but important owing to the oil works there, and anchored in midstream about six... About 5 o'clock we passed the tomb of the Prophet Ezra. It had a wonderful dome of turquoise-blue tiles. The colour is wonderful, and I believe they are unable to produce work like it nowadays, as the secret is lost. The tomb must be very old. The country is very bare and marshy, and we frequently stick on the mud... Reached Amara, our immediate base, about 2.30, and tied up there for the night. The bazaar was most picturesque and amusing. They have a large pontoon bridge across the river there, which swings open when anything wants to pass. The Arabs seem very friendly, but they are treacherous brutes.

The units of the 13th Division were landed beside the Tigris at Magil, 3 miles above Basra, and over the coming days began to embark for Sheikh Sa'ad, where the 13th Division was assembling. The men were put up in a tented camp where they began to weigh up their new home. The country was flat and it was the season when the Tigris overflowed its banks, turning vast areas into swamps. Lack of sufficient transport

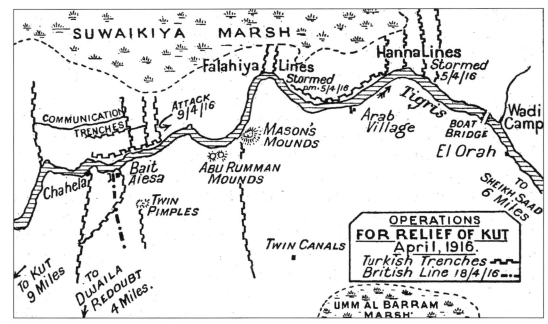

A map taken from the History of the South Wales Borderers *showing allied positions during the attempt to relieve Kut.*

pinned the British forces down to the course of the river. The 13th Division had arrived at a critical moment, as on 10 March the Turkish commander, Halil Pasha, wrote to General Townshend to attempt to gain his surrender. Time was running out for the besieged garrison at Kut.

The first casualty suffered by the Welsh troops within the 13th Division occurred on 10 March when Lance Corporal Herbert James Brickle (38286), the son of John and Elizabeth Brickle of 8 Monkton Village, Pembroke, died and was buried at sea. He was 39 years old and is commemorated on the Basra Memorial. Within less than a week, on 19 March two more men of the 8th Welsh died of sickness: Private John Ernest Cook (34245) of Ashford, Middlesex, and Private Archibald Lee (37683) of Barry.

General Gorringe, in command of the operations for the relief of Kut, planned to take Hanna, on the left bank of the Tigris, with the 13th Division, supported by the 7th Indian. He would then take Abu Rumman, on the right bank, with the 3rd Indian Division, which would be followed by the capture of Sannaiyat on the left bank. This preliminary operation should have been concluded by 8 April and was intended to lead to the relief of Kut. On the night of 31 March the 13th Division was ordered forward to take over trenches held by the 7th Indian Division in front of Hanna. The 8th Welsh were meanwhile attached to the 7th Indian Division to dig saps forward about 20 metres and then join them to form a new front-line trench. Work was carried out continuously both day and night and was completed in heavy rain.

By 4 April the rain had subsided and after dark the assaulting troops of 40 Brigade

26

of the 13th Division crept forward into the new trenches. The 4th SWB formed part of the third wave, which attacked at 4.55 am on the following day and watched as first the Wiltshires and then the 8th RWF dashed forward into Turkish rifle and machine-gun fire. At 5.15 am the artillery barrage subsided but the 4th SWB had already advanced under its own shellfire and crossed the Hanna trenches and, coming under heavy fire, Captain Hemingway, who was leading the charge, fell wounded. He was rescued by Captain Angus Buchanan. The attack on the next position at Fallahiyeh was postponed until 12.30 pm, when 38 and 39 brigades stormed the position, with a loss of 1,800 casualties suffered by the division, which then moved into reserve.

The 8th Welsh, who were employed in making tracks for guns during the action, suffered fifteen men wounded, but the other Welsh units had suffered more heavily. The 8th RWF had lost two officers – Captain Scott Powell and Second Lieutenant Leslie Spencer Gilbert – and twenty-one men. The 4th SWB had lost two officers – Lieutenant Stanley Mackenzie Bourne and Second Lieutenant Arthur Clarence Henley Field – and nine men killed. All these men are commemorated on the Basra Memorial.

For this action and also for gallantry during the coming days' fighting in Mesopotamia, three men from Welsh units were awarded the Victoria Cross, two from the 4th SWB and one from the 8th Welsh. The first award was for 5 April 1916 and was to Captain Angus Buchanan of the 4th SWB. He was born on 11 September 1894, the son of a doctor from Coleford, Gloucestershire and was educated at Monmouth School and at Jesus College, Oxford. He was commissioned in the 4th SWB and served in Gallipoli and Mesopotamia. He was awarded the Victoria Cross for his gallantry at the Fallahiyeh Lines on 5 April 1916:

Captain Angus Buchanan, VC, of the 4th SWB.

> For most conspicuous bravery. During an attack an officer was lying out in the open severely wounded about 150 yards from cover. Two men went to his assistance and one of them was hit at once. Captain Buchanan, on seeing this, immediately went out and, with the help of the other man, carried the wounded officer to cover under heavy machine gun fire. He then returned and brought in the wounded man, again under heavy fire. (*London Gazette*, 26 September 1916.)

Buchanan was also awarded the Military Cross. He was shot in the head in 1917 and blinded, but returned to his studies and worked in a solicitor's office in Oxford before his death at Coleford on 1 March 1944. His Victoria Cross is held in the collection of Lord Ashcroft.

The surprise attack had failed and the situation was so dangerous that the 13th Division was ordered back into the line on 7 April. On the night of 7/8 April the 7th Indian Division advanced and extended its line some 300 yards to form a jumping-off position for the 13th Division, which was to replace it the next night and attack.

At dawn on 9 April the 13th Division advanced with 38 and 40 brigades leading and 39 Brigade in support. When the attacking troops reached about 200 metres in front of the Turks they were met with heavy fire, but gallantly rushed forward into the Turkish trenches. However, with no support they were repelled and dug in just under 400 metres back from the Turks. Two companies of the 8th Welsh were then sent up with 40 Brigade and began sapping forward, moving the trenches about 250 metres further on.

Lieutenant Colonel Richard Courtney Brabazon Throckmorton of the 8th RWF, killed at Sanna-i-Yat on 9 April 1916.

During this failed attack of 9 April the 8th RWF had suffered terribly. Six officers – Lieutenant Colonel Richard Courtney Brabazon Throckmorton, Captain Gilbert Lloyd Sinnett-Jones, Lieutenant William McDowell Farmer and Second Lieutenants Howard Birch, William Houghton Harper and Mervyn Lepper, MC – and thirty-three men had been killed. Throckmorton had been detached from the 8th RWF to command the 5th Wiltshires and was shot dead during the attack. He was the heir to the Coughton Estate near Alcester and had served with the RWF since 24 August 1887.

Captain Gilbert Lloyd Sinnett-Jones was the son of James and Kate Sinnett-Jones of Caerwys Rectory, Flint. He was educated at Llandovery College between 1905 and 1911, and on leaving Llandovery College Gilbert entered St John's College, Oxford and was commissioned in the 8th RWF on 24 November 1914. He was wounded at Sari Bair and rejoined the battalion in Egypt. He was killed in action during the attack on Sannaiyat, on the old Babylonian Plain, in the third attempt to relieve the beleaguered Kut-al-Amara on 9 April 1916. Sinnett-Jones was 22 years old and is commemorated on the Basra Memorial. He is also commemorated on the Llandovery College War Memorial and at Caerwys. His brother James was killed the following year.

The second and third Welsh VCs of the Mesopotamia campaign were won during the battle as follows.

Private James Henry Fynn VC (11220) of the 4th SWB.

Private James Henry Fynn (11220) of the 4th SWB was born in St Clement, Truro on 24 November 1893, the son of Frederick John and Mary Baxter Fynn. He had moved to south Wales to work as a miner and lived at Frederick Street, Cwmtillery. In August 1914 he enlisted in the 4th SWB. Fynn was awarded the Victoria Cross for his bravery at Sannaiyat on 9 April 1916:

For most conspicuous bravery. After a night attack he was one of a small party which dug-in in front of our advanced line and about 300 yards from the enemy's trenches. Seeing several wounded men lying out in front he went out and bandaged them all under heavy fire, making several journeys in order to do so. He then went back to our advanced trench for a stretcher and, being unable to get one, he himself carried on his back a badly wounded man into safety. He then returned and, aided by another man who was wounded during the act, carried in another badly wounded man. He was under continuous fire while performing this gallant work. (*London Gazette*, 26 September 1916.)

Fynn was badly wounded and died later that day. He is commemorated on the Basra Memorial.

Captain Edgar Kinghorn Myles of the 8th Welsh was born at Wanstead, Essex on 29 July 1894. He had been commissioned in the 8th Welsh and saw service at Gallipoli prior to being attached to the 9th Worcesters and was awarded the Victoria Cross for his gallantry at Sannaiyat on 9 April 1916:

> For most conspicuous bravery. He went out alone on several occasions in front of our advanced trenches, and, under heavy rifle fire and at great personal risk, assisted wounded men lying in the open. On one occasion he carried in a wounded officer to a place of safety under circumstances of great danger. (*London Gazette*, 26 September 1916.)

Captain Edgar Kinghorn Myles, VC, of the 8th Welsh.

Captain Myles was also awarded the DSO later in the war (the VC was originally recommended for that action, but as no one had yet been awarded it twice in the war it was downgraded to the DSO):

> For conspicuous gallantry and devotion to duty. When all the officers except two had become casualties, he, for five hours, inspired confidence in the defence against two counter-attacks, and sent back most accurate and valuable reports of the situation. His courage and fine example were largely responsible for the steadiness of all ranks with him.

Myles died at Bishopsteignton, Devonshire on 31 January 1977, aged 82, and was buried at the crematorium in Torquay. His Victoria Cross is displayed at the Worcestershire Regiment Museum, Worcester.

Although the 4th SWB had gained two VCs in the space of five days, the battalion was almost annihilated. It had lost three officers – Captains Thomas Carnelly MacDonald Austin and Jack Farrow, and Second Lieutenant John Guith Morgan-Owen, thirty-three men killed and forty-three wounded, while the 8th Welsh had lost just one officer, Lieutenant William Frederick Dallas, who had been attached to the 6th East Lancs. The heavy losses were put down to the fact that the men had been cold while waiting for the signal to advance, and that recently-arrived reinforcements had been poorly trained.

The attack then switched to the other side of the Tigris, where the 3rd Indian Division held the 3-mile-long section of line between Rumman and Bait Issa. The country was flooded but the Turks had pushed a line between Bait Issa and the British along some dry ground. This was captured by the division on 12 April by wading through the floodwater and on the night of 15/16 April the British attacked, getting to within 500 metres of the main Turkish positions.

General Gorringe planned to hold the Turks at Sannaiyat with the 7th Indian Division, bring the 13th Division across the river to support the 3rd Indian Division and continue the attack. At dawn on 17 April the 3rd Division attacked the Bait Issa trenches and dug in before beating off a counter-attack. During the night the Turks attacked again, forcing two brigades of the 13th Division into the fighting, but the Turks failed to break through. The 13th Division then relieved the 3rd Division and on 19 April the advance began again but was hampered by heavy rain.

Gorringe thought that the Turks had sent troops from the Sannaiyat defences across the river, so a last attempt to advance was made by the 7th Indian Division on 22 April. Struggling through flooded defences and coming under heavy fire, the Indians were forced to withdraw.

Lieutenant Colonel Johnson of the 8th Welsh had meanwhile resumed command on returning from leave in England, and the battalion took part in this latest attack. Although a gallant effort was made to advance, heavy casualties and muddy terrain forced the Welsh to withdraw, with the loss of Sergeant Thomas Maurice Davies and seven other ranks killed, and Second Lieutenant Arnold and eleven men wounded.

The 'Tigris' Corps was by now shattered, short of men and exhausted. It had suffered more than 10,000 casualties in the space of less than two weeks, the weather had sapped the strength of the survivors and many men had fallen ill.

A last attempt to get food and supplies into Kut was made on 24 April, when the steamer *Jalna* tried to force its way upstream; but all the men on deck were killed and the steamer ran aground under Magasis Fort.

Meanwhile, T.E. Lawrence, a Welshman who later became known as Lawrence of Arabia, was sent, along with some other officers, to negotiate a deal with the Ottomans, offering £2 million in exchange for Townshend's troops. This was rejected, so the British asked for help from the Russians, who had a force of 20,000 men in Persia. However, by the time the Russians had begun their advance Townshend had surrendered on 29 April 1916 after a siege of 147 days. Around 13,000 British and Indian soldiers were taken into captivity, the majority of whom died of sickness.

Private Samuel Mathias Davies (37569) of the 8th Welsh from Grovesend, Swansea. Davies died on 21 April 1916 and is commemorated on the Basra Memorial.

Local men sent a series of graphic letters home in the days following the ending of the siege. Sergeant Albert Mallett of Pencoed wrote on 18 May:

We left Port Said for Mesopotamia on February 14th, arriving in the Persian Gulf on February 25th, then proceeded up the river Tigris on lighters, and got to a place called Shikes Saad [*sic*] on March 16th. It was there I got my next few letters only a week before going into action. I was very anxious about my people during the five intervening months, but I was fortunate enough to meet my brother Charley in Alexandria during January, and was pleased to hear that they were all in good health at home. I am sorry to say I have lost all my chums. I don't suppose we shall see poor Will Watkins and Arthur Greville again. Well, they died fighting like heroes for their King and country, and it was some fighting, I can tell you, in Gallipoli at that time, and I thank God for being spared through it all. I have been in some terrible battles there, but I won't say anything more about the Dardanelles, as I should like to forget it.

Sergeant Albert Mallett, 4th SWB, of Pencoed.

We moved up from Shikes Saad to the firing line, and got into the trenches on the 2nd of April. We had every support from our artillery (over 200 guns) behind us. This was the first position of the Turks we had to break in order to get to Kut to relieve Townshend. We moved to our position on the night of the 4th, and were to charge their first line sometime early in the morning. It was very little rest we got that night, I can assure you, as we were jammed in as tight as we could possibly be, and a man can't very well sleep standing up. I was luckier than some of them. I managed to get a blanket in the trench, and got into the traverse and lay down. I slept like a rock until someone pulled me up in the morning, and no sooner was I on my feet than we had the order to get over the parapet. We went over in fine style, I can tell you.

We had to take the first two lines, and stop until the artillery bombarded the third and fourth lines. Well, that was the worst part of it. Fancy lying down flat while over 200 guns were sending shells over at the rate of six shells a minute. For about half an hour it was a terrible row. After that was over, we took the third and fourth lines easily. It appears that the Turks 'smelled a rat' the night before, and cleared out, leaving a couple of hundred men behind. If they hadn't we should have captured about 30,000 Turks, or killed them, as nothing would have stopped us that morning. However, the Turks had very little start, and we soon caught up with them. We got out in extended order, and went for them, but they had good cover, and we had to dash across ground simply swept with machine gun and rifle fire. Nothing daunted, we went for them in good style. Our boys were dropping thick and fast all around. We were getting down to have a breather before making the last rush, when I got it through the right instep. The worst of it was, the bullets were simply pouring down amongst the wounded, and many a poor fellow was put right out where he was lying. Well, I could see a likely place for cover about 300 yards back, so I started to crawl there.

On the way I met a sergeant and another of our fellows. They were both wounded in the legs, so we laid down as flat as we could and dressed each other's wounds, as the blood was pouring from us. One of them was dressing my foot, when he got another bullet to the back, so we went for cover as quickly as we could. When we got there we found it was not deep enough, so we dug ourselves in with our entrenching tools.

Lieutenant H.M. Herbert wrote back to his father, the Reverend John Herbert, at Llanllawddog:

> Ever since March 11 we have not been in the same place for one whole day. We have been on the move all the time and have had hard and severe fighting, in fact the severest we have had in the whole campaign. I am quite fit and well again. Nearly all the others have had dysentery or fevers or something but I am still all right. Heat and dust storms all day and in the night time one is bitten to death by mosquitoes and sand flies; the temperature to-day is 108 in the shade... I can assure you that any man who holds out all through the summer in this country can say he has done his fair share. Not only have we to fight the Turk, but we have to fight malaria and dysentery and various other diseases which doctors can find no name for... It will be a Godsend to see a green field and trees again. It is impossible for anyone to imagine what a barren country this is.

With the fall of Kut, operations in Mesopotamia came to a standstill as the British did not have enough troops to continue the offensive. They were, however, too strong for the Turks to push them back towards Basra, so Lieutenant General Lake was ordered to consolidate his hold on the area and contain the Turkish forces opposite him. With the dreaded summer now taking hold, the Turkish commander knew that the British could not advance and in May withdrew some of his forces on the right bank of the Tigris to reinforce the Turkish troops operating against the Russians north-east of Baghdad and in Persia. However, the Russians, under General Baratov, were defeated by the Turks and the threat to Baghdad from this direction disappeared.

While the attempts to relieve Kut had been continuing in full swing, the British were establishing themselves on another front: Salonika.

Chapter 3

Salonika:
A New Front

By Christmas 1914 it had become apparent that neither the Germans nor the allies could break through on the Western Front, so both sides had turned their attention to other theatres of war. Part of the British effort had been to attempt to drive Turkey out of the war by forcing the passage of the Dardanelles Straits in order to bombard Constantinople, resulting in a Turkish surrender. However, with the Gallipoli campaign having stagnated into trench warfare, other avenues had to be considered.

The main British hope for the Middle East was to prevent the Turks from invading Egypt and seizing the Suez Canal, hence part of the reason for the ill-fated Gallipoli venture of the previous year. When that campaign was under way it had prompted the Germans to take action in the Balkans to crush Serbia, which would intimidate Rumania and secure the alliance of Bulgaria. A strong army, comprising Austrian and German troops, was assembled on the Danube at the end of September 1915 to invade Serbia from the north, while Bulgaria agreed to strike her from the east. Serbia had appealed to the allies for help and was supported by Greece.

With the failure of the Gallipoli campaign, the French also saw the sense of moving troops to Salonika to support the Serbs, putting the Greek King Constantine, a cousin of the Kaiser, in a delicate position. Because of the indecision of King Constantine, the British did not send troops to Salonika until after Bulgaria declared war on Serbia on 13 October and invaded Serbia the following day. The British then sent the 10th Irish Division from Gallipoli to Salonika, followed during the first week of November by the 22nd Division from France. Three other divisions – the 26th, 27th and 28th – were withdrawn from the Western Front in November and were eventually sent to Salonika.

The Greeks were loyal to King Constantine but also grateful to Britain for her help in liberating their country from the Turks, and it was only fear of the allied fleets that deterred the much more numerous Greek army from seizing Salonika and ousting the allies who had begun landing there in great numbers. Constantine finally agreed with Kitchener to allow the allied bases to be left alone.

Under attack by the Bulgarians from 14 October and then the combined Austro-German army from the north, the Serbs were soon in full retreat. Two French divisions were pushed hurriedly up the Vardar River in the hope of protecting the Serbian right but they arrived too late, the Bulgarians having pushed between the French and the Serbians.

On 28 October 1915, the 10th (Irish) Division moved into positions to the right of the French, but were outnumbered by the Germans and Bulgarians, who attacked on 7 December, forcing the allies to withdraw behind the Greek frontier. Meanwhile, the Serbs had managed to withdraw across the Albanian mountains and were evacuated to Corfu by the French, who then equipped them with French weapons, uniforms and equipment. Serbia was now in the possession of the enemy, who began to fortify the frontiers.

By the end of December 1915 the allies had begun constructing a huge entrenched camp in Salonika, known as the 'Birdcage'. It was here that the various Welsh units found themselves towards the end of 1915.

Among the earliest British battalions to arrive in Salonika was the 11th RWF under the command of Lieutenant Colonel George William David Bowen Lloyd, which landed on 5 November. The 11th Welsh, under the command of Lieutenant Colonel Albert Victor Cowley, landed at Salonika on 8 November. On the following day the 7th SWB under the command of Lieutenant Colonel James Grimwood, arrived, and then on 12 November the 8th SWB arrived, under the command of Lieutenant Colonel William Dennistoun Sword. The 1st Welsh reached Macedonia on 25 November after having been encamped in Egypt for three weeks and were commanded by Lieutenant Colonel Almeric Arthur William Spencer.

Captain Evan Ivor Glasbrook Richards, adjutant of the 11th Welsh, wrote about his impressions of Salonika:

Salonika, the town, was most interesting; it was so obviously eastern and mysterious; queer dark alleys; churches dating from the time when Christianity was young; wonderful pagan monuments; mosques and minarets; an amalgam of all races and all tongues. There one could see the Turk in fez and baggy trousers; the swarthy kilted Greek; the Jew in dignified gabardine as if he were Shylock himself come to life; handsome gipsy-like Serbs and Bulgars. Then the Allied Army itself – French, British, Italian, Russian, Serb, Indian, Chinese, never was so strangely a differing host of crusaders gathered together.

One had unforgettable pictures, the great stucco palaces so cheap and garish within, the painted ships, unchanged since the day of St. Paul, the inefficient railways. And over all the strange smell of the East, of the Arabian nights.

There were other peculiarities of that town. Greece was neutral and trains departed daily for Constantinople. Spies abounded openly. The population was not over friendly. Nevertheless it was fascinating and the pity was that we saw hardly anything of Salonika, outwardly a lonely white city extended to its grim medieval walls and abruptly stopped.

Then began Macedonia. Imagine the hilliest country of Wales and extend it to a horizon 5,000 feet high. Take away all trees, roads and civilization, replacing the towns by wretched poverty-stricken villages. Sear it with constant winds, freeze it in winter and scorch it in summer, and you have Macedonia. Only for two brief seasons was it tolerable – spring, which carpeted the plains with wild flowers, and autumn. For the rest we had great heat, much dust, and mules and mules and mules, flies by divisions, hills and the sense of monotony.

Our first introduction to this country was ominous. We were marched out of Salonika for about eight miles, where we met the D.A.A. and Q.M.G. of the Division. We asked him where we were to camp – it was now night – and with a sweep of his arm he indicated the broken moor, white under the stars, and said anywhere. We had the freehold of the country.

And by degrees we settled down to this strange land. Bell-tents were issued to us and for six weeks we wondered why we were at Salonika at all. Training, tactics, and musketry formed our days – Aldershot beneath another sky – the only detail that differed was the weather. Up to the 20th it had been delightfully mild and we could congratulate ourselves on wintering abroad. On the night of 20th November the temperature suddenly sank below freezing point, and on the 27th and 28th turned to biting sleet and snow. This was the same blizzard that wrought such ill at Suvla and was incredibly unpleasant. The temperature was zero, and the only training possible was brisk route marches and runs. Health of men and animals continued good, however, and on December 4th the cold was replaced by raw fogs and mists.

The 1st Welsh actually landed during this blizzard and bivouacked at Lembet in snow. All the Welsh units were then involved in digging in around the Birdcage. The British section of the Birdcage ran from the Galiko River, about 10 miles north-west of Salonika to Langaza, 10 miles north-east of the town, and then by a chain of lakes and marshes to Stavros on the Aegean Sea, some 30 miles distant.

The campaign was to be dogged with high levels of sickness, mostly malaria, and on 19 January 1916 Private Gwynne Griffith Prosser (15468) of the 11th Welsh became the first man from any of the Welsh units there to succumb to sickness and die. The 25-year-old from Cardiff is buried in Salonika (Lembet Road) Military Cemetery. Within days the 8th SWB lost its first man there when Private Tom Charles Jackson (16565) of St. Woolos, Newport died on 26 January, and on 29 January the 1st Welsh lost Private William Henry Orchard (38191) of 32 Harriet Street, Cathays.

The Welshmen spent their first St David's Day in Salonika playing sports against the other Welsh units, but there was barely anything of note taking place otherwise during these early days of the campaign.

Private Idris John Williams (13924) became the first Salonika casualty suffered by the 11th RWF when he died of typhus and pneumonia on 29 March 1916, aged just 19. Williams was born at Ffynonwen, Login, near Whitland, the son of David and Mary Ann Williams. The family had later moved to Rock House, Tumble and Williams had worked as an ironmonger's assistant at Carmarthen prior

Private Idris John Williams (13924), 11th RWF, from the mining town of Tumble in the Gwendraeth Valley.

to enlisting there into the 11th RWF. He is buried in Salonika (Lembet Road) Military Cemetery.

The 23rd Welsh arrived in Salonika under the command of Lieutenant Colonel Clifton Vincent Reynolds Wright on 13 July 1916 as the Pioneer Battalion of the 28th Division. Private Ieuan Hughes of Pontycymmer wrote about the voyage:

> Gibraltar looked imposing and massive, seen against a glorious Spanish sunset. The coast of Africa, which the transport passed close to so as to avoid the more usual route in case submarines should be about, was indescribably wild, rugged and majestic. While looking through my glass at the shore, I saw two lions on a hill, the base of which was washed by the surf. Thus, I judged the country thereabouts to be very wild.

The grave of Private Idris John Williams (13924), 11th RWF, at Salonika (Lembet Road) Military Cemetery.

> Very early one morning, just before daybreak I saw a lurid reflection in the sky far to the East. It was the lighthouse of the Mediterranean, the volcano Stromboli. And one thought kept coming to me, whoever would have thought, when I was reading of these things, that I should one day be actually see them? Arriving at Malta, we anchored alongside the *Megantic*, conveying Anzacs and Indian troops to one of the theatres of war... As soon as we had anchored, the bronze-skinned kiddies came round us in boats, begging us to throw silver coins (silver, if you please!) into the water. In after them they go, like so many fish. Malta soil has the appearance of impure chalk, and is in terraces rising from the shore. On these terraces are vineyards, and patches of olive trees relieve the monotony of the colour. In Valletta Harbour we heard a Maltese boy singing *Tipperary* in excellent English. When we left the harbour, it was with an escort of no fewer than four destroyers, for we were now entering the danger zone... Next day we arrived at Salonika, and port side, only a biscuit's throw from the ship, was a mine. One of the destroyers came up and exploded it. That evening we heard that the *Megantic*, the ship we had anchored alongside at Malta, had been sunk in the Adriatic. Next we arrived at Salonika, and marched up to the hills in sweltering heat. Our only rations were biscuits, bully, and marmalade. We slept where we could, and how we could. It was generally a case of 'A starlit sky my roof, and a growth of thistles my bed'. Then, one night came the storm! Don't talk of rain again, you good people of Blighty. I'll never forget the little bucketful that came my way that night.

Hughes took ill soon afterwards and was invalided back to Malta. Meanwhile, the work had finished on the Birdcage; but little else of note would take place at Salonika for several months.

Before we return to the early months of 1916 in France, where the forces were building up in readiness for a grand attack on the Somme, another force was building up for the campaign in Egypt.

Chapter 4

The Egyptian Expeditionary Force

In August 1914 the British garrison troops in Egypt were the 2nd Devonshires, 1st Worcestershires, 2nd Northamptonshires, 2nd Gordon Highlanders, 3rd Dragoon Guards, a battery of Royal Horse Artillery, a mountain battery and a field company of Royal Engineers. The situation on the Western Front required the instant recall of these troops and they were relieved on 27 September 1914 by the East Lancashire Division, Territorial Force. In October, Indian troops began to arrive.

Egypt, even after years of British administration, was still a province of the Ottoman Empire. The Khedive was actively pro-Turkish and when war was declared on Germany he went to Constantinople. Until Britain declared war on Turkey on 5 November, Germans could roam about Egypt at will and German ships could use its harbours. The aim of the British government was to suppress any rising that might break out and to defend Egypt from invasion as it was imperative that the Suez Canal be kept open to allow easy access to the Indian Ocean, so using Egypt as a base for operations against the Turks was the last thing they contemplated.

Egypt was declared a protectorate on 18 December, the reigning Khedive, Abbas Hilmi, was deposed and his uncle, Prince Hussein Kamel Pasha, was raised to the throne with the title of sultan. On the opposing side was the Turkish army: Djemal Pasha had been appointed commander-in-chief in Syria and Palestine, and his plan was to invade and conquer Egypt. The operation was placed in the hands of Colonel Djemal Bey, who had the German General Kress von Kressenstein as his chief of staff.

The Germans and the Turks hoped to provoke an Arab rising against the British through their allies, the Sultan of Darfur and the Grand Senussi. The first serious enemy attempt was in January 1915, when the Turks tried to cross the Suez Canal. However, from then until July 1916, when they again crossed the Sinai Desert, all the British military operations consisted of were the pursuit of a few tribesmen.

Some of the troops who had been evacuated from Gallipoli were rested in Egypt before moving to the Western Front, in particular the Australians and New Zealanders (ANZACs), who began embarking from Egypt to Marseilles and took up positions in Flanders. Many more were to remain in Egypt and so the Egyptian Expeditionary Force (EEF) was built up from March 1916 to counter the threat of the Turkish-backed Senussi tribesmen and to safeguard the Suez Canal, coming under the command of Sir Archibald Murray, who had arrived in Egypt on 9 January 1916. Murray arrived to find that a defensive scheme for the Suez Canal was already in place, after the attempt by the Turks to capture it in January 1915. The area had quietened down after the centre of the fighting shifted to Gallipoli but with Gallipoli evacuated, Egypt again became a crisis point.

Among the troops garrisoned in Egypt at the time were the 53rd (Welsh) Division and the Welsh Horse. Also included in the plans for the EEF were four more Welsh units: the 1st Mounted Division, which included the 1st/1st Denbighshire Hussars; the 1st/1st Montgomeryshire Yeomanry; the 1st/1st Pembroke Yeomanry; and the 1st/1st Glamorgan Yeomanry, including a number of Welsh artillery and medical units, entrained from Norfolk to sail for 'an unknown destination', while the 2nd Garrison Battalion, RWF sailed two days later for garrison duties. An article in the *Denbighshire Free Press* of 4 March 1916 stated:

> We learn that our county regiment, by the time this appears in print, will be on the briny ocean bound for somewhere in the East. They had a farewell service and celebration of Holy Communion and a parting address from their old chaplain, the Bishop of St Asaph, at Beccles Parish Church, on Tuesday. Wednesday evening about 200 of them paid honour to the Patron Saint by a good dinner with all the loyal toasts and a musical programme, with plenty of Welsh singing. That, they felt, was the best way of passing their last night in England. Our informant says 'All of us are in good spirits, and when our time comes we will bear up to the strenuous training that we have undergone since August 5th 1914.'

By 4 March 1916 the division had embarked aboard a fleet that included the transport ship HMT *Arcadian*, bound for Alexandria. The *Arcadian* was packed and contained the full complement of men of the Pembroke and Glamorgan Yeomanry, as well as the Shropshire Yeomanry. Their journey was fraught with danger, with German submarines known to be operating in the waters of the Mediterranean, but the *Arcadian* safely reached port on 14 March 1916. (*Arcadian* in her pre-war days was a luxury liner and had been the ship on which Sir Robert Baden-Powell fell in love with his future wife. The *Arcadian* was later sunk by the German submarine *UC-74* on 15 April 1917 while bringing troops to Salonika (see Chapter 16). Her captain was Wilhelm Marschall, who went on to take charge of the battleship *Scharnhorst* in the Second World War).

Upon disembarkation, the sea-weary troops marched to camp and some of the men settled down to write their first letters home from foreign soil. The *Arcadian* had also transported reinforcements bound for the 4th and 5th Welsh, so severely reduced on Gallipoli that the units had been merged temporarily into one battalion, the 4th/5th Welsh. A delighted Private John James John of the Pembroke Yeomanry bumped into two of his relatives who were part of this batch of recruits, as well as two old school friends from Llanddowror. In his first letter home to his uncle, Ben John of Parsons Lays Lodge, Laugharne, John wrote of the chance meeting and a résumé of the letter was printed in the local newspaper, *The Welshman*:

During the nine days and ten nights voyage he met on-board his Uncle, Trooper W. Jenkins, late of Cross Inn, also his cousin Trooper P.J. Saer, and Ptes Evan and John Hughes of Pantymenin, Llanddowror – now of the 4th Welsh. He says that they are encamped in a desert of sand with no sign of any village or town. The weather is so hot that they do nothing between the hours of 11 am and 4 pm. Still, we are all in the pink, and whilst not knowing what is in store for us in this far off country, we feel confident of doing our duty.

Once the various yeomanry regiments had arrived in Egypt, the 1st Mounted Division joined up with four other brigades of yeomanry who had fought at Gallipoli: the Highland Mounted Brigade, the South-Western Mounted Brigade, the Eastern Mounted Brigade and the South-Eastern Mounted Brigade. The strategic importance of Egypt lay in its location, guarding the vital Suez Canal and the North African oilfields, so Britain had no option but to make Egypt a protectorate and this was the role that these newly-arrived yeomen settled into.

After arriving in Egypt on 12 May 1916, Corporal Jones (35) of the Denbighshire Hussars wrote to the editor of his local newspaper, *Yr Adsain*:

Dear Editor,

Having seen my name, also that of H.V. Jones, Plas Bonwm, I thought we would write you a few lines to let you know how pleased we were to see our names in your valuable paper, as Jones receives it every week here. We are proud to think that so many have turned out to serve their King and Country from old Corwen, having left Corwen over 20 years I still have a great respect for my old home. We were pleased to have met a few Corwen boys out here looking well after their hard experience at the Peninsula. I was very sorry to see in your paper about my old schoolmaster missing but we pray to God that no harm has befell him as it would be a great loss to the children also to his many friends at Corwen and district. We find it rather lonely here on the desert, but we are in good health, we are about 3 miles from the Mediterranean Sea and manage to have a bathe each day. The heat is rather inconvenient as it's about 109 degrees in the shade, but we are getting climatized now. We haven't much news to tell you this time, we only hope that we shall live to see our old native town once more after this terrible war is over. Kindly remember us to any of our old friends at Corwen. We will now draw to a close. Wishing you and your valuable paper every success.

We remain your old Chums,

I.C. JONES & H.V. JONES

Meanwhile, Private Layton Richards of Pontycymmer, a member of the Glamorgan Yeomanry, wrote:

The natives are a filthy lot. It is wonderful how they manage to exist. The canteens are run by Greeks, who are absolute rotters; everything sold by them

Some of the Imperial Yeomanry members of the Pembroke Yeomanry in Egypt.

being frightfully dear except eggs and fruit. Now I realise I am from home, doing my own washing and mending and roughing it generally. Cultivation is carried on nearer the coast. The chief products are barley, wheat, oats, and rye, also a kind of clover. The implements used are very old and primitive, and indeed it is a wonder they are able to grow anything. The beasts of burden are the camel, ox, ass and mule, though horses are used in the cities. There are no wild beasts here except the jackal, numbers of which visit the camp nightly and kick up a horrid row. Holy day is celebrated by the natives on a Friday, but ours is still on the Sunday, of course, when we hold a Church Parade at 8.30 am. Our football team is still going strong – not been beaten yet, though we have drawn twice against the R.A.M.C. and 4th and 5th Welsh (3 points apiece). Also our choir is going to Cairo for three days to give concerts before the Sultan and Prince of Wales. Since writing the above we have been moved from Berni Salamai to a place some 150 miles south of Cairo. It is a fashionable town of 27,000 people, but not to my liking, for the temperature is some 15 degrees warmer than the other place! In fact it is really unbearable. We do nothing whatever after 8 am. We are encamped in the bed of the old river Nile, the present river being 200 yards or so away. The weather is telling on our boys; at least a score of them have gone to hospital with dysentery.

Some of the 3rd Line battalions of these regiments were by now in Ireland following the Easter Rising of 1916. The rising had been organized by the Military Council of the Irish Republican Brotherhood and began on Easter Monday, 24 April 1916, and lasted for six days. Members of the Irish Volunteers were joined by the Irish Citizen Army and seized key locations in Dublin before proclaiming the Irish Republic independent of the United Kingdom. There were other, mostly minor, actions in other parts of Ireland, so the British had rushed several army battalions out there to deal with the situation, rapidly bringing it under control by means of force.

The dividing line in the Sinai Desert was the Suez Canal, and Sir Archibald Murray had divided the canal into three zones of defence under the command of Major General Alexander Wilson, with centres at Suez, Ismailia and Qantara. The greatest threat here came from the Senussi tribesmen. Prior to 1906 the Senussi had been a relatively

British troops on the streets of Dublin.

peaceful religious sect who roamed the Sahara Desert, opposed to fanaticism. They had then become involved in resistance to the French occupation. In 1911 the Italians invaded Libya, occupying the coast while the Senussi maintained resistance inland and in Cyrenaica. During this period they generally maintained friendly relations with the British in Egypt.

The outbreak of war raised the tension. The Turks made strenuous efforts to persuade the Senussi to attack British-occupied Egypt from the west. In the summer of 1915 Turkish envoys, including Nuri Bey, the half-brother of Enver Pasha, and Jaafar Pasha, a Baghdadi Arab serving in the Turkish army, managed to gain influence over the Grand Senussi, Sayed Ahmed, and convinced him to begin hostilities against the British with Turkish support. The original plan was for a three-pronged attack on the British forces stationed here. The Senussi would mount attacks along the narrow strip of fertile land on the Egyptian coast, heading towards Alexandria, and in the band of oases 100 miles west of the Nile. At the same time the Emir of Darfur would launch an attack on the Sudan. In the event the three campaigns were fought separately and were defeated in turn.

The coastal campaign first began in November 1915. The British withdrew from Sollum and Sidi Barrani and concentrated their forces around Mersa Matruh. The Western Frontier Force, under Major General W.E. Peyton, was created from the garrison of Egypt, consisting of one cavalry and one infantry brigade, supported by a battery of horse artillery. They were outnumbered by the Senussi, who had 5,000 men trained to fight as infantry, supported by a larger number of irregular troops and with a small number of Turkish artillery and machine guns. Despite their advantage in numbers, the Senussi were defeated in encounters at Wadi Senba on 11 to 13 December, Wadi Majid on 25 December 1915 and Halazin on 23 January 1916.

The Senussi were finally defeated at Agagia on 26 February 1916, on the coast close to Sollum. The Western Frontier Force had been reinforced by the South African Brigade under Brigadier General H.T. Lukin. A column under his command was sent west to recapture Sollum, encountering and defeating the Senussi on their way west. Jaafar Pasha was captured during the battle and Sollum was reoccupied on 14 March 1916 by a mixed force of South African and yeomanry troops. Jaafar was kept in captivity in Egypt, but later in the war volunteered to join the forces under Emir Feisal, became commander of the Arab regulars during the revolt and then served as minister of war and prime minister of Iraq under the then King Feisal. Feisal was famously aided in his campaign by the renowned army officer Thomas Edward Lawrence, better known as Lawrence of Arabia, or El Aurens, who was the British liaison officer serving with Feisal's Arab army. However, small bands of Senussi tribesmen continued their fight. A fresh campaign against the oases started in February 1916. Sayyid Ahmed occupied the oases at Baharia, Farafra, Dakhla and Kharge, and forced the British to keep a sizeable garrison in Upper Egypt while a mobile force was organized to push him back.

On 20 March 1916 the South Wales Mounted Brigade became part of the 4th Dismounted Brigade and was attached to the Western Frontier Force. After a short stay at Wardan, on the banks of the Nile, it moved to the Wadi El Natrun, west of the Nile Delta, and was tasked with guarding the coastal strip, the gateway to Alexandria and to the Nile Delta, an area known as the Baharia front. The role of these newly-arrived troops was a simple peace-keeping one for the time being, and as garrison troops on the Suez Canal defences.

Captain Edward Lambton, Pembroke Yeomanry, died at Cairo on 28 March 1916.

The loss of the first officer of the Pembroke Yeomanry on active service occurred on 28 March 1916 when Captain Edward Lambton, a member of a well-known Pembrokeshire family, died in hospital at Cairo. He was born on 5 February 1877, the son of Lieutenant Colonel Francis William Lambton, of Brownslade, Pembrokeshire, late Scots Guards, and Lady Victoria Alexandrina Elizabeth, the eldest daughter of John Frederick Campbell, second Earl of Cawdor. He was educated at Wellington College and Cooper's Hill, prior to taking up a post as Director of Public Works for the Egyptian government in Cairo. Edward trained with an Egyptian cavalry unit prior to the war and returned to England, where he became a captain with the Pembroke Yeomanry. Two of his older brothers had been killed in South Africa during the Boer War.

The distribution of troops administered on the Suez Canal defences by April 1916, temporarily under the command of the 53rd (Welsh) Division HQ, was as follows:

ALAMEIN
1st Welsh Field Coy, Royal Engineers (Detach.)
53rd Division Signal Coy, R.E. (Detach.)

MOGHARA
  1st Denbighshire Yeomanry
ABBASSIA
  H.Q. 53rd Division and 53rd Signal Company
WADI EL NATRUN
  158th Brigade (less transport details)
  1st Welsh Fld Coy, R.E. (Detach.)
  3rd Welsh Field Ambulance (Section)
  53rd Division Train (Detach.)
BENI SALAMA
  53rd Divisional Artillery (less one battery)
  Details 53rd Division, R.E.
  159th Brigade
  Transport Details, 158th Brigade
  1st Pembroke Yeomanry
  1st Montgomery Yeomanry
  2nd Welsh Field Ambulance
  3rd Welsh Field Ambulance (less one section)
  53rd Division Casualty Clearing Station
  53rd Division Train Details and Bakery
  53rd Division, Mobile Veterinary Sect.
FAIYUM
  160th Brigade
  1st Welsh Field Ambulance
  53rd Division, Sanitary Sect. (less detachment)
  2nd/1st Welsh Field Coy, R.E.
  53rd Division, Train Details
  53rd Division, Cyclist Coy.
MINIA
  4th Dismounted Brigade
  4th Glamorganshire Battery Royal Field Artillery
SOHAG
  2nd/1st Cheshire Field Coy, R.E.
SUEZ
  53rd Divisional Train

In the meantime, the British were forming a regiment of mounted infantry. Members of the Australian Light Horse, which had been so badly handled during a futile charge across open ground at the Battle of the Nek in Gallipoli on 7 August 1915, had been moved to Egypt after the evacuation and had successfully taken part in mounted campaigns against the Senussi. With the extra horsemen now available to them due to the arrival of the yeomanry brigades, the Imperial Camel Corps was founded, with a core of six companies of Australian Light Horsemen from New South Wales. Formed alongside them were six British companies, all drawn from the yeomanry brigades. New Zealand personnel formed two additional companies. Later in the campaign motorized units were also formed, using men from the Imperial Camel Corps, to which a detachment of Pembroke Yeomanry and one of Glamorgan Yeomanry became attached. During July a detachment of thirty men under Lieutenant De Rutzen left the Pembroke Yeomanry to join the 6th Company, Imperial Camel Corps. With them went the regimental signal officer, Lieutenant F.S. Morgan, to become brigade signal officer to the Imperial Camel Brigade.

The loss of the first officer of the Glamorgan Yeomanry on active service occurred soon afterwards. Capel Lisle Aylett Branfill had been born on 29 August 1884, the son of Capel Aylett and Gwladys Gwendoline Branfill (née Miers) of The Plas, Crickhowell. He lived at Ynistawe, Clydach with his wife prior to the war. He was initially commissioned in the Glamorgan Yeomanry on 19 April 1909, and by the time the regiment landed

Captain Capel Lisle Aylett-Branfill, Glamorgan Yeomanry, died in Egypt on 11 May 1916.

in Egypt had been promoted to captain. He took ill due to the adverse desert conditions and succumbed to pneumonia in hospital at Cairo on 11 May 1916, aged 31. He is buried in Cairo War Memorial Cemetery. Capel's short life was full of tragedy. His wife, Susannah Hamilton Williams, was so distressed at the thought of him going to the front that she drowned herself and their infant child, Gwendoline, in a pool near her parent's home at Upton-upon-Severn on 24 January 1915.

The main body of the yeomanry was responsible for patrolling huge swathes of desert, either through the manning of outposts and blockhouses or by the use of converted Rolls-Royce armoured cars. Although this routine was relatively safe, it was difficult and dangerous work in a climate that bred ideal conditions for sickness. By night the men froze, by day their blood seemed to boil in the arid heat; and then they had to contend with sand, dust and the myriad flies. On top of all these unpleasantries, the Turks were building up a powerful force in the Middle East, which by mid-1916 had reached a strength of forty-three divisions, all in all over 650,000 men. On 19 July reconnaissance aircraft from the Royal Flying Corps had discovered that a large body of the enemy had moved from El Arish, and on the morning of the 20th cavalry patrols reported that Oghratina was held by strong forces of the enemy, who was entrenching.

The first member of the Montgomeryshire Yeomanry to die on active service was Private Thomas Leonard Evans (2309), the son of Rees and Jane Evans, who succumbed to illness on 7 July 1916. He was 23 years old and is buried in Cairo War Memorial Cemetery. The first death among the Denbighshire Hussars occurred during the campaigns against Gaza the following year.

We must now move back to France, where the troops were being massed for the Somme offensive.

Chapter 5

The Western Front:
The Build-Up to the Somme Offensive

While the aforementioned Welsh units were getting to grips with life in these far-off lands, back in France the allies were getting ready for the forthcoming Somme offensive. The 1st RWF were in positions at Bois Français, near Fricourt, on the Somme, when one of its young officers unwisely commented on the lack of casualties among its officers, prompting several officers present to touch wood to counter any bad luck. No officers of the battalion had been killed since Loos but this innocent comment was blamed for the deaths in quick succession of three officers over the coming days. On 18 March Second Lieutenant David Cuthbert Thomas was in charge of a working party that was repairing wire emplacements in no man's land when he was shot in the throat. He walked to the first-aid post for treatment but began choking and died shortly afterwards. The 20-year-old from Llanedy Vicarage is buried in Point 110 New Military Cemetery, Fricourt. Thomas was a close friend of the noted war poets Siegfried Sassoon and Robert Graves.

Second Lieutenant David Cuthbert Thomas, 1st RWF, the son of Reverend Evan and Ethelinda Thomas of Llanedy Rectory, Pontarddulais. Thomas was killed at Bois Français on 18 March 1916 and is buried in Point 110 New Military Cemetery, Fricourt. He was a close friend of the famed war poets Siegfried Sassoon and Robert Graves. His death left Sassoon, especially, very angry towards the Germans; an anger that led to his earning the Military Cross after a series of rash excursions into German territory. Robert Graves wrote a poem in memory of Thomas entitled Not Dead; *and he is mentioned in several poems and biographies written by both men, under the pseudonym of Dick Tiltwood in one. It was largely his death that famously soured Sassoon's attitude towards the war.*

The grave of Second Lieutenant David Cuthbert Thomas in Point 110 New Military Cemetery.

His death left Sassoon in particular very angry towards the Germans; an anger that led to his earning the Military Cross after a series of rash excursions into German territory. Robert Graves wrote a poem in memory of him entitled *Not Dead*, and Thomas is mentioned in several poems and biographies written by both men, under the pseudonym of Dick Tiltwood in one. It was largely his death that famously soured Sassoon's attitude towards the war.

On the following day a German trench mortar bombardment caused the instant deaths of the other two officers: Captain Mervyn Stronge Richardson of Wiltshire and Second Lieutenant David Pritchard of Dewsbury. The men were buried side by side in Point 110 Military Cemetery.

The 2nd SWB, commanded by Major Geoffrey Taunton Raikes, had been encamped in Egypt since being evacuated from Gallipoli, along with the remainder of the 29th Division, on 11 January 1916 and had moved to Alexandria on 9 March, where the battalion embarked aboard two transport ships: the SS *Karoa* and SS *Kingstonian*. Both ships sailed on the following day and arrived at Marseilles on 15 March 1916; the men entraining at 1 am on the following day for northern France. Two days later the men detrained at Pont-Remy and marched to billets at Domart. The Borderers trained here for almost two weeks before receiving orders on 1 April to move to Englebelmer, on the Somme. The entire 87 Brigade was inspected the following day and on 3 April took up the front line near Y Ravine, in front of the German stronghold of Beaumont Hamel. Unbeknown to the men of the 2nd SWB, one of their comrades, who had been hospitalized at Marseilles, died there during the day, becoming the battalion's first casualty in France. Private John Henry Wilson (14919) was from Brynmawr, Brecon and is buried in Mazargues War Cemetery, Marseilles.

The 29th Division was a battle-hardened and experienced unit, but the men had not faced a foe of the calibre of the Germans they were now facing and on 4 April the 2nd SWB came under trench mortar fire. Lance Corporal Thomas Davies (10789) became the first battle casualty that day, wounded by shrapnel and dying in the afternoon. He is buried in Miraumont Communal Cemetery.

On the following day a patrol was sent out under Lieutenant G.W. Phillimore but failed to return. At around 4 am the Borderers heard shots and machine-gun fire from the direction the patrol was last seen heading towards but they were not seen again. Later in the day Second Lieutenant Ballantine and two men were hit by shrapnel from a trench mortar shell: Ballantine suffered shellshock; the two men – Privates Reuben Hughes (11343) and William Holden (24705) – were killed. More shellfire followed later in the day; the Borderers were being given a hot reception but things were about to take a turn for the worse. [Phillimore was actually taken prisoner by the Germans and spent the rest of the war in Germany. He was repatriated on 12 November 1918.]

On the morning of 6 April another patrol was sent out to attempt to locate Phillimore and his party, but no trace could be found and the day was marked with intermittent shelling on the Borderers' lines. At 8 pm the 2nd SWB sent out another patrol, which retired an hour later after coming across hostile enemy patrols in no man's land. The patrol came back into the line at around 9 pm, just before a heavy artillery

Private David Hughes (14672), 2nd SWB, son of John and Margaret Hughes of Kidwelly. He married Mary Emily Musk at Seven Sisters in 1907 and the couple lived at 20 Bryndulais Row, Seven Sisters. Hughes worked at the Yniscedwen Tinplate Works at Ystalyfera and was one of twenty-nine men killed when the Germans raided the 2nd SWB trenches on 6 April 1916.

bombardment began to rain down around them, mostly on the communication trenches behind. The bombardment was followed by a trench raid by the Germans of RIR 119, who had crossed over the wire on the left of the 2nd SWB, and a desperate hand-to-hand fight began.

When the fighting ended, twenty-nine men of the 2nd SWB lay dead, while nineteen men had been captured and brought back to the German lines. The raid had been perfectly planned and executed by the Germans: the artillery fire suffered by the 2nd SWB on the previous days had been the German artillery registering their guns and testing the defences. The cost to RIR 119 was just three men killed by a grenade explosion and one man seriously wounded but successfully evacuated.

The event had been an embarrassment for the battalion, which felt forced to carry out a retaliatory raid on 30 April; however, this ended in failure due to poor planning. Three more men of the 2nd SWB were killed in the raid of 30 April: Lance Corporal Arthur Ernest Fry (10307) of Bristol, Private Harry Lloyd (13806) of High Ercall, Salop and Private Jim Tordoff (19690) of Castleford. The bodies of the three men were recovered from no man's land by the Germans and buried in Miraumont Communal Cemetery, where they still lie today.

Some of the men of RIR 119 and their prisoners from the 2nd SWB.

Mesnil Ridge Cemetery, Mesnil Martinsart. The cemetery contains the graves of twenty-seven of the 2nd SWB, men killed during the trench raid of 6 April 1916.

The Welsh Guards had, in the meantime, entrained for Calais on 16 March 1916 after a relatively quiet spell in the trenches around La Gorgue and spent the remainder of the month training and drilling. They moved to Wormhoudt ten days later, and on 5 March marched to Poperinghe prior to bathing in the communal baths at St. Jan-ter-Biezen on 6 March. The battalion war diary for the day makes some very interesting and uncomfortable reading:

> Also all battalion had baths in 6th Division baths in Poperinghe. Baths not to my mind satisfactory, consist of 2 vats each 10 ft. x 10 ft. and filled to a depth of 2 ft., then water changed every two hours, one vat going at any time. They take 120 men an hour, so it means 240 men in same water, not sanitary or nice. They say they tried separate tubs but not sufficient hot water. Men got change of clothes, wish they had not, as much of stuff they got was verminous. I saw the washing of clothes arrangements, and they first go through a disinfector, then stuffed or rather dipped in creosote, so they should be all right.

Washing usually did kill the lice that thrived in the trenches and infested the uniforms of the men, but the eggs laid by the lice in the clothes usually hatched as soon as they were put on a warm body and so the vicious, verminous cycle began all over again.

On 21 March the Welsh Guards at last returned to the trenches, taking up positions at Potijze and the Canal Bank. They suffered their first casualties here on 22 March when Private George Albert Lewis (1895), the son of John and Sarah Lewis of 40 Station Road, Burry Port, died after being shot through the lungs during the night. He is buried in Brandhoek Military Cemetery.

Private George Albert Lewis (1895), Welsh Guards, of Burry Port, shot through the lungs and died on 22 March 1916. He is buried in Brandhoek Military Cemetery.

Further south the 38th (Welsh) Division, still on the La Bassée Canal, was ramping up its training and had carried out its first trench raids. Trench raids were carried out for several reasons: to inflict casualties and take prisoners; to gain intelligence; to foster the offensive spirit; and to provide some excitement to relieve the monotony of trench warfare. Men on raiding parties felt as though they were picked men, as indeed they had to be; the life of the officer leading the raid depended on his men and vice versa. These men were often taken out of the trenches for specialized training, were given better rations, and lived together to foster team spirit.

On 9 April a platoon of the 16th Welsh attempted a raid on a machine-gun emplacement, tasked with laying a Bangalore torpedo to destroy it. Second Lieutenant A. Buist and one of his men succeeded in laying the device: it exploded, but the Germans were alert and threw a grenade at the raiding party, killing Second Lieutenant Oswald Morgan Williams and Private Fred Vagges (32789). Patrols under Second Lieutenants E. Williams and Leonard Tregaskis searched for Williams' body without success.

The grave of Private George Albert Lewis (1895) at Brandhoek Military Cemetery.

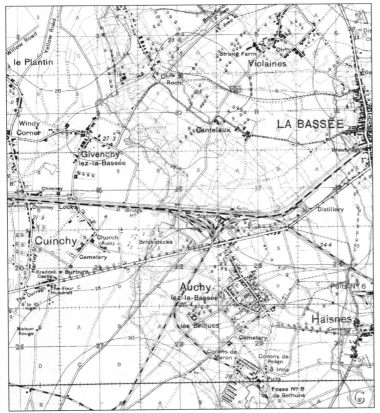

A section of a trench map showing the part of the line held by the 38th (Welsh) Division during March 1916 at La Bassée.

Second Lieutenant Oswald Morgan Williams was the son of Edwin and Mary Williams of School House, Risca, Monmouth. He was educated at Llandovery College from 1908 until 1912, and then at St John's College, Oxford, where he gained First Class Moderations in Mathematics. He enlisted in the army in 1914 and was commissioned in the 16th Welsh in early 1915. He was just 21 years old, and is commemorated on the Loos Memorial. Private Vagges, of Cardiff, is also commemorated on the Loos Memorial.

Second Lieutenant Oswald Morgan Williams, 16th Welsh.

At Ypres the 10th RWF had continued having a hard time of things at the Bluff, and went into rest billets at Thieushouk, near Caestre, on 5 April for the battered battalion to recuperate. The men received some cheering news during church parade on 23 April when the award of the Military Cross for Second Lieutenant Albert Nevitt was announced:

For conspicuous gallantry. When leading a bombing attack up a communication trench all but one of his men became casualties, but with this man he went on to within 10 yards of the enemy, when he was himself wounded. He had previously shown great daring on reconnaissance. (*London Gazette*, 16 May 1916.)

On 27 April the battalion had marched back to Kemmel and on the following morning at 1 am, took over the front line there. On the following day two German deserters were brought in and told their captors that they were about to be victims of a gas attack. All the men were warned and told that gas helmets were to be worn rolled up on the head and bayonets were to be fixed. At 12.30 am on 30 April the terrifying sound of gas being released from cylinders reached the ears of the Welshmen and a cloud was seen slowly moving towards them.

Gas sirens were sounded and the men came under rapid fire while they pulled their gas masks down, then the Germans attacked. Many of the advancing grey-clad soldiers were felled by machine-gun and rifle fire and also by artillery, although some managed to break the right of the 10th RWF line and were killed there during some fierce hand-to-hand fighting. By 1.20 am the gas had cleared and the situation was in hand, but after having suffered eleven men killed, about fifteen wounded and a further fifty suffering from the effects of gas, the Welshmen sent for reinforcements to cover the Regent Street dugouts and the GHQ line at Lindenhoek.

A memorial card for Lance Corporal Harry Dudley (23191), 10th RWF, of Coestfan, Barmouth, killed on 30 April 1916 and buried in Lindenhoek Chalet Military Cemetery.

Peering over the parapet, the men could see scores of dead Germans and also some wounded men, who were brought in for identification and interrogation, and watched as the German lines were pounded by heavy artillery.

While his countrymen were fighting gallantly at Kemmel, the ninth Welshman was about to be executed. Private Anthony O'Neil (15134) was the son of James Daniel and Sarah Ann O'Neil of 20 Castle Street, Neath. O'Neil had volunteered early in the war and joined the 1st SWB in France in November 1914. He was sentenced to death after deserting his post and was shot at Mazingarbe on 30 April 1916. He is buried in Mazingarbe Communal Cemetery Extension.

The 38th (Welsh) Division was still carrying out its quota of trench raids. On the night of 4/5 May the 10th Welsh in the Riez Bailleul sector placed a trench mortar barrage on the German wire before a party, led by Captain Robert Jesse Adams Roberts, went out to lay a Bangalore torpedo in position. Unfortunately, as was so often the case, the torpedo failed to explode and began to burn. It was important not to allow the Germans to recover the weapon, so Captain Roberts and Lance Corporal Samuel Jones (16623) made a gallant attempt to recover the torpedo. Although they failed to bring it back, Roberts was awarded the DSO and Jones the Military Medal (MM) for their actions. The citation for Roberts' DSO reads as follows:

The grave of Private Joseph O'Neil (15134), 1st SWB, executed at Mazingarbe on 30 April 1916 for desertion.

> For conspicuous gallantry. He led a party to lay a torpedo in the enemy's wire. When the torpedo failed to explode he made, with a lance-corporal, a very gallant attempt to get it back. When shown up by a bright flame emitted by the burning torpedo he was attacked at fifteen yards' distance by several of the enemy, but both he and his companion threw bombs which caused casualties, and got back safely. The torpedo was destroyed. (*London Gazette*, 30 May 1916.)

One of the most successful raids undertaken by the 38th (Welsh) Division during this early stage of the war was carried out by the 15th RWF at midnight on 7/8 May 1916. Captain Goronwy Owen led a party of three other officers and fifty-one NCOs and men out into no man's land with orders to 'Kill Germans; Take Prisoners; Capture or destroy Machine-guns; and To secure samples of German equipment, steel helmets, respirators, ammunition etc.'

Watches were synchronized and at 10.45 pm a reconnaissance party went out to cut the wire while the main raiding party assembled. By midnight nothing had been heard from this reconnaissance party, so a runner was sent out to see what was happening. He discovered that the party had come across a German wiring party and had to go to ground, so Captain Owen decided to lead the main raiding party out at 12.40 am to head off the Germans and carry out the raid. Upon moving out into no man's land they found that the Germans had gone, so Owen led his men across to the enemy wire, cutting several feet of it and passed silently through the gap. Owen crept on and saw a party of some twenty Germans in their trench, so returned to his men, led them through the wire and gave the order to attack at around 1.50 am. What followed then was a scene of horror, as men were stabbed, bayoneted and bludgeoned to death with clubs and spades. A large number of the Germans appeared to be unarmed and were thought to have been miners. Having dealt with these, a swift gathering of intelligence regarding the strength and layout of the trenches was carried out before the raiders made their way back. It was during the withdrawal that most of the following casualties were suffered. Two officers – Second Lieutenants Noel Osborne-Jones and Herbert Taggart – and four men were killed in the raid; Captain Goronwy Owen and nine men were wounded. Owen was subsequently awarded the DSO for his leadership during the raid: 'For conspicuous gallantry and determination in organising and leading a successful raid on the enemy's trenches. Many of the enemy were accounted for, and Captain Owen covered the withdrawal with great skill under heavy fire. Although slightly wounded, he gave assistance to wounded men.'

Second Lieutenant Noel Osborne-Jones, 15th RWF. Osborne-Jones was the son of Robert and Ada Mason Osborne-Jones of Brynawelon, Ystradmeurig. He was commissioned in the 15th RWF on 14 May 1915 and was killed while partaking in a midnight bombing raid on 8 May 1916. He was 21 years old and is commemorated on the Loos Memorial. He is also commemorated on a fine stained glass window in Ystradmeurig Church.

On 22 April the 25th Division moved to Neuville-St. Vaast; with it was its Pioneer Battalion, the 6th SWB. The Borderers were put to work constructing trenches near Zouave Valley, which lay west of Vimy Ridge. The battalion suffered several men killed and wounded during their first weeks at Zouave Valley due to intermittent German shellfire and on 13 May were put to work consolidating the lip of a crater. This work was extremely hazardous, so on 15 May the men rested all day in readiness to go out again and continue their work after dusk. During the night working parties from the battalion moved forward into no man's land and began work again on consolidating the crater and sapping communication trenches. The work did not go unnoticed, however, and the men came under heavy fire during the night, killing Second Lieutenant George William Jones and four men, and wounding Captain E. Lloyd, Second Lieutenants A.L. Amos and S. Evans, and thirteen men.

Second Lieutenant George William Jones was the son of William and Anne Jones of Dowlais. He was educated at Aberystwyth University prior to being commissioned in the 6th SWB. He was 24 years old when he was killed on 15 May 1916 and is buried at Écoivres Military Cemetery, Mont-St. Eloi.

On 17 May the 16th Welsh suffered the loss of the man who had raised the battalion, their CO, Lieutenant Colonel Frank Hill Gaskell. He was the son of Colonel J. Gaskell CBE, and Emily Mary Gaskell of Cardiff and the husband of Violet Gaskell of Boscobel, Llanishen, Cardiff. He was visiting his men in the trenches during the night when he was shot by a sniper and died later that day. Gaskell was a vastly experienced and well-respected officer who had seen active service during the Boer War. He is buried in Merville Communal Cemetery.

Lieutenant Colonel Frank Hill Gaskell, CO of the 16th Welsh, died of wounds at Merville on 17 May 1916.

The grave of Second Lieutenant George William Jones in Écoivres Military Cemetery, Mont-St. Eloi.

Just ten days later, on 27 May, Major Maurice Alexander Napier, second in command of the 10th Welsh was shot and killed by a sniper while supervising 200 men of his battalion who dug a trench 250 yards long in no man's land. Napier is buried in Rue-du-Bacquerot (13th London) Graveyard, Laventie.

The grave of Lieutenant Colonel Frank Hill Gaskell in Merville Communal Cemetery.

On 20 May 1916 the tenth Welshman of the war was executed. The man, Private John Thomas (12727), was the son of Mrs M. Davies of Lamphey, near Pembroke and was married with three children. Thomas was a reservist who had voluntarily re-enlisted and arrived in France on 3 February 1915, re-joining the 2nd Welsh. He had seen much bloodshed over the following months and had obviously had enough of this so he deserted, but was caught. At his trial Thomas pleaded that a man of his age, 44, should not be expected to be in the front line and carry out the same work as much younger men. However, the court showed no sympathy and Thomas was shot at Mazingarbe on 20 May 1916. He is buried in Mazingarbe Communal Cemetery Extension.

The grave of Private John Thomas (12727), 2nd Welsh, of Lamphey, near Pembroke.

The Canadian Corps was situated in positions near Ypres, between Hooge and Hill 60, around a feature named Mount Sorrel during the late spring of 1916. During the morning of 2 June the Canadians holding the Hill 62 position were hit by an intensive artillery bombardment that lasted until about 12.30 pm. At 1 pm a series of mines was detonated beneath the obliterated trenches at Mount Sorrel and the Germans attacked. At Sanctuary Wood the Princess Patricia's Canadian Light Infantry (PPCLI) held out bravely, but elsewhere the British and Canadians were overrun, losing both Mount Sorrel and Hill 62.

Reinforcements were rushed into the area and the Germans were forced to dig in and consolidate their gains before being counter-attacked by fresh Canadian units the following day. The advantage now, however, lay with the Germans, who now further dominated the heights overlooking Ypres and the salient, so Haig decided to reinforce the British units there, ordering several infantry and artillery units, much needed for the forthcoming Somme offensive, to Ypres. More than sixty of the Welsh contingent of the Canadian Corps were killed during the fighting that raged around Mount Sorrel from the German attack on 2 June until the Canadians moved south to the Somme in August.

Just a few miles to the south the 38th (Welsh) Division continued its policy of harassing the enemy. On 30 May the 13th RWF suffered one officer – Second Lieutenant Maurice Thomas Hughes – and six men killed, all of whom are buried in Rue-du-Bacquerot No. 1 Military Cemetery, Laventie.

On the night of 4/5 June a party of four officers and fifty-three men of the 10th Welsh attempted to raid the enemy trenches in the Laventie sector, using mats to cross the wire. However, these mats proved ineffective and the raiders found the enemy ready, suffering three men killed and all four officers – Captain Roberts and Second Lieutenants Tossell, Padgett and Brooker – and nine other ranks wounded while withdrawing.

A more successful raid was carried out on the same night by C Company of the 14th Welsh, consisting of three officers – Lieutenants Strange, Corker and Wilson – and thirty-nine men. At 11.02 pm the party crawled forward towards the German wire before silently making their way through. Corker and Wilson's parties jumped into the German trench, hoping to catch them unprepared. Wilson's party, on the right, initially found no Germans but then stumbled upon five enemy soldiers who were promptly bombed. Corker's party, on entering the trench, came into contact with the enemy who threw several bombs at them, wounding Corker. His men responded with their own bombs, and in the confusion a withdrawal was ordered.

The entire party regrouped in a nearby ditch before making their way back to the British trenches, where it was realized that Lieutenant Corker had not returned with his party. Lieutenants Strange and Wilson,

Lieutenant Francis Llewellyn Corker, 14th Welsh, the son of Alderman Thomas Taliesin and Rosa Corker of 6 Sketty Road, Swansea. He was wounded and reported missing during a trench raid on 5 June 1916.

accompanied by Corporal O'Brien, went back out to search for Corker but no trace of him could be found, although the body of Private William Williams (17569) of Lan Street, Morriston, who had died the previous night, was recovered.

Lieutenant Francis Llewellyn Corker was initially posted as wounded and missing, and one man, Private Daniel John Austin (17570), was killed during the raid. The next night Lieutenants Strange and Wilson went out again into no man's land under heavy fire in an attempt to locate Corker but found no trace. On 8 June his mother, who had suffered the death of her husband Alderman Thomas Taliesin Corker on 7 March 1916, received a telegram from the War Office to inform her that her son was missing. Only the previous day she had received a letter from young Corker telling her that he was alive and well, so considerable distress was caused in the Corker household in Swansea. Two weeks after Corker's disappearance, his mother received another letter from the British Red Cross:

Dear Madam,
In answer to your enquiry we beg to send you a report from Second-Lieutenant H. Lothaby, at Colchester Hospital, Étaples, who states: 'On the night of 4-5 June Lieut. F. Corker was in charge of a raiding party in front of — Church. They got into the German trenches where he was wounded. I was wounded myself, but Corporal O'Brien told the commanding officer this, and added that Lieut. Corker got out of the trench into No Man's Land, which was here about 250 yards wide. Search was made under Lieut. Strange without success. The C. O. subsequently told me that the grass in No Man's Land had grown very long, and it is possible that the Germans got him before our search party went out. Second-Lieutenant Wilson was also with the raiding party.'
We shall continue to make inquiries, the result of which will be sent you. Assuring you of our sympathy in your anxiety,
Yours faithfully,
J. BULTEEL.

Corker's family was not the only one in Swansea awaiting news from their loved ones. On the same day that Mrs Corker received her first telegram, the relatives of Private John Ferger (17510) of the same battalion received a similar telegram at their home at 13 Chapel Street, Swansea to inform them that he, too, was missing. Ferger had, in fact, been killed on 4 June, while Corker was later presumed to have been killed on 5 June. Both men are commemorated on the Loos Memorial. Even sadder for the Corker family, the youngest son, Thomas Gwyn Bevan Corker, died within months of his elder brother, aged just 6 years. Within one year the entire male generation of the Corker family had been wiped out.

On 5 June the 14th RWF lost Captain Hugh Powell Williams and nine men killed while in the trenches at Rue Tilleloy, following a heavy German artillery bombardment. One of the British shells that had been fired in retaliation also hit the 15th RWF position, bringing a section of the parapet down.

By now plans were under way to move the 38th (Welsh) Division down to the Somme and, complying with these orders, on 11 June the division was withdrawn from the line and began to move south, leaving XI Corps.

In the meantime the regular soldiers of the 2nd RWF were still in the infamous Givenchy sector. On 22 June the battalion was in the trenches at Cuinchy, enjoying a relatively peaceful day, when their peace was shattered in most dramatic style. A German mine had been dug beneath their positions and at around 1.30 pm exploded beneath their feet, throwing tons of earth, timber, men and material skywards. Frank Richards wrote of the experience in his classic memoir *Old Soldiers Never Die*:

I arrived back in my dug-out and about 1.30 am was woken up by a terrific explosion on our right front. The ground shook and rocked as if an earthquake had taken place. The enemy's artillery had also opened out and they were bombarding our right front, the majority of the shells being five-point-nines. The company stood-to: we knew that the enemy had exploded a mine on our extreme right but were not sure whether it was in our Battalion's area or not. All communication with the exception of D on our right had broken down. A little later the enemy shells began falling all along the Battalion's front and the lines went between us and D and also we lost touch with Battalion Headquarters in the rear. I made my way along the trench to D and met one of their signallers who told me that he had just repaired two breaks in the line. I asked if they were in touch with C or B. He replied that they hadn't received a sound since the mine went up. Word was now passed along the trench that the enemy had set off a mine under B Company. A and D were now being heavily bombarded and about an hour later word came that with the exception of eight men the whole of B had been blown up by the mine and that the enemy had made a rush to occupy the crater, but had been repulsed by C Company and the eight survivors of B.

One of the men gave me a full account of it and said that after the mine went off the enemy bombarded their lines with five-point-nines, and when they switched the barrage to the left, right and rear of them he had a pretty good idea that they were coming over to try and occupy the crater. Soon they did come over and into the trench. Some got around the rear to their left and there was some hand-to-hand fighting. A platoon officer of C lost his head and shouted, 'We'll have to surrender! They've got around the back of us.' 'Surrender my bloody arse!' shouted Hammer Lane. 'Get your men to meet them front and rear.' Captain Stanway with the rest of C Company then made a counter-attack and the show was soon over. One young officer of B who had escaped the mine had been killed in the fighting; a dagger had been driven up to the hilt in his belly. A young German officer and some of his men had been killed in the trench and a few prisoners had been taken. It was a big mine and the crater must have been a hundred feet across from lip to lip. The company commander of B, Captain Blair, was dug out alive on the lip of the crater, where he had been buried up to the neck. He was a man with many lives: he had been in the South African War, had been severely wounded on 2 September, when serving with the same company, and had only lately re-joined the Battalion. If the signallers of B had had a dug-out I might have stayed with them a couple of hours swapping yarns and brewing tea and would have gone West with them. Captain Stanway was awarded the D.S.O., which he had thoroughly earned before this affair. The platoon officer who shouted 'We'll have to surrender' was awarded the Military Cross. He really deserved something different. Lane was awarded the D.C.M.

Three officers – Captain Owen Price-Edwards and Second Lieutenants Arthur Chaplin Banks and Trevor Allington Crosland – and fifty-two men of the battalion were killed in the explosion and during the immediate fighting. Some of these men, including Banks, who was stabbed in the stomach by a German, were killed during the German assault that followed the explosion, and hundreds more were left wounded or shellshocked. Somehow the men fended off the German attack and with the utmost gallantry maintained their hold on their positions. In honour of the battalion, the resulting mine crater was officially named Red Dragon Crater and its scars can still be seen on the land today.

The bodies of Captain Owen Price-Edwards, Second Lieutenant Trevor Allington Crosland, Private William Chatwin (9181) of Birmingham, Private William Robert Hughes (10117) of Llanglydwen, Private Thomas Lewis, MM (11146) of Beaumaris, Private Bert Price (9204) of Newbridge-on-Wye, Private Frederick Vale (9696) of Birmingham and James Wyllie (5317) of Bangor as well as several unidentified bodies were among several discovered at different times after the war by farmers ploughing their fields and were reinterred at Cabaret Rouge Cemetery, Souchez. Twenty-nine of the men still lie somewhere in the remains of the crater and are commemorated on the Loos Memorial, while some are buried locally. Two DCM winners and two MM winners were among the dead. Among the many letters of

The Llanddulas War Memorial near Abergele. Second Lieutenant Arthur Chaplin Banks, 2nd RWF is among those commemorated on the base. He was 20 years old and was the son of Charles and Helen Agnes Banks of Arnold House, Llanddulas.

condolence sent out to the families of the dead men, Lieutenant Colonel Crawshay wrote to Trevor Crosland's father:

He was a splendid boy and one of the sort we can ill spare. On the night of 21st/22nd at 2 am the enemy blew an enormous mine. I regret to say that the

Second Lieutenant Trevor Allington Crosland, 2nd RWF, the son of Thomas Pearson Crosland and Charlotte Elizabeth Crosland of Newhouse Hall, Huddersfield and The White Cottage, Gresford. Educated at Harrow and at the Royal Military Academy, Sandhurst, Crosland was gazetted into the battalion on 12 August 1915. He was 19 years old when he was killed by the blowing of the Red Dragon Crater on 22 June 1916. His body was found by a farmer ploughing the land in July 1925 and was identified by several belongings, including a gold matchcase with his initials. He is buried in Cabaret Rouge British Cemetery, Souchez.

trench, in which your son was, was blown up. I am sad to say our casualties were heavy for the mine. They then attacked us after an intense barrage, but got badly defeated, leaving a certain number of dead in our trenches. It is really too sad, we all miss him, and everyone was very fond of him. I am afraid you will feel it very much. It will be some satisfaction to you to know he was a real soldier and leader of men.

The blowing of the mine also led to a tragedy further along the line. On the morning of 22 June 1916, Sapper William Hackett and four other miners of 254 Tunnelling Company, Royal Engineers, were driving a tunnel towards the enemy lines about 10 metres below the surface of the Givenchy battlefield. When the Germans blew the Red Dragon Mine a length of this tunnel collapsed, cutting off the five men. A rescue party was sent down to tunnel towards the trapped men and after two days of hard work the rescue party broke through into the collapsed section. Hackett helped three men to safety; however, one man, Private Thomas Collins (17572) of the 14th Welsh (Swansea Pals) was badly injured and unable to move. Hackett refused to leave the injured Collins and eventually the gallery collapsed, entombing both men.

Collins was just 22 years old and the son of Jack and Rachel Collins of 50 Shelley Crescent, Swansea. His body still lies beneath the silent fields of Givenchy today and he is commemorated on the Thiepval Memorial. His brother Daniel also fell during the war. Sapper Hackett was quite rightly posthumously awarded the Victoria Cross for his bravery in remaining with his injured comrade and sacrificing his own life. His citation reads:

For most conspicuous bravery when entombed with four others in a gallery owing to the explosion of an enemy mine. After working for 20 hours, a hole was made through fallen earth and broken timber, and the outside party was met. Sapper Hackett helped three of the

Private Thomas Collins (17572) of the 14th Welsh (Swansea Pals), who was trapped underground following the explosion of the Red Dragon Crater.

men through the hole and could easily have followed, but refused to leave the fourth, who had been seriously injured, saying: 'I am a tunneller, I must look after the others first.'

Hackett is commemorated on the Ploegsteert Memorial, while a recently erected memorial on the site of Red Dragon Crater commemorates this gallant man, the tunnellers and the tragic occurrence of 22 June 1916.

It is of note that another division with strong Welsh representation moved to France on 3 June. The 40th Division was a Bantam formation, formed mostly of men who had previously been deemed too short for overseas service. Attached to the division's 119 Brigade were the 19th RWF under Lieutenant Colonel Bryan John Jones, the 12th SWB under Lieutenant Colonel Edward A. Pope, the 17th Welsh under Lieutenant Colonel Charles Joseph Wilkie and the 18th Welsh under Lieutenant Colonel Richard Stirling Grant-Thorold; the brigade was known as the Welsh Bantam Brigade.

The division was attached to the 1st Division in the Loos area for instruction in trench warfare. When the 1st Division moved down to the Somme early in July, the 40th Division remained in the trenches in the Loos area.

Men of the 19th RWF prior to embarkation for France in June 1916.

Throughout the early months of 1916 the British had been taking up sections of the front along the Somme. On 1 March the British formed the Fourth Army under Lieutenant General Sir Henry Rawlinson, which took over the Somme front, the Third Army side stepping northwards. As more divisions made the move south, the allied strength on the Western Front at the beginning of the Battle of the Somme amounted to some 150 divisions – 95 French, 49 British and 6 Belgian – against 125 German divisions.

The Germans had launched an assault against the French at Verdun on 21 February, so the French Tenth Army was relieved by the British to enable the French to reinforce Verdun and the British line now ran continuously from Curlu on the Somme to the north of Ypres.

While on paper the British army now looked an impressive force, in reality the new divisions were inexperienced and sometimes poorly trained. The Germans held the advantage in terms of experience, artillery and holding the dominant ground along most of the Western Front.

General Joffre had suggested to Sir Douglas Haig that the British should launch their summer offensive at different points before commencing their main operations on the Somme, in order to wear the Germans down and to divert German reinforcements away from Verdun where the ground was soaked with French blood. Haig was not prepared to do this but proposed to carry out a series of minor attacks or large trench raids, and this is what we have seen being carried out further north.

The British army was developing apace during this period of the war. Steel helmets were issued to all the troops, reducing head injuries by some 75 per cent, while specialist machine-gunners within battalions were withdrawn to form Brigade Machine-Gun Companies, while Pioneer Battalions and Light Trench Mortar Batteries were also formed.

While this reorganization was going on throughout the BEF, the Royal Navy was about to engage in the biggest sea battle in its history.

Chapter 6

The Battle of Jutland

artly because of the need to cement its position as the most powerful naval force in the world, the Royal Navy had reacted to a naval race by Germany in the early years of the twentieth century as each side battled for supremacy. There was a simmering rivalry between the two navies as to who ruled the waves: the British knew that they were the greatest naval power, while the Germans wished to be at least their equal and this rivalry had seen the escalation of an expensive arms race.

Apart from smaller actions at sea during the early stages of the war, no major action had taken place between the two main fleets – the British Grand Fleet under the command of Admiral Sir John Jellicoe and the German High Seas Fleet under the command of Admiral Reinhard Scheer – as both parties were wary of what damage could be caused to them by the other and neither side could afford to lose a major sea battle.

This situation changed on 31 May when the two forces came together in the North Sea off Jutland, with catastrophic results. There were hundreds of Welshmen serving with the Royal Navy at the time, several of whom served aboard some of the most powerful warships in the world, including HMS *Queen Mary*, HMS *Lion*, HMS *Defence*, HMS *Black Prince*, HMS *Indefatigable* and HMS *Invincible*. Confidence ran high throughout both fleets, but the sailors of the Royal Navy were about to find out that this had been somewhat misplaced.

During the early months of the war the German High Seas Fleet staged hit-and-run actions against the English coast. As well as the sinking of British merchant shipping, the bombings of Scarborough, Hartlepool and Whitby and the bombardments of Yarmouth and Lowestoft had prompted the Royal Navy to keep a powerful force in the North Sea, both to counter any further threat to our coastal towns and also to keep the Germans penned into the Baltic.

On 30 May 1916 the Battlecruiser Fleet, under Vice Admiral Sir David Beatty, were carrying out a sweep from the Channel. Part of Beatty's force, the Fifth Battle Squadron, was commanded by the Welsh Rear Admiral Sir Hugh Evan-Thomas.

The German High Seas Fleet was commanded by Admiral Reinhard Scheer and was a powerful force comprising sixteen modern dreadnought battleships, six predreadnoughts, five battle-cruisers, eleven light cruisers and sixty-one destroyers. The British fleets totalled twenty-eight dreadnoughts, nine battle-cruisers, eight armoured cruisers, twenty-six light cruisers, seventy-nine destroyers and an aircraft carrier: on paper numerically superior, but three battleships were undergoing repairs and another's crew was judged as not being fully trained and so was not among the fleet.

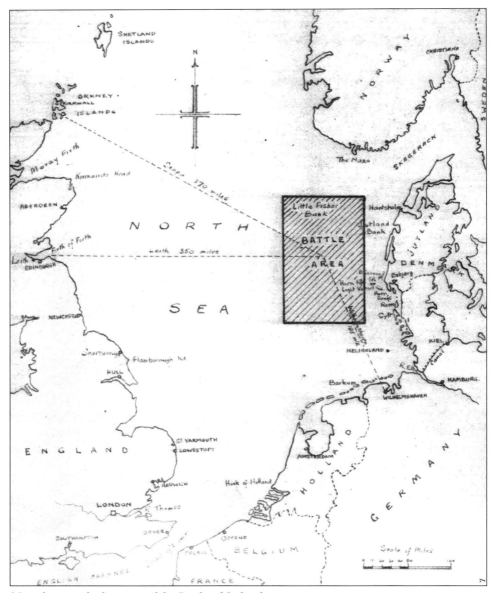

Map showing the location of the Battle of Jutland.

The intention of the German High Seas Fleet was to lure Beatty's battlecruiser squadrons into the path of the main German fleet, which was protected by a submarine screen. However, the British had intercepted German signals and as a result on 30 May Jellicoe sailed with the Grand Fleet to rendezvous with Beatty, passing over the German submarine positions before they had the chance to get into position.

On the afternoon of 31 May, Beatty encountered Hipper's battle-cruiser force and

*Rear Admiral Hugh Evan-Thomas, commander of the Fifth
Battle Squadron at Jutland. Evan-Thomas was born at The
Gnoll, Neath on 27 October 1862, the son of Charles Evan-
Thomas, High Sheriff of Brecknockshire. He joined the
Royal Navy as a cadet in 1876 and held his first command
by 1900. He commanded the dreadnought battleship*
Bellerophon *from 1908 to 1910, when he took command of
the Royal Naval College, Dartmouth. From 1913 to 1915 he
served as Rear Admiral in the First Battle Squadron before
being given command of the Fifth Battle Squadron which he
led at Jutland. Evan-Thomas died in 1928, aged 65, and
bequeathed The Gnoll to the townspeople of Neath.*
(Photograph courtesy of the National Portrait Gallery)

opened fire on them. The Germans drew Beatty's force into the path of the High Seas
Fleet and by the time Beatty had realized what was happening he had lost two battle-
cruisers from his force of six battlecruisers and four battleships. The battleships,
commanded by Evan-Thomas, were the last to turn and formed a rearguard as Beatty
withdrew, pursued by the German fleet. At 4.02 pm on 31 May 1916 that confidence
was shaken among the Royal Naval personnel when the battlecruiser *Indefatigable*
blew to smithereens after suffering direct hits in her magazines, taking 1,010 men to
the bottom in minutes. Soon after *Defence* blew up, with the loss of all her crew of
903 men, *Black Prince* sank with the loss of all hands and *Invincible* was sunk with
the loss of all but six of her crew. By nightfall fourteen British and eleven German
ships had been sunk, with heavy loss of life. Throughout the night Jellicoe manoeuvred
to cut the Germans off from their base in an attempt to continue the battle the next
morning, but under the cover of darkness the Germans slipped through the British
screen and steamed back into the safety of the Baltic.

Sporadic fighting continued throughout the night, as scattered ships fired occasional
salvoes at shadowy targets. A disastrous incident occurred when the 4th Destroyer
Flotilla spotted unknown ships off their starboard quarter. HMS *Tipperary* signalled to
the ships, which proved to be the German battleships *Westfalen*, *Nassau* and *Rheinland*
and three cruisers, and came under devastating fire. During the course of the one-sided
engagement, *Tipperary*, *Ardent* and *Fortune* were sunk; *Tipperary* with the loss of 185
hands of her crew of 197 including 3 Welshmen; *Ardent* with the loss of 78 of her crew
of 80 including 1 Welshman, and HMS *Fortune* with the loss of 67 of her crew of 68
including 1 Welshman. Also sunk during the night were the destroyers HMS *Turbulent*
with the loss of 90 hands and HMS *Sparrowhawk* with the loss of 6 hands.

Altogether the Royal Navy had suffered the loss of three battlecruisers,
Indefatigable, *Invincible* and *Queen Mary*; three cruisers, *Black Prince*, *Defence* and
Warrior; one flotilla leader, *Tipperary*; and seven destroyers, *Ardent*, *Fortune*, *Nestor*,

Nomad, Shark, Sparrowhawk and *Turbulent* sunk. Some 328 officers and 5,769 ratings had been killed, 25 officers and 485 ratings wounded, and 10 officers and 167 ratings taken prisoner. The British had lost more ships and sailors than the Germans but the Germans would never venture out in force again.

The Pembroke Dock built cruiser HMS *Warrior*, severely damaged, had been abandoned during the night after attempts to tow her failed and she sank in heavy seas at around 8.25 am with the loss of one officer and seventy ratings killed. She had been towed for 75 miles by HMS *Engadine* commanded by Lieutenant Commander Charles Robinson from Marchwiel, near Wrexham but had sunk so much that her top deck was only 4ft above the water. Robinson was later mentioned in despatches for his work in saving most of the crew of *Warrior*. This work was also aided by the arrival of the Cunard liner *Campania*, which aided in the tow and the evacuation of men from the doomed ship. Two officers and twenty-five men of *Warrior* returned to England safe; one of whom, from Swansea, died four days later. Richard Williams (8219/S) was born in Swansea on 31 October 1879 and was a Royal Naval Reservist. He rejoined the colours at Swansea in August 1914 and was posted as a stoker aboard HMS *Warrior*. He died at South Queensferry Hospital, Edinburgh on 6 June from shock following severe injuries, a broken leg and arm, received aboard *Warrior*. The body of the 47-year-old father of four was conveyed back to Swansea in an ornate black coffin and buried with full military honours at Danygraig Cemetery in Swansea. [There is some discrepancy regarding Richard's true age. His date of birth was given on his attestation papers as 31 October 1879 but his age at death was recorded as 47, therefore he may have lied about his age on enlistment and deducted ten years.] One of the men attending his funeral was a close friend from Swansea, Patrick O'Sullivan, who had also been wounded aboard *Warrior*. Seaman George Frederick Farmer (J701), a Bridgend man, was also among the survivors of *Warrior* and returned home on leave the week after the battle. Farmer continued to serve in the Royal Navy until January 1929 and died on 18 January 1978, aged 87.

Another Welsh survivor from *Warrior*, Able Seaman Edward John Lewis (231058), returned home on leave within a week of the battle and during a homecoming reception spoke proudly to his friends of the work done by his ship:

Lewis says little about the actual fighting – just that he was in the fore turret on the *Warrior* and that they did not forget to let it into the German vessels. The *Warrior* was disabled after a short, but hard fight of 17½ minutes' duration with several vessels of the German Battle Fleet. In the evening, about eight o'clock, Lewis says she was taken in tow by the *Engadine*, and about the same time the following morning was slipped, after 681 officers and men had been transferred. Lewis spoke highly of the good seamanship of officers and men of the *Engadine* in saving the *Warrior*'s crew. Ask him his impression of the issue of the fight, and he will tell you that the Germans suffered much more than the British, and that he believes the *Warrior* placed two German battle cruisers out of action before she was disabled. (*Brecon County Times*, 15 June 1916.)

Of the ships that returned safely to their ports, many had been hit by German shellfire, the worst being HMS *Warspite*, which had suffered thirteen direct hits from large projectiles.

At least 240 Welshmen are known to have been killed during the Battle of Jutland: 1 aboard HMS *Ardent*, 22 aboard HMS *Black Prince*, 1 aboard HMS *Broke*, 61 aboard HMS *Defence*, 1 aboard HMS *Fortune*, 77 aboard HMS *Indefatigable*, 30 aboard HMS *Invincible*, 3 aboard HMS *Lion*, 1 aboard HMS *Malaya*, 1 aboard HMS *Onslaught*, 1 aboard HMS *Princess Royal*, 33 aboard HMS *Queen Mary*, 1 aboard HMS *Southampton*, 3 aboard HMS *Tiger*, 3 aboard HMS *Tipperary* and 4 aboard HMS *Warrior*.

Lieutenant Commander the Honourable Hugh Cecil Robert Feilding, son of the 9th Earl of Denbigh, killed aboard HMS Defence *at the Battle of Jutland, 31 May 1916.*

This number included two members of the Welsh aristocracy, both of whom served aboard HMS *Defence*. The first was Midshipman the Honourable Bernard Michael Bailey, the son of the 2nd Baron Glanusk and Baroness Glanusk of Glanusk Park, Breconshire. He was just 17 years old. His brother, the Honourable Gerald Sergison Bailey, also fell. Their father was commanding the Brecknock Battalion, South Wales Borderers in Aden. The second was Lieutenant Commander the Honourable Hugh Cecil Robert Feilding, son of the 9th Earl of Denbigh and the Countess of Denbigh, the Honourable Cecilia Clifford, of Chudleigh, Devon. He was 29 years old.

Among the seventy-seven Welshmen killed during the sinking of HMS *Indefatigable* was Leading Seaman John Peters (Z/367). Peters was born on 22 December 1894, the son of James and Mary Peters of 3 Tregob, Llanelli. He was 21 years old when *Indefatigable* was blown apart after being hit by a salvo of huge shells from the German battleship SMS *Van Der Tann* struck the decks of *Indefatigable* and penetrated into the ammunition storage areas, tearing the ship apart. His brother Josiah was killed in 1918 while serving with the 14th Welsh.

Able Seaman John Peters (Z/367) of Llanelli, killed during the sinking of HMS Indefatigable.

Also killed aboard *Indefatigable* was Leading Seaman Bertram Treharne (Z/744). Treharne was born at Tumble on 26 March 1893, the son of William Treharne. His father then took up ownership of the Prince Albert Vaults at Pembroke Dock and moved his family there to live. Treharne enlisted on 10 April 1915 in the Royal Navy, and on 16 August 1915 was posted for duty with the Grand Fleet aboard HMS *Indefatigable*.

Leading Seaman Bertram Treharne (Z/744) of the Prince Albert Vaults, Pembroke Dock, killed during the sinking of HMS Indefatigable.

The final minutes of HMS Indefatigable *at the Battle of Jutland.*

One of the Welshmen who survived the battle was 17-year-old Trevor John, the son of William John of Grove Road, Bridgend. He served aboard HMS *Revenge* and wrote to his parents after the battle:

I should like to meet the one who said the *Revenge* went out to pick up wounded. They would have found a difference if they had been in it. I will tell you as much as I am allowed. We left our base with the Grand Fleet as quiet as we always do, and I never felt as well as I did then. We steamed about for a bit. While we were steaming we heard that battle cruisers were in touch with the enemy, and were holding them. We still steamed on, we being the second ship of the line, the Admiral being ahead of us. The next thing we heard was that the *Queen Elizabeth* class had got into the fight. This put fresh heart in us, as we had been afraid the Germans would run away before we had a chance to fire at them. At last we got in sound of the guns, and were simply dancing for joy. In my turret we were singing all the time until just before we opened fire. When we got in range the flagship opened fire first, and then we did. It was terrible to see. It was a lovely but awful sight to see ships on fire and sinking. I will never forget it. We kept on firing until they ran away. We claim to have sunk some enemy ships ourselves. Their losses must have been terrible. Anyway, we kept following them, as we should have liked to have finished them there and then, and we would have, if they had not run away. We met the Germans about half past five. Of course, they expected an easy victory over the battle cruisers, but found they could not beat them, let alone us. In the night our destroyers made attacks on them, and sunk some more. Next morning we steamed round the battle area, and down south, and found the Germans had gone home for another holiday. This will tell what sort of fleet you have looking after you: we fought on the 31st May, and patrolled all next day, came to our base, replenished, and were ready to put to sea on the night of the 2nd of June. I can't tell you anymore, but will if I ever get a chance of coming home. I was sorry about George Farmer. All they do at home for him he deserves, as it was a very rough time for our boys. I lost about two dozen chums on one ship that went down but wait till the next time we get a pop at them.

Another Welshman who survived the battle was Rear Admiral Sir Hugh Evan-Thomas, who commanded the 5th Battle Cruiser Squadron from his flagship, HMS *Barham*. Evan-Thomas was born at The Gnoll, Neath on 27 October 1862, the son of Charles Evan-Thomas, High Sheriff of Brecknockshire. He had a long and distinguished career in the Royal Navy after enlisting in 1877 at the age of 15. He was a close friend of Sir John Jellicoe and a cousin to Rear Admiral Sir Algernon Lyons and had commanded the Royal Naval College at Dartmouth prior to the war.

Evan-Thomas's command comprised five modern, extremely powerful battleships: HMS *Barham*, HMS *Valiant*, HMS *Warspite* and HMS *Malaya*. The fifth, HMS *Queen Elizabeth*, was in dock at the time of the battle but rejoined the squadron afterwards. Three of Evan-Thomas's ships received direct hits during the battle, while *Warspite* was almost lost after suffering damage to her steering and nearly foundered. Following the battle, Evan-Thomas was appointed a Companion of the Military Division of the Most Honourable Order of the Bath. In his despatch published on 15 September, Jellicoe specially recommended Evan-Thomas for further honours: 'Although Rear-Admiral Evan-Thomas has but recently received the C.B., I would draw attention to the fact that he commands a Battle Squadron which was closely engaged, and that he is, with the exception of Rear-Admiral Heath, the senior Rear-Admiral in the Grand Fleet.'

Evan-Thomas died on Thursday, 30 August 1928 and is commemorated in his home town of Neath. The town's war memorial was later erected in the grounds of the place he called home, in Gnoll Gardens.

Rear Admiral Sir Hugh Evan-Thomas, commander of the 5th Battle Cruiser Squadron at the Battle of Jutland. (Imperial War Museum)

Another famous Welshman who survived the battle was Horace Elliot Rose Stephens, who was a surgeon aboard Sir David Beatty's flagship, HMS *Lion*. Stephens later co-wrote a paper entitled 'Surgical Experiences in the Battle of Jutland', which was first published in the *Journal of the Royal Naval Medical Service* of October 1916.

Stephens was born on 4 January 1883, the son of the Reverend Horace Stephens, rector of Handley, Cheshire and was educated at Christ College, Brecon, Manchester University and at the London Hospital. He played rugby for Manchester University and also represented Cheshire and Lancashire. During 1910 he joined the Royal Navy as a surgeon and in August 1914 was appointed to HMS *Eclipse* before transferring to HMS *Lion* in April 1915. He was awarded the Croix de Guerre and OBE for his work during the war. He later served around the world with the Royal Navy and, following a period of illness in 1935, became Professor of Naval Hygiene and Director of Medical Studies at the RN Medical School at Greenwich. He retired on 4 January 1943 and died at home at Trearddur Bay, Anglesey on 18 February 1959. Part of his report, written in conjunction with Fleet Surgeon Alexander McLean, illustrated the horrors dealt with by the medical staff and also the difficulty of treating wounded men aboard a ship:

The medical organization on HMS *Lion* possessed two distributing stations for the shelter of the medical staff, stretcher parties, instruments, and medical stores. These were divided as equally as possible between the two stations. The forward station was small, though well protected. As it would accommodate not more than a dozen wounded, only walking patients proceeded to it. The after station was too small for the accommodation of wounded, so that stores and instruments were kept in it. During action the mess-deck, which was behind armour, received all the stretcher cases which were placed in bathrooms or on mess tables. The wounded were not carried further than necessary. Those wounded in turrets and isolated compartments were only moved out of the way, and were not brought to the mess deck until a lull occurred in the action... The part of the mess deck which had been thoroughly prepared for the reception of wounded could not be used at all, as it was rendered untenable by fumes and smoke at the outset of the action... Well-trained first-aid parties, made up of writers, cooks, stewards, and canteen hands, did most valuable work, as the rest of the ship's company shrank from dressing wounds, although they would tend fallen shipmates with brotherly affection.

Nearly all the casualties on this ship occurred within the first half hour. A few patients found their way to the fore station, but the majority remained on the mess-deck. During the first lull the medical officers made a tour of inspection of the ship. The scenes that greeted them beggared description. Most of the wounded had already been dressed. Tourniquets had been applied in one or two instances, though haemorrhage was less than might have been expected from the extensive lacerated wounds. As there was much water about the wounded were kept dry and warm on tables... During the evening ten of the desperately wounded and burned died. It was impossible to move any of the wounded during the night owing to the probability of a renewal of the action at dawn. Many of the wounded slept undisturbed.

Among the severe cases was that of R. B., aged 21 years. The left foot had been blown off by a shell. The surgeon probationer had trimmed and dressed the stump. There was a fearful shell wound of the left calf just below the knee, the bruising extending up the lower third of the thigh. The patient had lost much blood, was blanched and almost pulseless. He was given saline solution and brandy per rectum. The stump was dressed and treated with hypertonic salt solution. Four days later, as the patient had rallied, the stump, which was offensive, was amputated through the middle of the thigh. The stump became septic, and consequently one month later it was opened up and thoroughly cleansed. The flaps were dried and covered with bismuth and iodoform paste. Two days later there were signs of poisoning with iodoform. A severe secondary haemorrhage occurred, which necessitated the further opening of the wound. The bleeding was found to be derived from one of the perforating arteries, which was ligated. The patient slowly rallied, and six weeks later was able to get about on crutches.

Among the ships that had taken part in the Battle of Jutland was the armoured cruiser HMS *Hampshire*, which had been attached to the Second Cruiser Squadron. Upon returning to Scapa Flow she was boarded by Field Marshal Lord Kitchener and was ordered to take him to Archangel on a diplomatic mission.

Hampshire sailed from Scapa Flow during a gale at 4.45 pm on 5 June and went through the Pentland Firth before heading along the western coast of the Orkney Islands, where she met her escorts, the *Acasta*-class destroyers *Unity* and *Victor*. As the ships turned to the north-west a gale began to slow the destroyers, so *Hampshire* ordered them to return to Scapa Flow. At around 7.40 pm *Hampshire* struck a mine that had been laid by the German mine-laying submarine *U-75* on the night of 28/29 May and sank within fifteen minutes. Of the 655 crewmen and 7 passengers aboard, only 12 crewmen survived. Lord Kitchener and his staff were all lost.

At least fifteen Welshmen perished in the sinking of HMS *Hampshire*, including Fleet Surgeon Penry Garnons Williams of Abercamlais, Brecon. His brother, the former Welsh international rugby player Colonel Richard Davies Garnons Williams, was killed at Loos on 27 September 1915.

Chapter 7

The Battle of the Somme

In January 1916 the Somme sector had been chosen by the French commander General Joffre as the most suitable place for a joint offensive by the British and French. The offensive was planned to tie in with simultaneous attacks by the Russians and Italians and that these should start as soon as possible after 1 June 1916. On 4 June the Russians launched their Brusilov Offensive against the Austrians on a 200-mile front, relieving pressure on the Italians, who had suffered heavy losses on the Isonzo Front.

However, heavy French losses at Verdun led to the planned Franco-British offensive developing into a mainly British effort, although still with significant French support to the south of the River Somme, and over the months of May and June several divisions were moved into the area in readiness.

During this period of the war the allied thinking was that the only way of breaking through a defensive line was by first carrying out an artillery bombardment to smash the German defences and to follow this softening-up process with a massed infantry attack. Over the months prior to the launching of the offensive the forces deemed necessary to carry out such an attack were built up over a 22-mile front running from Maricourt in the south to Hannescamps, north of Gommecourt. The entire British sector behind this line was a seething mass of action, with lines of supply being built up and water supplies being readied for the vast number of troops, villages filling to bursting-point with tens of thousands of troops, artillery units being set up all along the front and casualty clearing stations and dressing stations established in order to tend to the impending casualties.

The preliminary artillery bombardment was carried out over several days prior to the launching of the battle, the date of which had been fixed for 29 June 1916. Over several months prior to the battle tunnelling companies of the Royal Engineers had been busy sapping tunnels beneath key German strongpoints and filling them with tons of ammonal and high explosive, ready to detonate them just prior to the infantry assaults.

Among the multitude of artillery batteries in the sector was a Welsh-raised unit, the 96th Siege Battery, Royal Garrison Artillery (RGA). The battery was one of several that had formed at Pembroke Dock, under the command of Major C.H.M. Sturges, on 1 January 1916. It was armed with four 6-inch, four 8-inch and four 9.2-inch howitzers and the nucleus of its men was drawn from officers and men of the Glamorgan and Pembroke Territorial RGA.

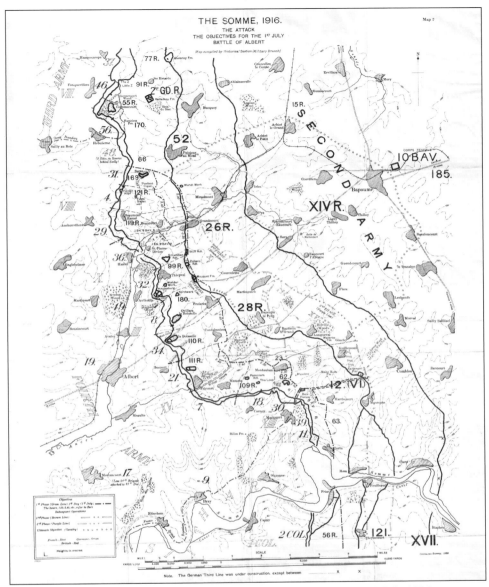

The positions of the German, British and French forces on the Somme, 1 July 1916.

On 4 February 1916 the battery entrained for Sheerness for training and on 20 May the first members of the battery began embarking from Southampton for Le Havre, while the guns went via rail to Avonmouth with a party of one officer and fourteen men. On 24 May the entire battery assembled at No. 3 Rest Camp, St. Martin's, Boulogne and four days later entrained for Doullens, in the rear of the Somme area. By 6 June the 96th Siege Battery was in place near St. Amand and on 25 June began

A British howitzer in action on the Somme, 1916.

bombarding the enemy positions in front of Gommecourt, the area earmarked for a diversionary attack by the 46th (North Midland) Division.

Over the coming days the battery began its bombardment of the Germans, and suffered its first casualty on 29 June when Sergeant William Rawlings (2393) was killed while digging up a gas shell. He is buried in St. Amand British Cemetery.

There were several Welsh units in place for the initial assault on 1 July. The 46th (North Midland) Division was in the line just north at Gommecourt, and included the 1st Monmouths as its Pioneer Battalion. The Royal Monmouth Royal Engineers were also in the sector carrying out work on railways and tunnels. The 29th Division, which included the 2nd SWB, was still holding the line opposite Beaumont Hamel. The 2nd Monmouths became the divisional Pioneer Battalion of the 29th Division on 1 May and so was in the same sector. The 49th (West Riding) Division was in reserve behind the 29th Division, and had the 3rd Monmouths as its Pioneer Battalion. The 19th (Western) Division, with the 9th RWF, 5th SWB and 9th Welsh, was to the south at Albert, in reserve for the assault on La Boisselle. The 7th Division, which included the 1st RWF, was still in positions at Bois Français, near Fricourt. The attack all along the line was launched at the same time, so we will look at the actions carried out by all the attacking formations from north to south, paying particular note of the Welsh involvement.

Preceded by the most destructive artillery barrage so far seen during the war, at 7.20 am on 1 July the sound of a massive explosion at Hawthorn Ridge heralded the blowing of one of eight large and eleven small mines that had been tunnelled under the German lines. Apart from one, which was blown some minutes later, the remainder were exploded as planned at 7.28 am and the infantry rose out of their trenches to attack at 7.30 am.

An exploding mine.

The 46th (North Midland) Division at Gommecourt was being used alongside the 56th (1st London) Division for a diversionary attack on Gommecourt to draw German attention away from the main assaults on Thiepval Ridge. Their attack was preceded by the release of smoke, but the wind was blowing the wrong way and the assaulting troops – 137 and 139 brigades – were tasked with capturing Gommecourt Wood, north east of the village, the 1st Monmouths were to follow up the attacking troops in order to consolidate any positions gained and to dig communication trenches.

At 7.30 am 137 and 139 brigades climbed out of their trenches and immediately came under heavy machine-gun fire from Gommecourt Wood and village. Only small parties of men reached the German wire, some getting through into the German trenches, but on the whole the attack was a catastrophe and by around 8 am it was realized that their attack had failed. Another attack was planned at 12.15 pm, but this was postponed until 3.30 pm due to the chaos. This final attack was carried out by only a small party of survivors and was soon brought to an abrupt halt. However, it was thought that 139 Brigade was still fighting in the German trenches and during the night a further attempt to advance to these men, who in fact were casualties, was ordered and the men reached the enemy wire before being withdrawn after suffering further losses. Together with the 56th Division, which had also failed, the British losses during the day at Gommecourt totalled some 2,206 killed, 3,766 wounded, 559 missing and 238 captured; a total of 6,769 men.

The 1st Monmouths had gallantly tried to consolidate what little positions were gained, but suffered more than 100 casualties during the day, 21 of them killed. The

Private William Small (3333), 1st Monmouths, the son of Robert and Elizabeth Small of 29 Agincourt Street, Newport. He died of wounds suffered at Gommecourt on 1 July 1916 aged 27 and is buried in Foncquevillers Military Cemetery.

remnants of the battalion moved out via Pommiers for billets at Berles, south-west of Arras, the following day. Most of the men killed, including Private William Small (3333), were from Newport, Monmouthshire.

To the south the 4th Division attacked between Serre and Beaumont Hamel and captured the Quadrilateral Redoubt, or *Heidenkopf* (named after a German commander), but could not exploit their gains due to the failures of the divisions on each flank. No further gains were made here and the positions were lost following a German counter-attack the following day. The division had suffered 4,700 casualties. The 31st Division was ordered to capture Serre and then turn north to form the northern defensive flank of the Fourth Army, and small groups of men from the Accrington Pals and the Sheffield City Battalion managed to reach Serre but were bombed back by the Germans.

To the south the 29th Division had faced an impossible task due to the firing of the Hawthorn Ridge Mine. The Germans, shellshocked as they were, knew an attack was imminent and were ready. The men had also been ordered to wear tin triangles, in the shape of the divisional crest, on their backs to allow them to be spotted more easily by their own spotters. (The blowing of the Hawthorn mine and the attack was captured on cinematic camera.) The division had been given the task of capturing Hawthorn Ridge and Y Ravine, a deep valley to its south, which had been heavily fortified by the Germans and contained a network of tunnels and dugouts.

The orders passed to the 2nd SWB for their attack on Y Ravine were simple: the battalion was to move back into the trenches from reserve at Englebelmer on the day before the attack and line up as follows:

> A Company in firing line from the left of the B2 sector up to and including B St.
>
> D Company in firing line from the right of the B2 sector to B St. exclusive.
>
> C Company in support and occupying the deep bombardment dugouts in Reserve trench and St. John's Road.
>
> B Company at Englebelmer.
>
> HQ Bombers. Four squads holding the Bomb trench in 1st Avenue – Haymarket – Clonmel Avenue and Carlisle Street. Two squads at Englebelmer.

The orders also specified the location of dugouts for HQ, a special gas party, Royal Engineers and signallers and gave specific orders for the companies to move into position on the night preceding the attack. Positions of machine guns and Lewis guns to cover the attack were also meticulously laid out, as well as the positions of Stokes mortars and details of the artillery bombardments. The final section of the plans laid out how the captured trenches would be consolidated, where HQ would move to and how ammunition and supplies would be brought up.

Everything appeared to be positive, and the men were confident that the artillery barrage would annihilate the German defences, making the assault something of a walkover. However, as things turned out, nothing could be further from the truth.

Two nights prior to the offensive Major Raikes, commanding the 2nd SWB, sent out wire-cutting patrols to cut through the German defences. The patrol on the battalion's left flank, led by Second Lieutenant John Bowler Karran, started out from a sunken road but came into contact with a German patrol. One German was shot dead, but the exchange of fire caused the Germans to send up flares and begin firing machine guns into the darkness. A red flare from the Germans was spotted which was the signal to their gunners and within minutes an artillery barrage crashed down in no man's land, forcing the patrol to return to the safety of their own trenches. Luckily there were no casualties suffered by the Borderers. Karran's report stated that they had found a deep German dugout that appeared to be much larger than those occupied by themselves. It would be these deep dugouts that would be the deciding factor on the first day of the forthcoming battle.

Second Lieutenant John Bowler Karran, 2nd SWB. A native of the Isle of Man, Karran was killed during his battalion's assault on Y Ravine on 1 July 1916.

As the debris from the blowing of the Hawthorn mine was still in the air, the men of the 2nd SWB arose from their trenches at 7.20 am and advanced through pre-cut gaps in the wire to attack Y Ravine, but the Germans had returned to their posts and the leading Borderers were mown down by machine-gun and rifle fire within 30 yards of their own front line and within less than ten minutes had lost 70 per cent of their strength. To make matters worse, the Germans then opened up a deadly barrage of shrapnel on the attacking troops. Not one man reached his objective and B Company was then sent over the top, meeting the same fate. The nearest the Borderers got to the German front line was when the survivors of A Company managed to close within just under 20 metres of them before being forced to ground.

The view over the battlefield crossed by the 29th Division on 1 July 1916, looking from the Newfoundland Caribou Memorial down towards Y Ravine and the cemetery.

Private David Thomas (18563), 2nd SWB, the son of Isaac and Mary Thomas of Llwynhelig, Farmers. He was 34 years old when he was killed on 1 July 1916 and is buried in Y Ravine Cemetery, Beaumont Hamel. His nephew Johnny was killed just ten days later.

The 2nd SWB had suffered heavy casualties during its charge towards Y Ravine. Ten officers – Captains Francis Seymour Blake, Alexander Arbuthnot Hughes and Robert John McLaren; Lieutenant Humphrey Pennefather Evans; Second Lieutenants George Henry Bowyer MC, David Fairweather Don, John Bowler Karran, Fred Rice, John Robinson and Thomas William Maurice Wells – and 125 men had been killed. Including those killed, wounded and missing, the battalion had lost 399 officers and men, mostly within ten minutes, and had been virtually annihilated. It was only because a 10 per cent battle reserve had been left at Englebelmer that enough men of the battalion survived to enable it to be later rebuilt.

Reports of the heroic efforts of the South Wales Borderers were published in the Welsh press within days of the battle. One man, Private Tucker, was wounded by a machine-gun bullet and lay out in the open throughout the day, afraid to move after seeing the Germans machine gun firing on any wounded comrades who tried to get up or made any noise. Another man stated:

It was a million times worse than hell, but splendid in spite of that. From the moment we showed ourselves over our own parapet we got it hell hot. The steadiness of our men under it all made one feel proud of being Welsh. It was often a question of passing between bullets that would shave you as clean as the smartest barber in the world, but our lads never showed fear. They pressed onward and upward towards the enemy position in front of us as though they were on manoeuvres. One terrible moment came when we were mid-way across 'No Man's Land'. Without the slightest warning the ground under our feet gave way, and we seemed to sink down and down until we hardly knew what to make of it. We had rushed into a series of carefully concealed pits that had been covered over to give us the impression that the ground was solid. At once we were raked by a murderous fire, and we suffered severely. There was, however, nothing that could be fairly done.

Corporal Walter Chase Upton (24817), 2nd SWB. A railway porter with the GWR prior to the war, Upton's body was later found lying in no man's land and was buried in Y Ravine Cemetery.

Private John Henry Evans (1404), 2nd Monmouths, the son of David Evans of 11 Tanycoed Terrace, Abercwmboi. Evans was 26 years old when he was killed on 1 July 1916 and is commemorated on the Thiepval Memorial.

The 1st Border Regiment was then ordered over the top at 8.15 am to support the 2nd SWB and climbed out of the support trenches only to be mown down by machine-gun fire before even reaching the original British front line. Just on this narrow sector two full battalions had been practically destroyed and to continue to attack such a strongly-defended position was obviously absolute folly; however, the Newfoundland Regiment was then ordered to attack and suffered the same fate. Some 14 officers and 296 other ranks were killed, died of wounds or were missing believed killed, and a further 12 officers and 362 other ranks were wounded; a total of 684 all ranks out of a fighting strength of about 929.

The 2nd Monmouths had gone into the line with only 200 steel helmets among the entire battalion. The rest of the men had been told to take helmets from the dead as soon as possible. Within half an hour of the opening of the battle, every member of the battalion had got hold of a helmet. Even with no ground being gained by the division, the 2nd Monmouths still suffered twenty-nine men killed without going into the attack themselves.

Altogether during the first day of the Battle of the Somme, the 29th Division had suffered 5,240 casualties, the second-highest suffered by any of the attacking divisions during that day.

The memorial to the 29th Division at the entrance to the Newfoundland Park.

To the south the 36th (Ulster) Division attacked between Thiepval and just north of the River Ancre including the Schwaben Redoubt, and gained one of the few victories of the day. Their artillery bombardment had been more successful than many on other parts of the front north of the Albert-Bapaume road and, the infantry had crept into no man's land before the attack, rushed the German front trench and then pressed on. However, the failures of the other divisions on both flanks meant that the Ulstermen were enfiladed by the Germans and the German artillery then began a barrage that isolated their forward troops. The German second line at Schwaben and Stuff redoubts were reached but the Ulstermen were forced back to the German front trench during the evening after losing around 5,104 casualties.

South of the Ulstermen, the Leipzig Salient and Thiepval village were attacked by the 32nd Division and captured the Leipzig Redoubt. The division was unable to press further due to heavy fire from the *Wunderwerk* (Wonder Work) German trench system and the capture of the redoubt was the only permanent success in the northern sector. The 49th Division, which included the 3rd Monmouths as its Pioneer Battalion, was in reserve and moved forward during mid-morning in support of the 32nd Division and attacked Thiepval through the 32nd Division area. It was then ordered to send any surplus units to support the 36th Division. The 32nd Division suffered 3,949 casualties and the 49th Division suffered 590 casualties; however, the 3rd Monmouths had suffered none.

The 8th Division attacked the Ovillers spur, north of the Albert-Bapaume road, having to cross 690 metres of no man's land up Mash Valley. A party of around 200 men reached the German second trench and then held about 270 metres of the front trench until 9.15 am. The troops were then forced back to their own front line following a German counter-attack. The 8th Division had lost 5,121 men, including eighteen Welshmen of the 2nd Devons.

The 34th Division attacked along the Albert-Bapaume road, following the blowing of the two largest mines either side of La Boiselle: Y Sap and Lochnagar. To the south of the road the British got into the newly-formed Lochnagar Crater but became pinned down. The Tyneside Scottish Brigade then attacked up Mash Valley against La Boiselle at the Glory Hole, with the Tyneside Irish Brigade in reserve ready to exploit any gains and to capture the second objective, from Contalmaison to Pozières.

The division advanced up Sausage Valley, south of La Boiselle, and almost reached Contalmaison, but had suffered heavy casualties and the survivors were surrounded and captured. The 34th Division had suffered the worst casualties of the day, losing 6,380 men. In reserve to both the 8th and 34th divisions was the 19th (Western) Division, which included the 9th RWF, 5th SWB and 9th Welsh.

The 19th Division had been given the following orders:

To capture the southern half of the second objective in case the 34th Division failed to get further than the first objective.

To capture the northern half of the second objective should the 8th Division fail to get beyond the first objective.

A view of Lochnagar Crater. It is impossible to sense the proportions of the crater from the photograph. It is huge, measuring about 91 metres in diameter and 21 metres in depth.

The Tyneside Irish Brigade advancing on 1 July 1916.

To capture the whole of the 'Intermediate' line if both the 8th and 34th Divisions were held up.

To capture the final objective should both the 8th and 34th Divisions take the first and second objectives but fail to get beyond the latter.

The first objective ran from a point just south-west of Peake Woods to the eastern outskirts of Ovillers, then north to the northern Corps boundary, about 1,000 metres south-west of Mouquet Farm. The second objective ran from just east of Peake Woods, past the western outskirts of Contalmaison, Contalmaison Wood and Pozières to a point about 140 metres south-east of Mouquet Farm. The dividing line between the 34th and 8th divisions ran through Mash Valley, between La Boisselle and Ovillers, so La

Boisselle and Contalmaison lay in the 34th Divisional area of attack and Ovillers and Pozières in the territory to be captured by the 8th Division.

The forward troops of the 19th Division had watched with morbid fascination as the attack was launched at 7.30 am:

> With almost as great a violence as when they began at 6.30 am, the guns suddenly ceased, long lines of khaki-clad figures leapt from their trenches and began to move quickly across No Man's Land. Immediately the sharp barking of scores of machine-guns filled the momentary silence as the guns lifted off the German front line, and in many places the advancing lines of troops were almost swept away. The first waves were followed closely by others, in many places suffering the same fate. South of Fricourt the attack went splendidly and rapid progress was made. Between Fricourt and La Boisselle the 21st Division, attacking from north of the village, after stubborn fighting swept the enemy back to his support trenches. But on the left of the 21st Division the 34th Division, attacking north and south of La Boisselle, succeeded only in penetrating the enemy's front line south of the village; little or no headway was made north of it. The 8th Division, on the left of the 34th fared even worse. By mid-day but little real progress had been made and no impression had been made on La Boisselle itself. The fighting had been of an extremely confused nature and no one could tell how far the troops had got, how much of the enemy's trench system had been captured or where exactly anybody or anything was, though subsequently some of the 34th Division dead were found beyond La Boisselle.

La Boisselle was still very strongly defended and, as the 34th and 8th divisions had both suffered heavily, the 19th Division was called upon to capture the village. The order to attack La Boisselle was received late in the afternoon of 1 July, and at 7.15 pm orders were issued from Divisional Headquarters: 'The 57th and 58th Brigades will attack at 10.30 pm tonight from the general line X.13 central–X.20 central, and will establish themselves on the line X.14.d.9.2–X.14.c.3.9. The dividing line between brigades will be the La Boisselle-Contalmaison road.'

The plan was for 58 Brigade to attack on the right and 57 Brigade on the left, gaining touch with each other on the La Boisselle to Contalmaison road just east of the village. Meanwhile 57 Brigade was to dig a trench to connect the western corner of La Boisselle with the British front line. Eight men from the 9th Welsh were killed while moving into position during the night, but as yet neither the 9th RWF nor 5th SWB had suffered any losses.

At 3 pm the battalions moved forward to their allotted positions in the front line, support and reserve trenches. The area held by the 34th Division was congested with parties of stretcher-bearers and wounded men, and it was impossible to get the fresh attacking troops of 57 and 58 brigades into position in the allotted time, thus delaying the start of the assault.

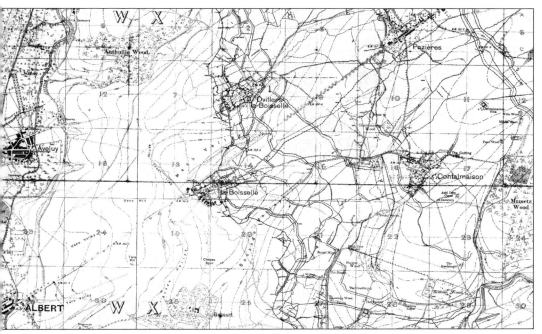

A section of a trench map showing the German positions around La Boisselle.

No. 58 Brigade formed up on the Tara-Usna line, with the 9th Cheshires on the right, 6th Wiltshires on the left, 9th RWF in the rear and in support of the Cheshires, and the 9th Welsh behind the Wiltshires. Only the 9th Cheshires, with orders to take up position from Lochnagar Street to Inch Street, reached their positions in time and their CO, Lieutenant Colonel Worgan, ordered B and D companies to reinforce troops of the 34th Division near the new crater. He then set out to find the remainder of the battalion and came across the 9th RWF, who had not received their orders, in the communication trenches.

Worgan returned to his battalion, where he received a telephone call to attack without delay and by 2.50 am on 2 July he moved the 9th Cheshires into the crater and the line beside it, and contact was made with the Germans.

We will leave the 19th Division for now to complete the happenings of the first day's fighting along the Somme front.

* * *

To the south of the 34th Division, the village of Fricourt lay in a bend in the front line where it turned eastwards for 2 miles before swinging south again to the Somme River. XV Corps was to attack either side of the village and surround it to avoid a frontal assault. The 7th Division sent its 20 Brigade in to capture the western edge of Mametz village and to create a defensive flank along the Willow Stream, facing Fricourt from the south, while 22 Brigade, to which the 1st RWF was attached, waited to exploit a German retirement from the village. The 1st RWF was ordered to support the attack

The 1st RWF advancing towards Mametz on 1 July 1916.

of 22 Brigade against Sunken Road Trench and as the assaulting battalions moved forward at 7.30 am the 1st RWF followed in support, reaching their allotted positions as follows: A Company at Sunken Road Trench; B Company, New Trench; and D Company in reserve at the Quarries. A brigade mobile reserve, under the command of Captain Edmund Dadd, was also in reserve.

The 21st Division advanced at 7.30 am to the north of Fricourt, ordered to reach the north bank of the Willow Stream beyond Fricourt and Fricourt Wood. Three mines, known as the Triple Tambour mines, were blown beneath the Tambour Salient to obscure the view of the Germans on the assaulting troops. The 21st Division made some progress and advanced beyond Fricourt, while 50 Brigade, 17th Division, held the front line opposite the village. During the first day the 21st Division suffered 4,256 casualties and 50 Brigade, 17th Division had suffered 1,155 casualties.

At 9 am Lieutenant Colonel Stockwell of the 1st RWF received orders for his battalion to advance at 10.30 am, so he passed his orders on to his company commanders to get ready; however, at 10 am the attack was delayed owing to the fact that the 7th and 21st division attacks had been held up on the right. Zero hour was subsequently set for 2.30 pm, when the 20th Manchesters attacked on the right of the 1st RWF but were immediately enfiladed by machine-gun fire and the remnants of the battalion reached Bois Français Trench and Bois Français Support, while a small party reached Sunken Road Trench.

The 20th Manchesters then sent a runner back to the 1st RWF asking for help, and Stockwell sent A Company forward via some craters to Bois Français in an attempt to outflank the German machine-gunners.

The village of Fricourt was still in German hands and the 20th Manchesters and A Company of the 1st RWF became jammed in the Bois Français trenches, so Captain Edmund Dadd and his brigade mobile reserve was called up to co-operate and clear Zinc Trench in order to safeguard the flank of the advanced troops.

Looking towards Bois Français over the remains of old trenches and reputedly a Second World War anti-aircraft gun emplacement.

At 7.45 pm a party of bombers from the 1st RWF under Lieutenant Stevens was ordered to advance and capture the Sunken Road and the Rectangle and place them in a state of defence and after a fierce fight this was carried out by 10.30 pm. The battalion moved its machine guns forward during the night. Just before midnight, news was received that the Germans had withdrawn and Stockwell asked permission to attack Wing Copse but was refused.

Casualties suffered during the first day of the battle among the 1st RWF amounted to just four men killed and thirty-five wounded. A large number of prisoners and a quantity of machine guns and trench mortars had been captured. The parents of one of the dead men, Private Frank Harris (31819) of Llandrindod Wells, received several letters from the friends of their obviously popular young son after his death on the opening day of the battle. Captain Edmund Dadd wrote:

I knew your son well, and as his Company Commander I feel I must say how deeply I feel for you in your bereavement. Your son was my company runner, which means that he could be relied upon to go anywhere under any circumstances, and

The grave of Private Frank Harris (31819), 1st RWF. Harris was the son of Arthur and Annie Harris of Weymouth Villa, Tremont Road, Llandrindod Wells. He was 18 years old when he was killed on the opening day of the Battle of the Somme and is buried in Dantzig Alley British Cemetery, Mametz.

the position is therefore considered a high honour. I had a long talk with him the night before the attack, and he was very cheerful, and quite looking forward to getting to close quarters with the Germans. He had no thought of personal danger at all. I was not actually with him when he was killed, but his platoon sergeant tells me that he was hit in the throat by a piece of shell just before the assault, and was killed instantly. He was buried by his comrades behind our lines the same night.

At the same time, three friends of Harris wrote the following:

We had both been very friendly since we got together some months ago. I was with your son 10 minutes before he got wounded. We were both together in the second German trench after we had captured it, and it was there he got hit with a German bomb. He was alive when he left the trenches for I was talking to the men, and they all had good hope of him recovering. He must have passed away in the hospital somewhere.

Frank and I became friends when we were sent to help the R.E. in the mines. Frank and myself were given a very dangerous job together. We had to stop together in the darkness for eight hours to listen if the Germans were working towards us, and ever since that we have been very good friends and always together when out of the trenches... I have taken part in five of the biggest battles that were ever fought, and I must say that I have been very lucky. Frank was in the battle of Fricourt, and it was then he got hit and also his other friend, Jack Hughes, of Stafford.

I am very sorry to tell you that Frank was killed straight out, and there was not a word from him. He was hit by taking a message to the German front line. We had taken the front line from them, and he was hit straight out. He was a pal of mine, and one of the best. He was a nice lad, I could have dropped down when I heard about it. I was only about 20 yards from him when he got hit and if he had been able he would have spoken to me and we might have had a chance to save him, but there was no hope.

Armed with the knowledge that the Germans had withdrawn from Fricourt, the 7th Division pushed on during the night to positions facing Mametz Wood and the Willow Stream. The division had suffered 3,380 casualties.

On the morning of 2 July the 1st RWF was ordered to seize Rose Alley and advanced in conjunction with the advance of the 17th Division on Fricourt. A Company occupied Rose Alley with little resistance, while B Company remained at Rectangle and Rectangle Support; D Company held the battalion's front line with a post at Wing Corner. The night was quiet, and casualties for 2 July amounted to just one man missing and four wounded.

The battalion rested in bivouacs in a valley north-west of Caftet Wood throughout most of 3 July and after dusk were ordered to consolidate a position on the southern edge of the as yet largely undefended Mametz Wood. The guide lost his way while leading the battalion forward under the cover of darkness and as a result it was daybreak on 4 July before they got into position, but were ordered to withdraw at 6 am and returned to their bivouacs.

Precious time and opportunity were being wasted during this period, enabling the Germans to reinforce their positions inside Mametz Wood. Siegfried Sassoon, still angered by the death several months earlier of his friend Lieutenant David Thomas, made a one man reconnaissance into the edge of Mametz Wood on 4 July, meeting Second Lieutenant Newton, known as 'Fernby' in his book *Memoirs of an Infantry Officer*. According to Robert Graves, Sassoon had thrown some grenades at a party of Germans before sitting down for several hours to read a book of poetry, and in the process held up a planned artillery bombardment for three hours while Lieutenant Colonel Stockwell awaited his report. This lack of sense of urgency was an error that would cost the 38th (Welsh) Division dearly over the coming days.

On 4 July the 1st RWF and Royal Irish were ordered to capture and consolidate a position running from Quadrangle Trench through Wood Trench to Strip Trench and during the evening attacked on a front running from the light railway into the wood and Bottom Alley. Four men were killed and twelve more wounded during the attack. At 12.45 am on 5 July the battalion moved towards Bottom Wood. Captain Edmund Dadd reported to Stockwell that A and B companies had captured Quadrangle Trench but that the Royal Irish had failed to capture Wood Trench, and it was found that the Germans covered the gap between the two with a machine gun. Lieutenant Stevens and Captain Dadd then took a party of bombers forward and cleared the communication trenches leading to Quadrangle Support and established a strongpoint that was reinforced by six Lewis guns.

The situation was chaotic but the 1st RWF beat off several counter-attacks during the day, losing nine men killed and two officers and fifty-five men wounded before being relieved during the night by the 14th RWF of the 38th (Welsh) Division, which had just moved up into positions south of Mametz Wood. The 1st RWF then marched into reserve via Mametz and Fricourt to bivouac 2 miles south of Méaulte. We shall look at the actions of the 38th (Welsh) Division in the next sub-chapter.

The southern flank of the British line was held by XIII Corps, which attacked Montauban with the 30th and 18th divisions and was the most successful area of operations for the British during the opening day. The 30th Division took its objectives by 1.00 pm and the 18th Division by 3.00 pm; Bernafay and Trônes Woods were captured by noon. The 30th Division had suffered 3,011 casualties, the 18th Division 3,115.

At the end of the opening day of the Somme offensive the British army had suffered almost 60,000 casualties, by far the greatest number it had ever suffered in one day in its entire history to then. Of these, almost 20,000 men were dead. Barely any ground had been captured and held on to, except in the southern area. Among this stupefying number of casualties were almost 400 Welshmen. Several major mistakes had been made. The British had underestimated the strength of the German defenders, who had sheltered safely below ground while the artillery had been pounding their lines, and the gap in the timings between the blowing of the mines and the infantry assault had given the German machine gunners ample time to return to their posts and reap a terrible harvest of death upon the British infantry. The latter had also been ordered to advance slowly across no man's land, loaded down with equipment such as entrenching tools, shovels and spades, therefore making easy targets for the Germans.

The day had been a disaster but instead of calling off the battle, it was continued the following day and other units were called into the line, among them the 38th (Welsh) Division, which was by now encamped near Heilly, in the Somme valley.

Two further Victoria Crosses were won during the day by men with Welsh connections. Major Stewart Walker Loudoun-Shand was the son of John Loudoun-Shand of Dulwich, London. He had served with the Pembroke Yeomanry during the Boer War and, on 12 December 1915, became second-in-command of the 10th Yorks. He was killed during the opening assault on the Somme on 1 July 1916 and is buried in Norfolk Cemetery, Bécordel-Bécourt. His citation reads as follows:

> For most conspicuous bravery. When his company attempted to climb over the parapet to attack the enemy's trenches, they were met by very fierce machine gun fire, which temporarily stopped their progress. Maj. Loudoun-Shand immediately leapt on the parapet, helped the men over it, and encouraged them in every way until he fell mortally wounded. Even then he insisted on being propped up in the trench, and went on encouraging the non-commissioned officers and men until he died. (*London Gazette*, 8 September 1916.)

Major Stewart Walker Loudon-Shand VC, a former member of the Pembroke Yeomanry.

The second was won by Major Lionel Wilmot Brabazon Rees of 32 Squadron, Royal Flying Corps. Rees was born at 5 Castle Street, Caernarfon in 1884, the son of Charles Herbert Rees, a colonel in the RWF, and his wife Leonora. He was educated at Eastbourne College before entering the Royal Military Academy at Woolwich in 1902 and was commissioned on 23 December 1903 in the Royal Garrison Artillery. He learned to fly in 1912 while attached to the West African Frontier Force and joined the Royal Flying Corps in August 1914. He soon gained a reputation as a fearless fighter, winning the Military Cross for two instances of gallantry:

> When flying a machine with one machine gun, accompanied by Flight-Sergeant Hargreaves, he sighted a large German biplane with two machine guns 2,000 feet below him. He spiralled down and dived at the enemy, who, having the faster machine, manoeuvred to get him broadside on and then opened heavy

fire. Despite this, Captain Rees pressed his attack and apparently succeeded in hitting the enemy's engine, for the machine made a quick turn, glided some distance and finally fell just inside the German lines near Herbécourt.

On 28 July he attacked and drove down a hostile monoplane despite the main spar of his machine having been shot through and the rear spar shattered. On 31 August, accompanied by Flight-Sergeant Hargreaves, he fought a German machine more powerful than his own for three-quarters of an hour, then returned for more ammunition and went out to the attack again, finally bringing the enemy's machine down, apparently wrecked. (*London Gazette*, 29 October 1915.)

Rees returned to England at the end of 1915 to take command of the Central Flying School Flight at Upavon and in June 1916 he took 32 Squadron to France. Within days he had gained the award of the Victoria Cross while on patrol on the opening day of the Somme offensive:

*Major Lionel Wilmot Brabazon Rees, 32 Squadron, RFC. (*IWM Q68027*)*

On 1 July 1916 at the Double Crassiers, France, Major Rees, whilst on flying duties, sighted what he thought was a bombing party of our machines returning home, but were in fact enemy aircraft. Major Rees was attacked by one of them, but after a short encounter it disappeared, damaged. The others then attacked him at long range, but he dispersed them, seriously damaging two of the machines. He chased two others but was wounded in the thigh, temporarily losing control of his aircraft. He righted it and closed with the enemy, using up all his ammunition, firing at very close range. He then returned home, landing his aircraft safely. (*London Gazette*, 5 August 1916.)

Rees continued on his glittering military career after the war and also served during the Second World War. His medals are part of the Lord Ashcroft collection.

On 2 July the majority of the units that had attacked on the previous day had been so badly depleted that they were moved back into reserve. At La Boisselle the 19th Division was now fully in position in readiness to restart the attack towards Contalmaison.

When dawn broke on 2 July the division was lined up as follows: 56 Brigade was in a reserve line south of Albert; 57 Brigade was in the front line opposite the northern end of the La Boisselle Salient, having been unable to carry out the attack owing to the state of the trenches and the impossibility of organizing it; 58 Brigade was in the front line opposite the southern end of the salient, with the 9th Cheshires in the German front line on the fringe of the village and the newly created Lochnagar Crater. North

British troops exploring a fresh crater.

of the 19th Division the 12th Division had relieved the 8th Division and everything was set for a fresh attack.

During the early afternoon the 7th East Lancs, the reserve battalion of 56 Brigade, was ordered to send two companies up to support the 34th Division in an attack on the Heligoland Redoubt. The combined force successfully captured the Redoubt, as well as almost 1,000 metres of German trenches.

* * *

Back on the 19th Division front, the attack on La Boisselle was planned to be carried out by 58 Brigade, with the 6th Wiltshires on the right and the 9th RWF on the left. The 9th Cheshires were on the right of the Wiltshires, whilst the 9th Welsh had received orders to provide carrying parties, with their bombers, under Second Lieutenant E.R. Kelly, being attached to the 9th RWF for the assault.

Zero hour was planned for 4 pm and as a diversion a preliminary artillery barrage fell on the village of Ovillers, followed by a smoke barrage. The Germans retaliated by firing a barrage in front of Ovillers, where they thought the assault would take place, while in the meantime 58 Brigade raced across no man's land towards La Boisselle.

By around 5 pm the Wiltshires had secured the western point of La Boisselle and the 9th RWF had taken German trenches to the south of the village. The 9th Welsh brought up supplies and munitions while the attackers regrouped in readiness for the next phase of their assault.

So far all had gone well; however, when the assault was resumed at a little after 5 pm the Germans had regrouped and fierce hand-to-hand fighting now took place within the trenches. The majority of the objectives in the village had been secured within one and a half hours of the first attack and the western edge of the village had been cleared of the enemy, while bombing parties fought their way towards the centre of the village.

By midnight the 9th RWF was holding the positions they had been ordered to take and parties of the 9th Welsh continued their work, bringing mostly trench mortar shells up in preparation for the continuation of the offensive on the following day.

By midnight on 2 July the 9th RWF had suffered comparatively lightly, with just one officer, Captain Ernest Kerrison Jones, and four men killed during the day's action. Captain Jones was the son of John Kerrison Jones of Glasfryn, Wrexham. He was regarded as one of the most brilliant students to have been educated at Grove Park School, Wrexham and had started his degree at in the University College, Oxford when war broke out. He volunteered to serve in the army and was commissioned in the 8th RWF, seeing service in Gallipoli before being invalided home wounded. He was then posted to the 9th RWF and was killed at La Boisselle on 2 July 1916, aged 24. He is commemorated on the Thiepval Memorial. The CO of the 9th RWF, Lieutenant Colonel Berners, wrote to his parents:

Captain Ernest Kerrison Jones, 9th RWF, killed near La Boiselle on 2 July 1916. He was the son of John Kerrison Jones of Glasfryn, Wrexham. He was 24 years old and is commemorated on the Thiepval Memorial.

I deeply regret having to tell you of the death of your son, who was killed while commanding A Company of my battalion in the recent fighting. On Sunday afternoon we were called upon to assault the German trenches opposing us, near the village of La Boisselle (near Albert). This involved a charge over some 150 yards of ground swept by machine guns. This was gallantly carried out by the battalion, and it was shortly after gaining the German line that your son was killed. We all of us regret his death greatly, and as his commanding officer I have lost the assistance of an officer of considerable ability and promise. In this fighting the brigade, I am proud to say, has earned the praise of the 4th Army Commander, but the success earned is due almost entirely to the young men who, like your son, have come forward and trained and led the men so splendidly. May I offer you my sincere sympathy in your loss.

The 9th RWF had been attacked by the Germans from their main point of resistance, a trench that ran about 50 metres east of the church, at around midnight but beat off the attack. Similar counter-attacks continued throughout the early hours of 3 June and the British troops could only admire the courage of the German bombers.

At 3 am on 3 July the 12th Division, on the left of the 19th Division, assaulted Ovillers, while 57 Brigade attacked towards the northern portion of La Boisselle. The

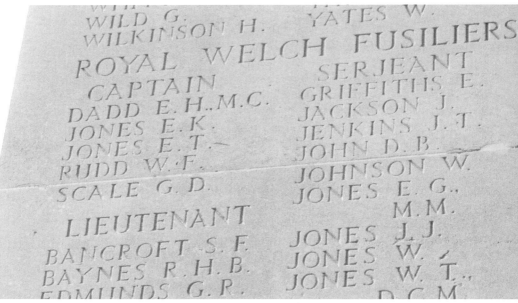

A section of the Thiepval Memorial showing the names of officers of the Royal Welsh Fusiliers, including Captain Ernest Kerrison Jones, who were killed on the Somme.

8th North Staffs and bombers from the 10th Worcesters attacked with men of the 8th Gloucesters and penetrated through La Boisselle before being forced back after running out of bombs. The first Victoria Cross to be won by the 19th Division occurred during this phase of the battle, when Private Thomas George Turrall (20572) of the 10th Worcesters:

> on his own initiative, stayed behind for three hours with his officer (Lieutenant R.W. Jennings), though under heavy fire from machine-guns and bombs. Finally, he succeeded in carrying him back to our lines. The enemy actually occupied the position in which Lieut. Jennings was wounded, and at one time he and Private Turrall were completely cut off from the battalion until a counter-attack drove the Germans back again. Having carried Lieut. Jennings to the Battalion Aid Post, Private Turrall returned at once to his company and continued to fight with great gallantry until the battalion was withdrawn.

By 5.30 am the division had made good progress and had reached a line of trenches that ran roughly just in front of the church, in touch with 58 Brigade on the right. The other three battalions of the brigade were in the village mopping up.

The 9th RWF had attacked simultaneously with 57 Brigade on their left and had encountered very strong opposition, although the battalion managed to push the line forward past the church, where they met up with the North Staffs of 57 Brigade. The whole of La Boisselle, with the exception of four houses on the eastern edge of it, had now been captured and at about 8.10 am Divisional Headquarters received a report that the village was clear of the enemy, although snipers still posed a threat throughout the day.

At around 8.30 am the Germans began a series of counter-attacks against 58 Brigade and the Wiltshires, Cheshires and 9th RWF were forced back. The 9th Welsh were sent up to reinforce the 9th RWF at around 11 am and, following fierce fighting, the positions had been regained by 12.30 pm. Captain Gardner took a party of fifty men to consolidate a crater and sent back intelligence pertaining to the situation facing the 9th Welsh and at 3.30 pm his party had consolidated a section of German trench adjoining the crater, at co-ordinates Z.20.A.0.5 to X.20.B.4.3. The remainder of the battalion then advanced to these positions and began work in consolidating more of the line, which came under heavy shellfire during the afternoon, and at 9 pm the 9th Welsh was ordered to withdraw back to the Tara to Usna line.

The division had by now gained a strong foothold in La Boisselle; to ensure enough men were in place the 7th Battalion, King's Own (Royal Lancaster Regiment) of 56 Brigade were placed under the orders of 58 Brigade and sent up to brigade reserve. [All further instances of 'King's Own' without a qualifier refer to this regiment.]

All the troops in the village then came under the command of Lieutenant Colonel Adrian Carton de Wiart, the CO of the 8th Gloucesters. It was his leadership during the German counter-attack on 3 July that saved the day for 57 Brigade. The commanding officers of the 8th North Staffords (Major C. Wedgwood) and 10th Worcesters (Lieutenant Colonel G.A. Royston Pigott) had been killed and Lieutenant Colonel R.M. Heath, commanding 10th Warwicks, was wounded, so Carton de Wiart took command of these battalions as well as his own and inspired the men of 57 Brigade to hold their ground. He was awarded the division's second Victoria Cross of the day for his actions in saving the situation:

> For most conspicuous bravery, coolness and determination during severe operations of a prolonged nature. It was owing in a great measure to his dauntless courage and inspiring example that a serious reverse was averted. He displayed the utmost energy and courage in forcing our attack home. After three other battalion Commanders had become casualties, he controlled their commands, and ensured that the ground won was maintained at all costs. He frequently exposed himself in the organisation of positions and of supplies, passing unflinchingly through fire barrage of the most intense nature. His gallantry was inspiring to all. (*London Gazette*, 9 September 1916.)

By the time darkness fell on 3 July all the units of the 19th Division counted their losses. All of them had suffered badly; the 9th RWF had lost two officers – Lieutenant Glyn Cadwallader Roberts and Second Lieutenant Charles Duncan McCammon – and forty-four men killed during the day.

Among the men killed was Sergeant William Jones (13664), the son of Richard and Sarah Jones of 20 Bryn Ogwy Terrace, Nantymoel. He was only 20 years old when he was killed on 3 July. Captain Lloyd Williams wrote to his parents:

It is with deep regret that I have to inform you that your son has been missing since the operations of July 2nd, when the battalion played a prominent and successful part in the attack on La Boisselle. Owing to the fierceness of the fighting I fear he has been killed, and buried by the men of another regiment. He was one of a number of hero-comrades who have given their lives for the fast-winning cause of honour.

Sergeant William Jones (13664), 9th RWF.

The 5th SWB had been exceedingly lucky and had lost just one man, who died of wounds during the day. Private Samuel Wainwright (13881) was from 16 Hewertson Street, Newport and he is buried in Heilly Station Cemetery, Méricourt-l'Abbé.

The 9th Welsh had also been lucky and had only lost three men killed during the day, but several officers had been wounded – Captain J.F.G. Cree, Lieutenant O.R.J. Green and Second Lieutenants E. R. Kelly and D. L. Davies – while seventy-seven men had been wounded and five were missing.

Lieutenant Oswald Robert John Green, known as 'Osey Green', was a well-respected officer who had been severely wounded. He was the son of William Arthur and Sophia Green of The Foundry, Aberystwyth, and the husband of Winifred Gwendoline Green of Buchland House, Neath Abbey. He was educated at Jasper House and at Aberystwyth University and was a holder of the Royal Humane Society Medal for life-saving. He was a well-regarded sportsman, excelling in swimming, cricket, golf and especially football, and was captain of Aberystwyth Town Football Club prior to the war. Green had suffered the loss of a leg during the fighting and died of his wounds on 5 July 1916, aged 35. He is buried in Heilly Station Cemetery, Méricourt-l'Abbé.

Private Samuel Wainwright (13881) of 16 Hewertson Street, Newport.

Lieutenant St. Helier Evans wrote of his death:

Capt. Whitty has injured a knee, Osey Green wounded, may lose a leg. They gave men a fine reception at Charing Cross. My leave will be hopelessly cancelled. Our Brigade helped to take la Boisselle and did well. I am very worried, Collicott was hit by a nose-cap from a shell of ours. Here we sit among corn, horses, and mules – all so safe. Our regiment is due to attack today; our losses are becoming heavy; Green is dead; Talbot has gone down with food poisoning. The men are in good spirits, having now an opportunity to pay off old debts, in short, Loos has to be avenged.

Lieutenant Oswald Robert John Green, 9th Welsh, of Aberystwyth.

Green's wife received the following letter from Lieutenant Colonel Cooke:

Dear Mrs. Green,

It is with the greatest sorrow and regret that I am writing to tell you of the death of your brave and gallant husband. He was severely wounded while we were occupying a gap in the line at La Boisselle on the 4th inst. The bombardment was so tremendous that we could not get him away at once, but we dispatched him as soon as it was possible. Our Regimental doctor attended him as soon as he was wounded, and we expected him to pull through. He, however, sank and died the next day. It is impossible to express to you in words our deep sorrow, and all the officers wish me to express their deepest sympathy in your sad bereavement. He was a most gallant fellow and feared nothing, and is a very great loss to the battalion and the Army, he was most popular with the men, who all loved him and would have followed him everywhere. Such men can ill be spared at such a time. He was buried at Heilly near Albert. Believe me with deep sympathy,

    Yours very sincerely,

    S.F. Cooke, Lieut. Col., commanding 9th Welsh Regiment.

Sporadic fighting continued throughout the night of 3/4 July but the 9th RWF and 9th Welsh of 58 Brigade remained in reserve in the Tara-Usna trenches.

The last assault on La Boisselle was launched by 56 and 57 brigades at 8.30 am on 4 July and, despite heavy fighting to clear dugouts, by 3 pm the entire village had at last been captured and cleared of the remaining Germans.

At 9 pm on 5 July orders were issued for several reliefs to take place: 57 Brigade was relieved by troops of the 12th and 25th divisions and moved back to Albert; 58 Brigade was to relieve 69 Brigade of the 23rd Division in a line of old German trenches; 56 Brigade was to remain in the line. By the early hours of 6 July, 57 Brigade was in Albert and 58 Brigade had completed the relief of 69 Brigade, 23rd Division.

The 9th Welsh and portions of the 58th Machine-Gun Company and Trench Mortar Battery took up the front line, while 56 Brigade came under attack at 7 am on 7 July. An hour later the 19th Division attacked towards Contalmaison in conjunction with the 23rd Division on their right and the 25th Division on their left and advanced the line forward. The attack was the first in which a creeping artillery barrage had been used and it proved to be a success, although some advanced parties of men advanced too quickly into their own bombardment. Despite several enemy counter-attacks, the division reached its objectives by 9.35 pm and the men began consolidating their gains on the outskirts of Contalmaison. During the day heavy fighting could be heard coming from the direction of Mametz Wood: the 38th (Welsh) Division had begun its assault on that wood.

During the advance on the 19th Division front on 7 July the 9th RWF lost six men killed. The 5th SWB had lost Lieutenant Clarence Espeut Lyon Hall, MC (a Jamaican) and three men killed, while the 9th Welsh had suffered dearly: two officers – Second Lieutenants Reginald Charles Cooke MC and Godfrey Gwilym Brychan Stephens – and thirty-two men were killed. Second Lieutenant Ivor Guest Rees of Llanelli was wounded and died after almost four weeks in hospital on 5 August. Captain Saunders, Lieutenant Lunn, Second Lieutenants A. Thomas, Goulding, and Pratt and 136 other ranks were also wounded. Lieutenant St. Helier Evans wrote to his mother to express his sorrow at the loss of his friend Reginald Cooke:

Saunders has stopped a bullet, it penetrated the shoulders, I hope he will come through; my friend with a somewhat saturnine smile, Cooke, Military Cross, is killed; this is too sad; we were together in D Company last year and we often went across on patrols; now he has gone across for the last time. I recall his dismay when we were in the Hun wire and I experienced an uncontrolled spasm of giggling; I have learnt since then that Stevens, who arrived from the S.W.B. a week ago, has fallen; Rees, another friend, is wounded in the head and badly. On the credit side, Contalmaison is ours. 390 prisoners went past, all looked bewildered and sickly; no more war for them until the next time. Their blue-grey uniform shows up more than our colour. One man bore a label 'Wanted by G.H.Q.' Some Hun officers murdered their escort and so, in turn, were shot. Our Brigade will be withdrawn shortly, we shall be glad to rejoin them. Russia's 'Push' will prevent the enemy moving troops to this front.

The other Green and I went up towards la Boiselle [*sic*] thinking it was ours, a sniper tried for us which deterred us from roaming in daylight in the old No Man's Land; nearby is a vast crater we blew on 1st July; the whole area is littered with debris, equipment soaked in blood, discarded weapons and all the aftermath of fierce scrapping. Every yard is pitted with shell holes; it is curious being able to disregard Communication Trenches and to be able to walk openly. Collicott proposed to get a wrist watch for me from a body or prisoner. I fear this lad has been wounded; Sgt. Owen says he is missing. This I refuse to believe, we must find out before writing to his mother. Later. We are in a wood, recovering from this bloody fighting, the weather is taking it out of us too, it was a long march (in the right direction), getting here where we may remain a week to recuperate. Fourteen of my platoon, including Sgt. Davies, are wounded or missing. We have lost sixty from the Company. Lunn went back with shattered nerves so I am left the only potential fighting body.

Among the other ranks killed with the 9th Welsh was Private David Stanley Davies (12120), the husband of Jane Davies of 9 Mount Pleasant Street, Dowlais. Like all but two of his comrades killed at Contalmaison on 7 July 1916, Davies has no known grave and is commemorated on the Thiepval Memorial. The only two men killed that day who have known burials are: Private William Albert Thomas (33674) of Collier's Row, Garnant, whose grave was found after the war and reinterred in Serre Road Cemetery

Private David Stanley Davies (12120), the husband of Jane Davies of 9 Mount Pleasant Street, Dowlais.

No. 1; and Private Henry William Phillips (38151), who enlisted in Aberystwyth and is buried in Bécourt Military Cemetery, Bécordel-Bécourt.

Also killed during the battle was the second son of Lord St David's, Captain Roland Erasmus Philipps MC. Philipps was born on 27 February 1890, the second son of John Philipps, the Right Honourable the 1st Viscount St David's PC and his wife, Leonora Gerstenberg, of 3 Richmond Terrace, Whitehall, London. He was educated at Winchester College and New College, Oxford. Philipps was an important early member of the Boy Scouts. In July 1912 he was appointed Assistant District Commissioner for East London. In 1913 he was appointed Commissioner for North-East London, and in November 1913 he was made responsible for all of East London. He was commissioned in the 9th Royal Fusiliers, which moved to France at the end of May 1915, attached to 36 Brigade, 12th Division. Their baptism of fire was at Ploegsteert Wood on 23 June 1915 and later at the Battle of Loos, by which time Philipps had been promoted to captain, had been awarded the MC and was wounded on 2 March 1916: 'For conspicuous gallantry and devotion to duty. Although wounded severely he kept his men well in hand, himself killing four of the enemy with his revolver. He stuck to his post and repelled three attacks.' (*London Gazette*, 14 April 1916.)

Captain the Honourable Roland Erasmus Philipps, MC, 9th Royal Fusiliers.

The division held the line at Loos until June, when they were moved in readiness for the Somme offensive. They relieved the badly damaged 8th Division at Ovillers-la-Boisselle on 1 July and took two lines of German trenches, but then stuttered to a halt. On 7 July 1916 the brigade attacked again, but was hit by German shell fire in Mash Valley. Philipps was buried by a shell that exploded in his trench while his battalion was awaiting the signal to attack, but was freed by his men in time to lead the assault, then fell wounded by shrapnel before being killed by a bullet in the head. He was 26 years old and is buried in Aveluy Communal Cemetery Extension. His brother Colwyn was killed in 1915. His commanding officer wrote to his father:

An irreparable loss has been suffered by the battalion in the death of your son. He was the finest natural leader of men that I have ever seen, and his courage, and dash and enthusiasm would have appeared fanatical were it not for the coolness and sane decision he displayed when his objective was obtained.

Philipps is commemorated on war memorials at Roch Castle and at Manorbier, and by the gift of the house he left for use by the Boy Scouts Association: Roland House in Stepney, London.

Listening to the battle was Sergeant Thomas Lewis Ebsworth (1994) of the 6th Welsh, who wrote home to his mother at the Beach Hotel in Pendine in a letter dated 7 July 1916:

I am glad to say I am so far tip-top. Well, I am writing you this now, and my word it is an experience. We are only 75 yards away from the Germans, and our chaps and they are blazing away. It is fairly quiet in the day for rifle fire, but the artillery shells are getting over our heads. At night it is like hell. God help anybody where these shells drop, but we are in very nice trenches – 7ft. high, with steps and periscopes. When you fire if you stop about a minute with your head up you are a goner. The snipers are on you, bang. It is fine to see the aeroplanes out and the fights with them. It is good weather so far, but we are afraid we are going to have rain. There is an awful mess here when it is raining. My pal has just popped up and had a shot. He just shouted to me 'I've sent them another souvenir, Tom. I hope they like them.' You'd not believe you can nearly get lost in these trenches! They are marvellous. One would not think, sitting where I am now, that to jump up suddenly would mean instant death. We are on a flat field with long grass and barbed wire between us. Our chaps caught two Germans cutting it, but they will never cut again. Next time you send, please put in a box of liquorice tablets as my throat is a little sore today. Hoping you are all well, and with fondest love to all, etc., etc.

Ebsworth went on to gain a commission in the 6th Welsh and won the French Croix de Guerre by the end of the war. By 1939 he had built up a successful bus company, Ebsworth Brothers, and regained his commission, helping to raise the local Home Guard battalion at Laugharne.

On 10 July the 19th Division moved to Millencourt for a well-deserved rest. It had performed a fine deed by capturing La Boisselle, and it was thought apt for one of the divisional memorials to be erected there after the war, west of the church. The division

The memorial cross to the 19th Division at La Boisselle, one of two such memorials on the Western Front. The other is near Messines, in Belgium.

had carried out a feat of arms of the highest order and had gained three Victoria Crosses in so doing.

On the same day that the 19th Division moved from the front for a rest, the 13th Battalion, Rifle Brigade of the 37th Division was gearing up for an assault on Contalmaison. The battalion was almost wiped out during its assault, losing its CO and most of the other officers. The second in command of the battalion was a member of the Welsh aristocracy, Sir Foster Hugh Egerton Cunliffe, 6th Baronet of Acton Park, Wrexham.

Cunliffe was born on 17 August 1875, the son of Sir Robert Cunliffe, 5th Baronet of Acton Park, Denbighshire and his wife Eleanor Sophia Egerton Leigh, daughter of Egerton Leigh. He was educated at Eton and at New College, Oxford and was a renowned cricketer, playing for Oxford and then for Middlesex. He became a lecturer in history at Oxford University and wrote *The History of the Boer War*. He was a JP for Denbigh prior to the war and had served with the Indian army. Cunliffe was commissioned in the 13th Battalion, Rifle Brigade (37th Division) as a captain on 13 December 1914. By the time of the Somme offensive he was second in command of the battalion, with the rank of major. He was seen to fall wounded after being shot during the battalion's attack on Contalmaison on 10 July 1916 and was later found dead. He is buried in Bapaume Post Military Cemetery, Albert.

After the death of Sir Foster Cunliffe, the estate was bought in 1917 by the diamond merchant and philanthropist Sir Bernard Oppenheimer, who opened a diamond-cutting training school and workshop in the grounds in order to give employment to injured ex-servicemen. He gifted 125 acres of the estate to the people of Wrexham, while the house and outbuildings were used for billeting troops of the Denbighshire Hussars.

(i) Mametz Wood

By the middle of June 1916 the units of the 38th (Welsh) Division commenced the move from their positions in Flanders to the Somme.

On 8 June the 14th RWF were relieved in the trenches by the 13th RWF and marched back to billets at Pont-du-Hem. The men rested for two days and undertook bathing parades before parading on 11 June prior to marching via Robermetz to Merville. On 12 June the battalion marched to Gonnehem, spent the following day resting, then marched onto Raimbert on 14 June, slowly working their way southwards to the Somme district. By 17 June the battalion had reached Monchy-Breton, where they began training in company formation. On 22 June the battalion marched to Tinques, where brigade training was carried out, alongside the 13th, 15th and 16th RWF.

Meanwhile, on the morning of 12 June 1916, the men of the 15th Welsh marched to La Pierrière, near Busnes and, after a much-deserved night's sleep, marched to Cauchy-à-la-Tour the following day. On 14 June the men marched to Béthencourt, where 114 Brigade assembled and the 15th Welsh began their brigade manoeuvres alongside the 10th, 13th and 14th Welsh.

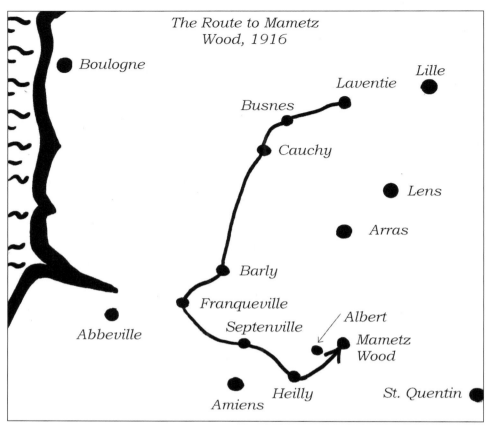

The movements of the 38th (Welsh) Division to the Somme, June 1916: the route taken by 114 Brigade.

On 15 June 1916 the 38th (Welsh) Division joined II Corps in the Third Army. While the three brigades had been carrying out their separate training regimes, trenches were being dug for the entire division to begin training. On 25 June the three brigades – 113, 114 and 115 – marched to Béthencourt where the entire division assembled to begin carrying out divisional manoeuvres. This training following a strictly laid down programme issued by GHQ. The troops were being trained in what were, at the time, thought of as revolutionary tactics; in the techniques of attacking on a large scale against the German trench lines, and in following through the attack and consolidation work once the lines had been broken. The constituent platoons and companies practised attacking over open ground in waves, with successive waves coming through them once the first had checked their attack, and the whole regime worked in conjunction with the assorted support arms: artillery, machine-gun companies, the service branches of signals, engineers and intelligence, and the Royal Flying Corps.

On 26 June 1916 the various components of the 38th (Welsh) Division began their long march towards the battle area. The route marched by each brigade was different. No. 113 Brigade had marched at battalion intervals from Bernaville to Puchevillers on

30 June and to Arquèves on the following day. The brigade then made an overnight march to Ribemont in the Somme valley on 3 July and the men had a day of rest there.

On 26 June, 114 Brigade had marched at intervals 20 miles to Barly, a small village sat on the main road from Arras to Doullens, where they bivouacked for the night in continuous rain. The brigade arrived at Franqueville by 27 June, and then the following day marched on to Septenville, where the men could hear the sounds of artillery fire: the awesome artillery barrage that marked the start of the first attacks of the Battle of the Somme opened up over the night of 30 June/1 July 1916. On the following morning, the day of 1 July 1916, deafened by the almost constant roar of artillery and the sound of gunfire from the front, 114 Brigade marched on to Hérrisart. Early in the morning of 3 July the men marched on to Franvillers, reaching Heilly in the Somme Valley on 4 July 1916 at 9.15 am.

115 Brigade had marched to Neuvillette on 26 June, then marched to Longuevillette the following day and Toutencourt on 30 June. On 1 July the brigade marched to Acheux, where it rested for a day before marching to Buire during the night of 3/4 July. The brigade was billetted in the village, where it awaited further orders.

The 38th (Welsh) Division now came under the command of XV Corps, under Sir Henry Horne, moving into XV Corps reserve. The area around the Somme valley was then – and is today – a beautiful and tranquil part of France, and the brigades set up camp along the valley overnight.

During May 1916 the 38th Casualty Clearing Station had set up at Heilly, where 114 Brigade was bivouacked. This was to be the main clearing station for the fighting in the Fricourt-Mametz area. The first casualties of the opening day of the Somme offensive had by now reached Heilly, and the constant stream of wounded and dying men must have been a great cause for concern to the men of the newly arrived 38th (Welsh) Division who watched as the medical staff became snowed under by the constant stream of casualties.

They left the greenery of the valley behind on 5 July 1916 when parties of officers from each battalion moved forwards through Fricourt to Mametz to reconnoitre the line the division was taking over and during the afternoon the entire division moved forward over the scorched and battered battlefield of the previous day's fighting through Morlancourt and south of Bécordel-Bécourt to positions south of Mametz Wood. Some units bivouacked at Carnoy, while others moved to Dantzig Alley and several battalion HQs were established in Pommiers Redoubt, a recently-captured German strongpoint.

During that night of 5/6 July 1916 the 38th (Welsh) Division took over the front from Bottom Wood along White Trench to Caterpillar Wood from the 7th Division, which had captured the ground during the day. It was during the relief that the division suffered its first Somme casualties, with six men killed: Private Frederick Emery (37298), 15th RWF, of

Private Frederick Emery (37298), 15th RWF, killed on 5 July 1916 while the 38th (Welsh) Division was relieving the 7th Division in trenches south of Mametz Wood. Emery was 28 years old and left a wife and young son.

Birkenhead; Private Henry Josiah Harris (22954), 15th RWF, of Victoria Park, London; Private Edward Jones (16775), 13th RWF, of Gwersyllt, Wrexham; Private Ernest William Tancock (22576), 15th RWF, of Holborn, London; Corporal George Wilkins (21552), 15th RWF, of Llanfyllin; and Second Lieutenant Wilfred Brynmor Williams, 16th Welsh, of Trewernen, Llantwit Fardre.

The sound of the terrible fighting and the continuous shellfire that echoed around the area of the battlefield must have been terrifying for the men. They had taken part in trench warfare but the trials facing them now were to be totally different from what anyone in the battalion, most probably within the whole division, had ever faced in their lives. The ground they were now treading had just recently been taken, with huge loss of life, and the bodies of men from both sides lay scattered over the ground.

Sir Ivor Philipps MP commander of the 38th (Welsh) Division and a close personal friend of David Lloyd George

This phase of the Somme offensive, the task set for the 38th (Welsh) Division, was to be the capture of Mametz Wood. It was well known that wood-fighting was a specialized and dangerous task, but just how deadly it would be was yet to be discovered. Major General Ivor Philipps, the commanding officer of the 38th (Welsh) Division, sent the following message to every man in the division:

You have worked hard for many months with an energy and zeal beyond praise to fit yourself for the task you have voluntarily undertaken. You have undergone the hardships of a winter campaign with fortitude. You have earned the praise of your corps commanders for your courage, discipline and devotion to duty. You have now held for six months a section of the British line in France, during which time you have not allowed one of the enemy to enter your trenches except as a prisoner, and on several occasions you have entered the enemy's lines. Eleven officers and 44 NCOs and men have already received awards from the King for gallant and distinguished conduct in the field. Your fellow countrymen at home are following your career with interest and admiration. I always believed that a really Welsh Division would be second to none. You have more than justified that belief. I feel that whatever the future may have in store for us I can rely upon you, because you have already given ample proof of your worth. During the short period in the training area you worked hard to qualify yourselves for still further efforts. I thank you most sincerely for the loyal and wholehearted way in which you have all supported me and for the way in which each of you has done his utmost to carry out the task allotted to him. With such a spirit animating all ranks we can one and all look forward with confidence to the future, whatever it may have in store for us. You are today relieving the 7th Division, which has attacked and captured German trenches on a front of little less than one mile and for a depth of about one and a quarter miles. In this attack the village of Mametz was captured, the enemy have suffered very heavy casualties, 1,500 German officers and men were taken prisoner and six field guns were captured.

The 1st Battalion, Royal Welsh Fusiliers and the 1st Battalion, Welsh Regiment of the 7th Division have both distinguished themselves in this attack, and I am confident that the young battalions of the famous Welsh regiments serving in the 38th (Welsh) Division will maintain the high standard for valour for which all three Welsh regiments have been renowned throughout the war.

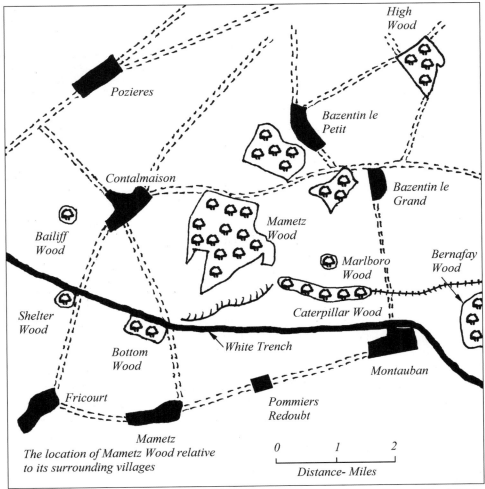

The location of Mametz Wood relative to its surrounding villages

A map showing the locations of Mametz Wood, showing Fricourt, Mametz, Bottom Wood, White Trench and Caterpillar Wood.

Sir Henry Horne had planned that 7 July would be the date for a general attack to capture Ovillers, Bailiff Wood, Contalmaison and Mametz Wood. The 19th Division, as we have previously seen, was to assault the trenches between La Boisselle and Bailiff Wood; the 23rd Division to attack Contalmaison; the 17th Division to seize Quadrangle Support at 2 am so as to be in position to attack Mametz Wood from the west; while the 38th (Welsh) Division was to attack and occupy the east of Mametz Wood, starting from Caterpillar Wood.

On 6 July 1916, the battalion officers of the 38th (Welsh) Division visited the ground in front of Mametz Wood and explored the area to prepare for the planned assault on the wood. One officer – Second Lieutenant James Hubert Waddington, 16th Welsh, of Briton Ferry – and thirty-seven men from the RWF of the division were killed during the day. Mametz Wood was, and still is, the largest wood on the Somme, covering an area of over 200 acres, with a maximum length of about a mile. It is situated on a low spur of the Bazentin Ridge and is overlooked by the valley that separated the two forces in the early days of July 1916.

Due to its situation on the opposite side of the valley, any attack made by the British forces would be initially downhill from their starting positions, then down a steep chalk bank ranging from 30ft to 50ft in height, and uphill across Death Valley to make contact with the enemy in the wood itself. The Germans were also able to bring flanking fire to bear on any approach to the wood from Flatiron and Sabot Copses to the east. The German second line was almost 300 metres beyond the northern edge of the wood and therefore it could be easily reinforced, since much of the movement would go unobserved due to the cover of the wood.

To the left was the area held by the 17th Division. To the right was the 18th Division, spread from Caterpillar Wood eastwards. The capture of Mametz Wood itself was to be the responsibility of the 38th (Welsh) Division, though support from the 17th

A view taken from behind White Trench overlooking Death Valley, the open ground over which the 38th (Welsh) Division attacked.

Mametz Wood-The Hammerhead

Flatiron Copse

Division on its left flank was essential. Facing the Welshmen was the Lehr Regiment of the Prussian Guard, holding the line from Mametz Wood to Flatiron Copse.

The task facing them was indeed immense. The Lehr Regiment was an elite unit, having seen action on the Eastern Front against the Russian Tsarist forces. They were concealed within the fringes of an unkempt, overgrown wood, which offered the benefit of a good defensive position with minimum effort. The wood itself was split by several overgrown pathways or 'rides' that crossed the wood both north-south and east-west, and the tangled mass of trees and undergrowth eliminated any real need for trenches and fortifications as machine-gun crews and snipers were easily hidden behind fallen trees and bushes.

If the Welshmen were to be able successfully to cross the open ground between themselves and the outskirts of the wood, any fighting that would then take place would be of a brutal, almost mediaeval, hand-to-hand nature, with bayonet, knife or trench club. The scene was set for a savage encounter that the survivors of both sides would never forget. Unknown, however, to the British, the outlook was also bleak on the side of the German defenders. An excerpt from the diary of a German officer captured at Mametz Wood on 13 July 1916 reads: 'The troops who had so far held the lines south of Mametz and south of Montauban had sustained severe losses from the intense enemy bombardment, which had been maintained for several days without a pause, and for the most part were already shot to pieces.'

The plan for the attack of 7 July was that the 17th Division would attack Acid Drop Copse on the left flank of the wood and act as support for the 38th (Welsh) Division whose task was to attack the Hammerhead on the right. Both divisions were to advance to the central ride and then turn north to sweep through the wood. In the 38th Division the responsibility for the attack was to rest on the shoulders of Brigadier General Evans and his 115 Brigade.

Mametz Wood from the site of Pommiers Redoubt. The undulations in the ground can be clearly seen. These gave some cover to the assaulting troops until they went over the crest of the ridge, when they immediately came under heavy machine-gun fire.

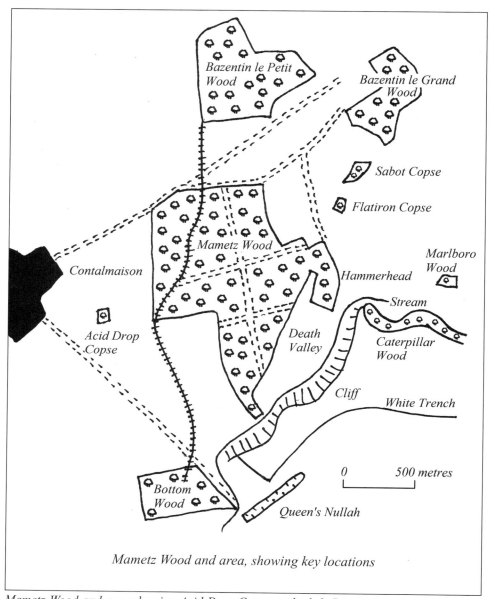

Mametz Wood and area, showing key locations

Mametz Wood and area showing Acid Drop Copse to the left, Bottom Wood, White Trench, Death Valley and Caterpillar Wood.

Evans had surveyed the ground and had decided to attack with two battalions squeezed into a single battalion frontage, with one spearheading the attack and one immediately following to the rear. A third battalion was to be in support at Caterpillar Wood and a fourth in reserve.

However, Evans' plans were not met with approval at XV Corps headquarters. They told him to assemble no more than two battalions at the western end of Caterpillar

Wood as any more would cause overcrowding and increase the risk of casualties from German artillery. The third battalion should be in support at Montauban, and the fourth further back. This compromised his plans somewhat, but Brigadier General Evans had no choice but to comply.

His revised plan put the 11th SWB on the left, near Caterpillar Wood in support of the main assault of the 16th Welsh on the right, on the ridge above the valley, who had received orders to attack the Hammerhead. The 10th SWB and 17th RWF were in reserve at Montauban Alley. Each battalion would have no more than a 250-metre frontage for the attack. Lieutenant Colonel Frank Smith of the 16th Welsh pointed out that the attack should be made before dawn as the battalion would be enfiladed from Flatiron Copse, but this request was overruled and he was told that the problem of flanking fire from the Germans was to be eased by the use of a smokescreen that would cover the attack.

On the night prior to the attack it rained heavily, and movement became very difficult in the resulting mud. An attack by 17th Division during the night had alerted the Germans to an attack on the wood. This attack was planned for 8.30 am on 7 July and, although the planned smokescreen did not appear, the 11th SWB and 16th Welsh moved over the crest of the ridge to the south of the wood but immediately came under fire from the German machine guns in Flatiron and Sabot Copses. Being on the right, the 16th Welsh had been more exposed to the enfilade fire and as the attacking waves came into sight of the German machine guns they were mown down. As a consequence, the casualties mounted and the attack died out some 250 metres short of the wood.

By 10 am the situation had deteriorated as the Germans increased shell and machine-gun fire across the approaches to the wood. The 10th SWB were ordered up in support but did not reach the battle area until after noon. Artillery support was offered but actually fell on the remnants of the 16th Welsh as they tried to push home the attack. The arrival of the 10th SWB did help a little in the afternoon but their commanding officer, Lieutenant Colonel Wilkinson, was killed in Caterpillar Wood as he brought his men forward. Gradually the attack faltered.

Brigadier General Evans received another order telling him that an attack was to be carried out at 5 pm when the wood was to be entered at all costs. He reported the gravity of the situation to Divisional Headquarters and they in turn reported to Corps Headquarters, who ordered a withdrawal to allow reorganization.

The attack by the 17th Division had also failed, and so the co-ordinated effort failed as a whole. It had cost 400 casualties in the three battalions engaged; and nothing at all had been achieved as these battle-weary units were withdrawn to lick their wounds and count the cost.

Of these 400 casualties suffered by the division during the first day of the battle, 183 men were killed. The 13th RWF had two men killed; the 14th RWF had four men killed; the 15th RWF had four men killed; the 16th RWF had three men killed; the 17th RWF had four men killed; the 10th SWB had lost its commanding officer, Lieutenant Colonel Sidney John Wilkinson DSO, killed; the 11th SWB had lost one officer – Lieutenant Thomas Price Hamer – and thirty men killed. The 16th Welsh had suffered the most, with five officers – Captain John Lewis Williams (who was badly wounded and died five days later), Lieutenants Arthur and Leonard Tregaskis, and Second Lieutenants John Edwin Howell of Trostre, Llanelli and Wilfred Brynmor Williams (killed on 5 July) – and 130 men, including three CSMs – Thomas John (23554), Richard Thomas (24093) and Albert William Willshire (23291) – killed. Captain H.P. Herdman, Lieutenants F. Bird, A.W. Gwyn and T. Otto Jones, and Second Lieutenants Lloyd and Lucas and 138 men had been wounded. The Cardiff City battalion had virtually ceased to exist as an organised unit.

Also killed during the attack was Corporal George Biddle (27369) of 115 Machine-Gun Company and two men of the 130th (St John's) Field Ambulance RAMC – Private William Houston (56231) of Bolton and Lance Corporal William James West (48217) of 20 George Street, Cwmcarn – who were killed while attempting to rescue wounded men.

The brothers Arthur and Leonard Tregaskis had both been working in Canada at the outbreak of war and returned home to Cardiff to enlist. They were both commissioned in the 16th Welsh, and were killed together in the wood on 7 July. These brave men are buried side by side in Flatiron Copse Cemetery.

The two brothers Tregaskis: Lieutenants Arthur and Leonard Tregaskis, sons of George Henry and Julia Anne Tregaskis of Taff's Well. The brothers worked for Spillers and Bakers in Canada prior to the war, their father being a director of the parent company, Spillers Nephews. They were killed on the same day in Mametz Wood and are buried together in Flatiron Copse Cemetery.

The graves of Arthur and Leonard Tregaskis in Flatiron Copse Cemetery.

Lieutenant Thomas Pryce Hamer, 11th SWB, was the son of Edward and Martha Hamer of Summerfield Park, Llanidloes, Montgomeryshire. He was a local celebrity prior to the war, played association football for Llanelli for two seasons and had represented Wales at international level, as well as being a wealthy industrialist. He was commissioned on 1 April 1915 and joined the 11th SWB. He was 33 years old when he was killed on 7 July 1916 and is commemorated on the Thiepval Memorial.

Lieutenant Thomas Pryce Hamer, 11th SWB, the son of Edward and Martha Hamer of Summerfield Park, Llanidloes, Montgomeryshire.

The name of Lieutenant Thomas Pryce Hamer, 11th SWB, on the Thiepval Memorial.

Also killed in the wood on 7 July was the fifth of thirteen Welsh international rugby players to fall during the war. CSM Richard Thomas (24093) was born at Ferndale on 14 October 1883. He played for Ferndale and Penygraig before moving to Mountain Ash and played for Glamorgan against South Africa in 1906. He gained his first Welsh cap that season after being selected to play against South Africa again, but had to wait until 1908 for his second cap against France. He won two further caps, one against Ireland that season and the last against Scotland in 1909. Thomas was a police sergeant when he enlisted in the 16th Welsh soon after its formation and was 31 years old when he was killed in Mametz Wood on 7 July 1916. He is commemorated on the Thiepval Memorial.

CSM Richard Thomas (24093), 16th Welsh, the fifth Welsh international rugby player to fall during the war.

General Haig was, quite unjustifiably, unimpressed by the performance of the division, which did not have the luxury of any form of command over the artillery bombardment (or rather the lack of it). The 121st Brigade, Royal Field Artillery of the 38th (Welsh) Division took part in the bombardment under the orders of the 7th Division. The 122nd Brigade came into action on 8 July under the same command, while 119th Brigade arrived on 8 July and 120th Brigade on 9 July, both under the orders of the 21st Division.

At the end of the day Lieutenant General Horne of XV Corps informed Haig that he was not happy with the conduct of Major General Philipps, who was removed from command on 9 July 1916. This was probably not helped by the fact that Philipps was a close friend and confidant of Haig's nemesis, David Lloyd George, who had negotiated his command of the 38th (Welsh) Division as a result of alleged family and political ties. Ivor Philipps did not fade away, however. After a successful business career in the City, he retired to the family seat at Cosheston, from where he supervised the restoration of the mighty Pembroke Castle. He died in August 1940.

Elsewhere on the front there was heavy fighting around Ovillers and Trônes Wood, while the French straightened out their line by the capture of Hardecourt.

A plan for a renewed attack on the wood on 9 July 1916 had been worked out by the 38th Divisional staff. The unused brigades, 113 and 114, were to be used. The whole of 114 Brigade was to provide the main attack on the central ride, while 113 Brigade was to capture Strip Trench. This plan was cancelled when Philipps was replaced and nothing of significance happened that day except for the command of the division passing to Major General Watts, although the division suffered a further thirteen men killed on 8 July and another forty-five killed on 9 July, mostly men of the 14th and 17th RWF while holding the frontline trenches facing the wood. An unsupported attack by the 17th Division on 9 July was completely unsuccessful.

The following day it was to be the turn of the 38th (Welsh) Division again. Major General Watts took over command of the division in the afternoon of 9 July 1916 and immediately set about organizing an attack on the wood. The attack was essentially the same as that worked out by Philipps the day before, but Watts placed importance on the equal status of the two brigades to be engaged, 113 and 114. The artillery plan, however, was changed and contained two novel features.

The first was that the initial barrage was to lift off the main German trenches to their rear, as if an infantry attack was to commence, and then to resume on them after a few minutes to catch the Germans as they emerged from their dugouts. This approach had been used successfully by the French further south but was an innovation for the British. Secondly, the use of a creeping barrage to accompany the attack was also planned. This was a timed lift of the artillery, keeping a screen of shellfire ahead of the advancing troops.

That apart, there was no complexity to the attack and the plan was simply relying on weight of numbers to overpower the German defenders. In this area it has been estimated that the Germans were outnumbered by as many as three to one and so the weight of numbers argument looked sensible. However, these figures took no account of the fact that the Germans were fighting from prepared defences and had numerous machine guns in supporting positions about the wood and, in general, had better-trained and more experienced men in the front line who had been on the Western Front for almost a year longer than the men of the 38th (Welsh) Division, who had limited trench experience.

However, the plan for the attack went ahead as follows. The 14th and 13th Welsh of 114 Brigade were to attack from the right. The 16th RWF of 113 Brigade was to lead the assault, and the 14th RWF of the same was to be close behind on the left. The 15th Welsh was in reserve at the Triangle, supplying work parties that carried Royal

Engineers' matériel, as well as being tasked with moving supplies to the front line and bringing German prisoners back with them as and when required.

At 3.30 am on 10 July the artillery barrage opened up, followed twenty minutes later by the planned smokescreen, which drifted from Strip Trench towards the north-east. Zero hour was fixed for 4.15 am and just after 4 am 114 Brigade started to move as they were further from the wood than 113 Brigade, who were at the Queen's Nullah. This caused some confusion in 113 Brigade area; however, Lieutenant Colonel Carden of the 16th RWF sorted this out in short order, leading his battalion off at 4.12 am and the attack was carried out with 'perfect steadiness'. In the time taken to sort this out, the 16th RWF lost some of the cover offered by the creeping artillery fire and subsequently the battalion lost heavily in the advance to the wood. Among the casualties was Lieutenant Colonel Ronald Carden himself. He had told his men prior to the attack: 'Boys, make your peace with God. We are going to take that position and some of us won't come back.' Carden had been wounded at the start of the attack but carried on right up to the edge of the wood, where he was shot again and fell dead. His body was later carried back by his men and Carden is now buried at Carnoy Military Cemetery.

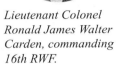

Lieutenant Colonel Ronald James Walter Carden, commanding 16th RWF.

On the right the 13th Welsh came under fire from the German machine-gun posts placed in the Hammerhead. They suffered heavy casualties and were beaten back on two occasions but a third attempt was made and they managed to get a foothold in the wood, although they had lost their CO. Lieutenant Colonel George D'Arcy Edwardes was killed while organizing an attack on a machine-gun post in the Hammerhead and second in command Major Charles Edward Bond was also killed. Command then devolved upon Captain Johnson. The 14th Welsh were attacking in the centre and were to some extent covered from enfilade fire by the flanking battalions and managed to reach the wood more or less as the artillery barrage was lifting from the edge. Lieutenant Frank James Hawkins, a former Welsh rugby international, personally charged and

Major Charles Edward Bond, 13th Welsh, a well-known man in Swansea and the cashier at the town's branch of the Capital and Counties Bank prior to the war. He became a recruiting officer in Swansea during the early months of the war before volunteering to serve with the 13th Welsh. He was killed during his battalion's initial charge against the wood on 10 July.

Lieutenant Frank James Hawkins, 14th Welsh, licensee of the Tynewydd Hotel, Porth. Hawkins had played rugby for Pontypridd and Wales. He was awarded the Military Cross for charging and capturing two machine-gun posts in Mametz Wood but was severely wounded. He died on 3 December 1960.

captured two machine-gun posts but was wounded in the process. (Hawkins was later awarded the MC for his gallantry.) Lieutenant John Edwards, 13th Welsh, of Penuwch, Cardigan was also awarded the MC for capturing another machine-gun post: 'He attacked three times a hostile machine-gun which was causing severe casualties. Finally, with a few men, he captured it, and killed the gun team. He was wounded later in the day.' (*London Gazette*, 22 September 1916.) On the left the 14th RWF had suffered heavily as it attacked close behind the 16th RWF, and Brigadier Price-Davies committed the 15th and 13th RWF to the attack almost immediately so that they were then in close support to the battalions already engaged. Lieutenant Colonel Oswald Swift Flower, CO of the 13th RWF, was mortally wounded during the fighting that followed, bayoneted in the stomach by a German. He was evacuated to Morlancourt, where he died on 12 July.

On the right, between 4.40 am and 5.10 am, Lieutenant Colonel P.E. Ricketts of the 10th Welsh had begun sending his battalion into the wood, making a total of seven out of eight battalions of the two brigades engaged in action. The attack was a reasonable success, with all the objectives being taken ahead of schedule, but it had not been without cost. Casualties had mounted throughout the first hour of the attack, so that in the seven battalions that went into battle five of the commanding officers had been killed or seriously wounded. Added to this was the loss of many of the junior officers, resulting in control of the thousands of men in the wood becoming increasingly difficult.

Meanwhile, the 16th RWF were held up at Point J by machine-gun fire from Quadrangle Alley, Wood Trench and Wood Support and Price-Davies ordered the last two companies of the 13th RWF forward to assist in the situation; they eventually cleared Wood Trench in conjunction with bombers of the 17th Division. However, Wood Support, which was a continuation of the first cross ride, was still in German hands.

To the right the Germans reinforced the Hammerhead, and this created havoc for a while among the attacking Welshmen. To ease this situation the 15th Welsh, under Major Percy Anthony, became the eighth battalion to be committed after being ordered from reserve at around 7 am to occupy the Hammerhead and be prepared to meet any German counter-attacks. Major Anthony led the battalion into the wood, leaving A Company behind in reserve, and set off to aid the 13th Welsh at point D-X.

The 15th Welsh were met with heavy machine-gun fire, but reached the wood with few casualties and pushed through the Hammerhead, establishing their positions on the eastern side. Major Anthony ordered two platoons of B Company to establish contact with the 13th Welsh on their left. No contact could be made, so a further platoon from A Company was sent forward under Major Phillips to push to points V, W and X. Phillips managed to get his men through and reported the objective gained and being consolidated, and left a reserve at D-X; however, the Germans got in behind the reserve and shot down two platoons, so Phillips' party of the 15th Welsh fell back to D-E, where they consolidated, getting in touch with the remainder of 114 Brigade on the first objective. Major Christian Gibson Phillips was killed during the retirement.

The grave of Major Christian Gibson Phillips, 15th Welsh, in Caterpillar Valley Cemetery, Longueval.

Major Christian Gibson Phillips, King's Own Royal Lancaster Regiment, attached to the 15th Welsh, killed at Mametz Wood on 10 July 1916. His grave was located, along with those of eight other men, by a graves registration unit after the war and he was reburied in Caterpillar Valley Cemetery.

During this time the Germans had entered the northern edge of the Hammerhead at Point X, bringing with them a machine-gun team; and another group of Germans had massed at Flatiron Copse ready for a counter-attack.

The German machine-gunners separated the two platoons of B Company from the platoon of A Company and almost annihilated them in the Hammerhead, leaving only four survivors who were led out of the wood by Captain Bertie Lewis of Carmarthen. During the carnage in the Hammerhead, Major Percy Anthony fell dead, shot by a sniper at around 8 am. His death was a sad loss to the battalion.

Major Percy Anthony, 15th Welsh. He was born on 3 May 1880 and was educated at Dulwich School, where he played cricket for the School XI. The talented batsman played for Herefordshire after leaving school and was invited to play first-class cricket for both Surrey and Worcestershire. However, he had decided on a military career and was commissioned in the army. The Boer War was raging in South Africa and Anthony served there, attached to the 2nd KSLI. Before the outbreak of the Great War he had given up military life and was in Malaya, where he had taken up rubber-planting. At the end of 1914 he returned to Britain and was commissioned in the 15th Welsh, fighting with them until his death at Mametz Wood. His grave was lost during the continued fighting in the area and so he is today commemorated on the Thiepval Memorial to the missing. His family owned the Hereford Times *newspaper.*

The machine-gunners also struck a party of men of the 129th Field Ambulance RAMC who were attempting to rescue the wounded, killing Second Lieutenant Raymond John Jones MB, a doctor from Llanrhaeadr-ym-Mochnant who had volunteered to serve with the 38th (Welsh) Division. Captain F. Tavinor Rees, his senior officer, wrote to his brother:

> He was my closest friend ever since I joined this ambulance 15 months ago. That is why I am writing to offer you my deepest sympathy. I feel his loss very much indeed. He was extremely popular with all ranks, and was held in deep affection by his brother officers. The Officer Commanding and the Padre will already have told you the circumstances of his death. All I need say is that he died in the performance of a very gallant duty – a deed that has won the admiration of all who know of it. We were the closest of possible friends and I shall always cherish his memory. We are going to erect an oak cross over his grave, the only tribute to his memory that is left us to pay. Will you and the other members of Raymond's family please accept this expression of condolence from a brother officer.

Jones was laid to rest in Carnoy Military Cemetery by the Reverend James Evans, with Lieutenant Colonel Mills Roberts, the CO of his unit, attending.

The survivors of the 15th Welsh pulled back to points D-E where they consolidated. In the meantime, the 14th Welsh, under the command of Lieutenant Colonel Hayes, had succeeded in capturing the central ride through the wood, though their right flank was held up since there was little by way of support.

A photograph, taken from a stereograph slide, showing the complete and utter devastation in part of Mametz Wood.

The remaining company of the 15th Welsh was sent in to aid the 10th Welsh, who had lost a company that had been attached to 113 Brigade. At 10.30 am, the 15th Welsh were at a line running from D-E but were hit by a strong German counter-attack and driven back to D-C where Lieutenant John Evans rallied the men, organizing a counter-attack that secured their positions and captured three German field guns in so doing. This action earned Lieutenant Evans of Llanelli the Military Cross. The attack then ground to a halt, and the next few hours were spent desperately clinging on to their precarious footholds in the wood while parties of men from the Royal Engineers and 19th Welsh dug a communication trench between Caterpillar Wood and the Hammerhead.

Sergeant Horace Frank Anderson (62650) of Aberdare, a member of the 124th Field Company, Royal Engineers.

A number of these men were killed by machine-gun fire from Flatiron Copse, including Sergeant Horace Frank Anderson (62650) of the 124th Field Company Royal Engineers. Anderson lived at 38 Trevor Street, Aberdare and had worked at the Powell Dyffryn Steam Coal Company as a draughtsman prior to the war. It was his 23rd birthday. No trace of him was ever found and he is commemorated on the Thiepval Memorial.

With the outcome of the battle hanging in the balance, Brigadier General Marden committed the reserves at his disposal to the attack. These were the 17th RWF, who went to support 113 Brigade on the left, and the 10th SWB, who had been in bivouac until 12 pm, went to support 114 Brigade on the right of the attack. They arrived in the fighting by about 2.40 pm, adding fresh impetus to the attack, and the 10th SWB soon reached a point to the north of the second cross ride and were able to get patrols out through the dense undergrowth to the northern edge of the wood. The 17th RWF, however, suffered a huge setback when their CO, Lieutenant Colonel John Arthur Ballard, was wounded on the way into the wood.

In the meantime, 114 Brigade was pushing further into the eastern half of the wood, led by the 14th Welsh. The undergrowth was so thick that progress was only possible in single file and so the 14th Welsh dug in, preparing positions ready for the next phase of the assault. The fragmented 15th Welsh were now moved up to replace the 14th Welsh at this new line and was hurriedly organized under Captain J.C. McDonald, digging a trench about 250 metres parallel to the northern edge of the wood, while the 14th Welsh were pulled back.

By 6.30 pm the 17th RWF had reached to within 20 to 30 metres of the northern edge of the wood and the Hammerhead had been taken by the 10th SWB as the German troops were forced to withdraw. The bulk of the wood east of the central ride was in the Welshmen's hands, though to the west it was necessary to turn a flank along the railway line facing the north-western corner of the wood.

The rest of the division came under heavy fire from the German second line and withdrew to the cover of the wood for some 200 to 300 metres. The day's fighting ended there; it left the men tired and jumpy, and throughout the night there was much wild firing as men shot at shadowy figures in the darkness.

At 5 am on the following day, 11 July, Brigadier Evans of 115 Brigade took over the command of all the troops in Mametz Wood, establishing his headquarters on the junction of the central ride with the first cross ride. He brought up into the wood the 16th Welsh and the remaining companies of the 11th SWB to replace some of the tired units of 113 and 114 brigades. The 13th and 14th Welsh were withdrawn to the Citadel in divisional reserve. Half the 19th Welsh with 100 men of the 14th RWF were in reserve.

It was around this time that Lieutenant James Frederick Venmore MC of the 14th RWF was killed. Venmore was born on 9 June 1888, the son of James Venmore, JP, of 200 Scotland Road, Liverpool. He was educated at Mill Hill School and Liverpool University and was an architect at Cemaes, Anglesey prior to the war. He was one of the first members of the 38th (Welsh) Division to have been awarded the MC:

Lieutenant James Frederick Venmore, MC, of the 14th RWF.

On the night of January 30th, 1916, Lieut. Venmore was on duty as patrol officer in front of the British trenches in France, when a sentry in the firing trench reported that three men in the advanced listening post had been wounded. Two of these men were just able to crawl back to the British lines over barbed wire, but the third man was too seriously wounded to follow, being shot through both legs. Lieut. Venmore volunteered to go to his assistance and took with him a non-commissioned officer (Corporal William Williams from Caernarfon), who is also awarded the Distinguished Conduct Medal. They went out under heavy fire over the parapet, and after great difficulty successfully brought the man over the wire and two ditches. This brave action was succeeded by a further gallant act on the following morning, when a message was received that a man had his arm blown off at another listening post, practically unapproachable by daylight. Lieut. Venmore again undertook to go to his aid, once more taking with him Corporal Williams. They crawled across the open ground in the face of heavy machine gun fire. The sufferer was reached, his wounds attended to, and he was subsequently brought to safety. Both the officer and his companion were most highly congratulated by the brigade and divisional officers.

The grave of Lieutenant James Frederick Venmore, MC, in Flatiron Copse Cemetery, Mametz.

Venmore was wounded and then killed in Mametz Wood on 11 July and is buried in Dantzig Alley British Cemetery, Mametz. He is commemorated on the Llanfechell War Memorial.

Evans was expected to complete the capture of the wood with the remaining tired troops at his disposal. He established a line, from the left, as follows: 16th RWF, 16th Welsh, 17th RWF, 11th SWB, 10th SWB.

An attack was planned for 3 pm with the 16th Welsh, 17th RWF and 11th SWB taking the lead. The centre left was expected to meet with the greatest difficulties. Evans had planned the attack without artillery support but at 2.45 pm an artillery barrage was opened that could not be stopped and Evans' infantry units began to suffer from the drop-shorts of 18-pounders firing on the limit of their range. This bombardment carried on until 3.30 pm.

As soon as the bombardment stopped, the battalions moved into action. The 11th SWB reached the north-east corner of the wood by 5.40 pm, relieving the battered the 15th Welsh who were placed in support on the Y-X transverse ride. The other two attacking units of 115 Brigade had much less luck and were held up.

With the attack again stagnant, Brigadier General Evans brought up the remnants of the 10th Welsh, 15th Welsh and the 16th RWF at around 6.30 pm to renew the attack, but after heavy fighting and reaching positions just 60 yards south of the wood's northern edge, heavy casualties due to artillery fire among these three battalions forced a withdrawal at around 2.30 am on 12 July. The attack had not been a success, although there was fierce fighting throughout the rest of the day. The German reaction to the attack was that they now realized that to continue to defend the wood was fruitless and costly and at 8 am orders were issued for their withdrawal.

Unknown to Brigadier General Evans, the evacuation of the 38th (Welsh) Division began as darkness fell, leaving only a few patrols within the boundary of the wood. As dawn broke on 12 July 1916 the units of 62 Brigade, 21st Division entered the wood to relieve the tired troops of the 38th (Welsh) Division and they very rapidly moved through it, which was hardly surprising since the Germans had already left the area after being soundly beaten by the Welshmen.

The fighting for Mametz Wood was over. It had cost the 38th (Welsh) Division about a third of its total infantry strength:

Killed: 46 officers and 556 other ranks.
Wounded: 138 officers and 2,668 other ranks.
Missing: 6 officers and 579 other ranks.
Total: 190 officers and 3,803 other ranks.

The individual infantry units had suffered as follows:

13th RWF: 3 officers – Lieutenant Colonel Oswald Swift Flower, Captain Edward William Lawrence (RAMC attached) and Lieutenant Harold Vivian Jones – and 49 men killed; 4 officers wounded.

14th RWF: 5 officers – Major Robert Henry Mills, Lieutenant James Frederick Venmore, MC, Second Lieutenants Adrian Hamilton Silverton Barrett, Brian Harrison and Alan Sheriff Roberts – and 58 men killed; 9 officers and 233 men wounded.

15th RWF: 2 officers – Lieutenant Roland Gwyn Rees and Second Lieutenant Reginald Henry Fleming – and 29 men killed; 7 officers and 132 men wounded. (Second Lieutenant Ceredig Ellis of Aberystwyth was wounded on 10 July and died of wounds on 19 July.)

16th RWF: 2 officers – Lieutenant Colonel Ronald James Walter Carden and Second Lieutenant Henry Hugh Tregarthen Rees – and 107 men killed; 5 officers and 196 men wounded.

17th RWF: 6 officers – Captain Hywel Williams, Lieutenant William Clifford Wright, Second Lieutenants Llewelyn Lewis, James Victor Sinnett-Jones, Thomas Oliver Thomas and Frederick William Walsh – and 38 men killed; 12 officers and 197 men wounded.

10th SWB: 2 officers – Second Lieutenants Maryon Jeffries Everton and Ralph Paton Taylor – and 32 men killed; 9 officers and 120 men wounded.

11th SWB: 3 officers – Captain Lawrence Reddrop Lewis, Second Lieutenants Arthur Stanley Fletcher and Stewart Alexander Miller-Hallett – and 25 men killed; 10 officers and 150 men wounded.

10th Welsh: 4 officers – Captain David Jones, Second Lieutenants Henry Benedict Cowie, Herbert Francis Jones and Thomas Yale Lloyd – and 68 men killed; 13 officers and 200 men wounded.

13th Welsh: 7 officers – Majors Charles Edward Bond and George D'Arcy Edwardes, Lieutenant William Stanley Goldsmith Jeffreys, Second Lieutenants Guy Danvers Mainwaring Crossman, Henry Mitchell Harvey, Thomas Paterson Purdie and Laurence Sinclair Rees – and 98 men killed; 6 officers and 168 other ranks wounded.

14th Welsh: 1 officer – Second Lieutenant Arthur Rosser – and 102 men killed; 11 officers and 286 men wounded.

15th Welsh: 4 officers – Majors Percy Anthony and Christian Gibson Phillips, Second Lieutenants John Reginald Hall and Clifton Malet Lucas – and 67 men killed; 4 officers and 119 men wounded.

16th Welsh: 2 officers – Captains Lyn Arthur Philip Harris and John Lewis Williams – and 22 men killed; 5 officers and 42 men wounded. (The battalion had also suffered grievous losses on 7 July.) John Lewis Williams was a former Welsh international rugby player.

19th Welsh: 1 officer – Second Lieutenant Walter Tessier Newlyn – and 27 men killed; 2 officers and 80 men wounded.

While many people have heard about the two Tregaskis brothers of the 16th Welsh who were killed on 7 July, the 15th Welsh lost two pairs of brothers killed during the fighting within the wood. Private James Jones (20026) and Corporal John Jones

The three Jones brothers of Llandovery: John, Daniel and James. John and James were killed together at Mametz Wood on 10 July, while Daniel survived the war.

(20027) were the sons of Daniel and Mary Jane Jones of 4 Towy Avenue, Llandovery. They had enlisted together at Llandovery, being given consecutive service numbers, and were killed together on 10 July. Neither of the men has a known grave, so they are both commemorated on the Thiepval Memorial.

Lance Corporal Henry Hardwidge (20649) and Corporal Thomas Hardwidge (26634) were the sons of John and Phoebe Hardwidge of 17 High Street, Ystradfodwg. They had both enlisted at different times at Ferndale in the 15th Welsh. Thomas was shot by a German sniper during the fighting within the Hammerhead and his brother Henry rushed to his side to give him water, but was himself shot by the same sniper. The two men died in each other's arms. They are buried side by side in Flatiron Copse Cemetery, Mametz. Both men were married. A third elder brother, Morgan, was killed later that year while serving on the Somme with the 2nd Welsh. Tom left behind his wife Annie and three children at 17 High Street, Ferndale and Henry left his wife Jennie and one child at 13 Lake Street, Ferndale.

A letter sent by their company commander to the widows of both men read: 'I had known them for nearly 12 months, for they were in my platoon. More cheerful, willing and capable soldiers I do not think it possible to find, and their presence is greatly missed by everyone in the platoon and by myself.'

The majority of the dead were buried within the wood where they fell, in what was named Mametz Wood Cemetery. Many of these graves within the wood were lost

The graves of the brothers Henry and Thomas Hardwidge in Flatiron Copse Cemetery.

during the continued fighting in the area during the course of the war and so the men are now commemorated on the Thiepval Memorial. There are scattered burials throughout the Somme which bear testament to the heavy fighting in Mametz Wood, at Heilly Station Cemetery, Caterpillar Valley Cemetery, Dantzig Alley Cemetery, Mametz and in Flatiron Copse Cemetery.

The author's great-uncle, Private Harry Montague Allen (20965) of Whitland, a railway worker at Llanelli prior to the war, enlisted on 17 April 1915 and was shot in the chest by a German sniper on 10 July during the fighting at the Hammerhead. The bullet passed through his pocket Bible into his chest, leaving the Bible holed and bloodstained. The Bible was sent to his parents along with his belongings. Allen was quickly evacuated to the 38th Casualty Clearing Station at Heilly, where he died the following day. The medical staff were so inundated with casualties during the opening days of the fighting on the Somme that the burials in much of the cemetery are too close together for individual headstones. As a result, he is commemorated along with two other men on one headstone.

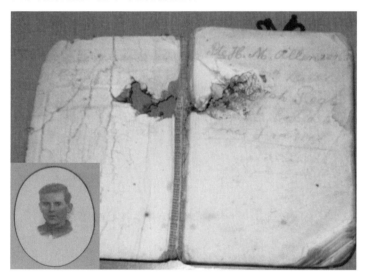

The pocket Bible that belonged to Private Harry Montague Allen (20965), 15th Welsh, of Whitland. Allen was shot through the Bible and evacuated to the 38th Casualty Clearing Station at Heilly, where he died on 11 July.

Another of the many men who died of wounds suffered at Mametz Wood over the coming days was the sixth of thirteen Welsh international rugby players to fall during the war. Captain John Lewis Williams was born on 3 January 1882, the son of Edward Lewis of Llwyncelyn, Whitchurch. He played for Cardiff and gained his first Welsh cap in 1906 against South Africa. Williams was one of the best of the Welsh internationals killed during the war, gaining

Captain John Lewis Williams, 16th Welsh, the sixth Welsh rugby international killed during the war.

seventeen caps in total, playing on the wing. He was wounded in Mametz Wood and died at Corbie on 12 July 1916, aged 34. He is buried in Corbie Communal Cemetery Extension.

Amongst the many tragic events that occurred to men within the wood was the death of Second Lieutenant William Harold Cullen. He was the son of Alfred and Elizabeth Cullen of 13 Noel Street, Nottingham. Cullen was educated at Nottingham High School and was a keen sportsman, being an excellent rower and a hockey and rugby player. He enlisted in the Royal Horse Artillery as a gunner in September 1914 and was commissioned in the Sherwood Foresters in March 1915. He then transferred in the 113th Company, Machine-Gun Corps, which was attached to the 38th (Welsh) Division. Cullen had taken his machine-gun team into Mametz Wood on 10 July and survived the first day's fighting only to become isolated inside the wood during the early hours of 11 July; he was mistaken for a German and shot dead by his own men. He was 26 years old and is commemorated on the Thiepval Memorial. We will never know how many men died in similar circumstances within the dark and overgrown confines of the wood, but doubtless Cullen was not the only man to suffer such a fate. Captain Glynn Jones of the 15th RWF saw a similar tragedy occur when one of his second lieutenants was shot in the undergrowth by his own men.

The grave of Captain John Lewis Williams, 16th Welsh, in Corbie Communal Cemetery Extension.

After the capture and consolidation of Mametz Wood, the entire 38th (Welsh) Division was relieved to a quiet part of the line, just to the north at Hébuterne, the brigades moving back to bivouac. In spite of the effort that had been expended in the capture of the wood, it was to get no credit for the work. The division was considered by some regular officers to have been of an inferior quality for a variety of reasons and all ignored the fact that the wood had fallen to them in a relatively short time. It was a political situation over which the men of the 38th (Welsh) Division had no control, and wild tales spread of the Welshmen's cowardice under fire.

Second Lieutenant William Harold Cullen of the 113th Company, Machine-Gun Corps. Isolated while fighting inside the wood, he was mistakenly shot dead by his own men.

Looking at how the men fought it is easy to see that this was blatantly untrue. Cowards do not run into machine-gun fire and die as those gallant Welshmen had done over those bloody days; the number of casualties suffered by the division at Mametz shows this. Also a succession of chances to capture the then lightly-defended wood after the initial advance of 1 July were not taken, and by the time the 38th (Welsh) Division had moved into position to attack the wood it was heavily defended and any momentum had been lost. If any blame were to be attached to the division, it was not the fault of the men who had spilt their blood on

Looking eastwards across Death Valley towards Flatiron Copse Cemetery, with Caterpillar Wood to the right. As the Welshmen crossed this bare ground they were struck by enfilade fire from Flatiron Copse in the distance.

the battlefield. Interestingly, later on in the Somme offensive, the smaller High Wood was to take two months and several divisions to clear; and no accusations were laid at the feet of those divisions.

Partly due to the unfounded criticism that followed the battle for Mametz Wood over the coming months and years, it took more than sixty years for the efforts of the 38th (Welsh) Division to be properly remembered, although a marble memorial was erected within Mametz Church after the war, following much deliberation. After a lot of hard work by members of the South Wales Branch of the Western Front Association, a splendid memorial in the form of the Welsh Dragon was erected at the spot from where the division first attacked. Appropriately, this magnificent piece of metalwork was created by the artist blacksmith David Peterson of St Clears, a man who once took a very interesting metalworking class in which the author was involved as a 15-year-old schoolboy.

The 38th (Welsh) Division Memorial overlooking Mametz Wood.

On the first parade that 114 Brigade carried out after being evacuated from Mametz Wood, the following 'Special Order of the Day' was read out to the men, written by Brigadier General T.O. Marden CMG, commanding 114 Infantry Brigade:

The Brigadier General congratulates all ranks on their achievements of the 10th of July when they firmly established the fighting reputation of the 114th Infantry Brigade by capturing the portion of the Mametz Wood allotted to them by the Divisional Commander, thereby gaining the thanks of the Commander-in-Chief for the performance of a task which called for a special effort.

Wood fighting is recognised as the most difficult form of fighting and it reflects the greatest credit on all engaged, that at the end of the day all Units in the Brigade were under their own Commanders.

The advance to the attack was carried out in perfect order by the 13th and 14th Welsh, to whom fell the majority of the Wood fighting, the severity of which is shown by the Casualty Lists.

The 10th and 15th Welsh showed equal steadiness in the advance when called on to support. The thanks of the Brigadier are especially due to Lieutenant Colonel J.H. Hayes, Commanding 14th Welsh, for his special work throughout the day, and to Captain A.P. Bowen, Brigade Major, for his Staff work and organising work in the Wood.

They are due to Lieutenant Colonel P.E. Ricketts, Commanding 10th Welsh, to Major D.A. Edwards, Commanding 13th Welsh, and to Major C.G. Phillips, Commanding 15th Welsh who all, unfortunately, became casualties during the action.

They are due, too, to those Officers and Non Commissioned Officers who assumed Command of Battalions, Companies and Platoons, when their leaders fell, and to others whose names have not yet been ascertained.

With such a splendid start, the 114th Infantry Brigade can look with confidence to the future, and with pride to the past.

T.O. Marden, Brigadier-General, Commanding 114th Infantry Brigade, 13 July 1916.

The 38th (Welsh) Division spent several days in bivouac before being moved north to positions between Serre and Hébuterne, and then spent a period training in northern France before being sent to Ypres later in the year. Just days after the 38th (Welsh) Division left the battlefield, on 15 July, troops of the 2nd RWF passed the wood while advancing towards the new front line near Bazentin-le-Petit. Various accounts written after the war by Siegfried Sassoon and Frank Richards spoke of the horrors that met them during their march, with the lingering smell of gas filling the valley, the shattered bodies of Welsh and German soldiers scattered over the devastated ground, and even the grisly sight of a South Wales Borderer and his German foe who had bayoneted each other at the same time and were both propped up by a tree. Torn bodies hung from branches and the stench of death was awful. The grounds within the woods are

The 38th (Welsh) Division Memorial in Mametz Church. The memorial was not dedicated until 1924 as the original church had been flattened during the war and had to be rebuilt. A campaign for its erection was carried out by the members of the Welsh Army Corps Committee under Lord Treowen, who had hoped for something grander in the form of a Welsh National Memorial, but despite the modest costs of £200 a great deal of work was needed to raise the money required.

still scarred with the remnants of battle; trench lines and shell holes are scattered throughout the wood, a testament to the men who died taking them.

Among the multitude of letters and poems written back to family members about their epic deeds in Mametz Wood, Corporal S.A. White of the Welsh Regiment sent a simple poem to the editor of the *Cambrian Daily Leader*:

> We reached that dread inferno
> And stormed the gates of hell.
> Why wonder when I tell you, we all went sort of mad.
> But yet took pity on the Huns, crying Mercy, kamerad,
> For tho' we all remembered the brutal deeds they'd done
> We deigned to show them mercy, tho' they had shown us none.
> We fought as Britons always do, the only way we know,
> A clean, fair fight, with right as might, no matter who the foe.
> So we battered them, and shattered them, until the wood was won.

Other, more famous, accounts were written by men such as David Jones of the 15th RWF, who wrote his well-known poem *In Parenthesis* about his experiences, and Captain Wyn Griffiths' epic book *Up to Mametz*; but the writings of 'lesser' poets,

122

such as Corporal White, are also of much interest. Other epic adventures would befall the 38th (Welsh) Division throughout the remainder of the war, but nothing would ever match up to the hell they suffered within the darkness of Mametz Wood. However, apart from their brief but relatively quiet spell at Hébuterne, the Battle of the Somme was over for them and it is time to look at the other Welsh units.

(ii) The Battle of Bazentin Ridge
The 2nd RWF had been in positions near Gorre since the blowing of the Red Dragon Mine and had begun plotting for a retaliatory trench raid to gain some vengeance for their fallen men. When the final artillery bombardment for the Somme offensive had started on the night of 30 June, the noise was so great that the men of the 2nd RWF could hear it from their positions. While their fellow countrymen were fighting desperately on the Somme, the 2nd RWF came up with a plan to attack the German salient at the Warren and all their officers got involved.

The plan involved D and A companies – some 200 men – who would assault from the west and north-west; A should push through to the reserve line and hold it while D mopped up and destroyed any points of tactical importance with the help of engineers of the 11th Field Company, Royal Engineers. B Company was to carry the necessary explosives, while C Company would hold the original line. At nightfall on 5 July the assaulting companies moved into position and at 10.30 pm the artillery barrage opened up on known machine-gun positions. The men of D and A companies set off 'like a pack of hounds' following white tape that had been laid out by the battalion scouts and at around 11.15 pm entered the German lines where a furious bombing fight began. Captain Higginson spotted some Germans disappearing into a dugout and shouted down for them to surrender. They replied by firing a rifle at him, so several grenades were lobbed down the steps into the dugout and an explosive charge was laid at the dugout entrance, sealing the fate of the Germans inside.

With German resistance now ended, the men began looting the trenches for anything of value for souvenirs, and forty-three prisoners of the 241st Saxon Regiment were hurried back. The raid was a complete success, although the battalion had suffered one officer – Lieutenant Raymond Archibald Robert Hollingbery – and eleven men killed, and forty wounded.

This was to be the last action in Flanders for the battalion for the time being, as on 7 July the 33rd Division received orders to move south to join the Somme offensive and the 2nd RWF left Béthune on 9 July, entraining for Longueau on the Somme under the command of Lieutenant Colonel Crawshay. On 10 July the battalion detrained and marched through Amiens towards Daours. On the afternoon of 12 July the 2nd RWF marched past Corbie, passing the transport of the 38th (Welsh) Division, which was withdrawing from Mametz, on the road and arrived at Buire in the afternoon. The division now joined XV Corps.

The 10th RWF of the 3rd Division had entrained at St. Omer on 1 July and arrived at Doullens. The division had then marched through Gézaincourt, Naours, Rainneville and Franvillers for Carnoy, reaching the latter on 13 July while the bombardment for the next phase of the offensive was under way. The 1st RWF of the 7th Division was at the Citadel, while the 19th Division had moved back to Albert. There would be another strong Welsh contingent involved in the next phase.

While the struggle for Mametz Wood was at its height, there had also been heavy fighting by the 30th Division for the possession of Trônes Wood which was on the right. The division eventually managed to secure the southern portion but, much like the 38th (Welsh) Division, had suffered so badly from the ordeals of fighting in woods that it had to be relieved on the night of 12/13 July by the 18th Division.

The South Africans entered the war in France in April and posted to the 9th (Scottish) Division. The first known Welshman to be killed in France while serving with the South Africans was Lance Corporal David Pugh (3278), the son of David and Sarah Pugh of Clover Hill Farm, Velfrey Road, Whitland. He had remained in South Africa after fighting in the Boer War and worked for the South African Railway at Cape Town. He enlisted on 17 August 1915 and joined the 4th (Scottish) South African Infantry Regiment, South African Expeditionary Force (SAEF). On 30 June the South African Brigade moved to Grove Town, south of Albert, where it watched the opening of the Battle of the Somme on 1 July. On the following night the South Africans entered the front line north-west of Maricourt and spent the coming days holding the trenches against German artillery fire. On Monday, 10 July 1916 the 4th South African Regiment

Lance Corporal David Pugh (3278), 4th (Scottish) South African Infantry Regiment.

attacked Trônes Wood in support of the 30th Division but came under heavy artillery fire. Pugh was killed here on that day, aged 42, and is commemorated on the Thiepval Memorial.

On 11 July a former officer of the Welsh Regiment was killed while commanding the 4th Regiment SAEF. Lieutenant Colonel Frank Aubrey Jones CMG DSO was born on 4 August 1873, the son of Arthur Mowbray Jones and Clara Belinda Jones. He was educated at the King's School, Ely and joined the Welsh Regiment on 28 September 1895. He served in Sierra Leone on the Protectorate Expedition and was severely wounded in South Africa during the Boer War. He was awarded the DSO in recognition of services during the operations in South Africa. He had retired soon after but volunteered to serve again on the outbreak of the Great War and was promoted to command the 4th Regiment SAEF. Jones was killed by a shell fragment while exiting his dugout in Bernafay Wood on 11 July 1916 and is buried in Péronne Road Cemetery, Maricourt. He was the first senior officer of the SAEF to be killed in France.

The grave of Lieutenant Colonel Frank Aubrey Jones, CMG DSO, CO of the 4th Regiment, SAEF, at Péronne Road Cemetery, Maricourt. (Delville Wood Memorial)

Meanwhile, on 10 July the 23rd Division had succeeded in capturing Contalmaison on the spur 900 metres west of Mametz Wood and the Germans had withdrawn to their second defensive line. The 21st Division relieved the 17th as well as the 38th (Welsh) Division at Mametz Wood on 12 July, while on the left the 1st Division, which included the 1st SWB, 2nd and 6th Welsh, replaced the 23rd Division on the night of 10/11 July.

The scene was set for an attack on the German second trench system on the front running from Trônes Wood to Contalmaison: fresh divisions were in position, and the date was fixed for 14 July. The 1st Division, which was to form a defensive flank to the west, had only its 1 Brigade in the front line at Contalmaison, 2 Brigade being in support and 3 Brigade in reserve at Albert.

The 2nd Welsh had reached Albert on 10 July after a six-day march from the Loos sector and was put up in billets in the town with the remainder of 3 Brigade. On 12 July a shell burst inside a house in which No. 15 Platoon was billeted, killing six men and wounding twenty-one others, two of whom died later that day. It was a tragic start to their Somme campaign. The dead men were Lance Corporal Thomas Llewellyn Evans (19612) of Morriston; Privates Thomas Henry Campbell (26502) of Bargoed, Edward Clabby (2495) of Cardiff, Benjamin Daniel Davies (13114) of Ferryside, Daniel James Griffiths (29032) of Cardigan and John Ward (8129) of Cardiff. All six men are buried in Albert Communal Cemetery Extension. The two men who died of wounds later in the day were Lance Sergeant William Donovan (569) of Dowlais, who is buried in Heilly Station Cemetery, Méricourt-l'Abbé, and Private Thomas Donovan (22766) of Gilfach Goch, who is buried in Warloy-Baillon Communal Cemetery Extension. Private Morgan Richards (38647) of Merthyr died of his wounds the following day on 13 July and is buried in Heilly Station Cemetery, Méricourt-l'Abbé.

Lance Sergeant William Donovan (569) of Dowlais. Mortally wounded by a shell that burst in his billets in Albert on 12 July 1916, he is buried in Heilly Station Cemetery, Méricourt-l'Abbé.

The grave of Private Thomas Donovan (22766) of Gilfach Goch in Warloy-Baillon Communal Cemetery Extension.

The 1st SWB, in the same brigade, had reached Albert on the same day and were pleased to find the 5th SWB, who were bivouacked in Baizeux Wood, and the 6th SWB also billeted in Albert. Officers of 3 Brigade then went forward to reconnoitre the positions near Contalmaison that had been taken over by 1 Brigade of the same division on 11/12 July.

In the early hours of 14 July the 1st RWF had moved from the Citadel to White Trench. At 3.30 am on 14 July, XIII Corps, comprising the 3rd and 9th divisions, attacked Delville Wood, Longueval and Bazentin-le-Grand, while XV Corps – the 7th

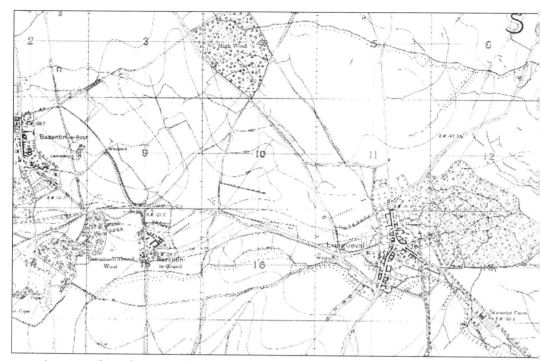

A section of trench map 57CSW3: Longueval, showing the positions of Bazentin le Petit, High Wood and Delville Woods.

and 21st divisions – attacked Bazentin-le-Grand wood and Bazentin-le-Petit Wood, its village and cemetery. The 18th Division formed a defensive flank to the east and the 1st Division a defensive flank to the west. The 10th RWF of the 3rd Division remained in reserve, as did the 1st RWF, who had been ordered to remain in White Trench until the attack began and then to advance and take over the positions of the assaulting battalions, the Warwicks and Royal Irish. At about 4.15 am the assault began and the 1st RWF went forward to occupy their positions in the Hammerhead of Mametz Wood, only to find there were no trenches in which to shelter. The Germans were bombarding the area and the Welshmen were forced to dig in to shell craters while under heavy fire.

At around 11 am the battalion received orders to advance after the cavalry and capture High Wood, which was about 1.5 miles away. The situation soon became dire. The Royal Irish were forced out of Bazentin-le-Petit and began falling back, and Germans began to exploit the gap in the line. A party of the Royal Irish rallied and advanced and at 12.30 pm the 2nd Gordon Highlanders and 1st RWF were ordered to attack: the former Bazentin-le-Petit; the latter the windmill and cemetery. Although the attack was successful, heavy fire was raining down all around, many casualties were suffered and the assaulting troops were forced to dig in to gain some shelter. A gallant attack was carried out on High Wood at 7 pm but this was easily beaten off and, with the situation worsening, the 33rd Division came up on the left of the 7th

Division. The 1st RWF had lost two officers – Lieutenants Richard Henry Beindge Baynes and Geoffrey Penney Morgan – and thirteen men killed, and four officers and twenty-eight men wounded during the day and spent the night in shell craters around Bazentin-le-Petit. Baynes and Morgan were buried near the windmill.

The front of the 1st Division ran from Bailiff Wood across the north of Contalmaison to a point midway between the village and Mametz Wood. On the right, the 21st Division line ran northward up to the north-west end of the wood and along its northern border. On the left of the 1st Division lay the 34th Division, almost 900 metres south of Pozières. This village was the key to the taking of Thiepval Ridge as it afforded the Germans a view over the ground to the south and south-east, the western slopes of the Contalmaison spur and extensive views north.

To attack Pozières it was imperative that Bazentin-le-Petit village and wood were captured, which would then enable Pozières to be attacked from the flank as well as from the front. On 14 July, while XV Corps were assaulting Bazentin-le-Petit, the 1st Division sent 2 Brigade from support to advance with the left of the 21st Division and they began to bomb up the German trenches from Bazentin Wood, sheltered by the rise of the Contalmaison spur from fire from Pozières. Sections of the German first and second lines were taken, but in the main the Germans defended stoutly. The 1st SWB moved into reserve at Lozenge Wood, north of Fricourt, and was shelled during the move, luckily suffering no casualties. The Borderers took over some old German dugouts, the elaborate construction and decoration of which, some with wallpaper and all with electric lighting, much amused the men. After settling in they began sending parties forward to carry ammunition, food and water to the assaulting troops ahead.

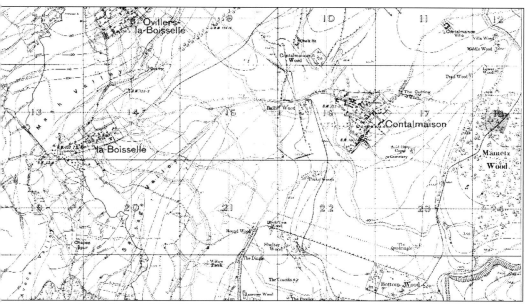

A section of trench map 57DSE4: Ovillers, showing the positions of Ovillers, Bailiff Wood, Contalmaison and Mametz Wood.

The fight for Bazentin Ridge also involved a large number of Welsh troops serving with a non-Welsh battalion, the 7th King's Shropshire Light Infantry (KSLI) of 8 Brigade, 3rd Division. The battalion had moved in the Somme sector from Ypres, reaching Carnoy by 7 July. Its officers spent the coming days observing the battle and reconnoitring the ground allocated to 8 Brigade to capture.

Their attack was launched at 3.30 am on 14 July, the 7th KSLI and 8th East Yorks leading the attack with the 1st Royal Scots Fusiliers in support, their objective being the enemy front trench and support line running through Bazentin-le-Grand, a distance of almost 1,300 metres. The preliminary bombardment fell short, causing casualties among the battalion, and when the whistles blew the men advanced only to find the wire uncut. The first wave was cut down by German machine-gun fire, then the second wave came forward only to find their advance blocked, affording the Germans an easy target.

Suffering terrible casualties, the survivors of the 7th KSLI withdrew to the safety of a sunken road some 200 metres from the Germans and could only watch in vain as their CO, Lieutenant Colonel Negus, together with two privates who lay wounded in the wire, were captured and brought in by the Germans. The remnants of the battalion were reorganized and at 11 am attacked again with the assistance of bombing parties and succeeded in breaking through the wire before reaching the enemy trenches, driving the Germans off and rescuing their CO.

The survivors of the battalion, consisting of just 6 officers and about 135 other ranks, consolidated and held the new line, beating off five counter-attacks, until 20 July, when they were relieved by the 1st RWF. Among the 8 officers and 163 men killed were 43 Welshmen, including another Welsh international rugby player, Corporal David Watts (13793).

Watts was born at Maesteg on 14 March 1886. He played for Maesteg and won four caps at forward during the 1914 season. The war interrupted a promising playing career and Watts enlisted in the 7th KSLI. He was 30 years old when he was killed on 14 July and is commemorated on the Thiepval Memorial.

The name of Corporal David Watts (13793), 7th KSLI, on the Thiepval Memorial. Watts was the seventh Welsh international rugby player to fall when he was killed at Bazentin le Petit on 14 July 1916.

Early on 15 July the 2nd Welsh were brought up from Albert to Mametz Wood, arriving at 9 am, and advanced in extended order from Mametz Wood to the south side of Bazentin Wood, where a shell wounded Lieutenant Bertram Victor Sinclair Cripps MC, and several battalion scouts.

The 2nd RWF also moved into Mametz Wood during the day, meeting up with their comrades from the 2nd Welsh. Frank Richards wrote:

The ruined village of Fricourt: the sight that greeted the men of the 2nd RWF on their way up to Mametz Wood.

We arrived on the Somme by a six days' march from the railhead, and early in the morning of the 15th July passed through Fricourt, where our First Battalion had broken through on 1st July, and arrived at the end of Mametz Wood, which had been captured some days before by the 38th Welsh Division which included four of our new service battalions. The enemy had been sending over tear-gas and the valley was thick with it. It smelt like strong onions which made our eyes and noses run very badly; we were soon coughing, sneezing and cursing. We rested in shell holes, the ground all around us being thick with dead of the troops who had been attacking Mametz Wood. The fighting was going on about three-quarters of a mile ahead of us.

The 2nd RWF lost Second Lieutenant Ernest Arthur Camies and Private Daniel Farrell (8799) killed during the day. Frank Richards and several other men of the battalion went scrounging in the wood to see what they could find and came out with several trench coats and some tins of Maconochie's stew [the ubiquitous 'meat and vegetable rations', with a somewhat dubious reputation].

At 11 am three companies of the 2nd Welsh were sent forward to aid in the assault of 1 Brigade, relieving them on the Contalmaison front. The battalion lost Second Lieutenant Henry Moore and three men killed and thirty-three men wounded. One of the dead was Private Thomas Henry James (27478) of Pontfaen, Fishguard, who had been awarded the DCM for Loos: 'For conspicuous gallantry in volunteering to cut through the enemy's wire within a few yards of his parapet, and carrying out his objective in spite of his patrol being seen and fired on.' (*London Gazette*, 15 March 1916.) (Private Frank Richards (6584), 2nd RWF, the aforementioned author of *Old Soldiers Never Die*, was awarded his DCM in the same *Gazette* issue: 'During a successful attack, Privates Richards and Barrett took their telephone over the parapet, established and maintained communication. They lay out in the open for three hours, and repaired the wire whenever it was cut.')

129

The Germans had steadied following their losses of the previous day and had defeated an assault by the 34th Division on Pozières during the afternoon. As a result, Brigadier General Davies, commanding 3 Brigade, ordered the 2nd Welsh to attack a trench that ran north-east to the Switch Line to prevent the Germans sending up reinforcements. The assault was delivered at 4 am the next day but the Germans held out and the attack failed with the loss of Second Lieutenant Reginald Mortimer Nicholls mortally wounded and ten men killed, six officers and forty-four men wounded. Lieutenant Wilfred York Price won the MC for pressing forward the attack even when wounded, and Second Lieutenant John Warren Davis won the same decoration for his gallantry in leading the bombing attack and during further fighting the following day. Captain Charles Pritchard Clayton wrote of Nicholls' death in his book *The Hungry One*:

Lieutenant Reginald Mortimer Nicholls, 2nd Welsh, of Bridgend, who died on 18 July 1916 of wounds suffered near High Wood. He is buried in Heilly Station Cemetery.

During the afternoon young Nicholls comes along from 'C' Company. He is usually a quiet fellow, but he is very cheery now for he is off to England, envied by all. It is not often that anyone gets away from the middle of active fighting. We cheer him along with the messages for London, and he hurries happily down the trench. He is no sooner out of sight than a few shells come screaming along. It is as if they have seen him. 'Mr Nicholls is hit, sir,' shouts one of the men. 'Poor fellow, right in the face it caught him.' 'Oh God, I'm killed.' That was all he said, then collapsed and died. I find it is true. It seems piercingly tragic, actually to be off with his leave ticket in his pocket, to be hit and know that he was dying. So many have died before they know.

Heavy fighting continued throughout 16 July and the Germans were pushed back to the road running from Bazentin to Contalmaison Villa. The 1st RWF was relieved from Bazentin-le-Petit during the afternoon, by which time their frontline position had become the second line, and met up again with their comrades of the 2nd RWF in Mametz Wood. The 1st RWF lost two men killed during the relief.

At midnight on 16/17 July 3 Brigade was ordered to attack again, the Gloucesters on the right with the Munsters on the left, and the 2nd Welsh were ordered to attack north-west when the Gloucesters passed them. The advance met with no opposition and the men advanced too far, so had to withdraw slightly and dug in along the Bazentin to Pozières road. The 2nd Welsh lost sixteen men killed during the night, four of them through a shell that burst on the battalion HQ dugout. Lieutenant Colonel Pritchard and Captain Dunn, the adjutant, luckily escaped. The German defenders of Ovillers surrendered on 16 July and the 48th Division was now approaching Pozières from the south.

The following days were very uncomfortable for the British as the Germans shelled their lines almost continuously. On 17 July the 1st RWF suffered four men killed, while the 2nd RWF lost seven killed, some from gas shells, and were forced to withdraw from the wood to bivouacs 100 metres south. The 6th Welsh, who were working on trench consolidation, lost two men killed, the 2nd Welsh twenty-eight men killed, Lieutenant Harman and fifty-one men wounded. The 1st SWB meanwhile were still in reserve and were relieved on 18 July, moving back to Lozenge Wood. The 2nd Welsh were also relieved during the night and went back into reserve at Albert. The 2nd RWF had been sent forward to Bazentin-le-Petit to take part in the assault on High Wood.

On the night of 19/20 July the 1st SWB was ordered to send working parties up to construct two keeps near Contalmaison. The men were heavily shelled and suffered four men killed and several wounded, Second Lieutenant Garnons-Williams distinguishing himself by going out under heavy fire to rescue one man. The battalion went back to Bécourt to rest on the following day.

Bazentin Ridge had been captured but High Wood, Longueval and Delville Wood were still the scenes of heavy fighting. The next phase would be the Battle for Pozières and the assault on Longueval Ridge, but in the meantime a disaster was about to unfold further north at Fromelles, where several Welshmen were about to lose their lives.

(iii) The Diversion: The Battle of Fromelles

With the launching of the Somme offensive on 1 July 1916, the British XI Corps and the ANZAC Corps had been ordered to launch an offensive on the Fromelles Salient, on the Aubers Ridge, to draw German reinforcements and attention away from the main offensive on the Somme.

The ANZAC Corps, especially the Australian contingent, had more than doubled in size since being evacuated from Gallipoli to Egypt. There they were joined by large numbers of fresh reinforcements, leading to the two original Australian divisions being expanded to four, while a further division, the 3rd Australian Division, was raised in Australia and sent straight on to Britain.

The Welsh contingent of the ANZAC Corps, consisting of some fifty or more men, spent St David's Day in Egypt singing the national anthem and other Welsh hymns while assembled around the Sphinx. From March 1916 the first of the divisions from Egypt began arriving in France, to positions around Fromelles for trench initiation.

The bulk of the ANZAC Corps made its way to the Somme in July 1916, leaving behind the 5th Australian Division, which held the Fromelles sector alongside the 61st (South Midland) Division.

The attack was planned to begin on 19 July 1916, its aim: '…an attack with a view to capturing and holding permanently 2,100 yards of the enemy's trenches from the Fauquissart road at N.19.a.4.3 to the enemy's salient at N.8.d.5.3 (the Sugarloaf position).'

In June 1916, the sector had been held by the 38th (Welsh) Division, who had been relieved by the 61st Division so that the 38th could move south to the Somme. Among the battalions that made up the 61st Division was the 2nd/7th Battalion, Royal

Some men of the 1st Australian Division at Fleurbaix, May 1916.

Warwickshire Regiment, a Territorial unit that had been made up to strength from a large draft of reinforcements from the 4th Welsh reserves.

At 5.50 am on 19 July 1916, the 2nd/7th Warwicks launched their assault across no man's land on the German positions opposite. They managed to successfully carry out their assault, capturing the German frontline trench and taking hundreds of German prisoners as they emerged from their deep dugouts. The units attacking alongside them failed to make headway, however, and the 2nd/7th Warwicks were left isolated, fighting a desperate defensive action. More than 380 men were killed in the ensuing fighting from that battalion alone.

Nearby, men of the 5th Australian Division had also launched their assault but had been massacred. The ground was littered with dead and dying men, but they could not be reached and most of them remained there for the next two years. The 61st Division had lost 1,547 casualties and the 5th Australian Division 5,533. At the end of the war, the local villagers gathered up the remains of the dead from the battlefield, and more than 400 of the Australian dead were buried in two pits at VC Corner. An unusual war cemetery was built on the site, incorporating the two mass graves, which is today called VC Corner Military Cemetery and Memorial. A wall at one end commemorates the names of the dead, plus another 1,000 Australian missing. The British missing are commemorated on the Loos Memorial.

In June 2008, acting on information discovered in the archives of the German Red Cross, archaeologists excavated a site at Pheasant Wood, near Fromelles in northern France, where there were believed to be several mass graves of Australian and British soldiers. These men were buried there by the Germans after they died in the futile assault on the German positions at Fromelles on 19 July 1916. Human remains were found during the preliminary dig, so from 5 May 2009 the authorities began to exhume these mass graves in an attempt to identify as many of the men as possible to afford them a decent burial in the new Fromelles (Pheasant Wood) Military Cemetery, which was specifically built for them.

The Welshmen known to have died while serving with the 61st Division at the Battle of Fromelles were Private James Ernest Davies (5949) of Llandovery, Lance Corporal Robert Clifford Davies (267414) of Llanelli, Private John Griffiths (5958) of Cardigan, Private Josiah Harries (5728) of Dafen, Lance Corporal Daniel Harris (5970) of Manordilo, Private Benjamin James (267174) of Merthyr, Private John Thomas Jones (5893) of Merthyr, Private Richard Morgan (1842) of Treharris, Private William Simon Rees (5962) of Ffairfach, Llandeilo and Lance Corporal Henry Percival Watkins (5948) of Milford Haven, all of the 2nd/7th Royal Warwicks.

Private John Griffiths (5958), 2/7th Royal Warwicks. He was the son of Thomas and Mary Griffiths of 27 Castle Street, Cardigan and worked as a butcher in the town prior to the war. He had enlisted at Cardigan in the 4th Welsh and was one of a large number of men posted to the 2/7th Royal Warwicks. He was killed on 19 July 1916 and is commemorated on the Loos Memorial. The regimental chaplain wrote a letter of condolence to his sisters in Cardigan, stating that John had been buried and a cross erected on his grave; however, his grave was obviously lost.

At least five Welshmen died while serving with the ANZACs at Fromelles, as described in the following paragraphs.

Major John Arthur Higgon of the Pembroke Yeomanry was born on 12 November 1873, the son of John Donald George Higgon of Scolton Manor, near Haverfordwest. He married Lurline May Moses, daughter of the Honourable Henry Moses, on 27 July 1900 in Hong Kong while serving with the RWF, and rose to the rank of captain. He became a major with the Pembroke Yeomanry before the outbreak of war, and while in Egypt volunteered to serve with the 32nd Battalion, AIF. He joined the AIF in Alexandria and then embarked on HMAT *Transylvania*, bound for Marseilles,

Major John Arthur Higgon of the Pembroke Yeomanry.

133

arriving on 23 June 1916. He took command of A Company and was killed while leading his men out of their trench on 19 July 1916. He is reported to have been standing on the parapet, shouting 'Come on boys', when a German bullet hit him between the eyes and he fell dead. His body was one of the few to be recovered from the battlefield and he is buried in Ration Farm Military Cemetery.

The grave of Major John Arthur Higgon in Ration Farm Military Cemetery.

Private Richard David Davies (4904) of the 53rd Battalion AIF was born at Strata Florida, Ceredigion in 1883, the son of Joseph Edward and Elizabeth Davies. The family had emigrated to Australia several years prior to the war and resided at 3 Attfield Street, Fremantle, Western Australia. Davies married Jessie Wilson at Freemantle in 1905, but three years later she left him to reside with an old boyfriend (however, this did not stop her from attempting to claim a widow's pension after her husband's death!). He enlisted at Holdsworthy, NSW on 22 September 1915 in the 1st Battalion, AIF and was sent to Egypt with the fifteenth batch of reinforcements to the battalion. On 20 April 1916 he was one of half the strength of the 1st Battalion that was transferred to make up the basis of the newly-formed 53rd Battalion, AIF. Davies was killed at Fromelles on 19 July 1916 and is commemorated on the VC Corner Australian Cemetery Memorial, Fromelles. He is possibly one of the men buried within the mass grave that was excavated at Fromelles several years ago.

Private Richard David Davies (4904) of the 53rd Battalion, AIF of Strata Florida, Ceredigion.

Sergeant William George Andrews (1503) of the 59th Battalion AIF was the son of George and Selina Andrews of Myrtle House, Caldicot. He had served in the Monmouthshire Regiment for five years before emigrating to Australia. He enlisted in Melbourne on 10 December 1914 in the 7th Battalion, AIF and served with the battalion at Gallipoli. He was shot in the shoulder at Lone Pine on 8 August 1915 and invalided to Alexandria. On 26 February he was released from hospital and joined the 59th Battalion AIF. His death at Fromelles on 19 July 1916 was particularly gruesome. Private Hayward, who was with him when he was killed, stated: 'We were the only two in No Man's Land, lying down waiting for the next wave to come up, when a shell hit Sergeant Andrews in the back and blew him to atoms and it was impossible to pick up the smallest particle of him.'

Six other men corroborated this story but another soldier, Private Russell, stated:

On July 19th, 1916 at Fromelles, Sergeant Andrews was hit in a communication trench behind our first line. He only lived for a short time after being hit. I saw him lying on a stretcher in the trench, badly wounded in the head, and was told that he died shortly before any attempt to move him could be made. The stretcher-bearers with him did all for him that could be done.

Andrews' father spent years attempting to get to the truth and wrote dozens of letters to former comrades of his son in an attempt to find out what had really happened to him. Whatever the case, Andrews has no known grave and is commemorated on the VC Corner Australian Cemetery and Memorial, Fromelles.

Private John Jones (1880) of the 30th Battalion AIF was the son of Ellis and Gwen Jones of Ffestiniog. He had emigrated to Australia to work in a gold mine and enlisted at Liverpool, NSW on 14 December 1915 in the 30th Battalion AIF. He was killed in action at Fromelles on 20 July 1916, aged 39, and is commemorated on the VC Corner Australian Cemetery and Memorial, Fromelles.

Private William Wood Brailsford (1050) of the 31st Battalion AIF was born in Llansteffan in 1885, the son of Thomas Stanley and Martha Anne Brailsford. He emigrated to Australia prior to the war and worked in Tasmania as an orchardist. On 6 April 1915 he enlisted at Claremont, Tasmania into the 2nd Pioneer Battalion AIF and embarked on HMAT *Ascanius* on 20 June 1915. He was part of a reinforcement batch bound for Gallipoli and arrived at Alexandria on 4 September 1915. He landed soon after at ANZAC Beach, Gallipoli, but by 25 September he was admitted to hospital suffering from gastritis and shipped from ANZAC to Heliopolis. It was not until the end of December that he was deemed fit enough to return to his unit, rejoining them at Ismailia. On 6 April 1916 he transferred to the 31st Battalion, AIF, which embarked at Alexandria on 16 May 1916 bound for Marseilles aboard HMAT *Hororata*, arriving on 23 May. The 31st Battalion was attached to 8 Brigade, 5th (Australian) Division. He was 31 years old when he was killed in action on 20 July 1916 and is buried in Rue-Petillon Military Cemetery, Fleurbaix.

A view of V.C. Corner Australian Military Cemetery and Memorial, Fromelles; a mass grave that contains the remains of 410 men whose remains were picked up from the battlefield after the war. The walls to the rear form a memorial to more than 1,100 Australian dead from the battle.

A view of the famous 'Cobbers' statue (erected in 1998) in Fromelles Memorial Park, commemorating the men who fell during the battle.

(iv) Delville Wood

Back on the Somme, by 18 July the British had worked their way forward and had taken hold of the southern edge of the ridge from Longueval to just south of Pozières, but had created a dangerous salient some 6 miles in depth on the south-eastern side from Longueval to Hem. The Germans had full observation over this ground from their positions between Guillemont and High Wood.

Sir Douglas Haig realized the dangers involved in holding this salient so he planned for the next phase of the offensive to straighten the line, which would involve the capture of Guillemont, Falfemont Farm and Leuze Wood, and then Ginchy and Bouleaux Wood, all very heavily defended strongpoints. To the west, the village and ridge of Pozières still needed to be captured.

Despite the diversionary attack at Fromelles, the Germans had brought several fresh divisions to the Somme to bolster their defences after realizing that the attack was a feint. Despite the huge loss of life already suffered, there was still a great deal more to come.

Various Welsh troops would be involved in much of the fighting but first we will look at the fighting for Longueval and Delville Wood, which involved the 1st RWF of 22 Brigade, 7th Division and the 10th RWF of 76 Brigade, 3rd Division.

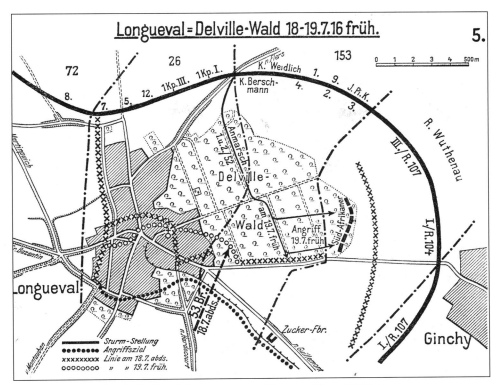

A German map of Delville Wood showing the positions on 18 and 19 July.

Delville Wood was known to the men who fought there as 'Devil's Wood' due to the ferocious fighting that took place there. The main part of the wood had been captured by South African troops on 15 July 1916, while much of Longueval had been captured by the 1st Gordon Highlanders and they held on despite numerous German counter-attacks, although some of the ground gained had been recovered by the Germans.

The 3rd Division was ordered to recapture Longueval and to clear Delville Wood. As part of the relieving force, the 2nd Suffolks were ordered to attack the west of Longueval and the 10th RWF was ordered to move into Delville Wood and to push through it from Prince's Street to the north of the wood. The wood was still congested with the survivors of the South African Brigade, so the order was given that there should be no firing.

The Suffolks assaulted at around 3 am on 20 July but appear to have lost two complete companies that had gone through the village but were not seen again. The 10th RWF had been ordered to parade at 10 pm on the previous night and were led into the wood by guides of 53 Brigade, 9th (Scottish) Division. It appears that the guides had no real idea of where the line was, so there was some confusion during the move towards the wood as the advancing men marched into heavy machine-gun fire. Lieutenant Colonel Long, commanding the 10th RWF, realized that the battalion might get scattered during the confusion, so he risked heavy casualties by ordering the men to close ranks, eventually reaching the south-west corner of the wood where South African guides met them.

It was then that their troubles began: a flurry of Very lights lit the sky, followed by machine-gun fire and Germans could be heard shouting from all directions. The guides had got lost in the confusion and the battalion was still nowhere near Prince's Street, so Long ordered three companies to deploy side-by-side and advance through the wood following a compass bearing. The Germans then attacked the Welshmen and heavy fighting ensued.

Staff Sergeant Joseph John Davies (31314) of Tipton, Staffordshire became separated from the battalion with a party of men, and won the first of two Victoria Crosses gained by the 10th RWF during the action. Davies had served with the 1st Welsh since 19 August 1909 and was wounded at Ypres. He returned to France to be posted to the 10th RWF:

Staff Sergeant Joseph John Davies (31314), 10th RWF.

> For most conspicuous bravery. Prior to an attack on the enemy in a wood he became separated with eight men from the rest of his company. When the enemy delivered their second counter attack his party was completely surrounded, but he got them into a shell hole, and, by throwing bombs and opening rapid fire, succeeded in routing them. Not content with this he followed them up in their retreat and bayoneted several of them. Corporal Davies set a magnificent example of pluck and determination. He has done other very gallant work, and was badly wounded in the second battle of Ypres. (*London Gazette*, 20 September 1916.)

The second Victoria Cross was won by Private Albert Hill (15280) of Hulme, Lancashire; a man reputedly only 5ft 3in tall:

> For most conspicuous bravery. When his battalion had deployed under very heavy fire for an attack on the enemy in a wood, he dashed forward when the order to charge was given, and, meeting two of the enemy suddenly, bayoneted them both. He was sent later by his platoon Sergeant to get into touch with the company, and, finding himself cut off and almost surrounded by some twenty of the enemy, attacked them with bombs, killing and wounding many and scattering the remainder. He then
>
> *Private Albert Hill (15280), 10th RWF.*
>
> joined a sergeant of his company and helped him to fight the way back to the lines. When he got back, hearing that his Company Officer and a scout were lying out wounded, he went out and assisted to bring in the wounded officer, two other men bringing in the scout. Finally, he himself captured and brought in as prisoners two of the enemy. His conduct throughout was magnificent. (*London Gazette*, 26 September 1916.)

The memorial to the two Victoria Cross winners, Davies and Hill, of the 10th RWF in Delville Wood.

Both men's medals are held by the Royal Welsh Fusiliers Museum, Caernarfon. There is a simple memorial within the wood commemorating the actions of both men.

If the hand-to-hand fighting with the Germans was not bad enough, the battalion also came under fire from the 11th Essex and suffered a number of casualties from this 'friendly fire' before the Essex men realized their mistake.

The fighting continued throughout the night and at 3 am on 21 July the battalion was relieved. During the action the 10th RWF had lost 4 officers – Captains George Penderell Blake and George Devereux Scale, and Second Lieutenants Leonard George Godfrey and Henry Page – and 84 men killed, 11 officers and 130 men wounded, and 50 men missing. The survivors remained in Breslau Trench between Carnoy and Montauban until 25 July, when they marched back to a camp at Bois des Tailles.

The men of the 10th RWF were not the only Welshmen to perform great acts of gallantry in the chaos of Delville Wood. Captain Ernest Emrys Isaac, a doctor from Carmarthen, was the medical officer of the 23rd (Sportsman's) Battalion, Royal Fusiliers, which was attached to 99 Brigade of the 2nd Division. The brigade moved into Delville Wood on 27 July and came under intensive artillery fire, trapping the 23rd Royal Fusiliers in the wood. Casualties mounted quickly and Isaac set to work gathering his staff and set up an aid post in the wood, where he began to treat the wounded.

Captain Ernest Emrys Isaac, RAMC, attached to the 23rd Royal Fusiliers. Isaac, a doctor from Carmarthen, who had worked at Colney Hatch Asylum in London prior to the war, gained his first Military Cross for bravery during the fighting in Delville Wood.

Despite terrible conditions, he stuck to his task throughout the day, earning himself what would be the first of two Military Crosses:

> For conspicuous gallantry and devotion to duty during operations. He tended the wounded in a very exposed position for 12 hours, some of them being wounded and one actually killed by shell-fire in his aid-post. At one time he had worked unceasingly for 35 hours without food, drink or rest, having divided up his food and water among those of the wounded who most needed it. (*London Gazette*, 20 October 1916.)

His second award, a Bar to the Military Cross, was awarded the following year 'For conspicuous gallantry and devotion to duty. He worked continuously under very heavy fire and was responsible for the successful evacuation of the wounded. He set a splendid example of courage and determination throughout the operations.' (*London Gazette*, 17 April 1917.) Isaac was a gifted singer, who had won a prize at the 1891 New Quay Eisteddfod.

Sergeant Jack Williams of Aberaman was another Welshman in an English battalion who was recognized for his gallantry at Delville Wood. Williams was serving with the 12th West Yorks, which had taken part in heavy fighting in the wood on 23 July. Williams was knocked over by an explosive bullet, which smashed his left shoulder. He was picked up by the stretcher-bearers, who began to carry him back to the aid post but a shrapnel shell burst nearby, killing the two bearers and wounding Williams in the leg. He was brought to the Torquay Red Cross Hospital the following week and after a long period of care recovered from his wounds. Williams, a local footballer, was awarded the Military Medal for gallantry performed in the action prior to his wounding.

(v) The Battle of Pozières Ridge – Guillemont – Capture of High Wood

As we have previously seen, heavy fighting for the possession of High Wood had continued since the capture of Mametz Wood on 12 July. Several assaults against High Wood, including a flamboyant cavalry charge by the 7th Dragoon Guards and the Indian 20th Deccan Horse, had been repulsed by the Germans and any small British gains had been recaptured by the Germans by 19 July.

Captain Robert Graves of the 2nd RWF was badly wounded when his battalion came under heavy shellfire near the cemetery at Bazentin-le-Petit and he was evacuated by stretcher to Mametz Wood, where he was thought to be dead. He luckily escaped being buried alive when he was seen breathing while being carried to his burial, but by then a letter informing his parents of his death had already been written and sent. (The incident later caused him much amusement and is covered in detail in his autobiography, *Goodbye To All That*.)

However, his battalion had no time to mourn him. 19 Brigade had been given orders to take High Wood and at 2 am on 20 July the 2nd Worcesters, 1st/5th Scottish Rifles and 1st Cameronians assaulted the wood with the 2nd RWF in reserve. A report reached

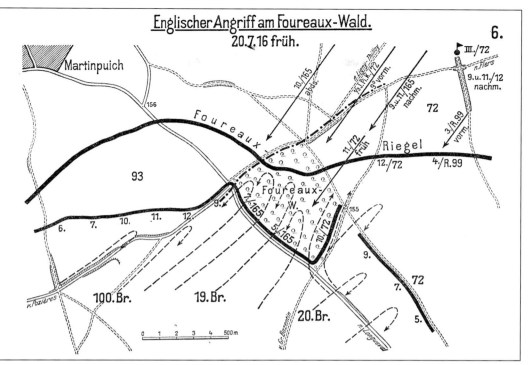

A German map of High Wood showing the action on 20 July.

Lieutenant Colonel Crawshay at 9 am informing them that the brigade had captured the southern half of the wood but that the Germans were counter-attacking from the north, so he ordered the 2nd RWF to advance and they commenced their assault at 2 pm. The 1st RWF had moved into support trenches in Bazentin-le-Grand the previous day and were fully aware of what was happening to their sister battalion. It moved into reserve the following morning, during which time Lieutenant Siegfried Sassoon was hospitalized; the two most famous RWF poets were now out of action.

Heavy casualties were suffered from the start when German shellfire rained down upon the battalion and when they entered the wood things soon began to get worse. The wood was ravaged, trees and foliage made the going difficult, while visibility was poor and the Germans defended stoutly. After several hours of hand-to-hand fighting Crawshay declared the southern portion of the wood secure and turned his men to attack the northern edge. During the afternoon a large number of Germans was spotted assembling beyond the Flers Road and at nightfall they attacked, breaking through the Royal Fusiliers, and enveloped B Company, 2nd RWF. Furious fighting continued throughout the night and at around 10 pm the battalion was relieved and marched back to Buire.

Casualties were exceedingly heavy for all the units involved. The 2nd RWF lost officers – Lieutenants Reginald Julian Albany Bowles (died of wounds in the afternoon) and Gwynne Rees Edmunds, Second Lieutenants Arthur George Lord and

141

Lieutenant Reginald Albany Bowles, 2nd RWF. Bowles was born in Burnley on 31 May 1891, the son of the Reverend Henry Albany and Louisa Alethea Bowles. He was educated at Haileybury and at Clare College, Cambridge and had served for five months as a second lieutenant with the Hampshire Regiment before resigning his commission to work as a traffic inspector with the Western Railway, Quiroga, Buenos Aires Province, Argentina. After the outbreak of war he returned to England to join the RWF.

George Rodney Heastey – and 53 men killed during the day, 8 officers and 180 men were wounded, and 29 were missing.

High Wood was not captured until 15 September 1916, making the capture of the larger Mametz Wood in six days something of a success; a comparison that never dawned on those who had condemned the 38th (Welsh) Division for their tardiness in capturing it.

The 1st RWF, relieved on 21 July, went back to La Chaussée and did not return to the line until 26 August. The 2nd RWF, relieved on 21 July, marched back to Buire, then to Fricourt Wood, and did not go back into action until 18 August. The 10th RWF, relieved from Breslau Trench on 25 July, did not go back into action until 17 August.

It was now the turn of some of the battalions of the SWB and Welsh Regiment to enter the fray once more.

Since its advance on 16/17 July the 1st Division had maintained its position to the east of Pozières, facing the enemy's switch line and a communication trench called Munster Alley, connecting it with the old German second system.

On 19 July the divisional pioneers, the 6th Welsh, left its billets in Albert to dig a new trench from Pozières to Bazentin-le-Petit Wood. The work was carried out throughout the day with little fuss, but on the return journey during the early hours of

A working party in the ruined village of Contalmaison.

20 July C Company was struck by a shell while marching through Contalmaison, killing eight men: Lance Corporal William David Jennings, MM (1595) of Landore, Privates William Ballard (1865) of Swansea, James Battenbough (2518) of Godreagaig, George Hooper (2469) of Gorseinon, Christopher Jones (2022) of Swansea, Ernest Percy Northcote (3300) of Swansea, Frederick Phillips (2598) of Ogmore Vale and Sydney Smith (2389) of Swansea. Seven others were wounded.

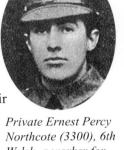

Private Ernest Percy Northcote (3300), 6th Welsh, a worker for the Great Western Railway at Landore prior to the war.

Throughout the next two days the 6th Welsh continued their backbreaking work, digging a zigzag trench between Gloster Trench and Munster Alley, ready for the attack on Pozières. The battalion suffered a continuous stream of wounded men and on 22 July moved into reserve for the attack on Pozières with orders to follow up the advance and dig communication trenches between Lancashire Trench and the Switch Line.

Meanwhile, to the north, the 29th Division had moved back into the Beaumont Hamel sector. The 2nd Monmouths suffered eight men killed on 22 July, while the bombardment of Pozières was at its height. Among the dead was Private Austin Charles Gunn (3493) of 40 Chepstow Road, Newport. The division, which included the 2nd SWB, was relieved and moved to Ypres during the night of 24/25 July, so Gunn, who is buried in Hamel Military Cemetery, Beaumont Hamel, became one of the last casualties suffered by the 2nd Monmouths on the Somme.

Private Austin Charles Gunn (3493) of 40 Chepstow Road, Newport.

Private James Mayberry Jones (26556) of the 2nd SWB was the last Somme casualty for his battalion. The 22-year-old son of David Enoch and Mary Anne Jones of 30 College Street, Lampeter was killed while on patrol at around 2 am on 22 July 1916 when the Germans launched a brief but fierce artillery bombardment. He is commemorated on the Thiepval Memorial.

Sir Douglas Haig had decided to transfer responsibility for Pozières to the Reserve Army of Lieutenant General Sir Hubert Gough, which was holding the line north of the Albert to Bapaume road, and three divisions of the ANZAC Corps had been put at his disposal. The 1st Australian Division had reached Albert on 18 July and had initially been ordered to attack the village on the following day. Major General Harold Walker, the divisional commander, realized the folly of the order and insisted that he should have time to prepare, so the date was set for the night of 22/23 July.

Private James Mayberry Jones (26556) of Lampeter, the last Somme casualty of the 2nd SWB.

The plan called for the Australians to attack Pozières from the south, while north of the Albert to Bapaume road the 48th (South Midland) Division would attack the German trenches west of the village and the British 1st Division would attack to the south.

The preparation for the attack involved a thorough bombardment of the village by high explosive, phosgene and tear gas. The infantry of the Australian 1st and 3rd brigades was scheduled to attack at 12.30 am on 23 July and had crept into position in no man's land behind the bombardment.

At zero hour the Australians advanced to the edge of the village through the ruined back gardens of the houses lining the south of the Albert to Bapaume road and after fierce fighting the survivors from the German garrison retreated to the northern edge of the village and to the OG lines to the east (OG stood for Old German; i.e. the two deep old German lines that ran just east of the village).

The OG lines were strongly defended, however, and the Australian assault failed due to a combination of stout defence and the deep dugouts and machine-gun posts that covered the village, so the 8th Battalion was sent in during the night of 23/24 July to secure the remaining portion towards the Windmill. On the western side of the village the Australians captured a strongpoint, which was nicknamed 'Gibraltar'. Much of the position still exists today, by the site of the 1st Australian Division Memorial on the western side of the village. The Windmill site also still exists, and is a memorial garden to the Australians who died here and in the ensuing attack on Mouquet Farm to the north.

An excavated entrance to the old German dugout 'Gibraltar'.

A contemporary photograph of the remains of 'Gibraltar', just after the capture of Pozières.

While the Australians were digging in to their newly-captured positions in Pozières, the British attack by the Fourth Army between Pozières and Guillemont had been a costly failure. This meant that Pozières became a focal point for the Germans, who began to bombard the village mercilessly prior to launching a series of counter-attacks on it. The taking of Pozières had been a huge success for the Australians, but the defence of it would prove to be a much more costly concern. When the Australian 1st Division, which had suffered 5,285 casualties on its first tour of Pozières, was relieved on 27 July, one observer noted: 'They looked like men who had been in Hell...drawn

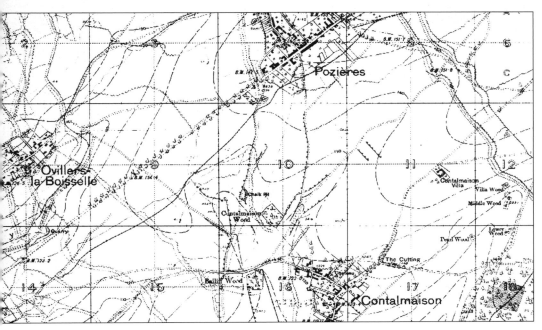

A section of trench map 57dSE4 Ovillers, showing the locations of Contalmaison, Pozières and Munster Alley (in map reference X 5 b, 6 a).

and haggard and so dazed that they appeared to be walking in a dream and their eyes looked glassy and starey.'

At least eight Welshmen were killed while fighting for the Australians at Pozières and the OG lines: Private Ernest Cadogan (4469), 2nd Battalion, of Cardiff (Villers Brettoneux Memorial); Private John Davies (2644), 5th Battalion, of Pontypridd (Pozières British Cemetery); Private Archie Eastham (3061), 3rd Battalion, of Cardiff (Pozières British Cemetery); Private Ronald Gifford Fishwick (3047), 1st Battalion, of Tenby (Villers Brettoneux Memorial); Private John Tudor Griffiths (5100), 9th Battalion, of Rhyl (Gordon Dump Cemetery); Private Gilbert Evan Wyndham Jones (4530), 11th Battalion, of Abergavenny (Pozières British Cemetery); Corporal Jack Northcott (1997), 11th Battalion, of Sully, Cardiff (Bécourt Military Cemetery); and Private Charles Taylor (2233), 1st Battalion, of Briton Ferry (Pozières British Cemetery).

*The road to Pozières, August 1916. (*AWM EZ0084*)*

While the Australians were storming Pozières, co-ordinated attacks by 1 and 2 brigades of the British 1st Division on 22 and 23 July against their positions were repulsed, so on 23 July 3 Brigade was brought up to relieve 2 Brigade, the 1st SWB and 1st Gloucesters taking up the front line, with the 2nd Welsh in support near Contalmaison and the Munsters in reserve. The only casualty suffered during the initial attacks on Munster Alley by the 1st SWB was when Captain Alexander Arthur Francis Loch, DSO was posted as missing on 22 July. The son of Francis Gisborne and Edith Mabel Loch of 14 Freeland Road, Ealing, London, Loch had been mentioned in despatches twice; his DSO citation reads:

For conspicuous gallantry and determination. When the enemy had bombed our grenadiers out of a new post, he led a counter-attack up our sap, and with a machine-gun dispersed some thirty of the enemy who had collected. He was twice wounded, and the man by his side was killed, but he hung on till nightfall, and eventually made the post bullet-proof under very heavy fire. (*London Gazette*, 28 March 1916.)

No trace of Loch was ever found, so he is commemorated on the Thiepval Memorial.

After ten days in reserve the 19th Division had moved back into action on 20 July, and the 9th Welsh moved up via Henincourt, Millencourt and Albert to dugouts in Bécourt Wood. On the following morning the 9th Welsh moved up into the southern edge of Mametz Wood, where it bivouacked. The 19th Division had been ordered to attack in conjunction with the 33rd Division on its right and the 1st Division on its left on 22 July, its objectives being the German Switch Line in its divisional area, which ran from the enemy's trench system east of Pozières in an easterly direction to the north-eastern corner of High Wood and then on to Morval. This line cut across the triangle formed by Martinpuich to the north, High Wood to the east and Bazentin-le-Petit to the south. At 3 pm on 22 July the Germans shelled Mametz Wood, killing four members of the 9th Welsh and wounding sixteen more, so the battalion moved to dugouts in the road south of the wood before taking up positions at Bazentin-le-Petit Cemetery on 23 July in support of the 9th RWF, who were in the line at High Wood.

The attack took place at 12.30 am on 23 July, when 56 and 57 brigades of the 19th Division advanced but got caught in heavy machine-gun fire from the front and flank and faltered. The remainder of the day was spent in consolidating the lines and at 9 pm 58 Brigade relieved the two brigades from the divisional front. During the night of 23/24 July the 5th SWB dug a new trench from north of the windmill at Bazentin-le-Petit to connect up with one that entered High Wood and while carrying out more entrenching on the following night lost five men killed by artillery fire.

Meanwhile the 38th (Welsh) Division, still at Hébuterne, had been enjoying a relatively peaceful time with a low casualty rate since withdrawing from Mametz Wood, but on 24 July lost twelve men killed, seven of whom were from the 10th Welsh. Although by now a peaceful sector, Hébuterne had seen its fair share of death and destruction in the early stage of the Somme offensive. Private Shanahan of the 15th Welsh said of the village:

The whole area had been turned inside out and upside down – disused and partially filled up trenches abounded. Spread about everywhere were the bodies of our chaps and the Germans. They lay about in all postures and were mutilated beyond description. They lay around like swedes the farmer had turned up from the soil and strewn around to dry. Some large shell holes were all but full of soldiers, bodies completely decomposed, but the uniforms keeping some semblance of the shape of a man.

By 1 August 1916 the division was back in northern France in billets at Merckeghem and on 3 August marched to Tatinghem, on the western side of St. Omer, where it was attached to the 2nd Army Central School of Instruction. On 13 August 1916 the Welshmen gathered along the roadside near Wormhoudt and were inspected by King

George V and the newly-promoted commander of the 38th (Welsh) Division, Major General Charles Guinand Blackader.

With Pozières having been secured by 24 July, General Gough pushed for the 2nd Australian Division to attack the OG lines north and east of the village, while simultaneously on the Australians' right, the British 1st Division was ordered to capture Munster Alley, the section of the Switch Line where it intersected the OG lines.

With the Australians on the left, at 2 am on 25 July the 1st SWB, supported by the 1st Gloucesters, made a simultaneous attack with the 3rd Australian Brigade; the latter attacked OG2 and the 1st SWB attacked Munster Alley. A party of the 17th Battalion, AIF got into a section of OG2 from the point where Munster Alley joined it to 100 metres to the north-west and dug in. The 1st SWB watched the preliminary artillery bombardment on Munster Alley from Sussex Trench, and as soon as the bombardment lifted at 2 am they attacked the Germans. Heavy machine-gun fire swept through the attacking company and the first assault was stopped dead. Four officers – Second Lieutenants Richard Harry Cole, Norman Evans, Hilary Francis Cleveland Skinner and David Aubrey Williams – and twenty-four men from the battalion had been killed within minutes, while eight officers and fifty-six men were wounded and seven missing.

Private William David Evans (33612), 1st SWB. The son of Daniel and Mary Ann Evans of Adam Street, Llechryd. He was 21 years old when he was killed at Munster Alley on 25 July 1916.

At 2.30 am the survivors were withdrawn and moved to support trenches near Peake Wood.

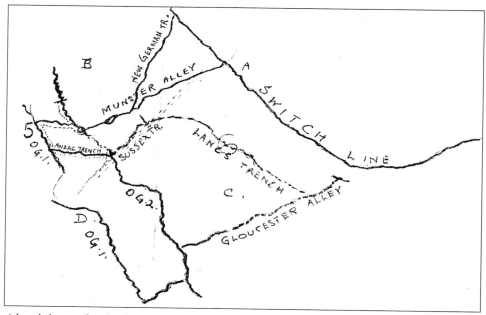

A hand-drawn sketch of Munster Alley Trench, taken from the 2nd Welsh War Diary.

The 2nd Welsh, who had been reinforced by a number of men of the 1st KSLI, were then sent up to relieve the Gloucesters, south-east of Pozières, with orders to carry out the attack over the open at 1 am on 26 July. The ground ahead of them was thick with wounded men and it was daybreak before the 2nd Welsh reached their positions with orders to attack Point 41, an area marked on their trench maps. Upon arrival the Welshmen found that the Australians held this position, the defences of which had been obliterated, and it was now possible to bomb up Munster Alley instead of attacking it over the open. The Australians agreed to let the 2nd Welsh use their trenches to initiate the attack and arranged to assist it with machine-gun fire.

At 3 pm on 26 July, supported by the machine guns and some artillery fire, B Company, under Captain Charles Pritchard Clayton, began to bomb its way up Munster Alley but within twenty metres started to encounter stiff German resistance. Fierce fighting continued throughout the day. Corporal William Archibald Morris (14582) of Carmarthen wrote:

On 26th July, 1916, I was with a bombing party. We were driving the enemy out of a trench known as the Switchback Trench, near Pozières, under heavy shell fire. The party being reduced considerably and there being a great shortage of bombs I myself went through heavy shell and machine-gun fire six times for bombs and the bombs I got kept my bombers in good supply, and our party succeeded in driving the enemy back. At this time I was shot through the chest. As I was lying there shot, I saw some officers pass me. They took charge of the party and carried on with the work. I do not know if I am being awarded the DCM for this particular work, or for previous deeds I have done in other battles by bringing wounded men in under heavy fire.

Corporal William Archibald Morris (14582), 2nd Welsh, of Carmarthen, awarded the DCM for his actions during the bombing up Munster Alley 'For conspicuous gallantry and devotion to duty in action. By his fine leadership a sap was held against hostile attacks. Though wounded he remained throwing bombs for two hours. He has displayed great bravery on other occasions.' (London Gazette, 22 September 1916)

Progress was very slow and demanding, but the situation became perilous when a supply of grenades arrived without detonators. With nothing with which to push the Germans further, the Germans counter-attacked and pushed the Welshmen back; but the Australians intervened, bringing up primed grenades and together with the bombers of the 2nd Welsh swept forward and regained all 140 metres that had been lost. The shattered men consolidated their positions during the night before being relieved and moved back to Millencourt at 4 am. The 23rd Division relieved the 1st Division the same night.

Casualties had been heavy within the 2nd Welsh: Lieutenant Calverley George Bewicke and 20 men were killed, Lieutenant Edward McGroarty taken prisoner, and 110 men were wounded. As well as the DCM that was awarded to Corporal Morris for the day's action, among the awards gained by the 2nd Welsh during the action were the Military Medal (MM) to regimental stretcher-bearer Cornelius Mack (6907) and three MCs to the following:

Private Thomas Price Nicholas (33673), 2nd Welsh. The son of Benjamin and Ellen Jane Nicholas of Clifton House, Newcastle, Bridgend, he was killed at Munster Alley on 26 July 1916. His grave was located after the war and he was reburied in Serre Road Cemetery No. 2.

Captain Charles Pritchard Clayton: 'For conspicuous gallantry in action. He displayed great coolness during a bombing attack, and commanded his company with marked ability. He set a fine example.' (*London Gazette*, 22 September 1916.)

Captain Cecil Walter Stanley Gardner: 'For conspicuous gallantry in action. He assisted in bombing down the enemy's trenches, in order to get into touch with the battalion on the flank. Later he consolidated the position under heavy fire and successfully held it.' (*London Gazette*, 22 September 1916.)

Lieutenant Lewis Henry Todd Walker: 'For conspicuous gallantry in action. When in charge of an advanced bombing party he kept up the spirits of his men by his fine example for six hours, and continued to make progress. All were exhausted after hard fighting.' (*London Gazette*, 22 September 1916.)

Ten men of the 5th SWB (19th Division) were killed during the day when 57 Brigade attacked the intermediate line between Pozières and High Wood once more. Also killed on the following day was Sergeant Herbert Roye Goldsby, MM (12854), 9th RWF, a Londoner who had worked as a farm hand at Nantgaredig and at Tycroes Colliery, near Ammanford prior to the war. His fiancée, Maggie John of Pontyshoot Cottage, Landore received news of his death soon afterwards in a letter stating he had been shot by a sniper and that he had been buried in a small cemetery nearby and a cross placed over his grave. He is commemorated on the Thiepval Memorial.

Sergeant Herbert Goldsby, MM (12854), 9th RWF. Goldsby was a miner at Tycroes Colliery prior to the war and had only recently been awarded the MM before being killed near High Wood on 27 July 1916.

The 19th Division was about to complete its first spell on the Somme and entrained for northern France on 2 August, moving into positions at Messines and Ploegsteert.

Another Welsh international rugby player would die during this period, not on the Somme but in the now more peaceful Calonne sector.

The 40th (Bantam) Division, which contained the all-Welsh 119 Brigade (18th and 19th RWF, 17th and 18th Welsh, and the 12th SWB), had arrived in France on 1 June 1916 and had initially moved to Maroc to learn its trade in the Loos sector before moving to Calonne-sur-la-Lys. On the night of 11/12 August Captain Pritchard of the 12th SWB took a party of men out and reconnoitred no man's land with the intention of carrying out a raid on the following night. With the plans in place, on the night of 12/13 August Pritchard, along with Second Lieutenants Enright and Wood, crawled out under the wire into no man's land with a raiding party, intent on capturing some German prisoners. The raid was a success, but Pritchard was badly wounded and died on 14 August. Four of his men were killed on the raid, three of whom are buried in Loos British Cemetery, while another wounded man died on the same day as Pritchard and is buried near him.

Captain Charles Meyrick 'Charlie' Pritchard, 12th SWB, the eighth Welsh rugby international to fall during the war.

Captain Charles Meyrick Pritchard was born in Newport on 30 September 1882. He joined Newport RFC in 1901 and won his first international cap at forward for Wales against Ireland in 1904. He played in thirteen more international matches and was a member of the 1905 team that defeated the All Blacks. He was commissioned into the 12th SWB on 31 May 1915 and by the time of his death had been promoted to captain. He is buried in Chocques Military Cemetery.

Back on the Somme, a draft of 176 men from the Welsh Regiment had joined the 1st SWB while the battalion was in reserve at the end of July, and the Welsh had received a batch of around 180 men of the SWB; a very peculiar but not rare occurrence. In August the men were swapped back to their original regiments. The 1st Division remained out of the line training and refitting until 12 August, when it relieved the 34th Division in the area between Bazentin-le-Petit and High Wood.

The 3rd Division was also just ending its spell in reserve. The 10th RWF had been in bivouacs at Méricourt-l'Abbé throughout much of August but on 11 August marched to Méaulte, and on 13 August carried out practice attacks after attending church parade. The battalion marched to Talus Wood on the following day, and its officers reconnoitred the Casement, Dublin and Chimpanzee trenches in the front near Guillemont before taking them over on 15 August and spent much of the day consolidating them, losing three men killed and four wounded.

During the following afternoon the battalion received orders for an attack on Lonely Trench by two companies of the battalion, in conjunction with two companies of the 12th West

The grave of Lance Corporal Robinson Hemingway (24259), 12th SWB, of Rotherham in Loos British Cemetery. He was one of four men killed in the trench raid on 13 August in which Charlie Pritchard was mortally wounded.

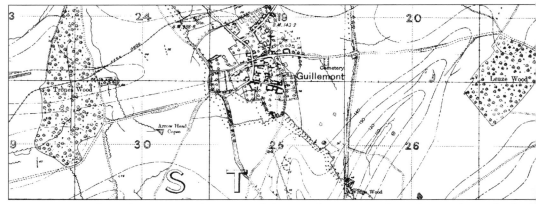

A section of trench map 57cSW3 Longueval showing the position of Lonely Trench, south of Guillemont, in the square marked 25.

Yorks. At 5 pm the men were issued with flares, smoke bombs, tools, wire-cutters and white bands and then at 8 pm B and C companies advanced up French Trench. The Germans had spotted the movement, so began laying down a heavy artillery barrage on the fusiliers who initially started to fall back, but the adjutant ordered the men forward and the front line was occupied by 9.30 pm. Tape had been laid in no man's land to guide the men, and by around 9.57 pm they were in position, ready to attack.

At 10 pm the battalion rose to attack. Watching his men advance was the CO, Major Samuel, who noted that the machine-gun fire seemed to be relatively light and that not many casualties had returned, so he assumed all was going well. At around 11 pm news came back that the left company had been held up, so a platoon of the 8th King's Own was sent up to help. It was then discovered that the attackers had been held up by the enemy wire between 12 to 50 metres short of Lonely Trench and that German bombers were causing disarray.

Samuel then received orders to mount a second attack, which he fixed for 4 am on 18 July in co-operation with the West Yorks and King's Own. By 5.52 am information was received that the second attack had also failed, and the attacking troops were then withdrawn after being relieved by the 7th KSLI. Heavy shelling accompanied the withdrawal, causing more casualties on the Fusiliers as they pulled back. What had happened to the men was very sketchy but it seems that a number of men under Captain Follit had reached their objectives but when Follit was wounded, the men had dug themselves in.

Casualties had been particularly heavy, which is why the attack had failed. The 10th RWF lost 5 officers – Lieutenant Stanley Fleming Bancroft, Second Lieutenants Ernest Dixon, John Edwyn Hughes, Arthur Owen Williams and Lewis Roberts Williams – and 116 men killed between

Private William Williams (15058), 10th RWF, of Wern Street, Clydach Vale, killed at Lonely Trench between 16 and 19 July 1916.

16 and 19 July, 8 officers (Captain Charles Albert Roy Follit, DSO, MM died of his wounds on 20 August) and well over 200 men wounded.

The battalion, which had lost almost all its attacking force of two companies, moved back to Chimpanzee Trench and on 21 August to Morlancourt to rebuild.

Sergeant Arthur Sproston (23059), 10th RWF, of Colwyn Bay, killed at Lonely Trench on 16 August 1916.

Troops in the Guillemont sector.

While the 10th RWF was severely handled at Lonely Trench, back at Pozières, 1 and 2 brigades of the 1st Division took part in a costly attack on Pozières Ridge between 16 and 18 August but were driven off their gains following a German counter-attack on 20 August. During that night the two brigades were relieved by 3 Brigade, which had been assisting the 6th Welsh in digging and trench consolidation, and the 2nd Welsh took up forward trenches on the right of the 2nd Royal Munsters and the 1st Gloucesters, while the 1st SWB took up support positions in OG1.

The 4th RWF, who had been having a relatively peaceful time as pioneers to the 47th (Second London) Division, lost ten men killed while working in the Caterpillar Valley/Mametz area between 15 and 20 August.

Private Alun Parry (8679), 4th RWF, of Gwaenysgor near Prestatyn, killed on 15 August 1916 and buried in Caterpillar Valley Cemetery, Longueval.

The 2nd RWF were also having a hard time of things after moving also moved back into the line, taking over trenches at High Wood on 19 August. During the day the battalion lost twelve men killed and fourteen wounded during a bombardment which was followed by a raid by the Germans, and on the following day two officers – Captain Caledon Robert John Ratcliffe Dolling and Second Lieutenant Philip Stanley Wilson – and twelve men were killed; nine more were wounded. Dolling, OC B Company, was killed by a shell. Wilson took over command of the company and was killed soon afterwards. Frank Richards made some interesting comments about Wilson's death in *Old Soldiers Never Die*. He did not name him but wrote of a newly-joined officer who was killed by a shell. Another five men were killed and twenty-four wounded during another bombardment on 21 August. The following morning the battalion was relieved, moving back to Bazentin-le-Petit, losing another seven men killed and nine wounded during the relief. The 2nd RWF was relieved on 28 August and the 2nd Division moved, in stages, away from the Somme.

The 2nd Welsh and 1st SWB remained in their trenches nearby from 20 to 28 August, working on consolidation and sapping forward. Both battalions suffered some casualties, mostly from the constant shellfire, but there was also some action in driving off German patrols. During this spell the 1st SWB lost an officer – Captain Francis Weldon Walshe MC – and 31 men killed; 52 men were wounded. The 2nd Welsh lost an officer – Second Lieutenant Harry Charles Reeves – and 51 men killed, 4 officers and 170 men wounded, while 46 men were evacuated with shellshock.

The 1st Division then moved to the right to take part in the final attacks on High Wood. The 15th (Scottish) Division moved to its left flank, while 3 Brigade went into reserve, the 1st SWB to Ribécourt and the 2nd Welsh to Albert until 5 September. The 6th Welsh, being the divisional Pioneer Battalion, had survived the fighting relatively unscathed so far, but had lost its CO, Lieutenant Colonel Cornelius Asgill Shaw Carleton, who was invalided with trench fever and Captain Frank Arthur Hinton assumed temporary command. The pioneers had been busy throughout the time their fellow Welsh units were in the line, digging trenches and building dugouts around Fricourt Wood and suffering casualties on a daily basis. Their worst day was suffered on 23 August when a party working near High Wood was caught in German shellfire, losing two men killed, two officers and nine men wounded.

Private Joseph Picking (12912), 1s SWB, of Pontyberem, killed near High Wood on 28 August 1916.

Meanwhile, on 26 August the 1st RWF moved back into the line after a long and welcome spell in reserve at La Chaussée and Dernancourt. The battalion left Dernancourt at 4.30 pm and marched via Fricourt, Mametz and Montauban to the north end of Bernafay Wood, now in the area that had seen the 10th RWF suffer so badly. They were led into positions at Beer Trench by guides from the 7th Rifle Brigade and 7th King's Royal Rifle Corps (KRRC). During the night the battalion received orders to push up towards the edge of Delville Wood by bombing their way forward, to gain touch with the 10th Durham Light Infantry (DLI) on their left and attack the German trench near Ginchy called Ale Alley, in conjunction with further assaults around High Wood.

Zero hour was fixed for 5 am on 27 August, but was delayed due to a lack of rifle grenades and the failure of the DLI to advance. By 8.25 am further orders were received to advance without the DLI and the 1st RWF bombed their way almost 100 metres up Beer Sap towards Ale Alley before consolidating their gains.

At 12.25 pm the DLI was ordered to carry out a co-ordinated attack in conjunction with the 1st RWF at 5 pm. In the meantime information was received that the Germans had constructed a new trench, which was promptly captured by D Company, 1st RWF. When the second assault was made at 5 pm the Germans responded by shelling the

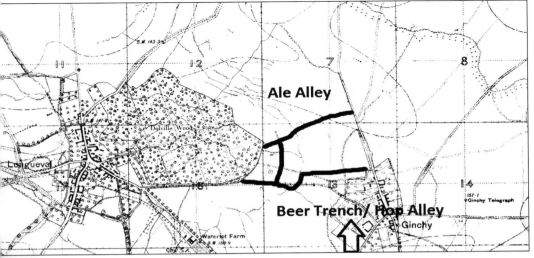

A section of trench map 57cSW3 Longueval, showing the position of Beer Trench, Ale Alley and Hop Alley.

attacking troops, causing heavy casualties. During the day nineteen men of the 1st RWF were killed, fifty-six had been wounded, one was missing and two were invalided sick. Another man had been despatched to a nearby prisoner of war camp after having been found to be under age!

During the following morning aerial photographs were sent forward to the battalion which raised some questions about the locations of the Germans. After a reconnaissance it was found that D Company had not captured the new German trench but rather an old disused trench and that they only held a small section. At noon a fresh bombing attack was organized under Captain Stevens and after a fierce fight almost 100 metres of trench were captured and consolidated throughout the night. A further twenty men were killed, thirty-nine wounded, five missing and five invalided sick.

Another attack was planned for 5 am on 29 August but was delayed until 2 pm due to troops being relieved on the left flank. Captain Stevens again led the assault, which was halted when it came under direct fire from a machine gun. The battalion consolidated what little ground it had taken during the day and during the night was relieved by the South Staffs and moved to a camp near Bonté Redoubt. A further eighteen men had been killed, Captain Kelsey-Fry and forty-eight men wounded, seven were missing and five more were sick. The battalion spent the next two days attempting to avoid German shellfire and on 1 September was ordered back into the front line following the loss of Ale Alley and a

Lance Corporal Reginald William Bamford Jones (29519), 1st RWF. The son of David and Louisa Jones of School House, Cockett, he was killed in action near Ginchy on 29 August 1916.

155

portion of Delville Wood to the Germans and a failed counter-attack by the South Staffs.

The battalion remained in Montauban Alley during 2 September, suffering several casualties from gas shells, while other units attacked the Germans without success and received orders to attack on the following day. The 7th Division was ordered to capture Ginchy and Pint Trench, while the 20th Division, on the right, was to capture Guillemont. The 1st RWF was allotted the capture of Pint Trench and took up positions on the edge of Delville Wood.

At 11 am on 3 September two parties of bombers from the battalion were sent forward to get ready to begin their assault, and fifteen minutes later Captain Dadd was ordered to get ready to take A Company forward to begin clearing out Hop and Ale alleys. Lieutenant Davies took over command of D Company from Captain E.T. Jones, who had suffered a loss of memory, probably due to shellshock. A creeping artillery barrage opened up at 12 pm and the attacking troops followed close behind, capturing Guillemont and Ginchy by around 1 pm. The attack had been held up by machine-gun fire on the left and at 1.25 pm Lieutenant C.M. Dobell, an officer who had been with the bombing party, returned to battalion HQ wounded, with news that their attack had been a complete failure. One hour later news came back that Captain Dadd, a well-respected member of the battalion, had been killed and that A Company had been held up, with no communications or support on its flanks.

The situation was dire. At 3.40 pm one company and four bomber sections of the 2nd Royal Irish were ordered to make a co-ordinated attack with the remainder of the 1st RWF, but this attack was postponed until 5.15 pm. This attack also failed due to heavy casualties, and news was brought back that of the two companies of the 1st RWF who had attacked earlier in the day only around thirty men were still alive. The Germans were now at Waterlot Farm and were able to lay down enfilade fire on the 1st RWF. By 8.45 pm the battalion received orders to get ready to be relieved and 20 Brigade was brought up by lorry to take over the attack.

The 1st RWF had suffered terrible casualties: 4 officers – Captains Edmund Hilton Dadd, MC and Edwin Tudor Jones; Second Lieutenants Joseph Ithel Jehu Davies and Hugh Jones – and 88 men killed, 7 officers and 129 men wounded, and 87 men missing. (Captain E.T. Jones had been reported missing but was later discovered to have been killed.)

The hardest loss to the battalion was undoubtedly the gallant Captain Edmund Hilton Dadd, the son of Stephen Thomas and Eva Elizabeth Dadd of 20 Wickham Gardens, Brockley, London. He was commissioned in the battalion from the Queen's Westminsters in November 1915 and had taken part in several raids prior to being promoted captain in July 1916. He is commemorated on the Thiepval Memorial. Dadd had only recently been awarded the MC for gallantry at Fricourt: 'For conspicuous gallantry during a counter-attack. When the senior Captain was wounded he took over the command of the attacking line and drove off the advancing enemy.' (*London Gazette*,

Captain Edmund Hilton Dadd, MC, 1st RWF, killed near Ginchy on 3 September 1916.

26 September 1916.)

Lieutenant Colonel Clifton Inglis Stockwell had the sad duty of writing to his parents, who had lost another son, Stephen, in Gallipoli on 5 July 1915: 'Edmund's death is a great loss to the battalion. He was my best Company Commander, and was a born soldier. We were all very much attached to him; he was most cheering under the most trying circumstances.'

The survivors withdrew during the morning of 4 September via Pommiers Redoubt to Bécordel and then on to Buire, before entraining at Albert on 8 September for Mérélessart in Flanders. Lieutenant Colonel Stockwell left the battalion to command 164 Brigade on 16 September and on 21 September the 1st RWF took over trenches in the Ploegsteert Wood sector under their new CO, Lieutenant Colonel William George Holmes.

During this period, on 31 August the 3rd Monmouths of the 49th Division were disbanded due to heavy losses, and its personnel were shared between the 1st and 2nd Monmouths.

The heavy fighting on 3 September also cost the life of another Welsh rugby international, the ninth to fall during the war. Second Lieutenant Horace Wyndham Thomas was born in Bridgend on 28 July 1890, the son of Reverend Morgan Thomas. He was educated at Monmouth Grammar School and at King's College, Cambridge, where he gained his Blue in 1912 during the Varsity match that saw Cambridge beat Oxford for the first time in seven years. He was picked for his first Welsh cap that year against South Africa. He also played for Swansea and the Barbarians and gained another Welsh cap in 1913 before joining the Mercantile Marine and was based in Calcutta, where he continued to play rugby and became captain of the Calcutta Football Club.

Second Lieutenant Horace Wyndham Thomas, 11th Rifle Brigade, killed at Guillemont on 3 September 1916.

In 1916 Horace returned to England and took up a commission in the Rifle Brigade on 13 January 1916. He was posted to the 11th Rifle Brigade, which was part of the 20th (Light) Division, in time for the Somme offensive. He was killed in action during the Battle of Guillemont on 3 September 1916 and is commemorated on the Thiepval Memorial.

With most of the other Welsh infantry units now in Flanders, the onus fell on the units of the 1st Division again. The 1st SWB of 3 Brigade remained in reserve until 2 September, when it moved to the north-east of Mametz Wood again and the 2nd Welsh joined them on 5 September. On 3 September 1 Brigade had attacked High Wood and captured some more ground and it now fell to 3 Brigade to continue the attack, so the 1st SWB relieved the 2nd Royal Munsters during the night of 3 September. On the following night officers of the battalion went forward to reconnoitre the wood prior to relieving 1 Brigade the following morning. The Borderers spent two relatively peaceful days at High Wood before being relieved by the 2nd Welsh on the morning of 8 September, while the 1st Gloucesters on the left relieved the Munsters. The 2nd Welsh were to assault north from within the wood, the Gloucesters were to attack north-east across the open, along the edge of the wood, while 44 Brigade, 15th Division, assaulted on the right.

Two companies of the 2nd Welsh, B and C, were to lead the attack, while D Company held their trenches, and A Company was detailed to carry bombs and tools. The preliminary artillery bombardment began at noon on 8 September and at zero hour, 6 pm, the assault began, covered by another bombardment and a new invention, the Livens Projector, which was operated by Z Company, Royal Engineers, and was used to hurl oil- or phosgene gas-filled drums that exploded on impact, spraying their flaming contents over the Germans. The Livens Projector had been invented to counter the German *flammenwerfer* (flame-thrower) and caused as much terror to the attacking Welshmen as it did to the Germans.

B Company managed to advance and captured over 100 metres of the German trenches, but C Company got held up by machine-gun fire and two attempts to advance failed. B Company began bombing out to each flank in its captured trench, but the Germans held firm. A Company was then sent forward to begin consolidation work and also to dig a new communication trench, but suffered heavy casualties from shellfire. The Welshmen then started to run out of grenades, so 100 boxes were brought forward by men of the Munsters. The Gloucesters' attack had also stalled and the 1st SWB were sent up to support them. The Germans then counter-attacked using the *flammenwerfer* and by midnight had driven the attackers back to their original positions.

Both the 1st SWB and 2nd Welsh suffered a large number of casualties. The 1st SWB lost 1 officer – Captain Gerald Watkins Brett Wileman – and 29 men killed, 3 officers and 72 men wounded. The 2nd Welsh lost 6 officers – Captains Alfred George Hayman, MC and John Oswin Turnbull, Lieutenants Conrad Clive Brockington and Henry Thompson White, and Second Lieutenants David Eleazor Price and Eric John Cecil Sear – and 49 men killed, while 4 officers and 132 men were wounded.

Lieutenant Henry Thompson White, 2nd Welsh. He was missing, presumed killed at High Wood on 8 September 1916.

Lieutenant Henry Thompson White, 2nd Welsh, was the son of John Davies and Lucy Thompson White, chemists, of Guildhall Square, Carmarthen. He worked for the London and County Bank in London as a bank clerk prior to the war and married Kathleen Marion Vereker in London on 16 August 1911. He enlisted in the 19th Royal Fusiliers and on 6 April 1915 was commissioned in the 3rd Welsh. He was posted to the 1st Welsh and was wounded at the Hohenzollern Redoubt in September 1915. After recovering he was posted to the 2nd Welsh. Although White was killed at High Wood on 8 September 1916, for over ninety years he has been incorrectly commemorated on the Jerusalem Memorial until research by the author proved to the CWGC that he was killed on the Somme. As a result, White will have his name engraved on the Commission's new Brookwood 1914–1918 Memorial in due course.

Captain Alfred George Hayman MC, 2nd Welsh was born on 26 February 1884, the son of Alfred and Ellen Hayman of Hapsford House, Frome. He was educated at Clifton and Malvern colleges before being commissioned in the Welsh in 1906. He resigned his commission in 1912 to become a rancher in Canada and at the outbreak of war enlisted in the Canadian Mounted Rifles. When he arrived back in England he rejoined the Welsh and served with the 2nd Welsh in France from February 1916. He is buried in Caterpillar Valley Cemetery and was awarded the MC for his gallantry during the action in which he was wounded and then died:

Private George Morris, MM (13108), 1st SWB, of 8 Long Row, Trynant, killed at High Wood on 8 September 1916.

For conspicuous gallantry during operations. He commanded his company in the front trenches during several days of very heavy shelling, and set a fine example, though he himself was buried three times [with earth as a result of shellfire]. He was wounded on the first day, but refused to be sent back. (*London Gazette*, 21 October 1916.)

The 2nd Welsh was relieved on the following day and marched back to Franvillers, while the 1st SWB was relieved on 10 September when the 1st Division was relieved by the 47th Division. The Germans withdrew to their second defensive system two days later but retained hold of the northern section of High Wood.

The Canadian Corps, under Sir Julian Byng, had moved to the Somme sector at the end of August and had begun preparing to take over the line north of Pozières from the Australian Corps, which moved to Ypres. One of the first known Welsh Somme casualties in the Canadian Corps was Private Hugh Albert Bunt. He was born at Pembroke Dock on 23 February 1878, the seventh child of Sidney and Sarah Bunt (née Kelsey). He emigrated to Canada prior to the war and enlisted at Valcartier into the 8th Battalion CEF, 'Little Black Devils'. Bunt had

Private Richard Henry Thomas (A25541), 8th Battalion, CEF of Machynlleth.

been involved in the first German gas attack at Gravenstafel on 24 April 1915, where the Canadians held a large gap in the line after French Colonial troops had fled. He was wounded at Mouquet Farm on 3 September and died at No. 3 Casualty Clearing Station on 8 September 1916. He is buried in Puchevillers British Cemetery.

Another Welsh Canadian of the same battalion as Bunt was killed in action at Mouquet Farm on that same day. Private Richard Henry Thomas (A25541) was born on 15 March 1886, the son of David and Jane Thomas of Gwynllys, Machynlleth. He emigrated to Canada with his wife Laura and worked as a bank clerk in

The grave of Private Hugh Albert Bunt (1005), 8th Battalion, CEF, at Puchevillers British Cemetery, one of the first Canadian Somme casualties from Wales.

Winnipeg and had been on leave in Machynlleth in April 1915. He is commemorated on the Vimy Memorial.

While the 1st Division was out of the line, the British began the next phase of their attempt to clear the Germans from Pozières Ridge: the 47th Division was now tasked with clearing High Wood. Attached to the division was the 4th RWF, serving as the divisional Pioneer Battalion. The division had been practising for their assault on the wood during the preceding days and when marching through Albert prior to relieving the 1st Division had been shocked by the devastation that they witnessed.

By this time there was no wood as such remaining: the ground by now contained only a mass of shattered tree trunks and everywhere was a scene of devastation. The division was to attack on 15 September and the 4th RWF was employed in digging assembly trenches ready for the attack, which would be a major offensive with Morval the objective of the Fourth Army (to which the Guards Division was attached). The New Zealand Division was on the right and the 50th Division on the left of the 47th.

At 6.30 am on 15 September the attack on High Wood was renewed once more and was finally successful. The 47th Division had finally cleared the wood and the 4th RWF began digging communication trenches and artillery tracks under heavy shellfire. The battalion was kept on this work continuously over the coming weeks, digging more assembly trenches for the forthcoming Battle of Le Transloy Ridge.

There is an impressive memorial to the 47th Division sited on the edge of High Wood. This memorial commemorates all the men of the division who fell during the fighting there, including the fourteen men of the 4th RWF who were killed while

The 47th (2nd London) Division Memorial at High Wood.

The ruins of Guillemont Railway Station: the scene of devastation facing the Welsh Guards.

carrying out such sterling work as digging the assembly and communication trenches that were necessary to capture and consolidate the wood.

(vi) The Welsh Guards: The Battles of Flers-Courcelette and Morval

The Welsh Guards had been in the Ypres sector over the preceding months and on 30 July marched to Bavinchove, where they entrained for Frévent. The Guards Division had been ordered to the Somme. The guardsmen marched to Halloy during the day and then on to Bus-lès-Artois, where they stayed from 1 to 6 August. The battalion marched to Arquèves, where it spent another three days, and on 9 August embussed for Mailly-Maillet. The intended destination for the Guards Division was the line between Beaumont Hamel and Serre.

The Welsh Guards lost five men killed during their short spell in the line here: Corporal William Simpson (267) of Bootle, Lance Corporal Joseph George Tanner (1224) of Newport, Guardsmen Frank Percy Beck (398) of Swansea, John Sidney Edwards (675) of Panteg, Ystalyfera and Edward Thomas Trehearne (2173) of Ruthin. Edwards and Trehearne were killed by a whizz-bang, a 77mm shell. The Welsh Guards' experiences here were mostly of clearing the trenches and burying the dead from the earlier fighting, so they were glad to be relieved on 19 August. By 25 August the Welsh Guards had reached Méricourt-l'Abbé. The Guards Division was heading to the brutal Ginchy/Guillemont sector, where the 10th RWF and 1st RWF had suffered so badly.

On 7 September the Welsh Guards moved to Ville-sur-Ancre, where they remained for two days, practising in an outpost scheme and night attack. The Guards Division had joined XIV Corps, which comprised the Guards, the 20th, 6th, 56th, 16th and 5th divisions. On 9 September the 16th Irish Division, with the 56th on its right, attacked Ginchy. The Welsh Guards had been ordered to relieve the left brigade of the 16th Division when it had captured Ginchy.

Complying with this plan, at 9 am on 9 September the Welsh Guards marched to Carnoy, over ground that had been trodden by innumerable Welsh soldiers during the previous weeks. The CO, Lieutenant Colonel William Murray Threipland, went forward to Bernafay Wood to arrange details for taking over the line that night and at 8 pm the battalion left for Ginchy, with two days' rations.

Lieutenant Colonel William Murray-Threipland, the man who raised the 1st Battalion, Welsh Guards.

The orders were that the Prince of Wales's Company and No. 2 Company should relieve 48 Brigade, which held a line to the north of Ginchy and was facing north-east. No. 3 Company was to move left and fill the gap between No. 2 and XV Corps and the 4th Grenadier Guards were to take the right flank.

The Welsh Guards arrived at Ginchy and encountered some Germans, who surrendered without hesitation, and around midnight a message arrived back at HQ stating that they had taken over the line from 48 Brigade. Major Harry Hickman Bromfield DSO was in command; Murray Threipland remained at HQ.

The guardsmen had taken over a line that ran along the outskirts of Ginchy, facing north-west. No one had moved up on the right flank of the Welsh Guards as the 4th Grenadiers had been unable to locate 47 Brigade to relieve it. Bromfield did not know the situation to his right, so sent patrols out to locate the Grenadiers but found only Germans and some shooting continued throughout the night. Due to the confusion suffered by 48 Brigade, owing to the 16th Division having been relieved in the dark, the Welsh Guards were facing in a different direction than they thought; a mistake that would prove costly.

Bromfield was quite rightly concerned about the battalion's situation, so at daybreak sent out another patrol under Sergeant Ashford, who came across some troops of 48 Brigade who were holding an isolated post. When Ashford returned to report his findings to Bromfield, the Germans attacked in strength from the north-east, hoping to recapture Ginchy.

The Welsh Guards were in danger of being isolated, so Bromfield ordered the right of the Prince of Wales's Company to fall back, but the Germans swept around them and a vicious fight ensued that was driven off by fire from 2 and 3 companies. At 10.30 am news of the situation ahead reached Murray Threipland and he sent half of No. 4 Company to fill the gap that existed between 48 Brigade and the Prince of Wales's Company, but the men came into contact with a party of Germans near Ginchy Church. By now the Germans were attacking towards the south-east of Ginchy, so Murray Threipland sent in the remainder of No. 4 Company. Heavy fighting continued past midday, when news reached HQ that Bromfield and two other officers had been killed.

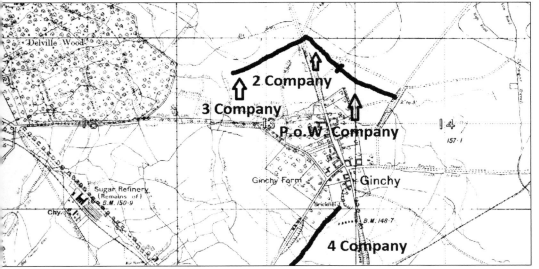

A section of trench map 57cSW3 Longueval, showing the positions taken up by the Welsh Guards on 19 September 1916. (Locations taken from war diary).

The survivors of the Prince of Wales's Company had joined up with No. 2 but scattered pockets of men were trapped in shell holes.

It appears that a company of the 1st Grenadiers had taken over a trench 120 metres east of Ginchy and was involved in a merciless bombing fight. Half of No. 4 Company was in the village on the east of the road and about 50 to 100 metres north of the ruins of the church, while the other half of No. 4 was on the left of the road and facing east; No. 2 and 3 companies held their original trenches.

Very heavy fighting continued throughout the day; and the Welsh Guards were reinforced by fifty men of the 2nd Scots Guards who had brought up a supply of grenades. At 10 pm two more companies of Scots Guards arrived. The line steadied during the night and the survivors of the Welsh Guards were relieved and went into reserve trenches north-west of Guillemont. The battalion had lost five officers – Major Harry Hickman Bromfield, DSO, Lieutenant John Wethered Power, Second Lieutenants Edward Luke Henry Bagot, Edward Cazalet and Alexander Pigott Wernher – and 73 men killed during the day; 5 officers and around 130 men were wounded.

Guardsman Thomas Benjamin Daniel (1933) of Nantgaredig, killed at Ginchy on 10 September 1916.

Major Harry Hickman Bromfield DSO was the son of Henry and Mary Elizabeth Bromfield of Stratford-upon-Avon. He married Ethel Philippa Philipps, the eldest daughter of Sir Charles and Lady Philipps of Picton Castle, in 1906. He had served with the SWB in the Boer War, gaining the DSO for his gallant leadership. He had been the chief constable of Radnorshire Constabulary prior to the war and volunteered to serve with the newly-formed Welsh Guards in 1915, joining the battalion at Esher. In July 1916 he took command of the Prince of Wales's Company from Viscount Clive, who had been promoted. Bromfield was killed during his first action on 10 September 1916, aged 47. He is commemorated on the Thiepval Memorial. Bromfield is also commemorated on the new Dyfed Powys Police War Memorial at Carmarthen and at St Mary's Church, Haverfordwest.

The XV Corps' attack to the left had failed, while 47 Brigade had lost direction; a disastrous chain of events had led to the Welsh Guards dealing with an impossible situation.

There were many acts of gallantry carried out during the Welsh Guards' first action on the Somme. Among the honours awarded to the battalion Sergeant Oswald Ashford (24) from Northwich was awarded the DCM: 'For conspicuous gallantry and skill in reorganising his company after all the officers had been killed or wounded. He also carried in a wounded officer under heavy fire.' (*London Gazette*, 14 November 1916.)

Major Harry Hickman Bromfield DSO, Welsh Guards, former Chief Constable of the Radnorshire Police.

Captain Henry Gordon Gooch Ashton was awarded the DSO:

For conspicuous gallantry in action. Owing to several casualties he found himself in command of three companies and some 50 men of other units. For many hours he was fighting the enemy on all sides, and had his men facing front and rear in the same trench. His great determination and fine leadership were largely responsible for the holding of the position. (*London Gazette*, 14 November 1916.)

The Welsh Guards moved to Bernafay Wood during the afternoon of 11 September to count their losses and on the following day moved to Happy Valley, near Fricourt, in pouring rain. A draft of 180 men arrived to help make up the losses suffered at Ginchy and on 14 September Murray Threipland attended a briefing at Brigade HQ, where he received his orders for another attack on 15 September.

The plan was that the Fourth Army should capture Morval, Lesboeufs, Gueudecourt and Flers, and that the Reserve Army should attack to the north and the French to the south. The Guards Division was to take Lesboeufs, with the 6th Division on their right and the 14th Division of XV Corps on their left. The Guards Division was to attack with 2 Brigade on the right and the 1st on the left, with 3 Brigade in support; the attack was to be in three stages, each of about 1,000 metres.

Complying with their part of the assault, 3 Guards Brigade moved to Trônes Wood on 15 September in reserve to the 1 and 2 Guards brigades, who were to attack alongside, as the Welsh Guards war diary states: 'the new so called tanks, otherwise known as caterpillars or crabs'. This was to be the first occasion that these new tanks would be used in action and the Guards Division was to have ten: one on the left flank of 1 Guards Brigade and the other nine in three columns. They were to start off from their positions forty minutes before zero hour and were timed to reach their first objective five minutes before the infantry. The men were fascinated by these strange

A tank advancing somewhere near Bapaume during the Somme offensive.

machines, some of which were parked in Happy Valley, and had watched in amusement as the noisy lumbering machines moved into their jumping-off positions.

1 and 2 Guards brigades, which had assembled at Ginchy, attacked at 6.20 am on 15 September, heading in a north-easterly direction from the north-west of Ginchy. Facing them just below Delville Wood were the trenches at Ale Alley and Hop Alley, which were still held by the Germans, who had fortified their positions with carefully-sited machine guns. To the east of Ginchy lay a German strongpoint known as the Quadrilateral. The tanks had been allotted to the Guards to deal with these positions; however, they failed to reach them.

The Germans, as ever, fought gallantly: both the attacking Guards brigades came under heavy fire but managed to take their first objective despite suffering terrible casualties; however, the attack then stalled. The 14th (Light) Division advanced on their left but there was a gap between the divisions. The 6th Division had advanced on the right with orders to take the Quadrilateral, but their attack failed due to the non-appearance of the tanks, which had all either broken down, become stuck or been destroyed. The latter position would take three more days of heavy fighting before it fell.

During the assault of 1 Guards Brigade near Ginchy, on 15 September the last remaining of the long line of Lord Marchers was brought to a sad end following the death of the only son and heir of Sir Marteine Owen Mowbray Lloyd, Lord Marcher of Kemes, and Katherine Helena Lloyd (née Dennistoun) of Bronwydd, Henllan. The title had been extant since the reign of King Edward I and entitled Lloyd to an estate of over 100,000 acres of land in Pembrokeshire, Ceredigion, Carmarthenshire and Glamorgan.

Marteine Kemes Arundel Lloyd was born in Bronwydd on 21 February 1890, and was educated at New Forest, Bournemouth and at Eton. He was commissioned into the Grenadier Guards in 1911, following his 21st birthday, which was celebrated at Bronwydd and was attended, among others, by Prince Alexander of Battenberg. Lloyd had acted as one of the guards of honour when King Edward VII was lying in state at Westminster Abbey. He landed in France on 4 October 1914 and joined his battalion, the 2nd Grenadier Guards, at Ypres. He was wounded soon after arriving in France during the same action in which Major Lawrence Vaughan Colby was killed, and was himself initially reported as missing believed killed, but was reputedly saved from death by a cat that curled itself around his neck and kept him warm overnight.

Captain Marteine Kemes Arundel Lloyd, 2nd Grenadier Guards.

Lloyd then spent several months in hospital and went back to France in January 1916, rejoining his battalion at Loos in the rank of captain. He was killed in action near Ginchy on 15 September 1916, aged 26, and is buried in Delville Wood Cemetery, Longueval. He is commemorated on war memorials at Aberbanc, Llangynllo, Newport, Pembrokeshire, the Church of the Holy Ghost, Basingstoke and at Eton, and his memorial scroll is also displayed in the parish church at Llangynllo, near a fine leaded-glass window that was unveiled in his memory on 17 December 1919 by General Sir Henry Mackinnon, dedicated by the Bishop of St David's.

The death of the heir to the title Lord Marcher of Kemes meant the end of the line of the last Welsh Marcher Lord, and also the end of a once powerful and thriving dynasty whose family home, Bronwydd, has since crumbled into decay and is a sad reminder of the continuing cost of the Great War to such families.

The plaque beneath the leaded window in St Cynllo's Church, Llangynllo, dedicated to Marteine Kemes Arundel Lloyd.

The CO of the 3rd Coldstream Guards, Lieutenant Colonel John Vaughan Campbell DSO gained the honour of being awarded the VC for his gallant leadership during the attack. John Vaughan Campbell was born in London on 31 October 1876, the son of Captain Ronald Campbell, brother of the Earl Cawdor. He was of mixed ancestry: his family was Scottish but had residences at Stackpole Court, Pembrokeshire and at Golden Grove, near Carmarthen. His father was killed in the Zulu Wars in 1879 while committing an act of gallantry that would have almost certainly won him the Victoria Cross if posthumous awards had then been awarded. Campbell followed in his father's footsteps and was commissioned into the Coldstream Guards on 5 September 1896. He served in the Boer War, in which he was awarded the DSO and was mentioned in despatches twice. He went to France with the 3rd Coldstream Guards after the outbreak of the Great War and was awarded the Victoria Cross for his gallantry at Ginchy on 15 September 1916:

Lieutenant Colonel John Vaughan Campbell VC DSO 3rd Coldstream Guards.

> For most conspicuous bravery and leading in an attack. Seeing that the first waves of his battalion had been decimated by machine gun and rifle fire he took personal command of the third line, rallied his men with the utmost gallantry, and led them against the enemy machine guns, capturing the guns and killing the personnel. Later in the day, after consultation with other unit commanders, he again rallied the survivors of this battalion, and at a critical moment led them through a very hostile fire barrage against the objective. He was one of the first to enter the enemy trench. His personal gallantry and initiative at a very critical moment turned the fortunes of the day and enabled his division to press on and capture objectives of the highest tactical importance. (*London Gazette*, 26 October 1916.)

On the same day, to the north the Canadian Corps attacked at Mouquet Farm and Courcelette. The Canadians had relieved the ANZACs at the beginning of the month and were faced with a landscape that had already been battered beyond all recognition. The Canadians made considerable gains during the day and on the following day, 11th Division attached to the Corps, captured Mouquet Farm, a position that had cost the lives of thousands of Australian troops. At least sixteen Welshmen were killed serving with the Canadians during this action.

The Welsh Guards were warned to attack on the following morning, so Murray Threipland moved the battalion slightly nearer to Ginchy and went forward to look at the ground. At 1 am on 16 September orders were given that the 1st Grenadiers and the Welsh Guards would attack the original second objective in conjunction with 61 Brigade on the right and that zero hour was 9.30 am.

During the night heavy rain fell all over the battlefield and, due to the congested trenches, the Welsh Guards were forced to move back to Ginchy to shelter rather than stay in the open and be in full view of the Germans when dawn broke.

When the attack started, Murray Threipland put No. 3 Company in reserve and the attack was carried out by the Prince of Wales's Company on the right and No. 2 on the left, with No. 4 in support. Again the assault was met with murderous fire, casualties were terrible and several officers were hit. Due to the confusion the Welsh Guards lost direction and mistook Gueudecourt for Lesboeufs, a mistake that made them swing left and come into contact with the Germans on the Flers to Lesboeufs Road, so they began to dig in. The 4th Grenadier Guards and the 3rd Coldstreams came up on each side, but the Guards were still almost 200 metres short of the second objective.

Sergeant Norman Carter (663), Welsh Guards, the son of Mr and Mrs Arthur Carter of 47 Carnarvon Road, Bangor. Carter was killed at Ginchy on 16 September 1916.

Thirty-five men had been killed, and Captains Clive and Ashton and another 111 men had been wounded. With the 3rd Guards Brigade badly depleted, during the night the line was relieved by the 20th (Light) Division.

Captain Clive was Percy Robert Herbert, Viscount Clive, the heir to the 4th Earl of Powis, George Charles Herbert. He was born in London on 3 December 1892. He had been shot in the thigh, fracturing his leg, so was evacuated to hospital in France before being brought home to Southampton and then to King Edward VII Hospital in London where he was operated on to remove the bullet. He subsequently suffered a haemorrhage and died on 31 October 1916 aged 23. He was buried with full military honours in Christ Church, Welshpool, accompanied by a band of the KSLI from Shrewsbury.

Captain Percy Robert Herbert, Viscount Clive.

It was still raining as the Welsh Guards withdrew to Carnoy and the ground was knee-deep in mud. Conditions were terrible and the battalion remained here, soaking wet, until 20 September, when it moved to Trônes Wood. The weather had taken its toll on the health of Murray Threipland, who remained in Carnoy, too ill to move, so Humphrey Dene assumed command of the Welsh Guards. Trônes Wood was full of dugouts and shelters, so the men managed to get under cover. They spent the next day providing working parties for the Royal Engineers before relieving the 4th Grenadiers and 2nd Scots Guards on 22 September.

During the night the men worked on digging a communication trench to connect with a battalion of the King's Own Yorkshire Light Infantry (KOYLI) on their left, and bombed a party of Germans out of a sap near Gas Alley. The Germans counter-attacked but the Welsh Guards met them with machine-gun fire.

The next two days were relatively quiet, although three men were killed on 24 September while the battalion was being relieved prior to the next assault on the following day: Lance Corporal William Goater Lloyd (731) of Carmarthen, Guardsmen

Guardsman Charles Edward Cheverton (2034), Welsh Guards. Cheverton was born on 28 September 1896, the son of William Henry and Alice Cheverton of Lax Lodge, Llanwenog. His brother William's life was saved at Fricourt when his pocket Bible took the force of a shell splinter that struck him in the chest.

Charles Edward Cherveton (2034) of Llanwenog and George Jesty (2473) of Cardiff.

The third attack was planned for 25 September, again using 1 and 2 Guards brigades, with the 3rd in reserve; however, the Welsh Guards were to remain in support of the assaulting battalions. Trench maps were issued with three lines marked in green, brown and blue; green was Needle Trench, brown the outskirts of Lesboeufs, and blue marking the far side of Lesboeufs. The 6th Division was on the right and the 21st on the left.

The 3 Brigade plan of attack was that the 2nd Scots and the 4th Grenadier Guards should advance to the brown line and, when that was captured, the 1st Grenadier Guards would go through and take the blue line, the Scots Guards looking after their right flank and the 4th Grenadiers their left. Two companies of the Welsh Guards were to move into the left of the green line and two remain in rear of the left flank.

At 12.35 pm on 25 September the attack began, following a creeping artillery barrage, and by 3 pm the 1st Grenadiers had reached the blue line, so the Welsh Guards advanced to the green line to consolidate. The 21st Division had failed to cover the left flank, so Humphrey Dene was ordered to cover it with the Prince of Wales's and No. 2 companies. After a lot of hard work the flank was formed and the men began consolidating.

There was a strongly defended German strongpoint at Needle Trench near Humphrey Dene's position, and on the following morning he received orders to support an attack on it by 62 Brigade. It was during this attack that the Welsh Guards saw their first tank in action when it advanced on Needle Trench and the entire garrison, some 400 men, surrendered. A further fifteen men were killed on 25 September and an officer and sixty-three men wounded; but the left flank of the Guards Division was now safe from danger.

During the day the Welsh Guards could see groups of Germans retreating towards Le Transloy, although snipers held out in isolated posts and made a nuisance of themselves. During the night 3 Guards Brigade was relieved and marched back to Trônes Wood. During the following day parties were sent out to bury the dead of the earlier fighting of 10 and 16 September and came across large numbers of German dead mixed up with their own men. The majority of the Welsh Guardsmen who were killed have no known graves and are commemorated on the Thiepval Memorial,

The Guards Division Memorial near Ginchy.

although several of the dead are buried in Guards' Cemetery, Lesboeufs. Several men who were missing since 16 September were found lying in crop fields.

The men of the Guards Division had given a good account of themselves under the worst conditions and were rightly proud of their achievements. On 29 September the Welsh Guards moved to a camp near Carnoy, where several officers and men rejoined it from hospital. The battalion then moved to Fricourt and on 30 September moved to St. Maulvis, where they enjoyed three days of doing absolutely nothing before leaving there for Morlancourt by bus.

For now their time on the Somme was over and the Welsh Guards were to enjoy a month out of the line; but for others the Somme offensive was still under way.

(vii) The Red Baron

While this fighting had been taking place on the Somme, on 17 September 1916 a Welshman serving with the Royal Flying Corps (RFC) would fall victim to a future fighter legend after becoming his first 'kill'.

Captain Tom Rees was the son of Thomas and Alice Rees of Troedyrhiw Villa, Devynock, Brecon. He had been commissioned in the 14th RWF and embarked for France in December 1915 before volunteering for service with the RFC. He became an observer with 11 Squadron, RFC, which was equipped with the F.E.2b.

On 17 September 1916, Rees was acting as observer to Second Lieutenant Lionel Bertram Frank Morris when their aircraft, serial no. 7018, was spotted by a flight of six German fighters, led by the flying ace Oswald Boelcke. One of the German pilots was an inexperienced flyer who had not yet shot down any enemy aircraft, and Boelcke allowed him to attack the inferior British aircraft.

A spirited fight ensued, with Morris flying a desperate evasive action, while Rees steadily defended them by firing his Lewis gun at the German. As Morris turned the aircraft away to head back to British lines, the German attacked again, firing bullets into the two men. The inexperienced German pilot reported seeing the observer (Rees) slump in his seat, and followed the stricken aircraft down to Flesquières airfield, where Morris managed to land.

Captain Tom Rees of Devynock, Brecon, the first victim of Baron Manfred von Richthofen, otherwise known as the Red Baron.

The Germans pulled Rees' body from the aircraft and Morris, badly wounded, was put into an ambulance that raced off to Cambrai. However, Morris died before the ambulance could reach its destination. He is buried at Porte-de-Paris Cemetery, Cambrai.

Rees was 21 years old and is buried at Villers-Plouich Communal Cemetery. Both men had just become the first victims of Baron Manfred von Richthofen, who would become better known as the Red Baron, the ace of all flying aces of the Great War. Richthofen would shoot down a further seventy-nine aircraft before being fatally shot and crash-landing his aircraft in 1918.

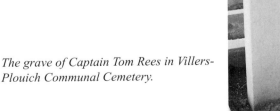

The grave of Captain Tom Rees in Villers-Plouich Communal Cemetery.

Chapter 8

The 38th (Welsh) Division at Ypres: Boesinghe and the Ypres Canal

W hile the Battle of the Somme was at its height, the 38th (Welsh) Division had completed its period of training at Wormhoudt, where it had been inspected by King George V, and had begun moving towards a new front on the far left northern flank of the British alongside the Ypres Canal, north of the city.

The division assembled in camps around Poperinghe before marching through the outskirts of Ypres towards Boesinghe to take over the defences along the canal bank on 19 August.

The Ypres sector had by now settled down and was thought of as a good place to send untrained or weak divisions. In the coming months little of note occurred for the 38th (Welsh) Division, although the various battalions within the division would take

Major General Blackader, the newly installed GOC of the 38th (Welsh) Division, talking to King George V during the inspection of his troops at Wormhoudt in July 1916.

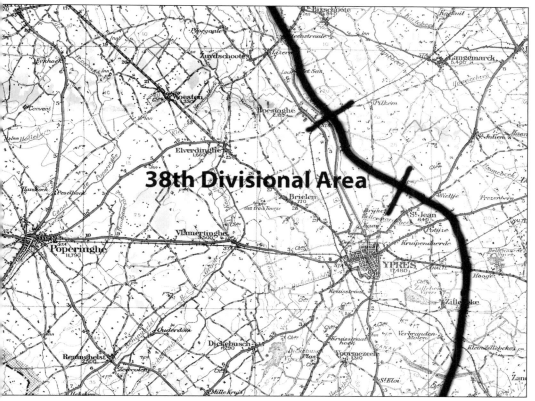

A map showing the position of the line taken over by the 38th (Welsh) Division in August 1916.

part in a number of trench raids of varying success and would also do some good work in consolidating and extending their defensive lines.

Even in this quieter sector, the steady stream of casualties continued. Since being relieved from Mametz Wood on 12 July up until the time it took over the Ypres Canal sector, the division had suffered 157 men killed or died of wounds. The majority had died of wounds suffered in Mametz Wood, but the spell at Hébuterne had seen twenty-two men killed.

On 18 August 1916 the division suffered its first Ypres casualty when Private Harry Hasell (29033) of the 14th Welsh was killed by a sniper while in an observation post on 18 August. Hasell was the son of Arthur and Sarah Ann Hasell of 69 High Street, Aberavon. Captain Milbourne Williams of the 14th Welsh was recovering from wounds he had suffered in Mametz Wood in

Private Harry Hasell (29033) of the 14th Welsh, the first casualty suffered by the 38th (Welsh) Division at Ypres.

173

Swansea when he read of Hasell's death and felt compelled to write to his parents a letter that caused some confusion:

I was so sorry to see in the paper that your son was killed in the attack on Mametz Wood on July 10th, and would like to offer you my sincerest sympathy. I was in charge of the company in which your son was on that date, and you have I no doubt heard how well our men advanced against a very strong position. I saw your son after I was wounded, as he helped to bandage my wounds and until I saw the announcement of his death in the paper I had hoped he might have come through safely. If you require any information, or if I can do anything for you, please let me know.

The article he had read did not state where Hasell had been killed; only that he had been shot dead and buried behind the lines. His parents had seen Hasell during a screening of *The Battle of the Somme* in a local cinema, in a scene in which the 14th Welsh were on parade. Nonetheless, Hasell was just 21 years old and is buried in Essex Farm Cemetery, a battlefield cemetery to the west of the Ypres Canal, and was the division's first casualty there.

Some 227 men from the division would be killed here between the death of Private Hasell and the end of 1916, mostly from trench raids and *minenwerfer* (trench mortar) attacks, but by Western Front standards this was peaceful. The Somme offensive still raged on to the south.

The grave of Private Harry Hasell (29033) in Essex Farm Cemetery.

Chapter 9

The Battle of Le Transloy
and the Battle of the Ancre

Following the success of the Anglo-French assault that had reached the Péronne to Bapaume road at Bouchavesnes, the capture of Morval, Lesboeufs and Gueudecourt and the capture of most of Thiepval Ridge by the end of September, Sir Douglas Haig instructed the Fourth Army to plan operations to advance towards Bapaume.

The plan was to gain Le Transloy on the right and Loupart Wood, north of the Albert to Bapaume road, on the left. The Reserve Army was to extend the attacks of the Fourth Army by making attacks on the Ancre valley, attacking from Thiepval Ridge towards Loupart Wood, Irles and Miraumont on the south bank and eastwards on the north bank of the Ancre, and also by attacking towards Puisieux on a front from Beaumont Hamel to Hébuterne, with the right flank meeting the attacks from the south at Miraumont, to envelop German troops in the upper Ancre valley. In the meantime the Third Army was to maintain the flank at Gommecourt.

The 1st Division had been holding the line north of High Wood and north-west of Flers since the capture of the former by the 47th (2nd London) Division and, while not undertaking any offensive actions, had continually suffered casualties. The 6th Welsh had been continually at work in the area throughout September, suffering casualties on a daily basis while carrying out the endless task of trench-digging. On 21 September a shell crashed near No. 5 Dump, killing one officer, Second Lieutenant John Herbert Morris. Three men were killed during the day and nineteen others wounded. Morris was the youngest son of Watkin Morris of 10 The Terrace, Cwmavon, the manager of the Duchy Colliery, Cwmavon. His uncle was Herbert Eccles, manager of the Briton Ferry Steelworks. Morris was educated at Llandovery College from 1904 until 1911. In 1915 he was commissioned from the RWF in the 6th Welsh and soon became a well-respected officer within the battalion. He was 25 years old and is buried at Flatiron Copse Cemetery.

The 1st Division was relieved on 28 September by the 47th Division, which had received orders to capture the strongpoint of Eaucourt l'Abbaye, and moved back to Fricourt. At 3.15 pm on 1 October the 47th Division attacked from assembly trenches dug once again by the 4th RWF in pouring rain. The history of the RWF states: 'The rain had turned the battlefield into a morass – they dug in mud, they lived in mud, with the bodies of the festering dead around them.'

The battalion suffered twelve men killed in these terrible conditions while consolidating trenches here before the division was relieved on 9 October, and four days later entrained at Albert for Vlamertinghe in the Ypres sector.

Another well-known Welshman, former Welsh international goalkeeper Lance Corporal Leigh Richmond Roose MM (PS/10898), 9th Royal Fusiliers, was killed during the battle. Roose was born on 27 November 1877, the son of Richmond Leigh Roose and Eliza Roose of Holt, Denbighshire. He studied at Aberystwyth University prior to the war, but interrupted his further studies to concentrate on his real love – football – and became a well-respected goalkeeper. He began his career at Aberystwyth FC before playing for several clubs, including Everton, Stoke, Celtic, Arsenal and Sunderland, and gained twenty-four international caps for Wales.

Lance Corporal Leigh Richmond Roose MM (PS/10898), 9th Royal Fusiliers.

Roose enlisted in the Royal Fusiliers at the outbreak of war under the name of Leigh Rouse, being posted to the 9th Royal Fusiliers. On 6 August his battalion was in the front line near Ration Trench, Pozières, when the Germans attacked using the *flammenwerfer*. Roose was at the forefront of his battalion's brave defence of their trench and was recommended for the MM.

On 7 October his battalion took part in an assault against Gueudecourt, a village that lies on the Le Sars to Le Transloy road, north-east of Flers and north-west of Lesboeufs. At some time during the attack Roose was killed. His body was never found and he is commemorated on the Thiepval Memorial.

The Gueudecourt Memorial, commemorating the actions of the Newfoundland Regiment during the Battle of Le Transloy.

The winter had begun to set in during the period of the Battle of Le Transloy, making the chance of any further successful attacks almost impossible. The conditions were terrible, the devastated ground was waterlogged and it was an immense task just to keep the troops in the front line supplied with food, water and ammunition.

The weather did not break until three days after the end of the Battle of Le Transloy on 18 October, by which time the allies had captured Le Transloy and Bouchavesnes. The British also attacked on the left, towards the marshy valley of the Ancre, where the high ground north of Thiepval overlooked the valley and gave the British good observation over the strong German positions held since 1 July around Beaumont Hamel. Realizing the importance of the position, the Germans made several counter-attacks to attempt to recapture the ground and heavy fighting took place round the Schwaben and Stuff redoubts.

While the Somme offensive was nearing its final phase, the 40th (Bantam) Division at Maroc was still undergoing its period of trench initiation. The sector was a known hot spot and the division had been suffering a constant drain of casualties since moving there. On 17 October the Welsh Brigade suffered its worst days of the war thus far, the majority of which were suffered when a heavy artillery barrage rained down on billets occupied by the troops in the north of Maroc. One officer – Second Lieutenant Kelyth Pierce Lloyd-Williams, 17th Welsh – was killed by a *minenwerfer* shell that fell on St James Keep, and eight men of the 18th Welsh were killed in their billets.

Lieutenant Kelyth Pierce Lloyd-Williams, 17th Welsh, the only son of Dr William and of Mrs Annie Lloyd Williams of Llwynybrain, Llanrug. He was educated at Towyn School, Shrewsbury School, Bangor University College and Clare College, Cambridge and was commissioned in the Welsh Regiment in 1915. He was killed in action on 17 October 1916 and is buried in Maroc British Cemetery, Grenay.

On the following day two men of the 19th RWF and two more of the 18th Welsh were killed, while on 19 October the CO of the 17th Welsh, Lieutenant Colonel Charles Joseph Wilkie, was killed along with Captain Charles Vyvyan Lyne when a high-explosive shell crashed into the trenches at South Street and St James Street while the two officers were inspecting their men. One of the battalion's junior officers wrote of Wilkie:

Colonel Wilkie was a man amongst men and a soldier amongst soldiers. His attributes as a man were only equalled by his

Lieutenant Colonel Charles Joseph Wilkie, CO of the 17th Welsh. A vastly experienced officer, his death was keenly felt by the battalion he had commanded since its formation.

exceptional and far-reaching capabilities as a soldier. In the field he was a leader with a knowledge and personality which created absolute faith and trustfulness, and in the orderly room his administration was just exemplary. I had the honour and privilege of serving under him as an officer from Dec. 1914, until June 1916. During the time I learned his character as a man and his qualities as a soldier. Both were the finest I have known, and during that period I heard no word of complaint or reproach against him from any rank. The officers, non-commissioned officers and men of the Welsh Regiment knew him first as a soldier, and secondly as a gentleman, and as such they loved him as only soldiers know how to love. They would have followed him through anything, and would have rejoiced to have had the chance to do so. They knew no injustice would be done to them provided Colonel Wilkie had a say in the matter. His loss will be felt amongst all ranks so deeply and so terribly that it is impossible for mere words to describe it.

Losing its two most senior officers was a terrible loss for the battalion but Captain Harry Percy Bright Gough, who assumed command, was a very able and respected officer.

Back on the Somme, two of the divisions containing Welsh troops that had left the sector after sustaining heavy casualties there were about to return, having rebuilt their strength.

On 4 October the 2nd SWB, with the 29th Division, was relieved from the trenches on the Ypres Canal banks and marched to L Camp, Poperinghe, before entraining for the Somme from Hopoutre on 7 October. During the evening the battalion detrained and marched to billets at Cardonette, north-east of Amiens. Over the coming days the battalion marched back to the Somme battlefront along the Bapaume road before spending a day training in Buire, and moving to Fricourt on 13 October, where the battalion trained for an attack on an unknown objective.

On 19 October the battalion marched to Bernafay Wood, where it bivouacked in heavy rain before moving out during the night to take up positions south-west of Gueudecourt, in Grease Trench. At around 1 am on 20 October the 2nd SWB were winding their way up to Grease Trench through a communication trench when the Germans opened up a heavy artillery barrage on them.

The battalion suffered heavy casualties, losing one officer – Second Lieutenant Ernest Thomas Samuel Bricknell – and nineteen men killed. Bricknell had been the head boy of Monmouth Grammar School, which named the school library in his honour. He was the son of Samuel and Fanny Bricknell of 4 Agincourt Square, Monmouth and was just 20 years old. He is buried in Longueval Road Cemetery. It was a savage welcome back to the Somme for a battalion with nothing but bad memories of it.

Their experience of life back on the Somme became no better on the following day. At 2.30 am a party of men of the King's Own Scottish Borderers (KOSB) were bringing rations up to the Borderers when they became victims of another artillery barrage. Second Lieutenant Beardshaw was sent down the trench with a party of men when he was mistakenly shot dead by friendly troops. Reginald Dudley Beardshaw

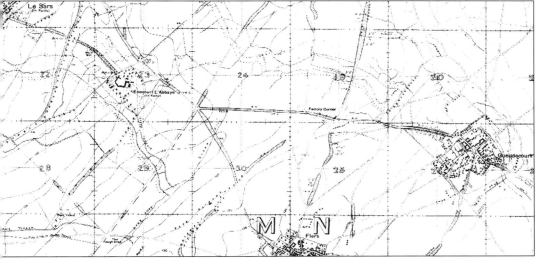

A section of trench map 57cSW1, Le Sars. Grease Trench was in map reference N 20 d, 21 c (square 20, bottom right quadrant).

was educated at Oxford and worked as a colliery official at Tondu. He married Elizabeth Whittingham of Aberkenfig in 1912 and was a well-known sportsman, excelling at tennis and rugby. He had served with the 2nd SWB in Gallipoli and was a well-respected officer. He is buried in Bulls Road Cemetery, Flers.

By the time the 2nd SWB was relieved after two days in Grease Trench, it had lost another officer – Second Lieutenant Charles Innes Wilton – and 16 men killed, 58 men wounded and 45 missing, with 4 men killed during their relief; 4 officers and 64 men were invalided out with trench foot. The wet weather was now a real issue for the men in the trenches. While in support trenches on 23 October the 2nd SWB lost another 75 men to hospital with trench foot, while 25 more were invalided out on the

Second Lieutenant Reginald Dudley Beardshaw, 2nd SWB, accidentally shot in the trenches near Gueudecourt.

following day and a further 18 on 25 October, by which time the strength of the battalion was down to 16 officers and 330 other ranks. At around 2 am on 26 October Lieutenant John Henry Harford was sent out with a patrol to see if the Germans had wired their trenches. Harford and two men were killed when the Germans discovered their presence and, after firing Very lights up to illuminate no man's land, began firing at the patrol.

Lieutenant John Henry Harford, 2nd SWB, of Falcondale, Lampeter.

Lieutenant John Henry Harford was born on 7 February 1896, the eldest son of Major John Charles Harford and Blanche Annabel Harford of Falcondale, Lampeter and of Blaise Castle. He was educated at Harrow prior to being commissioned in March 1915 in the 3rd SWB and had served in Gallipoli with the 2nd Royal Fusiliers before being wounded on 30 June 1915. He returned home to recover before being posted to France with the 2nd SWB. Harford was just 20 years old and is commemorated on the Thiepval Memorial. On the following night the battalion was relieved and moved to trenches near Delville Wood, then on 29 October moved to a camp near Pommier Redoubt and to newly-erected hutments at Fricourt the following day.

With the campaign slowing on all but the Ancre front, casualties for many of the Welsh units still on the Somme now began to lessen at long last. The 2nd Welsh had suffered the loss of one of its most promising officers on 23 October with the death of Lieutenant Basil Gordon Dawes Jones MC and another man, Private Stanley James Shepherd (17531), originally a member of the 14th Welsh (Swansea Pals), who died in captivity at Le Cateau. Basil Gordon Dawes Jones was born on 28 March 1897, the son of William Henry Dawes and Emily Georgina Dawes Jones (née Gordon) and was educated at Haileybury and the Royal Military College, Sandhurst. He was of a proud military heritage: his father was a lieutenant colonel in the Indian army, while his grandfather was Major General Sir Henry Gordon and his great-uncle was Major General Charles George Gordon of Khartoum. He had been awarded the MC while serving with the 2nd Welsh earlier in the Somme campaign: 'For conspicuous gallantry during operations. He did fine work in the front line trenches in command of machine guns under very heavy shell fire. He repeatedly made his way through heavy barrages to ensure the good work of his guns.' (*London Gazette*, 20 October 1916.)

The 2nd RWF had also returned to the Somme, along with the remainder of the 2nd Division and had taken over trenches at Foncquevillers and billets at Loucheux. On 14 October the division had been moved to Méricourt to join XIV Corps and on 21 October the 2nd RWF marched back to the Citadel, a tented camp beyond Méaulte, which the 1st RWF had known so well. The battalion was attached to the 4th Division on the 22nd and moved through Trônes Wood to join the division on the Lesboeufs to Morval front, and passed through the desolated villages of Guillemont and Ginchy without even noticing that these had once been small thriving communities. The battalion took up positions in touch with the French at Sailly-Saillisel, losing four men killed on 24 October and another four men on the 26th. Conditions were terrible: it was cold, wet and muddy and there was no possibility of hot food, so news that the battalion was to be relieved after dusk on 27 October cheered the men no end.

Some Welsh units, however, were about to get involved in the fighting in the Ancre valley. The 19th (Western) Division had been recuperating in the Bailleul area and was brought back to the Somme after being relieved by the 7th Division (1st RWF) at the end of September. By 6 October all the units had reached billets in the Marleux area, and on 7 October 56 and 58 brigade took over the front line from 152 Brigade of the 51st (Highland) Division, which ran from almost 600 metres north of John Copse to

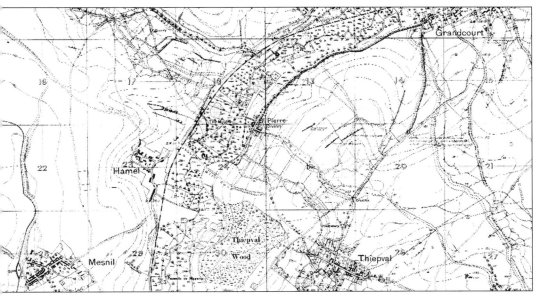

A section of trench map 57dSE1 & 2, Beaumont. Hessian Trench ran along squares R 20, 21, 22 and 23, which is off the map. The marshy valley facing the 19th Division can be seen centre left.

the sunken road east of Hébuterne. No. 56 Brigade was on the right and 58 on the left, each holding their position with one battalion.

By the middle of the month the division had been relieved and moved to Vadencourt (56 Brigade), Warloy (57 Brigade) and Herrisart (58 Brigade), with the 5th SWB at Bauchelles. On 21 October the brigades moved again: 56 and 57 brigades moved to the Brickfields, 58 Brigade to Bouzincourt and the 5th SWB to Toutencourt, before 57 Brigade relieved the 25th Division in Hessian Trench and Stuff Redoubt the following day. No. 56 Brigade took over the western portion of Hessian Trench and Schwaben Trench from the 39th Division. This line lay immediately south of the Ancre and faced the village of Grandcourt.

On 23 October the division received orders that large-scale operations were to be undertaken by the Reserve Army: the attack would be delivered eastwards from north of the Ancre and northwards from south of the river, from positions that had been captured during the Battle of the Ancre Heights. II Corps, to which the 19th Division now belonged, was to attack northwards. However, plans were delayed due to the bad weather that had made ground conditions treacherous. Even in the summer the valley is marshy and wet and, on top of this, the ground was filled with the stench of decaying corpses.

South of the line held by the 19th Division were the ruins of Thiepval and north was the object of their attack, Grandcourt, which was to be taken as soon as the weather allowed. The division's first Welsh casualty after moving back to the Somme occurred here when Sergeant John Richard Williams, 13282, 9th RWF of Llandudno was killed on 25 October. On the following day the Germans attacked 57 Brigade, but were beaten off and during the night 58 Brigade relieved both 56 and 57 brigades for a three-day spell three-day spell in the line, the 9th Welsh relieving the 9th Loyals (Loyal North Lancashire or LNL) in the Stuff Redoubt trenches and the 9th RWF in Regina and Hessian Trench, after marching through 3 miles of mud from their camp at Ovillers. The latter battalion was shelled during the move, losing one officer – Lieutenant Charles Gilbert Lawes – and two men killed. One of the men – Lance Corporal Charles Percival Harrop (29590) – was the son of John Harrop of the Westminster Collieries, Wrexham and of 22 King's Road, Colwyn Bay. He was educated at Grove Park School, Wrexham and had just received news that he was to return to England to train as an officer. Harrop and Lawes are commemorated on the Thiepval Memorial, while the third man – Private David Jones (31421) of Pontrhydfendigaed – is buried in Regina Trench Cemetery, Grandcourt.

Casualties from German shellfire continued throughout the coming days, resulting in the death of a former Llanidloes schoolmaster, John Gwilym Hughes. He was the son of John and Mary Hughes of Bangor and was educated at St Paul's School and Friars School and at the North Wales University College, Bangor. He had taught at Llanidloes County School and was a member of the Honourable Society of Cymmrodorion in Llanidloes before moving back to Bangor after gaining a position at Friars School. He was commissioned in the RWF in 1915 and joined the 9th RWF on 6 September 1916. Hughes was wounded on 28 October and died at Abbeville on 3 November, aged 35. He is buried in Abbeville Communal Cemetery Extension.

At sea the threat posed by German submarines was becoming critical. During the last weeks of October three merchant ships partly crewed by Welsh seamen were sunk while transporting vital supplies. On 20 October the SS *Bayreaulx* was torpedoed and sunk by *U-63* with the loss of twenty-six crew including nine Welsh; on 23 October the SS *Clearfield* was torpedoed and sunk by *U-55* with the loss of thirty-two lives including nine Welsh; on 24 October the SS *North Wales* was torpedoed and sunk by *U-69* with the loss of thirty lives including six Welsh. On 28 October the hospital ship SS *Galeka* struck a mine that had been laid by *UC-26* and sank while entering Le Havre. Nineteen men of the Royal Army Medical Corps were killed in the sinking, including three Welshmen: Private William Charles Bevan (44508) of Neath, Private Ernest George Cairns (59172) of Carmarthen and Private John Henry Roberts (52483) of Hirwaun. Those lost are commemorated on the Galeka Memorial in Ste. Marie Cemetery, Le Havre.

On the same day a converted herring drifter, HMS *Speedwell V*, which was based in Milford Haven, was on anti-submarine patrol off the south coast of Ireland when it was caught in a storm. While attempting to gain the safety of Rosslare Harbour she struck Splaugh Rock and broke up, sinking with the loss of her entire crew of ten. Three bodies were later washed ashore and buried in Kilscoran Church of Ireland churchyard, while the seven others are commemorated on the Portsmouth Naval Memorial. Four more Welsh sailors drowned following the loss of the SS *Adriatic* on 31 October. Her fate is unknown but she was declared a war loss, thus enabling her crew to be commemorated on the Tower Hill Memorial.

Back in France, during the last week of October Lord Llangattock, Major John McLean Rolls of the 1st Monmouthshire Battery RFA was badly wounded while carrying out observation work in the Somme sector. Rolls was born in London on 25 April 1870, the son of John Alan Rolls, 1st Baron Llangattock, JP, DL of The Hendre, Monmouth and his wife Georgiana Marcia, daughter of Sir Charles Fitzroy Maclean, 9th Baronet. His father had been MP for Monmouthshire for twelve years and had served as a captain in the Royal Gloucestershire Hussars before becoming honorary colonel of the 4th Welsh Brigade and mayor of Monmouth. Rolls was educated at Eton and Christ Church, taking his MA in 1896 and was called to the Bar in 1895, also serving with the 1st Monmouth Volunteer Artillery before retiring with the rank of captain and honorary major. He inherited the peerage on his father's death in 1912.

He rejoined the 4th Welsh Brigade, RFA in January 1915 in the rank of major and volunteered to serve in France. He died of his wounds at the Military Hospital at Boulogne on 31 October 1916, and is buried in Boulogne Eastern Cemetery. (Rolls was unmarried and his brother Henry Allan Rolls, the heir presumptive, had died just months earlier, while Charles Stewart Rolls, the youngest brother, who co-founded Rolls-Royce was killed in an air crash in 1910, so the title died with him.)

Back on the Somme the fighting was still raging. On 29 October the 9th Welsh got some form of retaliation when Second Lieutenants Benjamin Stewart Buckingham Thomas and G. Fitzsimmons took a party of twenty men out to bomb a German strongpoint that had been giving some trouble. Thomas was awarded the MC for the raid and Fitzsimmons was mentioned in despatches.

While the 19th Division was finding itself under pressure, the 10th RWF began its move back to the Somme with the 3rd Division after a period resting at Loos to join it in the planned offensive. The attack, the Battle of the Ancre, had been planned with the intention of capturing Miraumont, Beauregard, Serre, Pys, Irles and Achiet-le-Petit over three stages. The 19th Division was to assault over Grandcourt Trench to a line on the Miraumont to Beaucourt Road; the 3rd Division was to capture Serre and to form a defensive flank from John Copse across Pendant Trench to Puisieux Trench.

While the 3rd Division troops were moving into their sector in readiness for the offensive, back at Lesboeufs on 5 November the 2nd RWF, which had taken over Dewdrop Trench after being ordered to attack in conjunction with a French attack from Sailly-Saillisel, lost twenty-one men killed by machine guns and a German counter-barrage before digging in to some shell holes in front of their starting positions.

By now the weather had begun to take a turn for the better and Sir Douglas Haig made preparations for a final attack on Beaumont Hamel. The preliminary bombardment commenced on 11 November and continued until 5.45 am on 13 November when, in a dense fog, the attack began.

North of the River Ancre the 63rd (Royal Naval) Division attacked along the north of the Ancre Valley, capturing Beaucourt Station and Station Road; the 51st (Highland) Division attacked on its left flank, the 2nd Division attacked along Redan Ridge and the 3rd Division attacked towards Serre. At least thirty-eight Welshmen serving with the Royal Naval Division were killed during their attack on Beaucourt Station. The majority of these are buried in Ancre British Cemetery, while some are commemorated on the Thiepval Memorial.

The 10th RWF was one of the two assaulting battalions of 76 Brigade, 3rd Division and attacked alongside the 1st Gordon Highlanders, with the 3rd King's Own in support. The men were given hot tea, a swig of rum and a cheese sandwich before taking up their starting positions at John Copse.

At 5.45 am the 10th RWF advanced through thick fog towards the north of Serre, meeting little opposition initially but, when the artillery barrage moved forward, the ground to the left of the battalion came alive with Germans who had been sheltering in deep dugouts and began to pour machine-gun fire into the assaulting troops. The situation soon turned into chaos; the second objective line was easily reached, but the battalion became fragmented, with a party of men, supported by a number of Gordon Highlanders, taking the third line and two platoons under Captain Rudd advancing further into the fourth line. This small group of men was soon surrounded by the Germans who captured or killed them.

The next two waves met with the same fate but did not even reach the first German line, leaving the 10th RWF isolated. It was over an hour later before anyone reached the third line and only one man of the 10th RWF was to be found; it was now becoming clear that the attack had failed. Scattered survivors crept slowly back to safety throughout the day and gathered in Rob Roy Trench, where the survivors took stock of their losses. The 10th RWF had lost nine officers – Captain William Ferris Rudd, Second Lieutenants Arthur Edward Capell, David Davies, Howard Lock Harries, Henry Myrddin Jones, George Thomas, Herbert Gordon Thomas, Peter Williams and Richard Henry Williams – and eighty-eight men killed. Captain Bishop and 156 men were missing, while 3 officers and 102 men were wounded.

Captain William Ferris Rudd was the son of George Patrick Ferris Rudd of Plastangraig, Beddgelert and had been a master in the Mercantile Marine. He was commissioned on 6 October 1915 and joined the battalion in France on 31 August 1916. He is buried in Serre Road Cemetery No. 1. Many of the other ranks killed were fresh recruits who had been transferred from the second line regiments of the Denbigh and Montgomery Yeomanry following their disbanding in July. It was not until December that many of the bereaved families of these men heard any news of the fate suffered by their loved ones. The family of one man, Private Edward Lewis Bodycombe (54704) of Neath Abbey, received a letter from his captain who could only state that after a fierce engagement he did not return. Bodycombe had worked in the electrical department of the Cape Copper Works and was a well-known soloist and member of the St John's church choir

Corporal Thomas Reginald Knowles (29615), 10th RWF.

and had been in France only five weeks. Another man, Corporal Thomas Reginald Knowles (29615), the son of David Knowles of Arfryn, Park Street, Denbigh, was a solicitor who had been educated at Denbigh School and was a prominent local Liberal activist. Most of these men are commemorated on the Thiepval Memorial.

The 19th Division did not attack; instead it was ordered to hold position and contain the enemy in Stuff Redoubt. On the night of 14/15 November one company of the 9th Welsh carried out a successful but costly raid on German dugouts in Stump Road, losing Lieutenant John Wilfred Jones and five men killed, three officers and twenty men wounded. On 18 November 56 and 57 brigades attacked and captured Grandcourt while 58 Brigade was in reserve. The Battle of the Ancre was by now drawing to a close, but the 9th RWF suffered eight more men killed on 20 November, just after the battle officially ended and just days before the 19th Division was relieved from the front line.

The Somme offensive had been very costly for the allies, but it had also severely depleted the German forces and had succeeded in drawing German reinforcements away from Verdun, relieving pressure on the French.

The Battle of the Ancre had been a partial success for the British, but had cost them dearly. Among the Welshmen killed during the attack by the 63rd (Royal Naval) Division in the Ancre Valley was Able Seaman Jason Peters (Z/2331). He was born at Clynderwen on 9 September 1892, the son of Thomas and Margaret Peters of Jones Terrace. After the death of his father the family moved to Bethesda Cross, near Narberth. Peters was a collier and enlisted at Abertridwr on 3 November 1915 in the Royal Naval Volunteer Reserve (RNVR). He landed in France on 10 July 1916 and was posted to the Anson Battalion. Peters was killed during the assault on Beaucourt on 13 November 1916 and is commemorated on the Thiepval Memorial.

Able Seaman Jason Peters (Z/2331), Anson Battalion, Royal Naval Division.

One of many tragedies that occurred during the day was the case of one of the Welsh officers serving with the Royal Naval Division. Sub Lieutenant Edwin Leopold Arthur Dyett was born in Cardiff on 17 October 1895, the son of Commander Walter Henry Ross Dyett, Royal Naval Reserve. Dyett had enlisted in the RNVR on 24 June 1915 and then gained a commission before being posted to Nelson Battalion, RNVR. By his own admission he was not cut out for frontline duties, and had requested a transfer to a ship but this had been turned down. When the Royal Naval Division had launched its assault on Beaucourt on 13 November Dyett had been in reserve, but with mounting casualties he and another officer were sent forward as reinforcements. The pair reported to Advanced Brigade HQ and waited for over an hour before being instructed to move up through what must have seemed like hell, with artillery and gas shells falling all around them.

Sub Lieutenant Edwin Leopold Arthur Dyett, Nelson Battalion, Royal Naval Division.

The two men failed to make contact with their unit, so parted company to search alone. Dyett came across another officer who ordered him to follow him to the front line, but Dyett insisted on returning to HQ for fresh orders. The other officer, although of the same rank, filed a report against Dyett for refusing to follow a lawful order and this set off a chain reaction that ultimately led to Dyett being court-martialled. He was shot for desertion at Le Crotoy on 5 January 1917 and is buried in the communal cemetery there. Dyett was later pardoned but he had sadly become the only man of the Royal Naval Division, the eleventh Welshman and one of only three officers to be executed during the war.

Nothing more of note occurred during the last few weeks of 1916, except for the hanging of a Welsh soldier for murder. Frederick Brooks was an army reservist who had lived and worked as a collier at Gwaun-cae-Gurwen for several years prior to the war. He rejoined the colours at the outbreak of war and rejoined his old regiment, the Worcesters. He was stationed at Plymouth with the 5th (Reserve) Battalion when on 19 June 1916 he abducted and strangled a 12-year-old girl, Alice Clara Gregory. He was captured by the police soon after and was sentenced to death at the Devon Assizes at Plymouth on 3 November. The local MP John Williams attempted to gain Brooks a reprieve from his sentence, but on 12 December 1916 the 28-year-old was hung in Exeter.

While the local newspapers in south Wales reported on the death of Brooks, at the front each of the Welsh units in action continued suffering casualties almost daily while engaging in normal trench warfare. The 2nd Monmouths lost the Australian-born Captain Clive Warneford Taunton, who was killed in action on 25 November. He was born in Sydney and educated at Haileybury College, Melbourne. He then went to England to study engineering at Bristol University and was commissioned from there in the 2nd Monmouths. Taunton was 21 years old and is buried in Bernafay Wood British Cemetery, Montauban. Another former Bristol University student, Second Lieutenant Edward Frederick Lawlor of Salvador, Cyncoed Road, Cardiff was killed with the same battalion two days later and is buried in the AIF Burial Ground, Flers.

Two more commanding officers of the Welsh Regiment died before the year's end. Lieutenant Colonel Osborn Brace Pritchard, former CO of the 2nd Welsh, died on 27 November 1916 aged 48 and is buried in West Norwood Cemetery and Crematorium. Lieutenant Colonel George Frederick Pridham, CO of the 1st/5th Welsh, died while on active service in Egypt on 16 December 1916, aged 39. He was educated at Marlborough College and Sandhurst before being commissioned in the Welsh Regiment and had served throughout the Boer War. Four years later he joined the Egyptian army, in which he rose to command a battalion, and served in the campaign in Kordofan. He was a well-regarded polo-player and yachtsman, and took command of the 1st/5th Welsh on 26 February 1916.

Lieutenant Colonel Osborn Brace Pritchard, late CO of the 2nd Welsh. Wounded at Ypres on 24 November 1914, he died two years later.

Among the many Welsh troops still on the Somme, the Welsh Guards had moved back in the front on 7 November after a long spell of rest, Murray Threipland having rejoined after his spell in hospital. The battalion, was put to work in Trônes Wood and on the Carnoy to Montauban road, employed initially as road-builders but after a week taking over a section of frontline trenches near Gueudecourt, noted as being a particularly nasty section, on 14 November.

Guardsman John Henry Williams (2249) of Foel Gaer, near Bodfari, Denbighshire was the first to be wounded when their trenches were strafed by a German aircraft. He died on 15 November, aged 29, and is buried in Grove Town Cemetery, Méaulte. On the following day one officer and six men were wounded and another was evacuated with shellshock. The next two days were also hard for the Welsh Guards. On 17 November three men were killed, four wounded, and another was sent back with shellshock; on the 18th three men were killed, one died of wounds, four more were wounded and yet another man was evacuated with shellshock; while on the 19th seven men were killed, two officers and seven men were wounded, four were missing and another case of shellshock was recorded while the battalion was being relieved. Both officers were Scots Guards, attached to the Welsh; one Lieutenant Arthur Mervyn Jones, a Londoner, died on 21 November. He is buried in Grove Town Cemetery, Méaulte.

The battalion was relieved on 21 November and returned to hutments at Méaulte. It moved to hutments at Bronfay Farm on 2 December before occupying the front line again:

> The trenches fell to pieces, subsided within an hour. The whole country became a swamp, and from Haie Wood, between Combles and Morval, to the line, a distance of two and a half miles, each step forward was an effort. Everything possible was done to limit the traffic to the line – rations for the whole period were carried in by the relieving troops – but the absolutely necessary traffic cut up the soft muddy ground until men sank up to their knees in the puddled stuff. There was only one line along which anyone could move, and the track became wider and wider; but to leave the track altogether, especially as relief could only be done at night, meant a danger of getting lost in that bare, treeless country, with the even skyline. The march in was exhausting; much more so the march out, after three days in the mud without shelter of any sort or kind. A soup-kitchen was established by Sidney Jones, the padre, at Combles, and another at the railway siding, and they were great blessings. But the men arrived at Bronfay Camp wet to the skin. (*History of the Welsh Guards*)

During the remainder of the month another twenty-five men of the Welsh Guards died. Guardsman William George Aubrey (1301) was one of five men killed by a shell burst on 10 December. He was born at Burry Port on 16 December 1893, the son of John and Mary Aubrey

Guardsman William George Aubrey (1301), Welsh Guards, mortally wounded by a shell on 10 December 1916.

(née Watkins), and the brother of the Reverend John Aubrey of Rhoslwyn Villa, Penybank, Ammanford. Aubrey worked as a fireman at the New Dynant Colliery and enlisted at Kingston, Surrey in the Welsh Regiment before transferring to the Welsh Guards. He is buried in Bronfay Farm Military Cemetery, Bray-sur-Somme.

Seven more men were killed together on 27 December when the Germans shelled dugouts in which they were sheltering near Bouleaux Wood. They are all buried side-by-side in Bronfay Farm Military Cemetery. Among these was Guardsman Charles Tinklin (342) of Roath, Cardiff.

Guardsman Charles Tinklin (342) of Roath Cardiff.

Yet another tragic death, one among so many, yet still a massive blow to a family that had already lost two sons killed, was the death on Christmas Day of Private Morgan David Hardwidge (16172) of the 2nd Welsh. His younger brothers, Thomas and Henry Hardwidge, were killed at Mametz Wood with the 15th Welsh on 11 July. Unlike his brothers, the elder Hardwidge has no known grave and is commemorated on the Thiepval Memorial.

The worst casualties were, however, suffered by the 18th Welsh. The 40th (Bantam) Division was relieved from its positions at Maroc at the end of October and began the slow move south to the Somme. By 22 November the division had reached Gézaincourt and carried out some training before entraining for Edge Hill, near Buire-sur-l'Ancre. The division then marched to No. 14 Camp, located in Bois Celestins, near Chipilly, where it resumed training.

The various battalions of the all-Welsh 119 Brigade began taking turns in the line at Rancourt over the coming days. On 30 December the 18th Welsh, holding the front line near Bois de Saint-Pierre-Vaast, came under heavy shellfire, which exploded a French ammunition dump.

The 58th Divisions's memorial at Chipilly, in the valley of the Somme. The Division took part in the offensive of August 1918.

Shellfire at Bois de Saint-Pierre-Vaast, an old French sector near Rancourt taken over by the 40th (Bantam) Division in December 1916.

Eighteen men of the 18th Welsh were killed by the explosion of the dump, by far their worst day of the war thus far. The 17th Welsh watched the bombardment from the reserve lines and their war diary comments about the fire and smoke coming from the front. Among the dead was Private Samuel Fish (27849), a former miner at the Duffryn Amman Colliery. He was 27 years old and was buried in Priez Farm. His grave was among a large number in Combles German Cemetery and Priez Farm Cemetery that were lost during the course of the war and he is now among thirty men commemorated on special memorials in Guards' Cemetery, Combles.

Private Samuel Fish (27849), 18th Welsh.

During the following day the 17th Welsh relieved its sister battalion, the 18th Welsh, and losing two men killed and four wounded. Twenty-nine men were invalided sick on the previous day. These two men were the last fatalities suffered by Welsh units on the Western Front in 1916.

As 1916 drew to an end, the various Welsh units were scattered not only on the Western Front, but also in Egypt, Gibraltar, India, Mesopotamia and Salonika. The troops in Gibraltar and India were mainly on garrison duties, but the Welsh troops stationed in Egypt, Mesopotamia and Salonika had seen fighting throughout the year.

The Combles German Cemetery and Priez Farm Cemetery Memorial in Guards' Cemetery, Combles, together with some of the thirty special memorials to those whose graves were lost.

189

Chapter 10

Salonika:
The Campaign Continued

W hile the Somme offensive had been raging in France, the Salonika campaign burst into life. The allied plan throughout the summer of 1916 had been for an advance by the French up the Vardar Valley with the assistance of two Russian brigades, while the Serbians were to move on Monastir along with the Italians. The role of the British Salonika Army, under Lieutenant General George Milne CB DSO, was to defend Salonika from any attack from the north or east, and also to carry out subsidiary attacks to keep the enemy busy.

The British had taken over the 40-mile front from Lozista on the River Butkovo along the south side of Butkovo Lake and the right bank of the River Struma to Lake Tahinos. The terrain was rough and rocky, so the troops' first task was to build roads to supply the front.

The ruler of Greece, King Constantine, was still seen as pro-German by the allies who plotted against him. As a result, the Greek liberation movement, under the control of the politician Eleftherios Venizelos, used the situation to begin to undermine the king's powers and to align Greece with the allies. Constantine had ceded a Greek fort in Macedonia to the German-Bulgarian forces, giving Venizelos the ammunition he needed for the National Schism (or civil war) that followed. In August 1916, followers of Venizelos set up a provisional state in northern Greece with allied support with the aim of reclaiming the lost regions in Macedonia, effectively splitting Greece into two. Following a series of diplomatic negotiations and an armed confrontation in Athens between allied and royalist forces, the king abdicated and his second son Alexander, sympathetic to the allied cause, took his place.

The Welsh troops in Salonika were most probably oblivious to the political machinations that were going on in Athens when the British army moved forward at the end of May 1916. The 22nd Division, together with the 11th RWF, 7th SWB, 8th SWB and 11th Welsh, moving to support the French, advanced into the mountains to Janes, about 30 miles north of Salonika up the Galiko River. The 28th Division, with the 1st and 23rd Welsh, marched to take over a section of front in the swampy Struma Valley.

In a letter to the *Glamorgan Gazette*, Private Morgan Llewellyn of Pontycymmer, serving with the 30th Field Ambulance, 10th Division, wrote:

I am all right up to now. We felt the hardships in the winter a bit, especially in Servia, where we had very bad weather, snow and rain. We shall have them on the run next time. All the boys are eager to have another go at them, but we are giving Johnny the Bulgar and his German friend a rest now to finish his bit of gardening. The weather is getting better now, and we are getting to look as dark as Greeks. We take no notice of Zeppelin bombs out here – we got too used to them in Gallipoli. The only time they trouble us is when we hear of them being dropped on innocent children in England. I should like to send my best wishes and remembrances to all the Garw boys in France. Stick it, Cwmri!

The summer was blisteringly hot and the men had to undertake a lot of marching, dressed in their Mediterranean kit of shirts, shorts and sun-helmets, and they revelled in these fine conditions. However, there was much backbreaking work to do, and throughout June the 1st Welsh found itself employed on road-building duties before being ordered to take the left flank of the 28th Division front. Mosquitos and malaria soon became the soldier's worst enemy and all the Welsh units began to suffer from a lack of manpower as more and more men went sick. To illustrate the scale of the malaria problem, by 1 August the 1st Welsh alone had 8 officers and 236 other ranks admitted to hospital with the disease, while the overall strength of the battalion was just 280 all ranks.

Both the SWB battalions were also being employed as 'navvies' for most of June, constructing defences at the front. By the end of the month the 7th SWB had 150 men in hospital and another 100 sick in camp; the only medicine available was daily doses of quinine. As a result, when the 22nd Division moved to join the French all its units were severely short of manpower.

On 10 August the French, working in conjunction with the 22nd Division, launched an offensive towards Monastir and by the 18th had captured the outlying hills. At the end of the month the 22nd Division relieved the French and 67 Brigade, with its four Welsh battalions, took over the left sector. The British now held the whole line from Lake Tahinos to the Vardar; the 10th, 27th and 28th

Two Llanbadarn men, serving with the 7th SWB in Salonika.

divisions were on the Struma Valley front, while the 22nd and 26th divisions held the Doiran sector. The men of the 8th SWB then suffered an outbreak of sandfly fever, thought to have been contracted by taking over infected trenches, and as a result they were out of action for much of September.

On the Struma front, the Bulgarians continued their advance into Greek Macedonia towards Kavalla and Seres and so on 17 August a British Mounted Column, together with a French Mounted Detachment, was pushed across the Struma to locate them. The 28th Division sent 84 Brigade forward and on 22 August took up a defensive line on the right bank of the Struma River with the 1st Welsh in support. On 24 August the 23rd Welsh, under the command of Lieutenant Colonel Clifton Vincent Reynolds Wright, arrived at Salonika, becoming the Pioneer Battalion to the 28th Division and on 7 September moved to the front, one company being attached to the 1st Welsh in making a second line of defences. The 23rd Welsh suffered its first casualty of the campaign when Private William Wddyn Lewis (45665) died of dysentery on 21 September. Lewis was the son of David and Anne Lewis of 36 Hermon Road, Caerau and was a member of Penuel Calvinistic Methodist Church, Caerau. He is buried in Salonika (Lembet Road) Military Cemetery.

During September Private Haydn Phillips of the 11th Welsh wrote home to the editor of the *Aberdare Leader*:

> You are probably aware that we have started an offensive out here, and I may say that our bombardment of the various Bulgarian positions has been terrific, and the result is we have captured well-fortified hills and war materials, and also taken a number of prisoners who do not appear to be sorry at being taken captives by the British. The Russians, Serbians, Italians, French and British are fighting side by side, and the feeling shown towards each other out here is excellent. The weather is very warm here just now; almost every day it is over 100 degrees in the shade. Flies are a terrible nuisance here and so are mosquitoes; during the day especially one cannot rest unless covered with a mosquito net. We now wear helmets and shorts, which are much cooler than caps and trousers. A week yesterday a Bulgarian airman flew over our camp, and tried to drop bombs on us, but they fell just outside, and no one was injured. That is the second time they have tried to drop bombs on us, only last time a number of aeroplanes came over and it was a little more exciting. Quite a number of our fellows are down with fever, but I am pleased to say that I have enjoyed splendid health ever since I have been out here.

On 9 September a combined patrol led by two officers of the 7th SWB and twelve men of the 11th RWF went out during the night to scout Macukovo. More patrols went out on the following nights and a good picture was built up of the Bulgarian defences. This work was carried out in preparation for a planned assault against the Piton des Mitrailleuses, a salient north-east of Macukovo, on the night of 13/14 September. This would be the first attack by the 22nd Division and the first attack for the 11th RWF, who were to attack with 65 Brigade. Major General Gordon sent the Royal Welsh the following letter:

> You will be called upon to perform a most important operation to-morrow evening. You will be sure to meet the enemy (there are Germans opposed to us).

I trust that you will show that you can deal with Germans in the same effective manner as Welshmen have been doing in France ever since August 1914.

You must keep your presence of mind when the fight is warm. Do not fire wildly – aim low and fire slow. It rejoices the enemy to hear rifle ammunition being blazed off into the darkness high above his head. Look out for the enemy's counterattacks – they will certainly be delivered against your battalion. You are properly placed to repel them. Watch your flanks – keep constant touch. If rifle fire and bombing do not stop the enemy, a bayonet charge will certainly do so. Our enemy has courage of a brutal sort, but experience proves that they shrink from facing a British soldier who is prepared to use his bayonet with effect. From my heart I wish the Royal Welch Fusiliers Godspeed in their important work, upon the success of which much depends.

Finally, as a commander and a friend of all ranks, I urge upon each and all the pressing necessity to bear in mind the stern nature of the duty you are about to undertake.

I am well aware that among my battalions there are men of various Churches and forms of religious beliefs, but two years of unceasing war have to a great extent blotted out points where men differ as to religion, and the vital points common to all religions stand out as alone of eternal importance: the existence of God who loves all men; His Son and Saviour who died for us.

Let us all pray that our sins may be forgiven and commit our cause into God's hands. Then we may safely go to battle hopeful of victory.

God bless you all.

From your General and comrade,

Frederick Gordon

At 7.30 pm on 13 September the assaulting troops advanced through gaps in their wire. The 11th RWF advanced on the left flank, following a scouting party led by Captain Spooner. They reported Macukovo and Piton des Quatre Arbres clear of the enemy, so B Company took up a position in Bangor Ravine and Macukovo Ravine; D Company in the north-west of the village about Piton de l'Église; A Company continued the flank line to the River Vardar; C Company and Battalion HQ took up positions in a ravine about 400 metres south-west of Piton de l'église. All companies were in position by 9.30 pm, and D and A commenced entrenching and wiring while C carried up the materials for them.

The assaulting groups reached their assembly areas to the east of the village by 10 pm and sent patrols to examine the enemy's wire. The 9th East Lancs were the first to make contact with the enemy and the resulting fire-fight alerted the Germans, who turned a searchlight on to the river.

The returning scouts reported that the trenches had been manned in strength, but General Gordon approved the attack and at 2.10 am the assault began. The Dorsale and Piton des Mitrailleuses positions were captured by the troops of 65 Brigade, while the 11th RWF moved into Cardiff Ravine before attacking the German positions. Many

Germans attempted to flee into their deep dugouts, but were either captured or bombed out and the men began consolidating their gains under heavy shellfire. The Germans then counter-attacked behind their barrage and a fierce battle raged throughout much of the early morning. The Piton des Mitrailleuses position was lost and regained, but Bulgarian infantry had now arrived to reinforce the Germans and overwhelming numbers forced the British to withdraw.

Private Philip Vincent Cooper (14303), 11th Welsh, son of John and Jane Cooper of 78 De Burgh Street, Cardiff. He died of wounds on 14 September 1916 and is buried in Karasouli Military Cemetery.

The 11th RWF had suffered just one man killed – Private Richard Phillips (14312) of Pontypridd – but Captain Ronald Alan Spooner and three other ranks (all, oddly, from St Helens) died of wounds; Lieutenant W.S.B. Walker and twenty other ranks were wounded.

The 11th Welsh sent out a covering party to assist the stretcher-bearers during the withdrawal and lost eight men killed, all from Cardiff, and nine wounded, one of whom died several days later. In this action Private John Arthur Pearce (15441) became the first man in the battalion to be awarded the MM for his gallant work in rescuing the wounded.

Although a failure, much valuable intelligence had been gathered from the attack, so Major General Gordon decided to make another smaller-scale raid on the Dorsale positions. The 11th Welsh was chosen for the task. On the night of 22 October the raiders, in four parties, passed Macukovo and made their way by Bangor Ravine to their assembly positions. The German wire had been cut by shellfire, so the raiding party threaded its way through before deploying to assault its targets. The left flank, under Major Jones, occupied Cardiff Ravine and drove off a hostile patrol with the loss of three of his men. The right flank, under Captain Stewart, established itself on Double Hill, Petit Piton and Chapeau de Gendarme. Both were supported by the 67th Machine-Gun Company and a party of men of 127th Field Company, Royal Engineers, tasked with destroying machine-gun emplacements and dugouts.

The assault was supported by an artillery barrage, which brought down a retaliatory German barrage down on the British lines. Captain Evan Ivor Glasbrook Richards, the adjutant, wrote:

Undaunted, the four raiding parties under Captains Eynon and Morgan, Lieutenant Phillips and 2nd-Lieutenant Turner dashed through the gap and hurled themselves on the garrison. A Homeric struggle ensued, with our men victorious. The dugouts were bombed, 10 Germans (59th Regiment) being killed in one, and the only machine gun emplacement left standing was wrecked by the Royal Engineers attached to the party. A counter-attack was beaten off by bomb and bayonet. It was now 2 am and our guns were nearly out of ammunition. Colonel Wingate asked for five more minutes. Four minutes had elapsed when a runner came in to say that the raid was successful and the raiders leaving the trenches. It was a near thing. Many of the batteries were down to their last shell. Triumphantly, the raiders returned with 18 prisoners. 34 enemy dead had been counted in the Dorsale.

Casualties had been relatively light: Lieutenant Edgar Harold Holmes Turner and two men had been killed; Lieutenant F.C. Phillips and nineteen men were wounded.

During the withdrawal Private Hubert William 'Stokey' Lewis (16224) of Milford Haven became the fourteenth Welshman to win the Victoria Cross during the Great War. He had been badly wounded by a bomb in the raid and, while withdrawing, despite his injuries, he went back into the danger zone to rescue a wounded man, Lieutenant Turner:

> For most conspicuous bravery and devotion to duty during a raid. On reaching the enemy trenches Private Lewis was twice wounded, but refused to be attended to, and showed great gallantry in searching enemy dug-outs. He was again wounded and again refused attendance. At this point three of the enemy were observed to be approaching, and Private Lewis immediately attacked them single-handed, capturing all. Subsequently, during the retirement, he went to the assistance of a wounded man, and under heavy shell and rifle fire brought him to our lines, on reaching which he collapsed. Private Lewis showed throughout a brilliant example of courage, endurance and devotion to duty. (*London Gazette*, 15 December 1916. His medals form part of the Lord Ashcroft VC Collection.)

Private Hubert William 'Stokey' Lewis (16224), 11th Welsh, of Milford Haven.

The conditions seem to be aptly summed up in a short poem sent home by Private H.J. Evans of 20 Cadwaladr Street, Mountain Ash, who was serving with the 1st Welsh:

> Yes, we have our issue of lime juice,
> And we get our Bully Beef,
> And ferro-concrete Biscuits
> That smash up all our teeth.
>
> We get no eggs for breakfast,
> They send us only shells,
> We dive into our dug-outs
> And get laughed at by our pals.

Just a tiny bit of bacon –
Well, for sport, we call it ham;
Four fighting British Tommies
To a one pound tin of jam.

Sometimes we get some rooty,
You civilians call it bread,
It ain't as light as feathers
And it ain't exactly lead.

But we get it down us somehow,
And we never send it back,
Though it's smothered up with bits of lint
That gets rubbed off the sack.

The dust blows in our Dixies,
There's dirt upon our kit,
So can you really wonder
That a soldier's full of grit.

But we are not going to grumble
Because we are feeling well and fit,
And we have one great consolation
That we are doing our little bit.

With winter setting in, the remainder of 1916 was monotonous and uneventful apart from the occasional trench raid. The weakened battalions were hard pressed just to find enough men to man the trenches.

Chapter 11

Egypt

Nothing of great note had happened in Egypt since the defeat of the Senussi, but on 17 July 1916 it was noted by the allies that enemy aircraft were very active. A patrol by the RFC two days later discovered large numbers of Turkish troops at two oases, so 158 Brigade of the 53rd (Welsh) Division was ordered to Romani, a town that lies near Qatiya and the coast and was garrisoned by the 52nd (Lowland) Division. Romani marked the furthest point of the newly built desert railroad and was an important point for the British.

Sir Archibald Murray was now prepared for a Turkish attack, anticipating that it would be launched against the right of the Romani position. To the rear was the New Zealand Mounted Rifle Brigade at Dueidar and Hill 70, and at Hill 40 the 1st Dismounted Yeomanry Brigade, which had many Welshmen from the Welsh Yeomanry in its ranks.

No. 158 Brigade (5th, 6th and 7th RWF) arrived at Romani on 2 July. The 5th RWF was temporarily attached to 156 Brigade, 52nd Division, and the remainder of the brigade was responsible for the centre section of the Romani line.

The Romani railhead was an important oasis about 18 miles from Kantara and its defences ran from the coast, curling round the oasis of Romani. No. 158 Brigade was responsible for five posts in the line and the Herefords were detailed to hold them. To the right was 156 Brigade, to which the 5th RWF was attached and held in reserve. Beyond the line was a cavalry screen that had been established by the 1st Light Horse Brigade of the Anzac Mounted Division.

During the night of 3/4 August 1916 the advancing force, including both German and Turkish troops, launched an attack from Qatiya on Romani. The 1st Light Horse Brigade soon engaged them but was slowly forced to retire. At daybreak their line was reinforced by the 2nd Light Horse Brigade and by mid-morning the 5th Mounted Brigade, which included a number of Welsh Yeomanry members, and the New Zealand Mounted Rifles Brigade joined the battle.

The attackers had by now come within range of the 52nd (Lowland) Division defending Romani and the railway but with a co-ordinated effort the German and Turkish advance was checked. The allies attacked on the following morning and over the coming days the enemy was pushed back to their starting-point at Qatiya, pursued by the Anzac Mounted Division and the British Yeomanry. The pursuit ended on 12 August, when the German and Turkish forces abandoned their base at Bir el Abd and retreated back to El Arish.

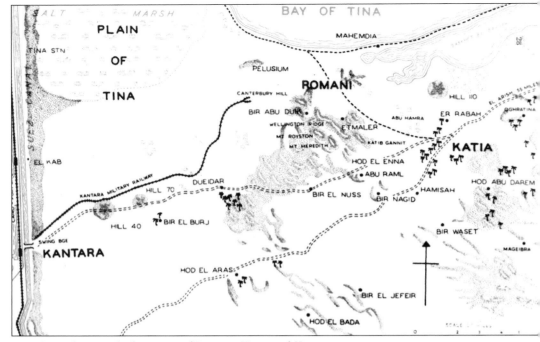

Map showing the locations of Romani, Katia and Kantara.

The Battle of Romani marked the last Turkish attempt to attack the Suez Canal defences and for the remainder of 1916 the allies began building up strength to go on the offensive in 1917. Among the 5th RWF, the only complete Welsh unit in action during the day, only one man died: Private Thomas Jones (3273), the son of Peter Jones of 7 New Street, Abergele. Two more men of the battalion died on the following day of wounds suffered during the battle: Private Jonathan Roberts (3646), the son of Jonathan and Mary Roberts of 4 Fern Bank, Northop Hall; and Private James Bewley (3660), the son of Edward and Margaret H. Bewley of Ash View, Alltami, Mold.

Private James Bewley (3660), 5th RWF, the son of Edward and Margaret H. Bewley of Ash View, Alltami, Mold

On 14 August 158 Brigade returned to Ferdan, on the Suez Canal, to rejoin the 53rd Division, which had its HQ at Ismailia.

According to all the contemporary reports on this time, it was a pleasant spell for the troops in Egypt. Men would sit on the edge of the canal and watch large steamers cautiously make their way up and down with lights on, some with orchestras playing and ladies singing. All the men were able to bathe daily and the weather was cooler.

The only other operation undertaken by any of the Welsh troops in Egypt during the year was in October, when Major General Dallas was ordered to attack Maghara. He formed a column of men of riding ability, which was to include a machine gun and Lewis-gun detachment from 160 Brigade. The Turks were encountered in the early morning of 15 October but, owing to a dense fog, did not engage them.

Christmas Day was celebrated at Romani by 158 and 159 brigades. Extra food and some beer had been brought up from Port Said but 160 Brigade, which was at Bir el Abd, had a miserable Christmas that was followed by several days of rain. Divisional HQ spent Christmas at Mahemdia, by the sea.

The division reorganized in December. The 2nd Welsh Brigade RFA, which had been numbered 266th, was renumbered the 267th and reorganized into a two-battery brigade, with six 18-pounders to each battery. The 4th Welsh Brigade RFA had been numbered 268th, was now renumbered 266th and given two batteries of six 18-pounders and one of four 4.5-inch howitzers. The 1st Cheshire Brigade RFA had been numbered 267th and was now renumbered 265th, with two 18-pounder batteries and one howitzer battery. The 1st Welsh (Howitzer) Brigade disappeared, with one battery going to the 265th and one to the 266th.

Changes were also made at higher levels. Sir Archibald Murray moved his general headquarters from Ismailia to Cairo, and Lieutenant General Sir Charles Dobell assumed command of the Eastern Force at Ismailia. Lieutenant General Sir Philip Chetwode arrived at the end of December to command the Desert Column, under Sir Charles Dobell.

On 20 January 1917 the 53rd (Welsh) Division marched from the canal in two columns, and on the last day of the month HQ arrived at El Arish. Meanwhile, 160 Brigade had rejoined on the line of march and was the first to arrive at El Arish, where the division took over a defensive line. On 28 February mounted troops entered Khan Yunus. The main British force was now on the frontier of Syria, while the yeomanry were being formed into a new formation, the 74th (Yeomanry) Division under the command of Major General Eric Girdwood, losing their identities as yeomanry regiments.

Over the New Year the three Dismounted Yeomanry brigades began to move east. The 2nd Dismounted Brigade reached El Arish by 6 March. The Lovat Scouts dropped out of the brigade in August 1916 and were replaced by the Ayr and Lanark Yeomanry in January 1917. The brigade was renamed 229 Brigade, commanded by Brigadier General R. Hoare DSO, and comprised the following:

16th Devonshires (Royal West Devon and Royal North Devon Yeomanry)
12th Somerset Light Infantry (West Somerset Yeomanry)
14th Black Watch (Fife and Forfar Yeomanry)
12th Royal Scots Fusiliers (Ayr and Lanark Yeomanry)
4th MG Company and 229th Light Trench Mortar Battery

The 3rd Dismounted Brigade went to Sidi Bishr on 2 April and to Deir al-Balah on the 9th. It was renamed 230 Brigade, commanded by Brigadier General A.J. McNeil DSO, and comprised the following:

10th Buffs (Royal East Kent and West Kent Yeomanry)
16th Royal Sussex (Sussex Yeomanry)
15th Suffolks (Suffolk Yeomanry)
12th Norfolks (Norfolk Yeomanry)
209th MG Company and 230th Light Trench Mortar Battery

The 4th Dismounted Brigade reached Khan Yunus on 10 April and became 231 Brigade, commanded by Brigadier General E.A. Herbert, and comprised the following:

10th KSLI (Shropshire and Cheshire Yeomanry)
24th RWF (Denbighshire Yeomanry)
25th RWF (Montgomeryshire and Welsh Horse Yeomanry)
24th Welsh (Pembroke and Glamorgan Yeomanry)
210th MG Company and 231st Light Trench Mortar Battery

The Divisional Artillery, which was the last formation to form, came under the command of Brigadier General L.J. Hext CMG, and comprised the following:

117th Brigade RFA (A, B, 366th and D Batteries)
44th Brigade RFA (340th, 382nd, 425th and D Batteries)
268th Brigade RFA
X74 and Y74 Medium Trench Mortar Batteries
74th Ammunition Column

The Divisional Engineers, commanded by Lieutenant Colonel R.P.T. Hawksley CMG DSO, comprised the following:

No. 5 (Royal Monmouth) Field Company
No. 5 (Royal Anglesey) Field Company
439th (Cheshire) Field Company
74th Divisional Signal Company

There were also additional units: the 447th, 448th, 449th and 450th companies RASC (Royal Army Service Corps) under Lieutenant Colonel J.G. Needham; the 261st MG Company; the 74th Employment Company; the 69th Mobile Veterinary Section; and A Squadron, 2nd County of London (Westminster Dragoons) Yeomanry, which later moved to Corps Cavalry.

This change from yeomen to infantry was a huge step that was received with good humour and inspired the divisional badge of the broken spur.

Sir Archibald Murray was now ready for the offensive into Syria and Palestine and had at his command the 52nd, 53rd, 54th and 74th Infantry divisions, the New Zealand and Australian Mounted Division, the Imperial Mounted Division and the Imperial Camel Corps on the Syrian Front. He organized this force into the Desert Column under Sir Philip Chetwode and the Eastern Force under Sir Charles Dobell.

Major General Girdwood and his staff arrived at El Arish on 4 March and marched his newly-formed division to Deir al-Balah, where his units took over sections of frontline trenches. There were now two divisions with a strong Welsh contingent in Egypt and the scene was set for the First Battle of Gaza.

Chapter 12

1917
The War Grinds Onwards

While 1916 had been a year of great losses for the allies, 1917 would be a year that continued to add numerous Welsh names to the casualty lists; several large-scale offensives launched: three in France at Arras, Ypres and Cambrai; the MEF would invade Syria, Gaza and Palestine; and the allies would go on the offensive in Salonika and Mesopotamia. All these campaigns would heavily involve Welsh units.

As the New Year dawned, there were thirty-five Welsh infantry battalions in action in France – 13 RWF, 7 SWB, 11 Welsh Regiment, 2 Monmouth Regiment and the Welsh Guards – as well as companies of the Royal Monmouthshire Royal Engineers, the Royal Anglesey Royal Engineers and companies of the Glamorgan Fortress Company, Royal Engineers and Royal Artillery, plus the associated Welsh support units in the 38th (Welsh) Division.

In Egypt were the Denbigh Yeomanry, Pembroke Yeomanry, Montgomeryshire Yeomanry, Glamorgan Yeomanry and the Welsh Horse Yeomanry; three battalions of the RWF (soon to be five, with the merging of the Montgomery and Welsh Horse Yeomanry and the reforming of the Denbigh Yeomanry into an RWF battalion); and two battalions of the Welsh Regiment (soon to be three, with the merging of the Glamorgan and Pembroke Yeomanry regiments). There were also garrison battalions of the RWF.

In Salonika these were one battalion of the RWF, two battalions of the SWB and three of the Welsh Regiment; while in Mesopotamia these were one battalion of the SWB and another of the Welsh Regiment.

While reorganization of the troops in Egypt would be of prime concern during the early weeks of 1917, the troops in France would have more pressing issues at hand.

On 8 January Brigadier General Robert Henry William Dunn, formerly of the RWF and former CO of the 2nd Brigade of the Welsh Army Corps, died at St Thomas' House, London. Dunn lived at Althrey, Bangor Isycoed and was the son of Major General

Brigadier General Robert Henry William Dunn, formerly of the RWF.

William Dunn RA. He joined the army in November 1876 and by 1902 had risen to lieutenant colonel after having seen active service in the Burmese expedition of 1885 to 1886. He became closely associated with the Volunteer and Territorial movements in North Wales after retiring from the regular army and on the outbreak of the war raised the North Wales Pals Battalion, RWF. In October 1914 he was promoted to command the 2nd Brigade of the Welsh Division. He is buried in Wrexham Cemetery.

At the Second Chantilly Conference held between 15 and 16 November 1916, the allies had decided that offensives should be launched on all fronts simultaneously in 1917 to prevent the enemy moving his forces from one theatre to another.

In December 1916 General Robert Nivelle, who had gained a great reputation during the defence of Verdun, succeeded Marshal Joseph Joffre as commander-in-chief of the French army and began planning for a French offensive in 1917 which, carried out in conjunction with a British offensive, would win the war for the allies. As part of this plan, Sir Douglas Haig agreed to take over 20 more miles of front from the French and the new British line during the winter ran down to Le Quesnoy, 26 miles south-west of Péronne.

Of all the Welsh units in France at the time, the 1st RWF was the first to suffer a large number of casualties. The battalion had wintered at Bertrancourt and spent the first week of the New Year supplying working parties in an attempt to keep the sodden trenches clear. On 5 January the battalion went into the line in the Ancre Valley, relieving the 2nd Gordons, and was warned to be ready for an assault on Muck Trench and Leave Avenue. The attack did not take place but the Fusiliers had a torrid few days, suffering from artillery bombardments and a slow stream of casualties. Further orders were received on 9 January for an assault on Leave Avenue and the Triangle, which was to be led by the 2nd Border Regiment.

The attack began at 2.30 am on 10 January; the Borderers had gained their objectives by about 5.30 am and began consolidating. At 1.25 pm the 1st RWF was ordered to relieve the 2nd Border Regiment and by dusk had completed the relief. Two men were killed and three died of wounds, while six more men were wounded during the day. On the following morning the battalion was ordered to send bombing parties forward to attack Munich Trench and heavy fighting continued throughout the day; the battalion suffered a further seven men killed, six wounded and one missing.

There were no major operations throughout the month but every Welsh unit was suffering a constant stream of so-called trench wastage, regular casualties occurring through their routine time in the trenches. The main operations during the month would occur overseas, but at sea another maritime disaster would create headlines in the newspapers.

Able Seaman John James, a Royal Naval Reservist from Cardigan, lost during the sinking of the HMS Laurentic *on 21 January 1917.*

On 21 January the converted White Star liner SS *Laurentic* was steaming off Lough Swilly, to the north of Ireland, when she struck two German-laid mines and sank with the loss of 354 passengers and crew. *Laurentic* had been one of White Star's most luxurious and fastest liners prior to the construction of the *Olympic*-class liners and served on the Liverpool to Canada route. She was in Canada when war was declared so had been requisitioned for use as a Canadian troop carrier. Among her crew were thirty-two Welshmen, only four of whom have known graves – Petty Officer Thomas James Collacott (142707) of Tenby, Engineer Lieutenant George Henry Daymond of Oswestry, painter Frederick Edwards and plumber Joseph Roberts, Mercantile Marine Reserve – whose bodies were recovered from the sea and buried in Upper Fahan (St Mura's) Church of Ireland Churchyard, County Donegal. *Laurentic* carried a cargo of 43 tons of gold ingots in her hold. Although a designated war grave, most of the ingots were salvaged in the years after the war by divers of the Royal Navy, the work beginning in 1919.

Captain Harry Love Jarman, 7th SWB. (Queen's University Archives, Canada)

In Salonika the 7th SWB lost two officers killed on 15 January when a stray shell crashed outside their officers' mess. Major John Bedward Royle, the son of Thomas Richard Popplewell Royle and Emma Royle of Hough Green House, Chester and the husband of Mary L. Royle of 2 Castle Hill Avenue, Folkestone was 43 years old. Captain Harry Love Jarman, the son of George and Betsy Jarman of Bancroft, Ontario was 24 years old. Jarman was a Canadian doctor who had volunteered to serve with the RAMC and was attached to the 7th SWB when he was killed. Both men are buried in Karasouli Military Cemetery.

Royle's son, Major John Popplewell Royle, served with 1 Wing, Glider Pilot Regiment and commanded Force John in the Normandy landings. He was killed at Arnhem on 20 September 1944.

Major John Bedward Royle, 7th SWB.

Chapter 13

Mesopotamia:
The Second Offensive

In Mesopotamia, following the embarrassment caused by the surrender of Major General Townshend in Kut, Lieutenant General Gorringe was sacked as commander of the Tigris Corps and replaced by Lieutenant General Sir Frederick Stanley Maude, later made commander of all allied forces in Mesopotamia in late July 1916, replacing Sir Percy Lake. Maude was ordered to capture Kut and make further advances in Mesopotamia, so over the winter his forces had begun marching to the River Hai along the right bank of the Tigris with the intention of cutting the enemy's lines of communication and securing the line along the Hai to prevent any Turkish assaults.

General Maude's preparations were complete by 13 December. His I Corps faced the enemy at a distance of 100 metres from the Sannaiyat defences on the left bank of the Tigris, and the line ran along the right bank of the river as far as Sinn Banks, where the Turks held the opposite side. The 14th Division continued the line to Maqasis, after

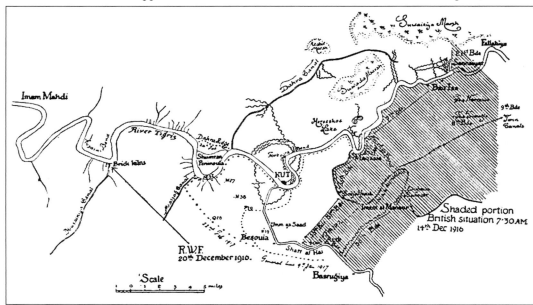

The situation facing the British in Mesopotamia, December 1916.

204

which it followed the Dujaila Depression to Imam and then to the Dujaila Redoubt. The 13th (Western) Division was concentrated at Imam and the cavalry south of Siam Abtar. Maude had superiority of numbers, so had planned to hold the Turks to their positions on the left bank of the Tigris by bombardments and threats of attack while he gradually encircled them on the right bank, round Kut, using the cavalry and III Corps.

Maude's plan started shortly after midnight on the night of 13/14 December when the cavalry surprised and drove back patrols of Turks and Arabs and crossed the River Hai at Basrugiya, about 3 miles south of Atab, at 6 am. The 13th Division sent 40 Brigade to Atab alongside the cavalry, crossing bridges erected by the 8th Welsh, who had also built a semicircle of twelve redoubts about 1 mile south of the Hai, which were occupied by 40 Brigade. Meanwhile 36 Brigade, 14th Division had followed 40 Brigade and occupied an old Turkish trench line, which ran from Dujaila Redoubt to the Hai at a point 2 miles south of Atab. III Corps was now covered from attack from the south by 36 and 40 brigades and from the west by the cavalry and the River Hai.

By the end of the year the British were well placed to continue the offensive in Mesopotamia. During the first week of January I Corps had sapped forward to within about 200 metres of the enemy and on 7 January the British and Indian brigades attacked, driving the Turks back over the river. The 8th RWF had been in camp for the first week of January and on 9 January moved into reserve to the 3rd Indian Division. The attack that day was only partially successful, the Turks counter-attacking strongly, and the battalion was held at the Pentagon and remained there until the 11th when it returned to Besouia.

The next phase involved the capture of the Hai Triangle. More ground on the west of the Hai had gradually been made good and 35 Brigade, 14th Division was now on the left of 39 Brigade, opposite the Hai defences. The 13th Division had been sapping forward since 11 January and the 8th Welsh had been actively employed in this, losing Second Lieutenant Harold Thomas John of 29 High Street, Gelligaer and eight men killed plus Second Lieutenant Kinley and twenty-four men wounded. The front line was now within assaulting distance of the apex of the Hai Triangle.

Plans to continue the offensive were then made. No. 40 Brigade took over the line opposite the apex of the Hai Salient on 12 January in trenches dug by the 4th SWB and found that no man's land was very wide, so work began to reduce the distance by sapping forward. This work meant that the original date of 20 January for the next offensive was postponed by five days.

On 15 January the 4th SWB lost an officer – Major Joseph Fairweather – and four men killed while digging trenches. Three of the four men were North Walians, showing that the recruitment area from which men had enlisted now meant nothing regarding the regiment to which they would be posted as they should have been serving with the RWF. (Major Fairweather's brother, Lieutenant Colonel James Macintyre Fairweather, was killed in action on 18 February 1917 at Rupira, in the Livingstone Range, Tanzania. Major Fairweather is buried in Amara War Cemetery.)

Digging continued every night and all the units involved suffered casualties from snipers, but by 24 January the sappers had moved forward by almost 600 metres.

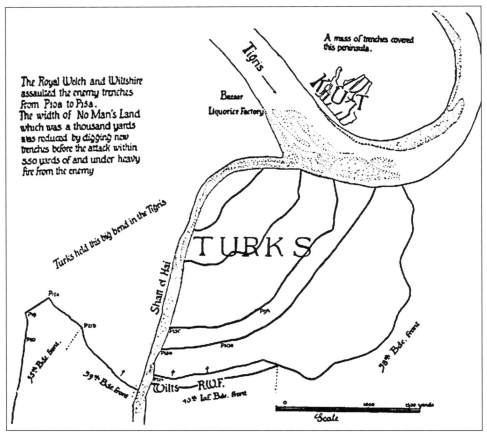

The Royal Welch and Wiltshire assaulted the enemy trenches from Pioa to Pisa.
The width of No Man's Land which was a thousand yards was reduced by digging new trenches before the attack within 550 yards of and under heavy fire from the enemy

A mass of trenches covered this peninsula.

Bazaar
Liquorice Factory

Turks held this big bend in the Tigris

Shatt el Hai

T U R K S

The capture of the Hai Triangle, January 1917.

At 9.30 am on 25 January the artillery barrage rained down on the Turkish second line and five minutes later moved on to their front line for ten minutes. By the time the guns stopped the assaulting troops were about 40 metres away from the Turkish trenches and after a gallant charge across no man's land entered the enemy trenches. Heavy fighting continued throughout the day and by nightfall the enemy's second line, at a width of about 1,000 metres, had been taken.

The heaviest casualties suffered by the Welsh units involved were among the 8th RWF, who lost two officers – Second Lieutenants Alfred William Hubbard and Robert Girard Sweetland (a Canadian) – and twenty-seven men killed; five men died of wounds on the following day and Lieutenant John Dyche died of wounds two days later. The 4th SWB had lost an officer – Second Lieutenant Roger Smith – and seven men killed, and three men killed the following day; while the 8th Welsh, who had been used as infantry during the action, lost Lieutenant Harold Frank Baggs and eight other ranks killed and twenty-seven other ranks wounded. Burial parties from 40 Brigade buried 380 Turks and took 108 prisoners.

The fighting of 25 January saw an action that resulted in the award of the Victoria Cross to a man who had been an inspector of taxes at Carmarthen prior to the war. Robert Edwin Phillips was born at West Bromwich on 11 April 1895. He had worked at Carmarthen Tax Office prior to the war, before enlisting in the Civil Service Rifles. Robert was initially commissioned in the 13th Battalion, Royal Warwickshire Regiment, before being posted to their 9th Battalion, which was in Mesopotamia. His Victoria Cross was awarded for gallantry near Kut, Mesopotamia:

Lieutenant Robert Edwin Phillips, VC, 9th Royal Warwicks, a former inspector of taxes at Carmarthen.

For most conspicuous bravery and devotion to duty. After his Commanding Officer had been mortally wounded in leading a counter-attack, Lt. Phillips went out under the most intense fire to his assistance, and eventually, with the help of a comrade, succeeded in bringing him back to our lines. Lt. Phillips had in the first instance tried to get a telephone wire across the open following the battalion in their counter-attack. This was impossible when the Signallers were killed. His Commanding Officer lay wounded in the open, and as the counter-attack had succeeded, he turned all his energies on getting him in. He showed sustained courage in its very highest form, and throughout he had but little chance of ever getting back alive. (*London Gazette*, 8 June 1917.)

Phillips never returned to work at Carmarthen and died at St Veep, Cornwall on 23 September 1968. His Victoria Cross is displayed at the Royal Regiment of Fusiliers Museum (Royal Warwickshire), Warwick.

The advance continued over the coming days. The 14th Division took to the offensive on the west of the Hai and after several days of hard fighting, in conjunction with the 13th Division, had captured the eastern side of the Hai Triangle by 3 February, a day that saw the 8th RWF suffer the tragic loss of its CO, Lieutenant Colonel Archibald Hay, Captain Philip Morgan Dunn and six men killed when the battalion advanced through the cover of darkness and as dawn broke had found itself too close to the enemy. Hay and Dunn were killed almost immediately as the Turks opened fire on the Fusiliers. Major Farrar had moved forward to take command of the battalion but was badly wounded later in the afternoon.

The bodies of Hay, Dunn and three men were brought back after dark and were buried in Bassonia Cemetery. Hay and Dunn now lie in Amara War Cemetery, where they were reinterred

Lieutenant Colonel Archibald Hay, 8th RWF. The son of Lieutenant General Sir Robert John Hay KCB and Lady Hay, he was killed at Dahra Bend on 3 February 1917, aged 44.

207

after the war. The 8th RWF then moved back to divisional reserve. Brigadier General A.C. Lewin wrote of Hay:

> The Brigadier-General Commanding desires to express his deep sorrow, which he knows is shared by every officer, N.C.O., and man of the brigade, on the death of the late Lieutenant-Colonel Hay, commanding the Royal Welch Fusiliers, who has fallen at the head of the battalion, which he raised at the outbreak of hostilities, trained, and subsequently so ably commanded during two years of active service, first in the Dardanelles, and later in Mesopotamia.

The Turks had by now fallen back on the liquorice factory and the line of trenches that stretched from there to the Dahra Bend. Fighting from 8 to 10 February, they lost the factory and now held only the Dahra Bend trenches.

On 13 February the 4th SWB lost two more officers killed: Lieutenant Frank Harrington Best and Second Lieutenant Frew Ferguson Evans.

On 15 February Welshmen of 40 Brigade, 8th RWF and 4th SWB, broke the centre of the enemy position and were followed up by troops of the 13th and 14th divisions, who completed the rout. More than 2,000 Turkish prisoners were taken and they were now forced back, taking up a position on the Dahra Ridge across the top of the Shumran Bend. The 8th RWF lost one

Lieutenant Percy Godfrey Herington, 8th RWF.

officer – Second Lieutenant Percy Godfrey Herington – and fifteen men killed during the action, eight dying of wounds on the following day, while the 4th SWB lost one officer – Second Lieutenant Glyn Lloyd Davies – and twenty-eight men killed during the action and four dying of wounds the following day.

Two days later Lieutenant General Cobbe VC launched an attack on the Sannaiyat positions, but the Turks held out until nightfall on 23 February following a surprise river crossing by the Norfolks and Ghurkhas that forced the Turks to withdraw again. By 25 February they were in full retreat, pursued by the 13th and 14th divisions and the cavalry and halted at Azizaya, midway between Kut and Baghdad, while the British supply lines were adjusted.

The advance began again on 5 March, pushing the Turks back from their defensive position at Ctesiphon to the line of the Diyala River, 8 miles south of Baghdad, which the Turks held in strength.

During the night of 7/8 March an attempt to cross at Diyala village was made by 38 Brigade, with the 8th Welsh and two field companies of Royal Engineers covered by artillery fire, but their pontoons were riddled by defensive fire, causing sixty-four casualties. General Maude then ordered the Cavalry Division to cross to the right bank and move straight on Baghdad, so a bridge was constructed at Bawi, 8 miles below Diyala and by nightfall on 8 March the cavalry had crossed. In the meantime 35 Brigade had advanced level with the Diyala and the 13th Division was ready to cross that river. On the following night the 6th Loyal North Lancs with two companies from the 8th Welsh and 72nd Company, Royal Engineers crossed the Diyala under murderous fire. A number of men of the Loyals got across and held on to their gains despite several counter-attacks, gaining the VC for Captain Oswald Austin Reid, a South African:

For most conspicuous bravery in the face of desperate circumstances. By his dauntless courage and gallant leadership he was able to consolidate a small post with the advanced troops, on the opposite side of a river to the main body, after his line of communications had been cut by the sinking of the pontoons. He maintained this position for thirty hours against constant attacks by bombs, machine gun and shell fire, with the full knowledge that repeated attempts at relief had failed, and that his ammunition was all but exhausted. It was greatly due to his tenacity that the passage of the river was effected on the following night. During the operations he was wounded. (*London Gazette*, 8 June 1917.)

For gallantry during these operations, Sergeant John Burnette Ainsworth (10526), 8th Welsh, of Cardiff received the MM, while the 8th Welsh lost one man killed and sixteen wounded during the river crossing.

More fighting on 9 March forced the Turks to withdraw from the left bank of the Tigris and during the night the 13th Division crossed the Diyala and advanced 4 miles to Qarara. By now the Turkish commander-in-chief, Haul Pasha, had decided that he could no longer defend Baghdad against the British so at dawn on 11 March he withdrew his troops, allowing General Maude to make a victorious entrance that day. The British began work on organizing defences around the city in case of a counter-attack and to organize it as a base for the capture of the rest of Mesopotamia.

Among the many letters sent home by the tired troops was one from Sergeant A.D. Price of Kenfig Hill:

Here I am, safe and sound; clean, healthy, but somewhat short of smokes. Yesterday we came into action in fine style in the open, and got peppered coming in, with their little 'pip-squeaks', but without a casualty. I have not been in the city yet, but we hear that the troops that marched through the town were loudly cheered and welcomed by the populace. I expect they have had enough of Turkish rule.

From here, all you can see of the city is the minarets and domes above the palm trees. Since my last letter, we have passed Ctesiphon with its fine old Roman arch that seems lost out here; have crossed the last Turkish line of defences, and are now in Baghdad. The river was the scene of a gallant stand by some of the Lancs. A small party of them crossed one night, and held on manfully against five counter-attacks, though their ammunition almost ran out, while we on the other side belched forth shrapnel on the enemy.

I had an egg yesterday – such a treat! Also some really nice dates. Tobacco is scarce, but I have been able to beg some every day so far. The people who come out to see us from the city are very liberal with their 'Salaam Aleukins'. We hear a few 'Good Mornings' and 'Good Nights'. No doubt, the Jews here will be busy teaching others what scraps of English they know.

When we squatted down before Kut on the 14th December, and slowly and methodically started to blow the Turk away, I never thought we would reach Baghdad. It seemed so remote, and even when we crossed the Tigris into Shumran and started pursuing the enemy, I was not very sanguine of reaching here, but we marched on, and marched on, and here we are. There was nothing really interesting to note during the march. One day was so much like another, unless it was our turn to be vanguard. Then we might come across the Turk. The only little thrill I can remember was when I first saw in the distance the Arch of Ctesiphon – Townsend's furthest point north.

Sapper W.B. Stephens of the 1/3rd Army Corps, RE Signals, wrote to his parents at Llangammarch Wells to inform them of his experiences, finishing off by explaining that he had been hospitalized after succumbing to malaria:

I was brought down to an Indian camp temporarily, where I was medically attended to by Captain Carey Evans I.M.S., F.R.C.S., whose engagement to Miss Olwen Lloyd George was recently announced. I was then removed to a British stationary hospital, where I am at present, swathed in bandages and a five weeks' beard on, 'some sight'. The treatment and accommodation is good, considering. It is not so hot during the day, and gets chilly at nights. We get the good news from the Western and other fronts daily by wireless. I met Fred Phillips, 'The Dot', he is quite well, also W. Ward of Talgarth.

Corporal W.E.A. Pugh of the RFC wrote a very long letter to his former headmaster at Presteigne County School in much more descriptive terms:

The land lying between the two rivers (Tigris and Euphrates) is, as you say, very fertile, but is only cultivated near to the river and that in some places. Great tracts of land in this area are lying waste only for the want of proper irrigation. Many years ago it was highly cultivated and the remains of enormous irrigation schemes are still to be seen in the presence of canals and barrages, but now with the exception of a few places, only land on the river banks are artificially irrigated, and these by very crude Arab water lifts, the water being lifted out of the river on skins (pulled by horses or bullocks) and distributed round the fields by little canals...

Of course, as you will know, Mesopotamia depends more upon her dates than almost anything else, and one sees date palms dotted all over the place, but coming up the Shatt al-Arab (the part where the two rivers run to the sea) there are tremendous date groves, in fact right from the sea to Qarmah, the banks are lined with date palms, after which one sees very few, in fact from Amarah to Kut, one hardly sees any date palms, nor sign of cultivation of any sort, and the Arab in this part lives in a very primitive fashion indeed, and is of a very bad character...

Here, right up to Bagdad, are grown dates, figs, oranges, mulberries, pomegranates, grapes, barley, wheat, opium, lettuce, cucumbers, peaches, apples and rice. I believe that much the same is grown on the Euphrates. (*Brecon & Radnor Express*, 23 August 1917.)

The campaign in Mesopotamia was far from over, but a very significant milestone had been reached. Meanwhile, another historic milestone was also reached in France during this time.

Chapter 14

The German Withdrawal to the Hindenburg Line

In France the German offensive at Verdun, coupled with the Somme offensive by the allies, had weakened the Germans in 1916. Paul von Hindenburg and Erich Ludendorff took control of the army when Erich von Falkenhayn was replaced in late August 1916 and had ordered the building of a new defensive line, east of the Somme battlefront from Arras to Laon, which became known as the Hindenburg Line (to the Germans the *Siegfriedstellung*). The Germans looked at their options but, deciding that they did not have enough manpower to launch an offensive, decided on a strategic withdrawal to the Hindenburg Line, which would shorten the front by over 25 miles and require fourteen fewer divisions to man it. They also decided on a scorched earth policy, to leave in their wake a desert that would afford no shelter or water to the British. This withdrawal would also affect any allied offensives planned as any spare manpower would be needed to rebuild roads, bridges and railways in the abandoned area. Crown Prince Rupprecht objected to this scorched earth policy and made his opinions very clear, even threatening resignation, but in the end, for sake of German unity, he was forced to follow Ludendorff's orders. The retirement to the Hindenburg Line was known as Operation ALBERICH.

The 2nd SWB had been in the front line at Morval and were relieved on 17 January, returning to Carnoy for a rest. The men were treated to a special anti-trench-foot bath, which had been recently put into place instead of the original remedy of whale oil, which was not to be used any more. On 22 January the Borderers went back into the line at Lesboeufs and found the time very hard going due to a heavy frost that had settled on this part of the line. The battalion moved through Guillemont on the night of 26/27 January and was ordered to prepare to take part in an assault on 27 January.

87 Brigade was selected to take part in a surprise attack on the second line of German trenches on a front of over 900 metres, bisected by the road running due south from Le Transloy to Combles. The artillery barrage commenced at 5.30 am on 27 January and the assaulting battalions moved forward, taking their objectives with scarcely any casualties. Six German officers and 395 men were captured, but the positions gained then became subject to an enemy counter-barrage. The 2nd SWB took over the Newfoundland Regiment's positions during the night and lost ten men killed and two officers wounded during the day's fighting. Another hard frost fell during the

night and on the following day the 2nd Monmouths moved up to begin consolidating the new trenches. The work was made all the harder due to the ground being frozen to 18in deep in places, but Lieutenant Colonel Bowen's pioneers carried out good work during the day, although twelve men were killed. The 2nd SWB lost another six men killed during the day.

One of the dead Monmouths was Sergeant Ralph Spencer Beddin (15668) of Abergavenny, who had been awarded the MM while serving with the 3rd Monmouths in 1916. Among the dead from the 2nd SWB was another MM winner, Private William Hopkin Davies (39678), the son of Thomas and Sarah Davies of 4 Colbourne Terrace, Swansea. He is buried in the AIF Burial Ground, Flers. Davies initially joined the Pembroke Yeomanry and had seen service in Dublin during the riots before being posted to France. He was a tin worker at the Cwmfelin Works prior to the war. His father was presented with his Military Medal by Lieutenant Colonel Symonds-Taylor during a ceremony in July that year.

Private Alfred Beynon (44156), 2nd SWB, of Llandebie. Beynon had served with the 9th Welsh and was wounded during their famous charge at Loos on 25 September. He was posted to the 2nd SWB after recovering from his wounds and was killed at Morval on 28 January 1917.

By now the 38th (Welsh) Division was settled into its period of routine trench warfare at Ypres. From 19 January the 19th Welsh worked on trench improvement along the canal bank. And on 28 January the men returned to their billets behind the front lines at Trois Tours. A German shell crashed into one of the huts, killing four men: Privates Alexander Butwell (32135) of Stepney, William Constable (32132) of Laugharne, Hayden Evans (2209) of Pontnewydd and William Henry George Springhall (32035) of Stratford, Essex. All four are buried together in Ferme-Olivier Cemetery.

William Constable was the son of Philip and Jane Constable of Horsepool Road, Laugharne. He worked in London prior to the war and enlisted in Finsbury into the RWF. He was among a number of men transferred to the 19th Welsh and had spent some time attached to 255 Tunnelling Company, Royal Engineers.

Back on the Somme the 2nd SWB was still in the firing line. The battalion moved back into the line for a three day tour in the Guillemont trenches on 3 February. On the following day the battalion came under heavy artillery fire and was isolated for a while, during which time enemy snipers caused a number of casualties: Second Lieutenant Walter Jones Sandys-Thomas and seven men were killed, and Captain Mundy was wounded.

Private William Constable (32132), 19th Welsh, shown here in his Boy Scout uniform in Laugharne prior to the war.

Sandys-Thomas was the son of Walter and Violet Sandys-Thomas of Llanthomas, Hay. He is buried in AIF Burial Ground, Flers. His younger brother, Lieutenant Charles Ivor Sandys-Thomas of the RFC, had been reported killed on 20 July 1916, although he had in fact been taken prisoner and survived the war.

Corporal Owen Morgan (10823), 2nd SWB, of Aberystwyth, killed at Guillemont on 4 February 1917.

Second Lieutenant Walter Jones Sandys-Thomas, 2nd SWB.

The German scorched earth operation began on 9 February 1917. Railways and roads were dug up, trees were felled, water wells were polluted, towns and villages were destroyed and mines and booby-traps were planted. The order to begin the withdrawal was issued by Ludendorff on 16 March. Construction of the Hindenburg Line was incomplete, so the Germans had to use delaying tactics to allow them time to finish off the work, although their scorched earth policy caused them tremendous embarrassment once the details of their destruction were used by the allied Press for propaganda purposes. Labour released from the building of the Hindenburg Line was then switched to work on the Hunding Stellung, which covered the Aisne front from La Fère to Rethel.

During February two former Welsh Regiment officers who had volunteered to serve with the RFC were killed in separate accidents. Second Lieutenant Robert Dykes Grossart, formerly of the 18th Welsh, was the son of Robert Fraser Grossart and Wilhelmina Gibson Grossart of Milton, Beattock, Dumfriesshire. He was at the University of Glasgow studying engineering when war broke out and enlisted in the Cameron Highlanders. He was commissioned in the 18th Welsh on 8 May 1915, but with his engineering training and a deep interest in aircraft engineering he volunteered to serve in the RFC and was sent back to England for pilot training, gaining his pilot's licence at Catterick on 10 December 1916. On 9 February Grossart was on a training flight in Yorkshire when his aircraft turned over and crashed into a field, bursting into flames and killing him. He was 25 years old and was brought home for burial in Kirkpatrick-Juxta Parish Churchyard.

Lieutenant George Trevor Brown, formerly of the 1st/6th Welsh, was the son of John S. Brown and Emily E. Brown of Oakleigh, Blackpill, Swansea. He had volunteered for pilot training and was killed during a flying accident in Wiltshire on 12 February 1917, aged 25. Brown is buried in Swansea (Oystermouth) Cemetery.

Also killed during this period was another member of the Welsh aristocracy, Second Lieutenant George Cecil Rowley, son of the 4th Baron Langford of Bodrhyddan Hall, Flintshire. Rowley was born on 18 August 1896, the second son of Hercules Edward Rowley, 4th Baron Langford, of Summerhill House, Co. Meath and of Bodrhyddan Hall. He was educated

Second Lieutenant Robert Dykes Grossart, 18th Welsh.

at Wellington College before being commissioned in the 5th Battalion, King's Royal Rifle Corps in January 1915 and was posted to France, joining their 1st Battalion. Rowley was killed in action during his battalion's attack on trenches to the south of Miraumont on 17 February 1917, aged 20, and is buried in Regina Trench Cemetery, Grandcourt.

At Ypres the 38th (Welsh) Division was starting to suffer a larger number of casualties as a result of German raids on their trenches. The 15th Welsh moved into the Canal Bank positions from reserve on 14 February and began settling in. At 1.30 am on the following day the Germans launched a heavy bombardment on their positions before several separate German raiding parties struck against some isolated outposts, killing four men, with two men missing and Second Lieutenant John Evans and fourteen men wounded. Three of the dead were from Bolton and the other from Ferndale. A fifth man, Private Ebenezer Davies (4200) of Talley, near Llandeilo, had been evacuated to the 46th Casualty Clearing Station near Proven, where he died of his wounds on the 20th. He was 36 years old and is buried within the military cemetery at Mendinghem.

Private Ebenezer Davies (4200), 15th Welsh, of Talley.

A constant stream of casualties occurred here on a daily basis for each of the division's units, but the worst incident so far occurred on 18 February when the 14th RWF sent out a raiding party with the intention of bombing a section of the German line opposite. The party was caught up in fierce fighting and was forced to return within ten minutes, with the loss of Second Lieutenant Enoch Lewis James and nineteen men killed. The officer leading the raid, Captain Harold Sydney Ormsby, an Australian from Sydney, was wounded early on but still led his men out. He was wounded again and brought back to his own lines but died during the day.

Second Lieutenant Enoch Lewis James was the son of Evan and Mary James of Omia Villa, New Quay. He served in the OTC prior to being commissioned in the RWF on 21 November 1916 and was posted to the 14th RWF after it had moved to Hébuterne. He was seen to fall wounded in the legs during the raid but was then seen no more. A sergeant later reported that he and James were among the last to return to their lines when they were caught by a German hand grenade. Many of the men killed on the raid were posted as missing initially, causing great distress to their families. One of the men, Private David Brees (55318) of Y Brandy, Dinas Mawddy, had lost a brother the previous year, and his anxious parents posted several notices in local newspapers asking for any information regarding the whereabouts of their lost son. No trace of him was ever found and Brees, together with ten of the men killed with him, is commemorated on the Menin Gate Memorial.

Second Lieutenant Enoch Lewis James, 14th RWF, of New Quay, Ceredigion.

A week later, at 2.45 am on 25 February, the Germans mounted a retaliatory raid and captured a prisoner. The 38th (Welsh) Division artillery was caught napping and took fifteen minutes to answer the SOS from the frontline troops being raided. As a result, the Germans managed to return to their own lines without suffering any casualties. The 14th RWF lost three officers – Lieutenants Stanley Jones and William John Williams, and Second Lieutenant Percy Francis Craddock – and ten men killed, while the 16th RWF lost five men killed, with a further nine wounded.

On the same day Private Thomas Edward Davies (25970) of the 17th RWF was killed while attached to the 177th Tunnelling Company, Royal Engineers. Davies was the son of John and Mary Ellen Davies of Canister Cottage, Overton, Ellesmere. He had worked as a miner prior to the war and lived at Barn Hill Cottage, Adwy, near Bersham, Wrexham. He landed in France with the 17th RWF on 4 December 1915 and had taken part in the assault on

Lieutenant Stanley Jones, 14th RWF, of Liverpool.

Mametz Wood. After the 38th (Welsh) Division had moved to Ypres, a number of experienced miners were attached to various Royal Engineer tunnelling companies and Davies was among them. He was killed while working on a tunnel in the Hooge sector on 25 February 1917 and is commemorated on RE Grave, Railway Wood, a memorial marking the spot where eight Royal Engineers of the 177th Tunnelling Company and four attached infantrymen, three of them attached from the RWF, were

R.E. Grave, Railway Wood.

killed in action underground during the defence of Ypres between November 1915 and August 1917.

After the closing of the Somme offensive at the end of 1916, the Germans had been left with a salient to defend and formed a defensive line from Le Transloy to Bucquoy called the Loupart Line. The British carried out a series of operations over the winter to seize tactical positions from which an attack on the Loupart Line could be launched in the spring and it was during these small assaults that the Welsh divisions mentioned earlier had suffered casualties during January 1917.

On 14 January the 1st RWF moved into reserve and had spent over two weeks at Rubempré carrying out various training routines. On 21 February the battalion moved back into the line in the Beaumont Hamel sector, supplying working parties around the White City. On 25 February sentries reported to battalion HQ that the Germans had evacuated their trenches at Ten Tree Alley and that Serre appeared to be deserted, so at 1.30 am the 1st RWF was sent in to support an advance by the 21st Manchesters and 1st South Staffs on Serre. Over the coming hours the three battalions stealthily made their way forward and concentrated in a valley north of the Serre Road in readiness to advance on Puisieux.

At 12 noon orders were received for 22 Brigade to advance on Soap Alley and pause for the 2nd Borders to pass through and assault City Trench. By the end of the day A Company, 1st RWF was in Serre and intelligence was gained stating that the Germans had indeed left the village and were intending to make a stand at nearby Puisieux. Unbeknown to the British, this was the beginning of the German withdrawal in this sector.

At 2 am on the following day, 26 February, the British artillery bombarded Puisieux and then the assault on the village began, with the 19th Division working on the left flank of the 7th Division. Heavy fighting continued throughout the day, while the Germans laid down a counter-barrage on the attacking troops in an attempt to slow them down. By the end of the day the 1st RWF had suffered eighteen men killed and thirty more wounded.

Further fighting continued around the village on the following day while clearing through the village, but the Germans held on to the northern part in strength and counter-attacked C Company, 1st RWF at 7.50 am in the attempt to slow their advance. The battalion continued its efforts to clear Puisieux throughout the day, losing two officers – Lieutenant John Bernard Pye Adams and Second Lieutenant William Williams – and eleven more men killed. Another officer, Lieutenant Frederick Mackay DCM, died of wounds the following day. Five more officers and twenty-two men wounded. The battalion was relieved during the night after clearing the village and marched to Mailly-Maillet before moving back to Bertrancourt.

Private Dan Ivor Price (40048), 1st RWF, of Abergwili. A former pupil at Carmarthen Grammar School, he was killed at Puisieux on 25 February 1917.

Lieutenant John Bernard Pye Adams, who was mortally wounded in Puisieux, was another of the famous diarists and writers with which

217

the RWF was blessed during the war. His book, *Nothing of Importance. A Record of Eight Months at the Front with a Welsh Battalion October 1915 to June 1916*, was published after his death and covers his time with the 1st RWF. He was the son of Harold John and Georgina Adams of St John's, Oakwood Avenue, Beckenham, Kent. He was buried in Couin New British Cemetery.

Further to the north was the 10th RWF, which had spent most of January and February training at Halloy and Béthonsart in the Arras sector. On 15 February the battalion moved back into the trenches following a heavy snowfall and enjoyed a relatively peaceful few days before returning to billets in Arras. It returned to the trenches on 26 February, suffering ten men wounded. On 28 February the battalion was being relieved by the 1st Royal Scots Fusiliers when it was hit by German artillery fire and lost ten men killed and nine wounded.

Among those killed was Private Thomas Oliver Owen (37787). He was the son of John and Alice Owen of Tal-y-Cafn Terrace, Eglwysfach, Denbighshire and worked with his father as a gardener at Bodnant Gardens prior to the war. Owen enlisted at Conway in the Royal Welsh Fusiliers and was posted to the 10th RWF, probably after the battalion had been moved out of the Somme sector. He was 23 years old when he was killed on 28 February and is commemorated on the Arras Memorial. He is also commemorated on the Eglwysfach War Memorial.

The medals and a photograph of Private Thomas Oliver Owen (37787), 10th RWF, of Eglwysfach.

The German retreat had now begun in earnest on the Somme. By the end of February Gommecourt, Puisieux, Miraumont and Warlencourt had been taken, and on 10 March Irles, the last obstacle to the Loupart Line, had been captured. The only part taken in these actions by the Welsh was an attack by the 9th Welsh of the 19th Division on St David's Day, on a portion of the trench system north of Puisieux called Knife and Fork Trench. The portion of the enemy's trench that was captured, Berg Graben Trench, was renamed St David's Trench in honour of the occasion. Casualties were light, amounting to three men killed, and one officer and thirty other ranks wounded. Second Lieutenant Theodore George Alexander Lima, who was wounded, gained the MC 'For conspicuous gallantry and devotion to duty as sniping officer. He set a splendid example throughout, and was largely responsible that so few casualties were sustained. He was severely wounded.' (*London Gazette*, 17 April 1917.) Other Welsh units were luckier, spending the third St David's Day of the war enjoying their usual celebratory meals.

On 2 March the 2nd Monmouths, still in the Somme sector with the 46th (North Midland) Division, suffered the death of the CO, Lieutenant Colonel Alfred John Hamilton Bowen, DSO and Private Samuel Gwyn Davies (266150) of Pontypool at Sailly-Saillisel. Bowen was the son of Alfred Edward and Emily Marianne Bowen of Usk, Monmouthshire. He had been awarded the DSO twice prior to his death for actions described in the following citations:

> On the 13th May 1915, east of Ypres, though wounded in two places in the head before dawn, he refused to leave his company, and continued to command it with conspicuous ability. After the action was over and the battalion returned to La Brique, he was found to be suffering from two other wounds in the body. He was then sent to hospital. (*London Gazette*, 3 July 1915.)

The grave of Lieutenant Colonel Alfred John Hamilton Bowen DSO, 2nd Monmouths, in Guards Cemetery, Combles.

> For conspicuous gallantry and devotion to duty. He, with great personal gallantry, supervised the difficult task of consolidation throughout the whole night, and continually went round his working parties. He was mainly responsible for the excellent work carried out. (*London Gazette*, 9 March 1917.)

Bowen was 31 years old and is buried in Guards' Cemetery, Combles.

During the day another Welsh RFC pilot was killed. Second Lieutenant Cyril Stephen Cravos was born in Cardiff in 1895, the son of Joseph and Rebecca Cravos. He was educated at Ampleforth, where he excelled at rugby and boxing. He joined the Honourable Artillery Company (HAC) in February 1915 and was commissioned in the 21st Welsh on 12 August 1915 before volunteering to join the RFC, gaining his pilot's licence in November 1916. He was posted to 5 Squadron, RFC in France. On 2 March 1917 he took off with his observer Flight Sergeant A.G. Shepherd in B.E.2.e Serial 7192 and was reported as missing over the Gommecourt sector. Both men were found dead in their crashed aircraft and were buried by the Germans in Moyenneville German Cemetery near Arras before being relocated to Douchy-les-Ayette British Cemetery after the war.

The Welsh Guards had moved back into the Frégicourt sector on the right of Sailly-Saillisel and opposite Saint-Pierre-Vaast Wood on 26 January after almost two weeks at Billon Farm Camp and began another spell in the trenches. The war diary for 5 March mentioned the extreme cold, and the desertion to the Germans of Private Pearson, who 'went off his head' after being hit by a shell fragment on the previous day, but does not mention the six men killed. On the following day seven more men were killed and another five on the 8th by German artillery fire. Dudley Ward wrote of this period:

> This was one of the hardest tours of duty the battalion ever had. Heavy guns, field-guns, and trench-mortars fired continuously at the British line; the line was blown in, and the men occupied shell-holes where they could; enemy snipers waited to catch men moving from one hole to another, and, until the divisional artillery found them with shrapnel, did some damage. Communication was almost impossible. Rowlands, the signaller, was twice blown up and buried and the men he was working with killed, but he carried on, merely asking, as this was his first experience in the line, if it was always like this. Humphrey Dene stormed for retaliation and more retaliation, for counter-battery work and ever more, and for four days a fierce artillery battle raged. In the midst of all this C.S.M. Pearce did good sniping, and seemed on the whole to be rather enjoying himself. Sergt. Ashford was badly wounded in this action, and Cpl Parker, an excellent sniper, so injured that he afterwards died. There is no greater test of discipline and determination than a prolonged and furious bombardment. In the four days there were one officer (Jenkins) and seventy-nine other ranks as casualties. When the 2nd Battalion Scots Guards relieved on the 8th the fire was dying down.

The Germans were apparently using up their artillery shells before they withdrew, to save carting hundreds of tonnes of shells back with them. Nonetheless, on 17 March the British began advancing behind the Germans along the whole line from Arras to Le Quesnoy, meeting occasional pockets of resistance, and by 9 April the British front line had been established opposite the Hindenburg front line, at a distance varying from three-quarters of a mile on the north to 5 miles further south.

During this period, the 38th (Welsh) Division endured a constant drain in terms of casualties. The 14th Welsh lost two of its most gallant officers. Second Lieutenant Arthur Frederick Hastings Kelk MC, the son of Reverend Arthur Hastings Kelk and Bessie Grace Kelk of Goldsborough Rectory, Knaresborough, Yorkshire was killed on

9 March. Kelk had studied for his BA at Magdalene College, Cambridge and lived in Swansea prior to the war. He gained the MC for gallantry during a trench raid on 17 November 1916: 'For conspicuous gallantry in action. He hastily reorganised the men, led them to their objective, and was instrumental in finding and capturing the majority of prisoners taken.' (*London Gazette*, 9 January 1917.) Kelk is buried in Bard Cottage Cemetery.

Second Lieutenant John David Vaughan MC, the son of Henry and Rachel Vaughan of 44 Mansel Street, Burry Port was killed on 18 March. He had also gained the MC for gallantry during a trench raid on 17 November 1916: 'For conspicuous gallantry in action. He carried out a daring reconnaissance with great courage and determination, obtaining most valuable information.' (*London Gazette*, 9 January 1917.) He is buried in Ferme-Olivier Cemetery.

Lance Corporal Richard Osmond (19345), 10th Welsh, of Stanleytown, killed on the Canal Bank on 22 March 1917 and buried in Bard Cottage Cemetery.

At 4.20 am on 22 March the 10th Welsh, in the Canal Bank trenches, began being heavily shelled by the Germans. Within minutes two strong German trench-raiding parties forced their way into their trenches and a bombing fight ensued. The Welshmen drove the Germans off but lost two men taken prisoner and one officer – Lieutenant Edgar Hadfield – and seven men killed. One of the dead men, Private Benjamin Rees (18144) of Treorchy, had fallen in love with a young lady named Freda May Phillips while based at Rhyl early in the war and married her at Winchester on 11 March 1915. Many men of the 38th (Welsh) Division met their future wives while based in North Wales. All the dead men, apart from one, are buried in Bard Cottage Cemetery.

While the 38th (Welsh) Division lost men at Ypres and the Welsh units in the Somme sector were beginning the advance towards the Hindenburg Line, the war in Palestine became far more active.

Chapter 15

Palestine:
The First Battle of Gaza

While the 74th (Yeomanry) Division was forming under Major General Girdwood, the 53rd (Welsh) Division was ready for action. During 1916 the British had advanced across the desert and defeated the Senussi. The Suez Canal was safe and the desert railway and water pipeline were well under way, so the scene was set for the next phase of the offensive, the attack on the Turkish stronghold of Gaza, some 18 miles away. Originally the British government had no immediate policy for Palestine but with orders for pressure on all fronts during 1917, Sir Archibald Murray began planning for an attack on Gaza.

By the beginning of March 1917, the Desert Column, comprising the Australian and New Zealand Mounted Division and the Imperial Mounted Division, was at Khan Yunis with HQ at Sheikh Zoweid, while Eastern Force Headquarters and the infantry – 52nd, 53rd, 54th divisions and 229 Brigade of the 74th Division – were at El Arish. The force was short of artillery but there were still almost 100 guns available. The Turks held a defensive line from Gaza on the sea to the railway which here was some 17 miles to the east.

Palestine had four parallel features: between the sea and the great Arabian Desert there is a long Maritime Plain, a central range of mountains, the Jordan Valley and the eastern range of mountains. There is a break in the central range, where the Plain of Esdraelon connects the Maritime Plain with the Jordan Valley.

The Turks had their left flank on Beersheba at the foot of the central range and on the edge of the desert, while Murray's troops were on the coast, with their lines of communication running back through the province of Sinai along the coastal route. He decided that an attack along the coast towards Gaza was the safest proposition, as lines of communication would be more easily protected along the coast and that water would be more readily available. Murray rebuilt the Desert Column, which now comprised the Australian and New Zealand Mounted Division, the Imperial Mounted Division and the 53rd Welsh Division. With his other two infantry divisions, the 52nd and 54th, in support, the stage was set for the First Battle of Gaza, the objects of which were to seize the line of the Wadi Ghuzze and cover the advance of the railway, to prevent the enemy from retiring without a fight and to capture Gaza by a *coup de main* and cut off its garrison.

Sir Archibald Murray decided not to attack towards Beersheba but along the coast, where railway construction would be faster and water more plentiful. During the night

Sketch map showing the British dispositions at the First Battle of Gaza.

of 25/26 March, Dobell's troops moved into position in readiness for the battle. Two mounted divisions and the 53rd (Welsh) Division moved to Deir al-Balah, the camel brigade to Abassan el Kebir, the 54th Division to the El Taire hill and the 52nd Division to Khan Yunis, with one brigade at In Seirat.

During the early hours of 26 March the troops began to move out, covered by a thick mist that had fortuitously rolled in from the sea. The Australian and New Zealand Mounted Division left Deir al-Balah, crossed the Wadi Ghuzze, followed by the Imperial Mounted Division, and headed for Beit Durdis, 5 miles east of Gaza, while the Imperial Mounted Division made for El Menclur on the Wadi Sheria. The leading troops then deployed to the sea, thus closing the exit from Gaza. At the same time the 54th Division crossed the Wadi Ghuzze and occupied the Sheikh Abbas Ridge, while on the left the 53rd Division advanced towards Ali Muntar. The orders issued to the 53rd Division were plain and simple:

The Division will attack the Ali Muntar position as follows:

160th Brigade along the main ridge from the south-west on Ali Muntar.
158th Brigade from the east, also on Ali Muntar.
159th Brigade, less one battalion, on the hill north-east of Ali Muntar, indicated
   to G.O.C. 159th Brigade, at the same time covering the right of the 158th
   Brigade.
The artillery of the division will support the attack under order of the C.R.A.
The G.O.C. 159th Brigade will detail one battalion in Divisional Reserve at
   Mansura.

The 5th RWF led the assault of 158 Brigade, while on the El Sire Ridge, Brigadier General Butler advanced with 160 Brigade; however, the artillery was not ready for action and 159 Brigade had not yet arrived. The 5th RWF reached a line opposite the Ali Muntar defences before spreading out on a two-company front, followed by the 6th and 7th RWF, and began to advance across the open valley between Mansura and the El Sire Ridge and up the crest of the ridge to the mosque of Ali Muntar. Their advance was seen by the Turks and was watched by the Anzac Mounted Division from the far side of the Gaza-Beersheba road.

The three battalions were required to perform a wheel to the left before advancing down a slope about 750 metres from Ali Muntar and came under shrapnel fire, followed by rifle and machine-gun fire from Green Hill and Ali Muntar. It was obvious that these positions were strongly held and the 5th RWF found that it had advanced with no cover on either flank. When the 6th and 7th RWF came into the line it was found that the brigade had gone too far north and as a result the Herefords were sent to assault Green Hill at 1.45 pm.

In the meantime, 159 Brigade arrived at Mansura half an hour after the attack had been launched and the 5th Welsh and 4th Cheshires were forced to advance on the double to attack Clay Hill. The Herefords then moved off while the whole line of 158 Brigade advanced, with 159 Brigade making a diagonal advance across their rear to extend the attack to the right.

The advance of 160 Brigade along the El Sire Ridge had already been brought to a standstill. The brigade had to advance across a trench system known as the Labyrinth, which was surrounded by cactus hedge and olive groves. The brigade advanced with the Sussex on the right and the Middlesex on the left, with the Queen's in reserve. The Labyrinth was captured at 1.30 pm and the Middlesex began consolidating on a ridge half a mile south of Gaza, the advance having stopped. The Sussex suffered heavy casualties and their advance had also stalled.

By this time the advance of 158 Brigade had also been held up and the three battalions were being hit by flank fire from Green Hill. By now 159 Brigade had come up on the right of the 7th RWF, with the 5th Welsh and 4th Cheshires advancing along the Gaza-Beersheba road, but a gap appeared between them and the 4th Welsh were sent forward to fill it. The brigade managed to advance a little further but with inadequate artillery support, got held up by Turks firing into them from the thick cactus hedges between Clay Hill and Ali Muntar.

The attack of the 53rd (Welsh) Division had now come to a standstill, so both the mounted divisions that were covering the advance of the infantry on Gaza were sent in to attack the town. Major General Chauvel ordered the Camel Corps to replace the Imperial Mounted Division who took over from the Anzac Division, but it was not until 4 am that the Anzac Division began to advance on the town and by then came news that the Turks were massing in the distance.

While the Anzac Division was getting ready to advance on Gaza, 161 Brigade, which had been lost in the fog, had arrived at El Sire at around 3.30 pm. Together with the arrival of a field artillery brigade, this allowed Major General Dallas to release the 7th Cheshires from divisional support to join 159 Brigade, and also allowed them artillery support. This brigade was heavily engaged in the cactus hedges on Clay Hill and below Ali Muntar Hill.

The 5th Welsh, on the flank of the brigade, had suffered heavy casualties so the 7th Cheshires were sent up to help them. While they were advancing, Captain Walker of the 7th RWF, together with Lieutenants Latham and Fletcher and about forty men, joined with Captain A.H. Lee and Lieutenant R.H. Taylor of the 5th Welsh and forty of their men and charged the Turkish line, breaking through their positions east of the mosque after some heavy hand-to-hand fighting. Just then the 7th Cheshires arrived and helped to consolidate the position before laying down fire on the Turkish trenches to the west and began clearing cactus gardens around their position, which then afforded them a fine view over Gaza. Captain Lee of the 5th Welsh said:

Our great concern was a certain cactus hedge, from which machine guns might wipe us all out as soon as we got level with it. A small party was sent off to investigate, and all being reported well we got on a few yards further, leaving some behind (hit) at every rush forward. Worn out and heavily laden [besides their packs the men carried extra rations, a second water bottle, and extra bandoliers of ammunition], the prospect of having to rush the entrenched and steep slopes was not a pleasant one, but with bayonets fixed and revolvers cocked, off we went with a cheer. The Turks vacated their trenches and ran. The top of the hill was reached and we rounded up many Turks. Those who ran were fired at and some bowled over. On looking round we found ourselves behind Turks who were still firing on other oncoming troops, and we got some fine firing at their backs, until they withdrew. Our party had reached the top, I suppose unobserved, at any rate for a while, for we were troubled by British shells and rifle fire from converging troops. These troubles soon ceased, and Colonel Lawrence of the Cheshires came along and took command of the situation...water shortage was serious, and parties were sent off to collect water bottles from the dead, and ammunition from the wounded and dead.

During this action near the mosque, the artillery began shelling Turkish machine-gun positions on the 159 Brigade front, enabling the 4th and 5th Welsh, together with the 6th Cheshires, to storm and capture Clay Hill. The Anzac Division had also advanced from the north by now, and the New Zealand Brigade had advanced from Jabalieh towards Ali Muntar.

The Turks were now under extreme pressure, so General Dallas ordered 161 Brigade to attack Green Hill at around 4 pm and within an hour the Turks had fled into Gaza. By 6 pm the British had taken Clay Hill, Ali Muntar, Green Hill and the Labyrinth. The Australians and New Zealanders were fighting amongst the streets of Gaza.

This was an important moment when the outcome of the battle lay in the balance. Lieutenant General Chetwode, after consulting with Dobell, was worried about news of large numbers of Turks advancing from Abu Hureyra. He decided that if Gaza was not captured before 6 pm he would withdraw the mounted troops, also concerned that they had not been able to water their horses and he made the fatal mistake of pressing his order to withdraw. It was only afterwards that it became known that the 4th Field Company, RE had moved forward to sink wells and had ample water available for both horses and troops, but by then it was too late as they were withdrawing past the engineers, who had to dismantle their gear and follow the retreat.

If the attack had been maintained, then Gaza could have fallen during the night but Chetwode's lack of conviction had cost the British their chance of victory. All the troops really had to do was hold their positions during the night, take advantage of some sleep and be watered overnight and the attack on Gaza would have been completed on the following day; however, it was not to be.

The lack of communication between each division had been the real issue. Chetwode did not realize how successful the 53rd (Welsh) Division's advance had been. General Dallas of the 53rd was not aware of the location of the 54th Division and it galled Dallas to see the hard work of his division come to nothing. He ordered the 53rd Division to occupy the line from Sheikh Abbas through Mansura, north of El Sheluf to Tel el-Ajjul, and sent a message back to General Chetwode informing him this at 9.30 pm but later followed his orders to withdraw the division. Lieutenant Ashton of the 7th RWF wrote:

However, orders were orders, and the necessary instructions were sent to units, and at midnight the withdrawal was begun. As a matter of fact, small parties of heroes had pushed down the slope into Gaza, notably one under Walker and George Latham of the 7th R.W.F. and never got the order, only coming away at dawn, when they found that there was no one else about. One such party met some Anzac cavalry, who had come right through the town, from north to south. It showed to what a pitch the Turks had sunk. The whole remnant of the garrison and Gaza itself was like a large plum, and no one to pick it... We got back behind our cliff edge at Mansura somewhere about 2 a.m., and literally fell asleep in a heap across each other.

By 3.30 am 159 Brigade had occupied its new position and just over half an hour later so had 160 and 161 brigades. By then General Dallas had been further annoyed after learning that the 54th Division had actually closed the gap up to the 53rd and he could have safely kept the division on the line it had attained. Later in the morning Chetwode caused more annoyance by ordering General Dallas to re-occupy Ali Muntar after finding out all the facts himself!

By the end of the fighting of 26 March, the Welsh battalions had suffered the following casualties:

Lieutenant Thomas Bate, 5th RWF, killed at Gaza on 26 March 1917.

5th RWF: 3 officers – Lieutenants Thomas Bate and Evan Llewelyn Thomas, and Second Lieutenant Evelyn Llewelyn Hustler Jones – and 56 men killed; 9 officers and 186 men wounded.

6th RWF: 2 officers – Second Lieutenants Walter Ernest Ireland and Arthur Llewelyn Williams – and 15 men killed; 11 officers and 138 men wounded.

7th RWF: 7 officers – Captain Ivor Thomas Lloyd-Jones; Lieutenants Horace William Fletcher, and Vivian Gwynne James; Second Lieutenants Evan Walter Davies, Owen Gwilym Jones, Arthur Rogers and Robert Parry – and 95 men killed; 7 officers and 219 men wounded.

4th Welsh: 1 officer – Second Lieutenant Frederick James Mansel Bryant – and 54 men killed; 12 officers and 150 men wounded.

5th Welsh: 2 officers – Captain Thomas Glyn Llewelyn Phillips and Second Lieutenant Oscar Reginald Frankenstein – and 68 men killed; 16 officers and 210 men wounded.

Several more officers and men from each battalion died of wounds over the coming days, including Major Harry Hartley Waite Southey of the 5th Welsh, who died four days later.

Despite suffering these heavy casualties, on the following morning the 53rd Division moved forward to retake the positions they had been ordered to surrender on the previous night. 160 Brigade had barely reached its position after marching all night when it received orders to turn around and go forward again. The 7th Essex of 161 Brigade re-occupied Green Hill and Ali Muntar, while the Queen's pushed forward on their left and the Herefords on the right, taking up the positions gained by 158 Brigade on the previous day. The 7th RWF took the right flank, joining with the 54th Division.

As the Herefords pushed forward onto Ali Muntar Hill, the Essex retired into them, being pushed back by a Turkish counter-attack that recaptured Ali Muntar and Green Hill. Reinforcements were sent up to stem the Turks but the 5th and 7th RWF, isolated in the valley, had also been forced to withdraw to conform to the new line by 4 pm. The withdrawal of these troops proved to be a costly error that allowed the German

General von Kressenstein to reinforce Gaza. The battle ground to a close by 27 March, the allies withdrawing to Deir al-Balah and Khan Yunus. In an attempt to mitigate the failure, Murray over-estimated the Turkish losses, stating in his despatches:

> The total result of the first Battle of Gaza, which gave us 950 Turkish and German prisoners, and two Austrian field guns, caused the enemy losses which I estimate at 8,000, and cost us under 4,000 casualties, of which a large proportion were only slightly wounded, was that my primary and secondary objects were completely attained, but the failure to attain the third object, the capture of Gaza, owing to the delay caused by the fog on the 26th, and the waterless nature of the country round Gaza, prevented a most successful operation from becoming a complete disaster to the enemy. [Murray had considerably over-estimated the Turkish casualties; in reality they were around 2,450.]

The soldiers who had fought so valiantly felt that they had been betrayed, having victory pulled from their grasp. Corporal William Jones of Carmarthen who was serving with the 4th Welsh wrote:

> We have had a fight at last, and have given the Turks something to remember us by. I am pleased to say that I got through all right, just slightly grazed on the head and arm, but am now as fit as ever. I suppose you have read about the fight in the papers. The 4th Welsh have made a name for themselves that will never die. We have unfortunately lost a lot of brave comrades, but they died a glorious death. The Turks were trenched in a fort, and we had to advance for hours under a rain of bullets, but we drove them out with our bayonets. What a fight it was! We captured their general and hundreds of prisoners, Germans as well. Don't worry, little mother, I thank God I am alive. It is now like a dream. I think I went mad in the fight. Our colonel and officers were great. We have only one officer left of our company. We were seven N.C.O.s in my platoon, and I am the only one left now; the other six were knocked out. Our colonel is proud of us. He said that we were the best men he had ever had. We lost about 200 of our boys, but I can tell you the Turks lost more. We made them pay for what they did. I am all right. What I miss is a fag. The people of Wales can be proud of their men; I do not think there ever was such a grand victory. The men were heroes.

The First Battle of Gaza had been lost, but planning was already under way for a second attempt. Meanwhile, back in France, preparations were in full swing for a major offensive at Arras.

Chapter 16

The Battle of Arras

For the troops on the Somme sector, the period between 9 February and 16 March was dominated by the Germans' strategic withdrawal to the Hindenburg Line. The allied policy for 1917 was to carry out a series of co-ordinated offensives on all fronts, and over the winter much planning had been carried out to enable the French to assault further south on the Aisne, while the British would reluctantly carry out an offensive on a wide front running from Arras down to the Somme.

However, a series of incidents complicated the allied plan. One was the dismissal of General Joffre by the French and his replacement by General Robert Nivelle. Another was the German withdrawal to the Hindenburg Line.

While High Command decided on the best option for the offensive, there were still several Welsh units on the Somme following the German withdrawal. The 40th (Bantam) Division had been in France since June 1916 and, although it had suffered a large number of casualties, had not yet taken part in a major battle. In November 1916 Brigadier General F.P. Crozier DSO took command of the all-Welsh 119 Brigade, which took over trenches in the Somme sector, south of Rancourt, opposite the German trenches in the wood of Saint-Pierre-Vaast, 7 miles south of Bapaume on the Péronne road.

The 40th Division was well-placed to follow the German withdrawal and while advancing from the line it had held near Rancourt, in the direction of Gouzeaucourt, much work was carried out in road-building. The Germans had now strengthened their defences to slow down the pursuit, and the 40th Division was set for its first battle.

The 7th Division, which included the 1st RWF, had been out of the line when the Germans had begun their withdrawal and were moved back to the northern Somme sector to follow the Germans, reaching positions around St. Leger, some 8 miles south of Arras, by 19 March. The 3rd Division, with the 10th RWF, was also being moved there, as was the 29th Division with the 2nd SWB. The 1st Division, 1st SWB, 2nd and 6th Welsh remained in the Somme sector to repair damaged infrastructure, while the 19th (Western) Division, 9th RWF, 5th SWB and 9th Welsh and the 38th (Welsh) Division were further north, out of the current battle area.

The new French commander, Nivelle, had elaborated on the original French offensive plan for the Aisne. His new plan, the Nivelle Offensive, was intended to break through the German defences on the Aisne within two days, in conjunction with a British offensive at Arras and the French Third Army at St. Quentin who would divert German reserves from the Aisne and the Champagne. The main offensive was to be delivered by the French on the Chemin des Dames Ridge, with a subsidiary attack by their Fourth Army in the Champagne sector, and was intended to follow up the meeting of the French and British armies following their expected breakthroughs and allow Nivelle to drive the Germans back to the border.

Three British armies were already concentrated in the Arras sector and were deployed roughly north to south: the First Army under General Sir Henry Horne, the Third Army under General Sir Edmund Allenby and the Fifth Army under General Sir Hubert Gough. The plan for the offensive had been devised by Allenby. Since the middle of 1916 major underground operations had been in progress, making use of the existing underground caverns and systems in Arras and the Vimy sector to the north. The objective for the British was the German-held town of Cambrai, with the Douai Plain to the north. The German withdrawal had merely impeded the plans.

Private Griffith David Jones (53638), 1st RWF, of Eglwyswrw, killed at Croisilles on 30 March 1917.

The first Welsh unit to be involved in the area, but not in the main battle which had not yet begun, was the 1st RWF, which had been at Mailly-Maillet for much of March. The 1st RWF went into the line on 16 March and on the night of 29/30 March took up positions opposite the village of Croisilles, which the Germans had decided to defend. During the afternoon patrols were sent out as reports had been received that the Germans had withdrawn, but before they entered the village they came under fire and were forced to retreat. Two companies of the 1st RWF were relieved during the late afternoon, but some confusion surrounded the relief of the other two companies and during the evening Second Lieutenant Etienne Howard Dove and eight men were killed, while one officer and fourteen men were wounded.

Just a day later, at Ypres the 38th (Welsh) Division was still holding its positions along the Canal Bank. Attached to the division was the 122nd Brigade Royal Field Artillery, a formation that had been raised in Wales specifically for the division. On 2 April several officers from their B Battery were in their billets when a shell crashed into their mess, killing two of them: Major Brinley Richard Lewis and Second Lieutenant David Alexander Carnegie were killed in the blast. Both men are buried in Ferme-Olivier Cemetery.

Carnegie was the son of Lieutenant Colonel the Honourable Douglas Carnegie, the second son of the 9th Earl of Northesk and Margaret Jean, his wife, of Fair Oak, Petersfield, Hants. Major Brinley Richard Lewis, 'Bryn' Lewis, was a former Welsh international rugby player, the

Major Brinley Richard Lewis of B Battery, 122nd Brigade RFA, the tenth Welsh international rugby player to be killed during the war.

tenth to be killed during the war. Lewis was born in Pontardawe on 4 January 1891, the son of David and Margaret Lewis. He was educated at Swansea Grammar School and at Cambridge University, where he won three Blues. He played club rugby for Newport and gained the first of his two caps against Ireland in 1912. He joined the Glamorgan Yeomanry in October 1914 and was commissioned in the RFA early in 1915. Lewis was 26 years old when he was killed on 2 April 1917.

The grave of Major Brinley Richard Lewis at Ferme Olivier Cemetery.

Within the week, on 8 March, the second Welsh airman fell victim to the guns of the Red Baron, Manfred von Richthofen. Second Lieutenant Guy Everingham was born in Barry on 28 June 1894, the eldest son of William and Patricia Florence Everingham. The family then moved to Vaenor, Hawarden Road, Colwyn Bay, where Everingham and his younger brother Robin were raised. Everingham enlisted in the 13th RWF in October 1914, was soon commissioned on 25 February 1915 and joined the battalion in France in March 1916. He saw action during the assault on Mametz Wood that year but when the 38th (Welsh) Division moved to Ypres he volunteered to join the RFC, training as an observer. He married Gladys Annie Brown of Lynwood, St David's Place, Llandudno while on leave on 19 February 1917 before returning to France with 16 Squadron. On 8 April 1917, during 'Bloody April', as it was known among the RFC, Everingham was flying as observer to Second Lieutenant Keith Ingleby in B.E.2e, serial A2815 on a photographic reconnaissance over Vimy Ridge when they were attacked by Manfred von Richthofen. At 4.40 pm their aircraft came hurtling into the ground behind German lines, killing both men. Everingham was 22 years old and is buried next to Ingleby in Bois-Carré British Cemetery, Thélus, Pas-de-Calais. His brother Robin (1098) was killed on Gallipoli with the Welsh Horse in 1915.

Second Lieutenant Guy Everingham of Colwyn Bay, the second Welsh airman killed by the Red Baron.

No. 16 Squadron was among twenty-five RFC squadrons that suffered a great number of aircraft shot down while carrying out this sort of work over the Arras front during the month, work that was vital for the forthcoming battle. During April 1917, the British lost 245 aircraft, with 211 air crew killed or missing and 108 taken prisoner.

Among those killed was another Welsh airman, the third Welsh victim of von Richthofen. Second Lieutenant George Orme Smart was born on 17 August 1886, the son of Arthur and Edith Smart of Coverpoint, Llansannan. He joined the RFC early in the war and first served as an air mechanic before learning to fly at the Brooklands Military School, gaining his pilot's certificate on 20 October 1916. He joined 60

Squadron, RFC, which had recently been equipped with Nieuport Scouts, in France. On 7 April Smart took off from Filscamp Farm aerodrome aboard his Nieuport 17, serial A6645, as part of a flight from his squadron that had been despatched to photograph German positions south of Arras. Smart was shot down by von Richthofen near Neuville-Vitasse and crashed on the British side of the lines. He was Richthofen's thirty-seventh aerial victory. Smart was buried by his aircraft by British troops but his grave was lost and he is today commemorated on the Arras Flying Services Memorial. He is also commemorated at Bolton and on the Llansannan War Memorial.

Second Lieutenant George Orme Smart of Llansannan, the third Welsh airman killed by the Red Baron.

Back on the ground, preparations were well under way for the launch of the offensive. Only one Welsh battalion would be heavily involved on the first day: the 10th RWF of the 3rd Division.

The 10th RWF, now under the command of Lieutenant Colonel Geoffrey Lee Compton-Smith, had been inspected by Sir Douglas Haig on 6 March and spent the rest of the month training and playing rugby. It left Wanquetin at 7 pm on 6 April and marched to Arras, taking up billets in the cellars of the Rue Ronville, next to the station. The battalion's officers spent the coming days reconnoitring the lines and received their orders. At 7 pm on 8 April the battalion moved out of Arras and took up their assembly positions by 11 pm.

Zero hour was set for 5 am on 9 April and the 10th RWF had been ordered to follow the Gordon Highlanders, who were to lead the assault, then to advance through them to capture Devil Wood, a position to the north-west of Tilloy, marked by a black line on the trench maps with which the company commanders had been issued.

The assault went to plan at 5.30 am and the Gordons advanced behind a creeping barrage with the 10th RWF behind. The Germans launched a heavy counter-barrage eight minutes later but it fell behind the RWF and the first objectives were soon captured. While the Gordons consolidated, A and C companies, 10th RWF followed the creeping barrage and worked their way through the wood, capturing a large number of prisoners and machine guns.

While the battalion began consolidating its gains, 9 Brigade came through to continue the advance on Neuvilly Trench, followed by 8 Brigade, who continued the advance towards the Feuchy to Wancourt line. This is when the assault stalled. The Germans were determined to defend their positions and stood firm at Chapel Road and the attack was called off until the next morning.

The 10th RWF had successfully captured its objectives but had lost nineteen men killed in doing so. Two officers were mortally wounded. Lieutenant Edward Evans of Porthmadog (RAMC attached) died of his wounds on 9 April and Second Lieutenant John Charles Edmunds-Davies of Lampeter died of his wounds on 12 April. Three other officers were wounded by a shell.

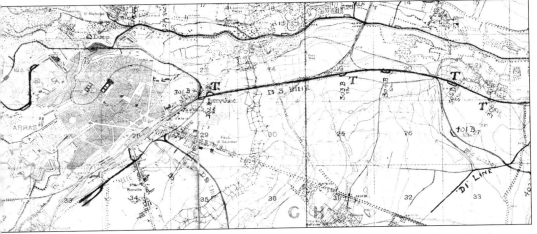

A section of trench map 51bNW, Arras, showing the position of Devil Wood on the right edge of Square G36.

Second Lieutenant Edmunds-Davies was born in 1894, the son of Alderman Walter Davies, JP and Agnes Davies of London House, Harford Square, Lampeter. He was commissioned in the Royal Welsh Fusiliers on 26 July 1915, prior to being sent to France on 11 March 1916, joining the 10th RWF. While on leave in October 1916 he married Olive Gwynedd Davies of Priory Street, Carmarthen. Edmunds-Davies was wounded at Devil Wood on 9 April and died of his wounds in hospital on 12 April 1917. He is buried in Abbeville Communal Cemetery Extension, France. After the war his widow Olive married Captain James Ira Thomas Jones, the famous Welsh air ace from St Clears.

Second Lieutenant John Charles Edmunds-Davies, 10th RWF, of Lampeter.

This was not the end of the fighting for the 10th RWF. The battalion remained in its positions throughout the first night of the battle and on the following day received orders to move forward, advancing to Feuchy Chapel in readiness for an attack on Guémappe the following day. The assault on the village began at 7 am on 11 April and was carried out by 76 Brigade, with the 10th RWF in support. The attack was soon held up, mainly due to inadequate artillery support, but later in the afternoon the 1st Gordons of 76 Brigade made another charge with artillery support. Again there was no breakthrough and the Germans poured artillery fire down on the attacking units throughout the day.

The 10th RWF lost another officer – Second Lieutenant Evan Williams – and 16 men killed, and by the time it was relieved during the night of the 11th, lost a total of 3 officers killed and 10 wounded, 35 men killed and 164 wounded, with 5 men missing. On the following morning Wancourt fell to the 56th Division.

Wednesday, 11 April also saw the opening day of the Battle of Bullecourt, to the south. Bullecourt was part of a strongly defended section of the Hindenburg Line, but following the failure of the British to penetrate the defences further east, General Hubert Gough was ordered to attack here.

Among his forces were the 4th Australian and 62nd British divisions but the attack had been hastily planned. The 4th Australian Division moved into position by 9 April and its officers began reconnoitring the positions facing them. Two of the division's units were the 15th and 16th Battalions AIF which moved into the villages of Favreuil and Noreuil respectively. The plan was for the division to attack two sectors of the German front between Bullecourt and Quéant, with the 16th and 14th battalions taking on the Hindenburg Line and the 15th and 13th tasked with passing through them to attack and capture Riencourt. The officers' patrols, including the famous Captain Albert Jacka VC MC, of the 14th Battalion, reported that the enemy wire had been smashed in places but was mostly still intact and that the garrison of Bullecourt was very strong and advised that any attack on the village would be useless without artillery support and the wire being cut. At 11 pm on the 9th the attacking battalions received orders to attack on the following day with the support of tanks, but the tanks failed to show up and the attack was postponed until 11 April.

At 2.15 am the assaulting troops moved into their assembly positions, where they were joined by the tanks; but even before zero hour two tanks were quickly disabled, one being stuck in a sunken road and another with engine trouble. At 4.30 am the remaining three tanks allotted to the 16th Battalion set off, followed by four waves of infantry. Two of the tanks started opening fire too early, giving away the Australians to the Germans, so the Australians pushed on to their first objective, with just one tank making it there, only to be disabled by a shell. By about 5.15 am the first objectives had been taken, but there was now no tank support and the Australians were being cut down by machine-gun fire from the front and from their flanks. Eventually the Australians were forced to retreat, taking 3,300 casualties. Some 1,170 Australians were taken prisoner; the largest number captured in a single engagement during the war.

Among the dead were at least four Welshmen: Lance Corporal Thomas Jackson David (6486), 15th Battalion AIF, whose parents were from Laugharne; Sergeant Arthur Richard Evans (1483) 15th Battalion AIF of Newtown; Private Edward Humphrey Rees (5416), 16th Battalion AIF of Treorchy; and Lance Corporal David Samson (3548), 16th Battalion AIF of Llanglydwen, Pembrokeshire.

Both Thomas Jackson David and David Samson had brothers serving with the AIF who were also killed: Private Robert Craig David (2161) was killed on the Somme on 5 February 1917, while Lance Corporal Benjamin Samson (4118) was killed at Ypres on 30 September 1917.

Among the 1,170 prisoners taken by the Germans at Bullecourt was Private William Joseph Harrington (6525), 16th Battalion AIF, the son of Joseph and Kezia Harrington of Tudor Lodge, Manorbier, Pembrokeshire. He died in captivity in Germany on 10 May of wounds suffered at Bullecourt on 11 April and is buried in Hamburg War Cemetery. He too lost a brother, Private Reginald Humphrey Harrington (7020), 16th Battalion AIF, who was killed at Ypres on 6 August 1917.

The 'Digger' Memorial at Bullecourt.

Also killed during this period was the son of the 7th Earl of Shannon, Second Lieutenant Richard Bernard Boyle of Monachty Mansion, Llanbadarn Trefeglwys. Boyle was born in Ireland on 13 November 1897, the son of Richard Henry and Nellie Boyle (née Thompson). Upon the death of his grandfather, Henry Boyle, on 8 February 1890, his father became the 7th Earl of Shannon and the family took up residence in the family seat at Castlemartyr, Ireland.

Boyle lost both his father and mother prior to the war, his father dying at Monachty on 11 December 1906 and his mother dying at sea after falling from a steamer in the Bay of Biscay on 11 April 1910. He was educated at the Royal Military College, Sandhurst before being commissioned in the Royal Fusiliers in 1916 and was posted to the 4th Royal Fusiliers in France. The battalion was attached to 9 Brigade, 3rd Division. Boyle saw his first major action at Arras, during an attack south of the Arras to Cambrai road, taking command of a company of his battalion after his company commander, Captain Furnie, had been badly wounded. Taking part in heavy fighting over the following days, the battalion had moved towards its objective of Guémappe, and on 13 April 1917 launched an assault on the strongly-defended village. Boyle was killed while leading the right support company of the 4th Royal Fusiliers during the attack on the village that day. He was 19 years old and is commemorated on the Arras Memorial. Upon his death, the title of 8th Earl of Shannon passed to his younger brother, Richard Henry Boyle. Boyle is also commemorated on his father's grave at Llanbadarn Trefeglwys.

The greatest successes of the first day of Arras had seen to the north of the Scarpe, where the Canadian Corps and XVII Corps made big advances through the forward part of the Hindenburg Line.

In the week leading up to the battle, British and Canadian artillery had smashed the enemy positions on the ridge and were well placed to support the infantry assault. Attacking together for the first time, the four Canadian divisions stormed the ridge at 5.30 am on 9 April 1917. Three more days of costly battle delivered the final victory. The Canadian operation was an important success but had cost 3,598 Canadian dead and another 7,000 wounded.

Second Lieutenant Richard Bernard Boyle, 4th RWF, of Monachty Mansion, Llanbadarn Trefeglwys, Ceredigion.

Among the Canadians killed on the first day were at least sixteen Welshmen, including two officers – Lieutenant Charles Stanley Bevan, MM, 16th CEF of Wrexham (Quatre-Vents Military Cemetery, Estrée-Cauchy) and Major Walter Thomas Hooper of Cardiff (Givenchy-en-Gohelle Canadian Cemetery, Souchez) – and fourteen other ranks; the men from all corners of Wales.

While the Battle of Arras was raging, another maritime disaster occurred when on 10 April the hospital ship SS *Salta*, returning to pick up wounded from Le Havre, struck a mine that had been laid by *UC-26* and sank with the loss of nine nurses, forty-two members of the RAMC and seventy-nine crew. The crew included four men and a woman from Wales, plus one RAMC orderly, Private Walter William Elul Barnsley (36560) of the Griffin Temperance Hotel, Blaenau-Festiniog. The woman was Stewardess Miss Frances J. England from Leeswood, near Mold, who managed to get into the water but became exhausted in the strong seas and drowned. All six are commemorated on the Salta Memorial within Ste. Marie Cemetery.

The grave of Private Charles Ambrose Flowerday (642662), 1st CEF, of Milford Haven, at Nine Elms British Cemetery.

The weather had been abysmal during the first week of the offensive and 13 April was the first day fine enough to make use of the Royal Flying Corps. A patrol of RE8s of 59 Squadron left their airfield at 8.15 am to carry out a photographic reconnaissance of the line from Quiéry-la-Motte to Étaing. This sector was close to Douai, where von Richthofen's squadron was based and a mix-up occurred with the squadron's fighter escort that left the six aircraft unguarded. All were shot down within minutes. Among the casualties suffered during the catastrophe was Lieutenant Charles Herbert Morris, the son of William Morris of Severn Villa, Welshpool. He was commissioned in the RWF but had volunteered to join the RFC. Morris was serving as the observer aboard RE8, serial A3216 when it was shot down at Étaing. The 25-year-old is commemorated on the Arras Flying Services Memorial. His brother Edwin Morris (2024), Canadian Cavalry Brigade, had died of wounds on 5 October 1916 and is buried in Étaples Military Cemetery. The brothers are commemorated on memorials at Christ Church, Welshpool and also at Rhyl.

A month earlier, on 2 March 1917, the 2nd SWB (29th Division) had marched from Méaulte to Bonnay to undergo a period of training after being relieved by the Guards Division. On 19 March the division had begun to move out of the Somme sector and the 2nd SWB marched to Le Quesnoy. Ten days later the battalion marched to Vignacourt and began marching in stages to the Arras sector, along with the remainder of the 29th Division, moving through Montrelet, Occoches, Lucheux, Estrée-Wamin and Monchiet before taking up positions in the line facing the strongly defended village of Monchy-le-Preux on 12 April and relieving the 5th Berkshires. The village lies 5 miles south-east of Arras, to the north of the Cambrai road, and is set on an elevated position; this made it easy to defend yet it was a vital position for the British to capture as it guarded the approaches to Cambrai.

On the following day the battalion relieved the 12th West Yorks, just south of Monchy, in readiness for an assault on the village. Four men were killed during the move and during the following morning the battalion extended its line, relieving the 4th Worcesters. Nine more men were killed during the day and on 15 April D Company HQ was blown up by a German shell, burying seven officers and killing Captain Charles Percy Owens. Six of the officers were dug out alive, but two had to be sent back to Arras with shellshock. The 2nd SWB remained in their positions here over the coming days, in support the 29th Division's assault on the village.

In the meantime a tragedy had occurred in the Mediterranean. On 15 April 1917 the requisitioned troopship SS *Arcadian* was en route from Salonika to Alexandria with 1,335 troops and crewmen aboard. The ship was 26 miles north-east of the Greek island of Milos when she was struck by a torpedo from the German submarine *UC-74* and sank within six minutes with the loss of 279 lives. Four lifeboats were lowered before she sank. Among the dead were forty-one men of the RWF, mostly reinforcements for the 24th RWF, plus one soldier of the 4th SWB and four Welsh members of the Army Service Corps. The ages of some of these men are interesting as they show the increase of the age limit due to manpower shortages: Private Edward John Jenkins (63794) of 6 Woodland Road, Barry was 38, and Private George Robert Jamieson (63668) of Carmarthen Road, Swansea was 40. Jamieson had only enlisted four months earlier, so was probably a conscript. He was a draper at Carlton Terrace prior to the war.

On 21 April the 40th (Bantam) Division, with its all-Welsh 119 Brigade, made an assault against the heavily defended outskirts of Villers-Plouich, while the 8th Division attacked Gonnelieu, on the right flank.

The attack was led by 119 Brigade. The 19th RWF on the right and the 12th SWB on the left attacked astride the railway, while the 18th Welsh remained in support in the British front line. The 17th Welsh held the line of resistance further back. The attack was successful but a platoon of B Company, 18th Welsh was called on to mop up a party of the enemy who had been passed over by the 12th SWB and who had opened fire on their backs with machine guns while they were still advancing. B Company did this efficiently, though with the loss of two killed and Captain Gibbs and nineteen men wounded.

Having consolidated the positions gained, the 18th Welsh relieved the 19th RWF on the right, the 17th Welsh relieved the 12th SWB on the left and the division prepared to attack again on 24 April.

Casualties had been remarkably light. The 19th RWF had lost nine men killed; the 12th SWB had lost an officer – Captain Oscar David Morris – and twenty-four men killed; the 17th Welsh 1 officer, Second Lieutenant Gerald Ratcliffe Jackman; and the 18th Welsh four men killed. There were two Anglesey men among the RWF dead: Corporal Owen Jones Roberts (29399) of Llanbedrgoch and Private John Jones (28428) of Penterfyn, Llantrisant.

With Gonnelieu now captured, the Germans now held a line Beaucamp through Villers-Plouich to La Vacquerie. Villers-Plouich lies in a valley between the other two villages, which are on higher ground. 120 Brigade was given the task of seizing Beaucamp and Villers-Plouich, while 119 Brigade attacked the high ground on the right. On 22 and 23 April officers of the 18th Welsh reconnoitred the ground and at 11.30 pm on the 23rd established a position on the spur, which would secure the flank of the advance of the 17th Welsh on the following day.

CSM Stanley Frederick Chard (23353), 12th SWB, of Kimberley Terrace, Newport, killed near Villers Plouich on 21 April 1917.

The 2nd RWF was also in action by now. The battalion had crossed paths with the 12th SWB and 18th Welsh when relieved from the line at Suzanne the previous month and had spent the last fortnight of the month training. During the first weeks of April the battalion began to move from the Somme with the remainder of the 33rd Division and moved into the Hindenburg Line via Villers-Bocage, Beauval, Lucheux, Saulty, Basseux and Henin before moving into the front line opposite Fontaine-lès-Croisilles on 13 April. The battalion HQ found safe dugouts in a long tunnel that was allegedly two miles long, known as Tunnel Trench, which formed part of the Hindenburg Line. Siegfried Sassoon was wounded here on 16 April. Frank Richards tells the story in *Old Soldiers Never Die*:

> The following morning one hundred bombers of the Battalion under the command of Mr. Sassoon were sent to the Cameronians to assist in a bombing attack on the Hindenburg Trench on our right. A considerable part of it was captured but was lost again during the day when the enemy made a counter attack. During the operations Mr. Sassoon was shot through the top of the shoulder. Late in the day I was conversing with an old soldier and one of the few survivors of old B Company who had taken part in the bombing raid. He said, 'God strike me pink, Dick, it would have done your eyes good to have seen young Sassoon in that bombing stunt. He put me in mind of Mr. Fletcher.

It was a bloody treat to see the way he took the lead. He was the best officer I have seen in the line or out since Mr. Fletcher, and it's wicked how the good officers get killed or wounded and the rotten ones are still left crawling about. If he don't get the Victoria Cross for this stunt I'm a bloody Dutch man; he thoroughly earned it this morning.' This was the universal opinion of everyone who had taken part in the stunt, but the only decoration Mr. Sassoon received was a decorated shoulder where the bullet went through. He hadn't been long with the Battalion, but long enough to win the respect of every man that knew him.

Sassoon did share that element of respect towards some of his men. However, he had only rejoined the battalion on 12 March and noted: 'Posted to B Company. I found myself in command of No. 8 Platoon (which included eight Joneses)... A recent draft had added a collection of undersized half-wits to the depleted battalion. Several men in my platoon seemed barely capable of carrying the weight of their equipment.'

The battalion was relieved from Tunnel Trench on 17 April, before moving back up on the night of 22 April in readiness for an attack by the 1st/4th Suffolks the following morning. The assault began at 4.45 am but was brought to a halt by machine-gun fire. Runners from the 2nd RWF went forward with supplies of bombs for the Suffolks but at 10.30 am the Germans counter-attacked and forced the Suffolks back. A bombing party from the 2nd RWF under Captain Owen advanced and held the Germans up for a while but heavy casualties were suffered throughout the day. At 6.25 pm the RWF supported another assault, this time by the 5th Scottish Rifles, but only a small number of men got over the barricade before they too were forced back and then established an outpost line some 450 metres in front of the Germans.

The 2nd RWF had suffered heavily during the day: four officers – Captain John Morris Owen of Oswestry, Second Lieutenants Stewart Lenton Blaxley of Northampton, James Battle Jackson of Ilford and Arthur Phillips of Bridgend – and thirty-seven men were killed, and eight officers and seventy men were wounded. Among the wounded was one of Sassoon's closest friends, Second Lieutenant Robert H. 'Bobby' Hanmer, while among the dead was one of the battalion's most decorated soldiers, Sergeant Thomas Hughes DCM, MM (9836) of Worthen, Shropshire. His DCM had been awarded whilst in the Ypres Salient: 'For conspicuous gallantry displayed on night patrols, particularly on the night of 27th-28th March 1915, when he was wounded.' (London Gazette, 3 June 1915.) His MM had been awarded for the Somme. He is buried in Wancourt British Cemetery.

The battalion was relieved by the 20th Royal Fusiliers on the following day and moved back to bivouacs at Boiry-Becquerelle.

In the meantime the 2nd Monmouths were hard at work on the 29th Division's front at Monchy. On 23 April the division assaulted Monchy-le-Preux again: the 2nd SWB was the assaulting battalion in 87 Brigade and at 4.45 am went over the top, storming the German frontline trench before advancing about 250 metres further and consolidating. The artillery barrage fell short, causing British casualties, while the battalion, in an advanced position, was subject to considerable sniping during the day and beat off a counter-attack before being relieved during the night by the 1st Lancashire Fusiliers. The 2nd SWB suffered terrible casualties: seven officers – Captain Philip Aubrey Hill; Lieutenant Bernard Lynton Shaw; Second Lieutenants Horace Yelverton Chadfield Clarke, John Elvet Harries, Daniel Idwal Hopkins, William Bryant Nightingale and Reginald Phillips – and seventy-two men were killed. Among the men were two brothers: Private George Henry Crook (45245) and Private Percival John Crook (45246) of Enfield, Middlesex. Both men are commemorated on the Arras Memorial. Sadly, only three men out of the seventy-nine have known graves: Sergeant John Hobby (10368) of Talgarth is buried in Tilloy British Cemetery, Tilloy-lès-Mofflaines; Private Charles Bradbury (34232) of Failsworth, Lancashire is buried in Canadian Cemetery No. 2, Neuville-St. Vaast; and Private Jonathan Heels (40785) of Halton, Buckinghamshire is buried in Cabaret-Rouge British Cemetery, Souchez.

Second Lieutenant John Elvet Harries was born at Solva on 1 July 1897, the son of James Harries of Lochwryler, Pen-y-cwm. He was educated at St David's County School and at Cardiff before joining the Royal Military College, Sandhurst in 1915. He was commissioned in the 2nd SWB in April 1916 and was wounded on the Somme in July 1916. He was just 19 years old when he was killed at Monchy on 23 April.

Second Lieutenant John Elvet Harries, 2nd SWB, of Pen-y-Cwm, Solva.

Captain Philip Aubrey Hill was born in Crickhowell, Brecknockshire on 13 December 1873. Educated at Uppingham and Caius College, Cambridge, he was employed as a schoolmaster. Having served in the Cambridge University Rifle Volunteers, he was commissioned in the Brecknock Battalion on 15 September 1914 and posted to the 2nd SWB on 22 January 1917. He was 43 years old when he fell on 23 April.

The 2nd Monmouths lost one officer – Second Lieutenant Raymond Alfred Cruickshank – and fourteen men killed while helping to consolidate the ground gained. Cruikshank was born on 15 March 1893 and educated at Earl Street School, Tredegar and Durham Road School, Newport and had married Gladys Maud Green at Newport on 14 December 1914. He then went to work in Canada and enlisted in the 61st CEF. He embarked for England and applied for a commission, joining the 2nd Monmouths on 28 December 1916. He was wounded on 9 April but remained on duty and was killed by a shell while leading his platoon at Monchy on 23 April. His men carried his body back and buried him in Dury Crucifix Cemetery, while five of his men are buried in Vis-en-Artois British Cemetery, Haucourt.

Second Lieutenant Raymon Alfred Cruickshank, 2nd Monmouths, of Tredegar.

A Welshman serving with the French Foreign Legion was also killed on 23 April. Sydney Carew Puddicombe was the eldest son of Sydney Dunsterville Puddicombe and Frances Andrews, and the grandson of James Puddicombe, of the Ivy Bush Inn, King Street, Carmarthen. The family had moved to Asnières-sur-Seine, a suburb of northern Paris, some years prior to the war. Puddicombe enlisted in Paris in August 1914 in the 1st Battalion, French Foreign Legion. He was mortally wounded on the Chemin des Dames during the Nivelle offensive and died in a hospital near Châlons-sur-Marne on 23 April 1917, aged 25. He is buried in the French Military Cemetery at De-l'Est, Châlons-en-Champagne Cimetiére de L'Est.

The young Sydney Puddicombe with his father and grandfather.

As we have seen, the 40th (Bantam) Division was in position ready for the assault on Villers-Plouich by 23 April. Their attack began at 4.15 am on 24 April and met with little opposition except at Beaucamp. The 17th Welsh had to make an advance of about a mile and dig themselves in on the top of the spur, 550 metres east of Villers-Plouich and about 900 metres west of La Vacquerie, but was held up by uncut wire in front of its objective. Coming under heavy machine-gun fire, the men forced their way through and began bombing the German trenches, capturing the position by 9.40 am. The fighting was not over, however, as the Germans began bombarding Villers-Plouich and the battalion of 120 Brigade that had captured the village was forced to retire, so the 17th Welsh covered their withdrawal while working to consolidate their position, which was later named Rhondda Hill, Welsh Ridge.

During the attack the 17th Welsh lost an officer – Captain Colin Turner Young – and thirty men killed, three officers and fifty-eight men wounded. The 18th Welsh, in support, lost just three men wounded. Young, the son of Howard and Mabel Young of 29 Mark Lane, London, played rugby for Rosslyn Park prior to the war and would have fitted well into the battalion. He is buried in Fins New British Cemetery, Sorel-le-Grand.

Unusually, all but one of the men of the 17th Welsh killed at Villers-Plouich on 24 April have known graves. One man is commemorated on the Thiepval Memorial. In Fifteen Ravine Cemetery at Villers-Plouich is a headstone marked 'A Soldier of the Great War, Welsh Regiment. 24th April 1917'. This can only be the grave of Private Fred Holland (46417) of Newport, Monmouth. The author has presented the case to the CWGC in the hope that this headstone can be correctly engraved with his details. [While writing this book, on 30 November 2015 the author received a letter from the Ministry of Defence confirming that they agreed with my conclusion and on 23 March 2016 a new headstone was erected for Private Holland in a moving ceremony attended by surviving relatives from Newport.]

Private Oswald John Payne (25457), the son of John and Eliza Payne, of 17, Mackintosh Place, Aberfan. Killed on 24 April 1917 and is buried in Fifteen Ravine British Cemetery, Villers-Plouich.

The battalion was well rewarded for its efforts: Second Lieutenant Leslie Arthur Walton was awarded the DSO and Croix de Guerre:

> For conspicuous gallantry and devotion to duty. He showed a marked contempt for danger, and when the company was held up he was seriously wounded whilst engaging an enemy sniper. In spite of this he dashed forward at the head of his men, and was responsible for capturing eleven prisoners who had been holding up the advance. (*London Gazette*, 16 August 1917.)

Captain Harry Percy Bright Gough was awarded the first of two MCs that he would gain during the war: 'For conspicuous gallantry and devotion to duty. He led his company in the most gallant manner, and was largely responsible for the success of the operations. He set a splendid example to his men.' (*London Gazette*, 26 July 1917.)

Private Philip John Phillips (25964) was awarded the MM and French Croix de Guerre.

The grave of 'A Soldier of the Great War, Welsh Regiment. 24th April 1917' in Fifteen Ravine Cemetery. This is the grave of Private Fred Holland (46417) of Newport, Monmouth and by the time of the publication of this book, will be marked with a new headstone bearing his name.

On 28 April a battalion that had received a large draft of men from the Welsh Regiment, the 10th Lincolnshires (Grimsby Chums) of the 34th Division, made an attack on the Rouex Chemical Works. The attack started at 4.15 am but the battalion was subjected to mortar and machine-gun fire almost immediately and quickly faltered. The Germans counter-attacked at 8 am but were beaten off. The battalion suffered 420 men killed, missing and wounded during the day, including four Welshmen: Private Charles Edward Agate (37902) of Tonypandy, Private William James Bird (40956) of Margam, Private Benjamin Thomas (2532) of Ynyshir and Private Albert Vallance (34842) of Ynysybwl.

Of all of the Welsh units at Arras, the 10th RWF had been continuously holding the line at Monchy since 24 April and suffered a continual drain of casualties throughout the remainder of the month until relieved on 15 May, losing three officers – Captain William John Douglas Hale, Second Lieutenants Henry Curran and Edwin Gordon Williams – and forty-six more men killed. Second Lieutenant Edwin Gordon Williams was the son of William and Elizabeth Williams of Abertillery. He was educated at Aberystwyth University and graduated BA with first-class honours in history in 1915. He was commissioned in the RWF in January 1917. Williams had only recently joined the 10th RWF before being wounded at Monchy and died of wounds on 13 May 1917. He was 23 years old and is buried at Étaples Military Cemetery. The battalion then moved to Berlancourt for a rest having suffered the heaviest casualties of any Welsh unit thus far at Arras.

The grave of Private William James Bird (40956), the son of Walter and Mary Ann Bird of 14 Carmarthen Row, Margam at Roeux British Cemetery. Bird had served with the 15th Welsh (Carmarthen Pals) prior to being transferred to the 10th Lincolnshires.

In the meantime the 15th Welsh, still at Ypres with the 38th (Welsh) Division, had been practising for a trench raid on a German strongpoint that had been causing

Captain William John Douglas Hale, 10th RWF, of Whitchurch, Cardiff, killed on 28 April 1917 and buried in Feuchy Chapel British Cemetery, Wancourt.

trouble. The strongpoint was Morteldje Estaminet and on 22 April Captain Daniel had taken a party of specially-selected men to Burgomaster Farm, where they commenced training on a scale model of the battlefield. Nightly patrols by the men over the ground that they were to assault helped them to familiarize themselves with the nature of the terrain and by the night of 29 April 1917 the men were ready and waiting.

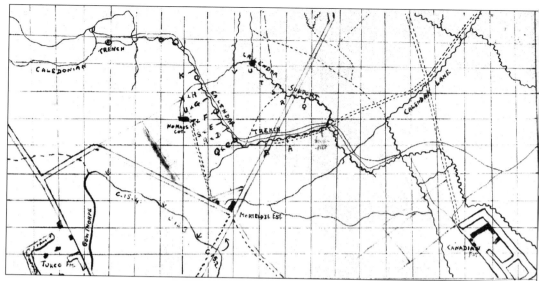

Sketch map showing the area of the Morteldje Trench Raid. (The National Archives)

At 9.30 pm on 29 April, a patrol was sent out to ensure that the Germans were still in their positions and two hours later they returned with the news that the unsuspecting Germans were in the line working, with a wiring party at work near No Man's Cot. The codename 'Bridge' signalling that the raid was to be carried out was relayed to Brigade HQ and the raiding party moved into the line.

A pre-arranged artillery barrage began at 10.45 pm, killing the German wiring party and forcing the defenders of the estaminet to shelter and the raiders moved into the front line fifteen minutes later. At 12.28 am another barrage began on the German lines and the raiders advanced, swarming into the German trenches. The barrage kept up a screen around the estaminet to prevent German reinforcements coming up and by 1 am the raiders withdrew, having captured ten German prisoners plus a quantity of maps and a machine gun, blown up several concrete emplacements and killed a large number of Germans. [The story is told in full by the author in *Carmarthen Pals*.]

However, a heavy price was paid for these sketch maps and ten prisoners, with eleven men having been killed and more wounded. Several men were decorated for their roles in the raid, notably the commander, Captain James Arthur Daniel, who was awarded the MC: 'For conspicuous gallantry and devotion to duty. He commanded a raiding party with great success. To his

Private John Davies (20630), 15th Welsh, the husband of Hannah Davies of Brynheulog, Beulah, Cardiganshire. He died of wounds suffered during the trench raid on the Mortjelde Estaminet on 1 May 1917.

careful training beforehand and gallant leading during the raid much of the success is due.' (*London Gazette*, 26 July 1917.)

On the same day, at Arras, a B.E.2e, serial 2738 belonging to 12 Squadron was on patrol near Roeux when it came under attack by Manfred von Richthofen. The aircraft was piloted by Second Lieutenant David Evan Davies and had taken off from its base at Avesnes-le-Comte at around 7.45 pm along with another aircraft in order to support an artillery shoot. Von Richthofen had already shot down two aircraft that day before Davies fell under his guns and crashed to the ground, killing Davies and his observer, Second Lieutenant George Henry Rathbone of Montreal. Davies and Rathbone had become the fifty-first victims of von Richthofen (and Davies his fifth Welsh victim). His brother Lothar shot down the other B.E.2e. Von Richthofen shot down another aircraft soon afterwards, notching up his fifty-second 'kill'.

Davies, who was just 19 years old, was the son of Shem and Mary Davies of 175 Crogan Hill, Cadoxton, Barry. He was educated at Barry Grammar School, then at Cardiff University, graduating with a masters degree in science. He gained a post in the Civil Service and was posted to the West Indies, but in August 1914 returned home and enlisted in the Royal Welsh Fusiliers. He was later commissioned and volunteered to join the RFC, gaining his pilot's licence before joining 12 Squadron in 1917. Both Davies and Rathbone are commemorated on the Arras Flying Memorial.

On the following day one of the war's most epic 'secret' encounters occurred at sea, earning the award of the Victoria Cross for a New Zealander who was based at Milford Haven.

Lieutenant Commander William Edward Sanders was the son of Edward Helman Cook and Emma Jane Sanders of Alexander Street, Auckland. At the outbreak of war he was serving in the Mercantile Marine and at the end of 1915 joined the Royal Naval Reserve, serving as second mate of the *Hebbern Jan*. Sanders was a gifted sailor and was commissioned a sub lieutenant in the Royal Naval Reserve on 19 April 1916. He attended a gunnery course before being appointed to HMS *Sabrina* on 11 June 1916 and later served on HMS *Idaho*, before transferring to the Q-ship HMS *Helgoland Morley* as second-in-command on 6 September 1916. He received rapid promotion and was appointed to command another Q-ship, HMS *Prize*, on 5 February 1917, gaining the rank of lieutenant commander on 25 April 1917. *Prize* was the first vessel to be captured from the Germans by the Royal Navy during the war, hence the name, and was a three-masted schooner. Her purpose as a Q-ship was to lure U-boats to the surface and then attack them with its hidden guns, a method that proved highly successful. Sanders was billetted with his crew at Milford Haven and it was during one of his missions from there aboard *Prize* that he won his VC.

Lieutenant Commander William Edward Sanders, VC, DSO.

At midnight on 30 April 1917, HMS *Prize* was on patrol south of the Irish coast when she was sighted and engaged by the U-boat *U-93*. Pretending to abandon ship, a crew was launched in a boat and pulled clear of the *Prize*, which was then shelled for half an hour by *U-93*. The ship was hit many times, being holed at the waterline in three places and the engine room was set on fire, but Sanders bravely held his fire until the submarine moved in for the kill. When the enemy had closed to within 80 metres, Sanders gave the order to fire. The bewildered Germans turned their ship away to escape but their commander was knocked overboard by the body of one of his men who had been hit by a shell. When the submarine was 180 metres from *Prize*, another shell badly damaged her and she stopped and appeared to sink. The submarine commander and two others of his crew were picked up by *Prize*, whose crew were busy repairing the badly-damaged ship before she limped back to the safety of Kinsale. *U-93* was claimed as sunk, but her second-in-command managed to regain control and brought it safely home to Germany, where he told the story about HMS *Prize* and her tactics.

While *Prize* was in port the First Sea Lord, Admiral Sir John Jellicoe, offered Sanders command of a destroyer of his choosing, but Sanders preferred to remain where he was and returned to sea aboard the newly-repaired *Prize* in May 1917. His award of the VC was gazetted while he was at sea on his third patrol and due to the secrecy surrounding the Q-ships simply read: 'In recognition of his conspicuous gallantry, consummate coolness, and skill in command of one of H.M. Ships in action.' (*London Gazette*, 22 June 1917.)

On 14 August 1917 *Prize* was on her fourth patrol when she was spotted and identified by *U-43*, the commander of which had been briefed of her attack on *U-93*, which fired two torpedoes at her, blowing the Q-ship apart. No trace of Sanders or any of the crew of *Prize* was found. Sanders was posthumously awarded the DSO, which was presented to his father, along with his VC, by the Governor General of New Zealand in June 1918. As well as being commemorated on several memorials in his native New Zealand, Sanders is commemorated on the war memorial at Hamilton Terrace, Milford Haven and in St Katherine's Church in the town.

Deck hand John McClelland of 22 Greville Road, Milford Haven was awarded the DSM for the same action that saw Sanders gain his VC. McClelland was not aboard *Prize* when she was sunk on 14 August 1917 and died in 1972, aged 77.

While great gallantry was being performed in the Irish Sea, it was now the turn of the 1st RWF to re-enter the battle in France. The 7th Division had been in reserve at Courcelles during the Battle of Bullecourt in April and on 2 May moved into position to support a fresh assault on the village. The 62nd Division attacked the village at 3.45 am on 3 May but, after entering Bullecourt, was beaten back to their original position.

Deck-hand John McClelland, DSM (9629SA), Royal Naval Reserve, the son of William and Kate McClelland of 22 Greville Road, Milford.

The 1st RWF received its orders during the day for another attack, which would involve 22 Brigade. The 1st RWF would attack on the left and the Honourable Artillery Company (HAC) was to attack on the right and capture a trench running through the centre of the village, then the 20th Manchesters and 2nd Warwickshires would pass through and carry on the advance to the Hindenburg Line to the rear of the village. Zero hour was set at midnight on 3/4 May and the RWF began slowly to advance. A party of men under Second Lieutenant Soames entered the enemy trench on the right flank whilst on the left the battalion was held up by wire. The HAC had been slow to advance but on their right the Australians had not moved and at 2.30 am on 4 May the HAC retired, leaving a small party of men isolated in the village.

The 1st RWF held out, clinging on to posts in front of the German wire and at 3.10 am the Manchesters and Warwickshires passed through but also failed to gain their objectives. It was extremely dark, confusion reigned throughout the early hours and it was not until midday that some sort of order was brought about and all the dotted groups of men were found. Heavy fighting continued throughout the day and by nightfall the 1st RWF had lost four officers – Second Lieutenants Daniel Thomas Jones, Arthur Starkey Lewis, Alfred Montague Syrett and David Arthur Thomas – and thirty-eight men killed, with sixty-five wounded during the day.

Second Lieutenant David Arthur Thomas was the son of the Reverend David E. Thomas and Jennie Thomas of Brynllwyfen, Llansteffan. Prior to the war he had worked on the staff of Lloyds Bank in Llanelli and enlisted in the Welsh Regiment some time in 1915. He was commissioned from the Welsh into the RWF and joined the 1st RWF in France on 23 January 1917. Thomas was only 22 years old when he was killed at Bullecourt and is commemorated on the Arras Memorial. Second Lieutenant Arthur Starkey Lewis was another banker from Conway, who had worked in Canada prior to the war.

Second Lieutenant David Arthur Thomas, 1st RWF, of Llansteffan.

The battalion was relieved during the night, moving back to Courcelles until 13 May.

In the Mediterranean another naval disaster unfolded during the same day. The Cunard liner SS *Transylvania* was requisitioned by the Admiralty at the outbreak of war for use as a troopship. On 4 May 1917 she was sailing from Marseilles to Alexandria with a full complement of troops, escorted by the Japanese destroyers *Matsu* and *Sakaki*, when she was hit by a torpedo that was fired by the U-boat *U-63* while some 2 miles south of Cape Vado, near Savona, in the Gulf of Genoa. The *Matsu* came alongside to take off troops, but the Germans fired another torpedo, which hit *Transylvania* and sank her immediately, with the loss of 412 lives. Among the dead were twenty-one officers and men of the 5th RWF and twenty-eight men of the 5th Welsh, as well as several Welshmen from other units such as the Black Watch and RAMC.

Many of the bodies were recovered at Savona and buried two days later in a special plot in the town cemetery, while others are buried elsewhere in Italy, France, Monaco

The Savona Memorial, in front of which are several rows of graves of men killed during the sinking of the SS Transylvania.

and Spain. The body of one man, Private Herbert Pritchard Thomas (53067), 5th RWF, was recovered and buried in Oneglia Town Cemetery. Savona Town Cemetery contains eighty-five Commonwealth burials from the Great War, all but two of them casualties from the *Transylvania*, including nine of the Welsh contingent. Within the cemetery is the Savona Memorial, which commemorates a further 275 casualties who died when the *Transylvania* sank but whose graves are unknown.

Among the dead was Private George Church DCM (8377), 5th Welsh of 63 Daisy Street, Canton, Cardiff, who had been awarded the DCM for his gallantry at Givenchy with the 2nd Welsh on 25 January 1915: 'For conspicuous gallantry on the 25th January 1915, at Givenchy when, under a very heavy shell fire, he went forward to open communications with the Gloucestershire Regiment, and for gallant conduct and devotion to duty on many previous occasions in the firing line.' (*London Gazette*, 30 June 1915.) He is buried in Savona Town Cemetery.

The 40th (Bantam) Division was also on its way

The grave of Private George Church, DCM (8377), 5th Welsh, in Savona Town Cemetery.

248

back to the Arras battlefield after a brief rest following its ordeals at Villers-Plouich. On 4 May the Welsh 119 Brigade received orders to attack La Vacquerie; the 17th Welsh would attack alongside the 12th SWB, with the 19th RWF allotted the task of mopping-up.

At 11 pm the 17th Welsh moved off, led by guides from the 12th SWB, via a sunken road at the north end of Gouzeaucourt, ordered to mount an extensive two-hour raid on the enemy lines at La Vacquerie and retire at 1 am, the object being 'To inflict loss on the enemy, lower his morale, and secure prisoners and material'.

A rolling barrage preceded the assault and was well-aimed, apart from a few stray shells that fell short, causing some casualties. The Germans also retaliated with a barrage of high-explosive shells. Nonetheless, the first companies forced their way into the village, gaining all their objectives, clearing out the enemy and taking a number of prisoners from the 459th Infantry Regiment. At 1 am the raiders withdrew, collecting the wounded and bringing back as much booty as the men could carry.

The 17th Welsh had suffered very lightly, with one officer – Second Lieutenant J.H.T. Mathias – and twenty-three men wounded. Two were thought to have been killed and one missing, but these men had been taken prisoner by the Germans and survived. The 19th RWF lost nine men killed, while the 12th SWB had one officer – Captain Arthur Guy Osborn – and seventeen men killed.

Captain Osborn was a former schoolteacher and an original member of the Birmingham Pals and was commissioned in the 12th SWB on 19 July 1915. He is buried in Fins New British Cemetery, Sorel-le-Grand. He left behind a legacy of written material that is now held by the Imperial War Museum. Oddly, only one of the RWF men killed was a Welshman – Private Edward William Jones (29384) of Wrexham – while eleven of the SWB were Welsh.

At Ypres on the same day the 5th SWB of the 19th (Western) Division had its four companies working at Cavalry Barracks, Zillebeke Tramways and Sanctuary Wood.

At 9 am the Germans launched a heavy bombardment on their company at Cavalry Barracks, killing one officer – Lieutenant William Clifton Raymont – and twenty-one men, and wounding three others. The battalion war diary for the day recorded the names and numbers of all the dead, a very rare occurrence, especially during this period of the war. All the men are buried in Vlamertinghe Military Cemetery, except for one man, who is buried in Railway Dugouts Burial Ground (Transport Farm).

Among the dead was Private Joachim Bonner (14540), the son of Evan and Sarah Bonner of 3 Brewer Street, Aberystwyth. He lived with his uncle and worked as a miner at Pontycymmer prior to enlisting at Bridgend in the 5th SWB. He was 27 years old when he was killed on 6 May 1917 and is buried in Vlamertinghe Military Cemetery.

Private Joachim Bonner (14540), 5th SWB, of Aberystwyth.

Eight members of the 9th RWF were killed in similar circumstances here on 12 May when a series of shells crashed into their position; seven are buried side by side in Vlamertinghe and one is buried in Lijssenthoek after being evacuated to a CCS there. Among the casualties was Lance Corporal Thomas Latham (23399) of New Brighton Row, Northop Hall, Flintshire, a collier hewer prior to the war. He enlisted in the North Wales Pals Battalion on 22 February 1915 but had later been posted to the 9th RWF.

An officer of the 9th Welsh wrote of this period at Ypres, which the 19th Division was just about to leave:

The grave of Lance Corporal Thomas Latham (23399) of New Brighton Row, Northop Hall, Flintshire, in Vlamertinghe Military Cemetery.

> We moved by train which decanted us just short of Ypres. We marched through Ypres by night (leaving 'C' and 'D' Companies in Ypres) through the Lille Gate, past Shrapnel Corner, and relieved a battalion of the 23rd Division in close support of the Zillebeke sector of the line, having our headquarters at the Tuileries.
>
> So much has been written of Ypres that our opinions are hardly called for. Everyone who passed through the town formed his own opinion of the place, but all agree that it was an uncanny place. To us, on our move up to the line, though it was a bright moonlight night, it seemed a city of the dead. Not a soul was met in the streets and the only sound was the whine and crash of an occasional shell followed by a clatter of falling bricks and masonry. Troops we knew were billeted in the city, but none were about by night. In the moonlight the city had a peculiar beauty of its own. Shells by the thousand had fallen among its buildings and yet in the dim light little damage appeared on the exterior, but when one looked closely at the houses one saw that only shells remained – the interiors were gutted.
>
> By day the City looked gaunt and evil: from a distance the buildings seemed to be undamaged but, as one got closer, windows and doors showed charred and black interiors like the sunken eye-holes of a rotting corpse.

The worst days for Ypres were yet to come, but would have to wait until the Arras offensive drew to a close.

Another member of the Welsh aristocracy was killed during this period. Major John Burgh Talbot Leighton MC was born on 9 February 1892, the elder son of Sir Bryan Baldwyn Mawddwy Leighton, 9th Baronet, of Loton Park, Shrewsbury. He was

The ruins of Ypres before its total destruction.

educated at Eton and Sandhurst prior to being commissioned in the Scots Guards in 1912 and had gained his pilot's certificate prior to the outbreak of war, when he joined the RFC and flew to France in November 1914 with 6 Squadron. He fought in France for nine months before being posted to Egypt, gaining the Military Cross there while attached to 14 Squadron during a mission over Jifjaffa: 'For conspicuous gallantry and skill. He took photographs at a height of 200 feet while his Observer engaged the enemy with rifle fire. On other occasions he has done fine and gallant work.' (*London Gazette*, 30 May 1916.)

Leighton returned to England to take command of 62 Squadron and then 23 Squadron and died of wounds on 7 May 1917, aged 25. He is buried in Varennes Military Cemetery, the resting place of a large number of Welshmen from the 38th (Welsh) Division.

The 1st RWF was about to go back into action at Bullecourt. The battalion had been in camp at Courcelles since 6 May and on 11 May moved to another camp at Sapignies for company training. On 13

Major John Burgh Talbot Leighton, MC, 23 Squadron.

May the battalion was ordered to a position at Homme Mort in support of an assault by the 21st Manchesters on a German strongpoint called Red Patch. At 6 pm the battalion moved into position via the windmill; but while taking up their positions an SOS flare was sent up by the British troops in Bullecourt and a messenger was hurriedly sent to stop the battalion advancing any further. The assault on Red Patch had failed and so the 1st RWF was ordered to move forward to attempt to storm the position the following morning.

At 2.10 am on 14 May B and D companies, 1st RWF attacked Red Patch but were beaten off and ordered to reorganize before attempting a second assault at 4 am. This again failed, but several outposts were established from which a third assault was made under the cover of a Stokes mortar barrage at 6.15 am. Heavy fighting raged throughout the day, with HQ receiving numerous reports asking for ammunition and for more bombs and rifle grenades, and by about 4 pm the battalion was ordered to stand fast and be prepared to be relieved.

Three officers – Chaplain 4th Class Maurice Berkeley Peel, MC (RACD attached), and Second Lieutenants Richard Parry Evans and Lewis George Madley – and twenty-four men were killed during the day. Second Lieutenant Ralph Royds Brocklebank was among four officers and sixty-nine men wounded; Brocklebank died two days later, on 16 May.

The most heartfelt loss to the battalion was the chaplain, Reverend the Honourable Maurice Berkeley Peel MC, the son of Viscount Peel, Speaker of the House of Commons. He was born on 23 April 1873 and educated at Winchester and New College, Oxford. He had held a commission in the 4th Volunteer Battalion of the Queen's Royal West Surrey Regiment and was ordained in 1899, becoming curate of St Simon Zelotes, Bethnal Green, then vicar of Wrestlingworth and Eyeworth and Rector of St Paul's, Beckenham.

Reverend Peel volunteered to serve as a chaplain in France early in the war and was awarded his first MC while serving with the 7th Division at Festubert in 1915 when he fell wounded while leading an attack by the 1st RWF (*London Gazette*, 18 February 1915). He returned home and after recovery rejoined the battalion, gaining a second MC for gallantry during the capture of Puisieux:

Reverend the Honourable Maurice Berkeley Peel, MC.

> For conspicuous gallantry and devotion to duty. He went out to the advanced patrols with two stretcher bearers and succeeded in bringing in several wounded men. Later, he worked for thirty-six hours in front of the captured position and rescued many wounded under very heavy fire. (*London Gazette*, 17 April 1917.)

Peel was killed by a sniper at Bullecourt while attempting to rescue a wounded man on 14 May and three days later his body was recovered and buried in Quéant Road Cemetery, Buissy. Two of his cousins – Captain Alan Ralph Peel and Lieutenant Robert Lloyd Peel MC of Taliaris, Carmarthenshire – also fell, while his son, Major David Peel MC, was killed in Belgium while serving with the 2nd Irish Guards during the Second World War.

Another thirteen men from the 1st RWF were killed the following day after a series of German counter-attacks, with a further twenty-five men wounded and fifteen missing. The battalion was relieved on the morning of 16 May.

The 2nd SWB was about to return to the fray with the 29th Division. We last saw the battalion being relieved from Monchy-le-Preux on 25 April, and it had moved to various locations around Arras before moving back to Monchy on 15 May.

The battalion was ordered to attack the enemy trenches opposite their brigade front on 19 May, so the previous night moved forward through Orchard Trench to Chain Trench in preparation for the assault. This began at 9 pm, with the 1st Border Regiment on the left, the 1st Royal Dublin Fusiliers on the right and the 2nd SWB in the centre, with one company attached to the Borders. As the men climbed out of their trenches, the first line was immediately brought down by machine-gun fire and Captain Benjamin Jones Davies fell dead. The men charged on, gaining a foothold almost 100 metres in front, but were forced to go to ground due to fire from a machine gun to the left. Sergeant Albert White (24866) then rushed forward under a hail of bullets, accompanied by Lance Corporal Arthur William John Norvell (44571), in an attempt to put the machine gun out of action; but both were killed within a few feet of the gun.

The attack had now stalled and during the night the survivors crawled back to their own lines. Two officers – Captain Benjamin Jones Davies of Llandyssul and Second Lieutenant Vavasor Jones of Porthmadog – and thirty men were killed, one officer and twenty-six men wounded and twenty were missing.

Second Lieutenant Vavasor Jones was the son of Captain Morris and Ellen Jones of Ael-y-Gath, Porthmadog. He was educated at Porthmadog County School and had worked at the Alliance Assurance Company at Wrexham and at Southampton. He enlisted in the Inns of Court OTC in 1915 and was commissioned in the RWF on 5 September 1916.

Jones spent some time home on leave with his uncle at Bethesda before embarking for France in March 1917 and was 27 years old when he was killed at Monchy on 19 May 1917. He is buried in Dury Crucifix Cemetery.

Second Lieutenant Vavasor Jones, 2nd SWB, of Portmadoc.

Sergeant Albert White, who was killed while attempting to charge the machine gun that had stopped the assault, was posthumously awarded the Victoria Cross:

For most conspicuous bravery and devotion to duty. Realising during an attack that one of the enemy's machine guns, which had previously been located, would probably hold up the whole advance of his Company, Serjt. White, without the slightest hesitation and regardless of all personal danger, dashed ahead of his Company to capture the gun. When within a few yards of the gun he fell riddled with bullets, having thus willingly sacrificed his life in order that he might secure the success of the operations and the welfare of his comrades. (*London Gazette*, 27 June 1917.)

None of the men killed during the day have known graves apart from Vavasor Jones

The name of Sergeant Albert White, VC (24866), 2nd SWB, on the Arras Memorial.

and all are commemorated on the Arras Memorial. The battalion returned to Arras upon being relieved.

Back at Ypres, the 16th Welsh had moved from L Camp to Boesinghe on 19 May for a spell in the front lines. Their first four days were very quiet, with nothing of note happening except for the discovery of the body of Private John William Cooper (55420) in a shell hole full of water behind the front line on 22 May. He was buried in Ferme-Olivier. However, this peaceful spell did not last long as on the following day, 23 May, the Germans shelled the positions held by the 16th Welsh, killing seven men and wounding eight more, with one dying the following day; the worst casualties suffered in a single day by the battalion since Mametz Wood the previous year. The seven men are buried side-by-side in Ferme-Olivier, while the man who died the following day – Private William George Christopher (54893) – is buried in Mendinghem Military Cemetery.

Back at Arras the 2nd RWF was about to re-enter the fray, having enjoyed a brief rest at Adinfer and Moyenneville. On 15 May the battalion moved into positions near St. Leger before taking over positions in the Hindenburg Line at Croisilles on 19 May. On 22 May the battalion was relieved and took part in a parade in which a large number of gallantry awards were presented to members of the battalion and attended a sports event at Achiet-le-Petit on 24 May, the battalion winning the tug-of-war.

The battalion moved back into the front line soon after in preparation for an assault on a section of the Hindenburg Support Line between Plum Lane and Oldenburg Lane at Fontaine-lès-Croisilles. The battalion attacked at 1.55 pm on 27 May on a two-company frontage following a creeping barrage and managed to reach their objectives on the left before being enfiladed by a large party of Germans who had pushed through a gap between the 2nd RWF and the Cameronians. Suffering heavy casualties and in danger of being isolated, the men withdrew following the issuing of orders from an unknown person and by 2.45 pm were back in their own front line.

The survivors were quickly reorganized in case of a German counter-attack but the Germans were beaten off by artillery fire. The 2nd RWF had suffered heavy casualties: five officers – Lieutenants Thomas Rothsey Connings, MC and Edward Leslie Orme, and Second Lieutenants Thomas Edward George Davies, William Owen Lewis and Thomas Benjamin Williams – and sixty-eight men were killed; four officers and seventy-six men were wounded and a large number were missing. The battalion was relieved the following day and on 31 May went into rest billets at Bailleulval.

Second Lieutenant Thomas Edward George Davies, known as 'Teg' Davies by his fellow officers, was one of the battalion's real characters. He was born on 15 January 1887, the son of Reverend and Mrs Thomas Davies of Mumbles. He was educated at Cardiff University and became a schoolteacher in Slough. He applied for a commission as early as 31 December 1914 but was rejected and enlisted in the Army Service Corps as a motor driver. He married Lilian Martha Brickwood in 1915 and they had a child, born on 29 January 1916. He applied again for a commission and was posted to the 2nd RWF on 29 August 1916. Davies was 30 years old when he was killed on 27 May and is buried in Bailleul Road East Cemetery, St. Laurent-Blangy. Captain Dunn recalled in *The War the Infantry Knew* an occasion during October 1916 when the battalion held its last formal mess of the war:

Private William Davies MM (5540), 2nd RWF. The son of Thomas and Hannah Davies of Penybont Cottage, Llanwenog, he was killed on 21 May 1917.

One of the few incidents recalled about it is 'Teg' Davies' hearty voice bridging a silence that fell upon the generally talkative company at dinner, to say: 'I'm a bastard Saxon myself'. The C.O. was shocked; but Teg was an unconscious droll. Shortly before this he poured out the whole of Higginson's last pint of champagne, drank it off, drew his hand along his lips and said, 'I don't like these light French wines; I prefer roodge veen [vin rouge] and grenadine to that.'

Another Welshman killed during this time was far from famous, but his image became immortalized when he was selected to aid the Royal Naval Division's Recruiting, featuring prominently in one of their posters. Able Seaman Simon Owen James (Wales Z/881) was born in Cwmavon on 22 April 1895, the son of Samuel and Rachel James of Preswylfa. He enlisted on 1 May 1915 and was posted overseas with a draft for the MEF on 5 October 1915. He joined C Company of the Anson Battalion, Royal Naval Division, and went to France with the division in 1916. James was killed in action while bringing up supplies to the front on 26 May 1917 and was buried by his comrades beside the

A famous Royal Naval Division recruiting poster, featuring the image of Able Seaman Simon Owen James of Cwmavon.

road. His grave was later lost and he is commemorated on the Arras Memorial. The poster in due course became amongst the most famous of all the Royal Naval Division recruiting posters used during the war.

The Battle of Arras was now over, officially lasting from 9 April to 16 May 1917. For now the main attention would move further north, to the Ypres Salient, but Arras would see fighting again before the year's end.

While the Battle of Arras was drawing to a close, another Welshman became the twelfth man of Welsh descent or of a Welsh unit to be executed during the war. Private George Watkins (8139) was an army reservist and had served with the 2nd Welsh since the outbreak of war. He had seen some severe fighting and was transferred to the 13th Welsh at some time. He had obviously had enough of war when he deserted his battalion in January 1917. Watkins was apprehended after three months on the run and was tried by court martial for desertion. Watkins was sentenced to death by firing squad and was executed on 15 May 1917. He is buried in Ferme-Olivier Cemetery. On that same day his comrades from the 13th Welsh were celebrating the award of several gallantry medals to men who had taken part in a successful trench raid in the previous month.

The grave of Private George Watkins (8139), 13th Welsh, at Ferme Olivier Cemetery.

Chapter 17

The Battle of Messines

The Messines to Wytschaete Ridge lies midway between Armentières and Ypres and was a tactically important location due to its prominent views over the battlefield. Its capture was necessary before any offensive could be launched further north in the Ypres Salient against the Passchendaele Ridge. Messines Ridge divides the valleys of the Lys and the Yser rivers and links to a ridge that stretches from Wytschaete north-eastwards to the Ypres to Menin road and northwards, via Passchendaele, to Staden.

The village of Messines, situated on the southern spur of the ridge, commands a wide view of the valley of the Lys, which allowed the Germans to enfilade the British lines south, while Wytschaete, situated on the highest part of the ridge, commanded a view of the town of Ypres and the entire British position in the Ypres Salient.

The ridge was defended by a trench system that ran along the western foot in a curve from the Lys opposite Frelinghien, almost to the Menin Road, then turned north-west past Hooge and Wieltje, with a second defence system following the crest of the ridge. There were also two diagonal trenches: the Oosttaverne Line, which lay slightly east of the village of Oosttaverne; and the Warneton Line, crossing the Lys at Warneton, running parallel with the Oosttaverne Line a mile east of it.

Although the Germans were well entrenched with concrete emplacements and pill boxes supporting the trenches, the British had been hard at work beneath them for months. Tunnelling companies of the Royal Engineers, Canadian, British, Australian and New Zealand had laid twenty-six mines with 454 tons of ammonal explosive beneath tactical German positions along the ridge. Of these, one was lost to German counter-mining and another was abandoned after it proved impractical to work.

The RFC had also been hard at work, photographing and mapping the German defences and a large force had been built up for the assault.

During May, the 4th Australian, 11th (Northern) and 24th British divisions were moved north from Arras to become reserve divisions for the formations of the Second Army that were preparing to attack Messines Ridge. To support the infantry, seventy-two tanks were brought into the area under conditions of great secrecy.

The 25th Division was to attack the front between the Wulverghem to Messines road and the Wulverghem to Wytschaete road, facing 1,100 metres of the German front line. The 47th (2nd London) Division was to attack with two brigades along either side of the Ypres to Comines Canal. The 19th (Western) Division was to attack the front bordered on the south by the Vierstraat to Wytschaete road and on the north by the

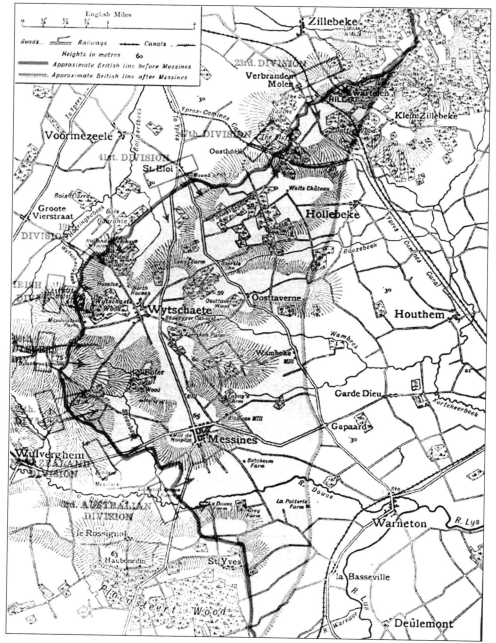

The lines before and after the Battle of Messines, June 1917.

Diependaal Beek. The 16th (Irish) Division was to attack on their right and the 41st Division on the left of the 19th Division. The Welsh units involved included the 9th RWF, 5th SWB and 9th Welsh of the 19th Division, the 6th SWB of the 25th Division and the 4th RWF of the 47th Division.

The orders for the assault by the 19th Division contained the following essential points: 58 Brigade on the right and 56 Brigade on the left were to capture the three first objectives, the red, blue and green lines; 57 Brigade was then to pass through and capture the fourth objective, the black line, and then to push forward an outpost line. The divisional assault was to be covered by an artillery barrage and then an indirect machine-gun barrage was provided for the first time.

58 Brigade was to attack with the 6th Wilts on the right and the 9th RWF on the left, who were to capture the red line; the 9th Welsh on the right and the 9th Cheshires on the left were then to pass through and capture the blue and green lines. 56 Brigade was to attack with the 7th Lancs on the right and the 7th LNLs on the left to capture the red line, with the 7th East Lancs on the right and 7th South Lancs on the left to capture the blue and green lines.

Once the green line had been captured the four battalions of 57 Brigade were to attack and capture the black line, advancing from right to left – 10th Worcesters, 8th Gloucesters, 10th Warwicks and 8th North Staffords – and were then to push forward outposts. Once the positions had been attained, the Royal Engineers and 5th SWB were to follow up the attack and construct strongpoints and consolidate the newly captured positions.

During the night of 6/7 June all the units moved forward to their assembly positions and by 2.45 am were ready to go. Zero hour was at 3.10 am and the signal to go would be the blowing of nineteen of the underground mines. On the front facing the 19th Division three mines lay beneath the Hollandscheschuur Salient, to destroy a position named the Nag's Nose.

At zero hour the ground beneath the men trembled and shook as the Royal Engineers fired the nineteen mines, creating the largest ever man made explosions [to date] and the earth beneath the German strongpoints burst into the air in a sheet of flame that looked like water spouts to the stunned onlookers. Men could see the gruesome sight of bodies being hurled into the air among the debris as they rose from their trenches to advance under their artillery and machine-gun barrage.

The German survivors were, quite understandably, traumatized by what had happened and put up little opposition to the assaulting troops. The infantry of the 19th Division got across No Man's Land easily and were shocked at the devastation they encountered when they reached the remains of the German lines. Lieutenant St. Helier Evans of the 9th Welsh wrote:

We went over the top at 3.30. Three large mines on our immediate front, and there were others, were blown. In one a whole company of Huns went up. Cheers. We were to have taken the 3rd and 4th lines, but it was all too simple, we just walked into them, thanks to the guns blasting every inch. This most intense barrage cleared the way and what Huns were left ran up to us with their hands up. They are too demoralized to make a big counter attack, just yet, the first twenty-four hours is the critical time. Hope they will not attempt it. May be moving further up this evening. Most of the Hun guns are drawn back and what they have left are firing at extreme range.

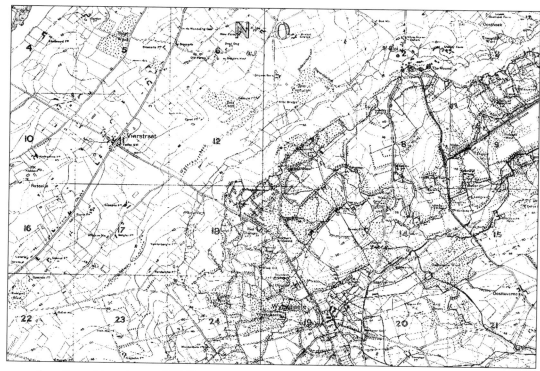

A section of trench map 28SW2-5A, Wytschaete, showing the Hollandscheschuur Salient, the apex of which is in square N12, the objective for the 19th Division.

With limited opposition, by 5.32 am the blue line had been captured and consolidation of it was under way; however, the advance to the green line saw the assaulting troops walk into their own barrage. They were hurriedly recalled and waited until the barrage had moved forward before advancing again and by 7.30 am that line had also been captured and a portion of the black line was also taken.

Reports sent back from the assaulting troops confirmed that the Germans were in such a state of shock that they either surrendered or, those who were in a fit state to do so, ran away. The final advance made by 57 Brigade moved through and by 10.15 am had occupied the black and mauve line, which ran roughly along the eastern edge of Oosttaverne Wood.

Because the assault had been so successful, Corps HQ decided to push further forward to take advantage of the situation and issued orders to advance at 3.10 pm and capture Oosttaverne Village and the Oosttaverne Line, from Polka Estaminet to about 600 metres east of Odonto Trench. The attack was hurriedly arranged and orders sent forward to the front line troops for 56 and 58 brigades to relieve 57 Brigade and concentrate north west of Oosttaverne Wood before carrying out the assault. This was carried out successfully and the division made contact with the 3rd Australian Division on the right and the 24th Division on the left.

The day had been a complete success, but from around 5 pm the front-line troops began suffering casualties from their own artillery barrage, which began falling short, and were forced to withdraw to the Odonto Line for a while before moving forward to occupy their original line later in the evening. Patrols were sent out during the night and succeeded in capturing a number of prisoners and by midday on 8 June the first atage of the Battle of Messines was over. The offensive ended on 14 June.

The 19th Division lost 51 officers and 1,358 men killed, wounded and missing and had captured 1,253 prisoners, fourteen artillery pieces, fourteen machine guns and thirty-six trench mortars.

The 9th RWF lost sixteen men killed, the 5th SWB eight men killed and the 9th Welsh twenty men killed. Among the dead of the 9th RWF was a former coal miner, Private George Pullen (200708), the son of Margaret Ellen Gibbons of 19 Tower Hill, Acrefair, Ruabon, who had been awarded the DCM while serving at Loos with the 4th RWF. He was the second man from Ruabon to gain the DCM and was honoured by a presentation in Cefn Drill Hall while home on sick leave in November 1915 after being gassed. He is commemorated on the Menin Gate Memorial. The citation for his DCM reads:

> For conspicuous gallantry on the 25th of September 1915, at Loos when, on his own initiative, he successfully carried a telephone wire to the German trenches, and in returning brought in some prisoners. Later he assisted to bring in a wounded man under very heavy shell fire. He was ultimately wounded when close to the trenches. (*London Gazette*, 16 November 1915.)

Another of the fallen was Private Thomas Milton Mason (23127), the son of Joseph and Annie Mason of 86 Quarella Road, Bridgend. He lived at Cilgerran prior to the war and enlisted in London in the 15th RWF, for some reason under the name of John Davies. He was later transferred to the 9th RWF and moved to France with the battalion in July 1915. He was 31 years old when he was killed at Messines on 7 June 1917 and is buried in Croonaert Chapel Cemetery alongside six of his fallen comrades. His CO wrote to his parents:

Private Thomas Milton Mason (23127), 9th RWF.

The grave of Private Thomas Milton Mason at Croonaert Chapel Cemetery. The grave is named for John Davies, his alias, but his correct name is engraved at the top of the headstone.

Your son was a very brave soldier always cheerful and willing and very popular with officers and men. You have the sincere sympathy of everyone here in your sad bereavement. It may console you to know that during his period as a stretcher bearer he saved many lives by his fearless conduct.

Among the fallen of the 5th SWB was Private William Owen Thomas (29616), the son of David and Hetty Thomas of Penanteryn, Blaenporth. He married Elizabeth Jones of Glandwr, Beulah while home on leave in 1916. He was 25 years old when he was killed on 7 June 1917 and is buried in Wytschaete Military Cemetery. His widow Elizabeth later married David T. Owen and the couple resided at Furze Hill, Cefneithin.

Private William Owen Thomas (29616), 5th SWB, of Blaenporth.

Among the fallen of the 9th Welsh was Lance Corporal William Henry Davies (10058), the son of William James and Margaret Davies of 7 Philip Street, Robert's Town, Aberdare. Davies had seen eight years' active service, having served in India and Egypt, and went to France with the 2nd Welsh in August 1914. He was wounded on 28 March 1915 and spent eleven months in Chelsea Hospital before being posted to the 9th Welsh. He was 27 years old when he was killed on 7 June 1917 and is buried in Klein-Vierstraat British Cemetery.

Three Welshmen were killed during the attack by the New Zealand division during the day: Corporal Mathew Michael Lane (71863), Auckland Regiment, of Pontypool; Private Lloyd George Williams

Lance Corporal William Henry Davies (10058), 9th Welsh, of Robertstown.

The ruins of Messines after the battle. The mound to the right is the ruins of the church, the cellars of which were once well-known by Adolf Hitler, who had been stationed there earlier in the war.

'The Ruins of Messines Church in December 1914', a painting by Adolf Hitler.

(24090), Auckland Regiment, of Llanrwst; and Rifleman Robert Williams (30416), New Zealand Rifle Brigade, of Port Dinorwic. Two Welshmen were killed with the Australians: Private Evan Archibald Davies (1481), 35th Battalion, of Aberdare; and Private Robert Saunders Williams (1580), 52nd Battalion, of Pwllheli. (Corporal Lane was originally buried by his comrades in a battlefield grave halfway between the village of Messines and a position named Hill 3. His grave was never located after the war, so he is commemorated alongside his adopted countrymen on the Messines Ridge (New Zealand) Memorial.)

At least three Welsh airmen were killed during the battle while carrying out reconnaissance work in the area.

Second Lieutenant Gwynonfryn Albert Haydn Davies was the son of Elias and Annie Davies of 59 Newall Street, Abertillery. He was commissioned in the Monmouth Regiment on 13 December 1915 and in August 1916 transferred to 45 Squadron, RFC. On 7 June 1917 Davies was an observer in the Sopwith 1½ Strutter serial A8296 piloted

263

by Second Lieutenant A.E.J. Dobson when it crashed on a road west of Deûlémont. They were both originally reported as missing but were later found to have been killed in the crash. Davies is commemorated on the Arras Flying Services Memorial.

Second Lieutenant Archibald Vincent Shirley was born on 17 May 1887, the son of Walter Rayner Shirley of Leckwith, Cardiff. He was educated at Rugby and studied for a degree in jurisprudence at Exeter College, Oxford prior to the war. He was among the first officers commissioned in the Welsh Horse Yeomanry after its formation and served in Gallipoli and Egypt until volunteering to serve with the RFC in October 1916. He trained as a pilot and was posted to 66 Squadron, Royal Flying Corps, which flew the Sopwith Scout. Shirley was killed in aerial combat over Roulers on 8 June 1917 when his Scout collided with another flown by Second Lieutenant Robertson and both came crashing to earth. Both men were

Second Lieutenant Archibald Vincent Shirley, 66 Squadron, Royal Flying Corps.

buried at Roulers by the Germans, but their graves were later lost and both men are commemorated on the Arras Flying Services Memorial.

The Arras Flying Services Memorial, within Faubourg d'Amiens Cemetery, Arras.

Lieutenant Bernard Sanderson Marshall MC was born on 24 November 1894, the son of Henry John and Helen Marshall of Lynwood, Mumbles. He was educated at Abingdon School and studied for his engineering degree in London prior to volunteering to serve with the Royal Engineers at the outbreak of war. Marshall was commissioned in the 5th SWB in December 1914 and served with the battalion in France, winning an MC on 13 May 1916: 'For gallant conduct and devotion to duty when consolidating a crater. Though badly hit in the arm he carried on till exhausted. He had his wound dressed and returned to superintend his working parties.' (*London Gazette*, 25 July 1916.)

Upon recovering from his wounds, he transferred to the Royal Flying Corps and, after gaining his flying certificate, went back to France to join 20 Squadron, RFC. He had only been back in France for a month when he went out on patrol on 7 June and attacked a flight of enemy aircraft. After a brief fight, Marshall was hit in the head by shrapnel and crashed his aircraft into a canal near Lille. His observer, Second Airman C.P. Lloyd, was thrown clear of the wreckage and captured by the Germans. Marshall has no known grave and is commemorated on the Arras Flying Services Memorial.

With Messines Ridge captured, the stage was set for the next phase of the offensive, the Third Battle of Ypres on 7 June had witnessed an action that saw another Welshman gain the Victoria Cross.

Seaman William Williams was born in Amlwch, Anglesey on 5 October 1917 and served with the Royal Naval Reserve aboard HMS *Pargust*. *Pargust* was one of the Q-ships, a former collier that had been requisitioned by the Admiralty and converted for use as a decoy in anti-submarine work. She was assigned to special service duty and was based at Queenstown, in southern Ireland, for anti-submarine duties in the South-West Approaches.

On 7 June 1917 *Pargust* was on patrol west of Valentia Island when she encountered U-boat *UC-29*, which had already sunk three ships in the area. The submarine fired a torpedo that struck *Pargust* in her engine room. Her captain, Commander Gordon Campbell, used this as a ploy to tempt the submarine to surface and sink *Pargust* by using its deck gun, as was normal practice. His crew was rushed on deck, masquerading as a panic-stricken Merchant Navy crew, to lead the Germans into believing they were facing no opposition; and the submarine duly surfaced and closed in for the kill.

At around 8.36 am *Pargust's* crew pulled the canvas covers off her gun and opened fire on the unsuspecting submarine, damaging the conning tower, and the Germans

Seaman William Williams VC, of Amlwch, Anglesey.

began to abandon ship. Within four minutes the submarine had sunk with the loss of all but two of her crew. *Pargust* was disabled but remained afloat and was towed back to Queenstown.

William Williams had already been awarded the Distinguished Service Medal (DSM) for his gallantry during an earlier operation and was awarded the Victoria Cross for his gallantry following the torpedoing of *UC-29*:

> The King has been graciously pleased to approve of the award of the following honours, decorations and medals to Officers and men for services in action with enemy submarines:- To receive the Victoria Cross. Lieut. Ronald Neil Stuart, D.S.O., R.N.R.. Sea. William Williams, R.N.R., O.N. 6224A. Lieutenant Stuart and Seaman Williams were selected by the officers and ship's company respectively of one of H.M. Ships to receive the Victoria Cross under Rule 13 of the Royal Warrant dated the 29th January, 1856. (*London Gazette*, 20 July 1917.)

Williams was awarded a Bar to his DSM just a few months later. He died in Holyhead on 22 October 1965 and is buried in Amlwch. His medals are displayed at the National Museum of Wales, Cardiff.

Chapter 18

The Prelude to the
Third Battle of Ypres

By the time the Battle of Arras had drawn to an end the French had become increasingly disheartened following the failure of the Aisne Champagne offensives to live up to expectations. The United States declared war on Germany on 6 April 1917 as a consequence of Germany's unrestricted submarine policy and the Zimmerman telegram; but it would be almost a year before they would be in a position to send troops to France.

An offensive at Ypres had been planned in conjunction with another along the Flanders coast in order to capture the ports of Ostend and Zeebrugge, important bases for enemy submarines, but this second offensive depended on success at Ypres. The front on which the offensive was to be delivered extended from Dêulémont on the River Lys, northwards to beyond Steenstraat, a distance of over 15 miles, and was to be carried out in conjunction with the French, who relieved the Belgian army on the front from Boesinghe to Nordschoete, some 3 miles north of Steenstraat.

The front was too large to be controlled by one army commander, so was divided into two sections: the Fifth Army under General Sir Hubert Gough, was allotted half the front from the Zillebeke to Zandvoorde road in the south to Boesinghe in the north, while the Second Army, under General Plumer, had the southern half.

Several Welsh units were to take place in the opening assault: the 38th (Welsh) Division was to attack from the positions it had held along the Ypres Canal for the last twelve months, while to their left flank the Guards Division, with the Welsh Guards, had been allotted the front between them and the French.

While the Battle of Messines was under way, the troops in the Salient took advantage of the diversion of German attention provided by the battle. The 15th Welsh opened this preparatory work on the night of 25/26 May when they began digging and wiring a new trench about 250 metres long, 140 metres in advance of their original positions and just 45 metres from the enemy trenches at Caesar's Nose.

All the battalions of the 38th (Welsh) Division continued this work over the coming days, toiling in No Man's Land under extreme danger and enduring a constant flow of casualties, mostly from hostile artillery fire. On one particularly unpleasant day the 14th RWF lost eight men killed on 24 June while holding the line on the Canal Bank; the 16th Welsh lost two men killed; and the 19th Welsh the loss of two officers – Captain Arthur Ernest Evans and Second Lieutenant Howell Morgan Williams – who

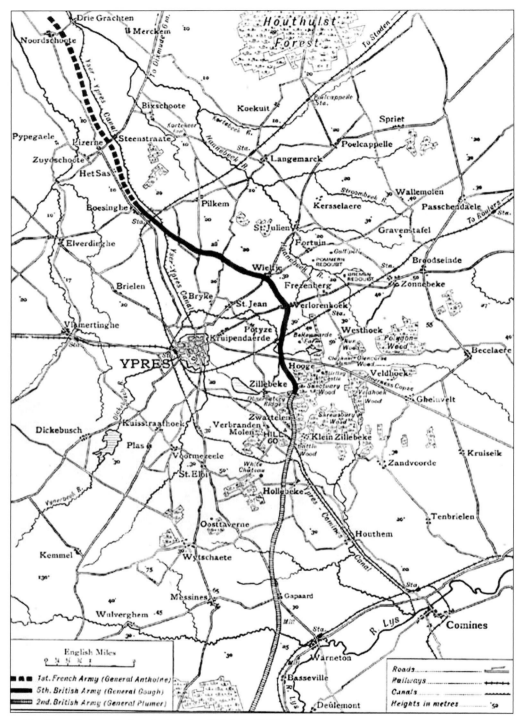

The Ypres Salient before the battle of 31 July 1917.

were killed while having tea in their dugout when it was hit by a shell.

Evans was the son of Henry and Marie Evans of 6 Rosehill Terrace, Swansea. He was well known throughout south Wales, having worked for the borough surveyor's office, he had worked at Llandeilo, Swansea and Cardiff and was a Freeman of the latter. He returned home from South America to enlist in the army and joined the Welsh Regiment in May 1915, serving under Major Richard Lloyd George before embarking for France with the 19th Welsh in December 1915. He was 31 years old and is buried in Bard Cottage Cemetery, alongside Williams.

Captain Arthur Ernest Evans, 19th Welsh, of Swansea.

In June 1917 the division left the salient, handing over their portion of the line to the 29th Division, and entrained from Poperinghe for St. Omer, then marching to billets at Tatinghem in the St. Hilaire area in northern France. Here, a replica of the trenches and strongpoints to be attacked was laid out on the ground between Enquin and Liettres and the brigades were drilled over these in their respective roles. Opportunity was also taken to practise the machine-gun barrage and this practice found to be extremely useful as none of the machine-gunners had as yet done any firing for extended bursts.

While the division was undergoing its period of training in preparation for the forthcoming offensive, other Welsh units were continuously at work on other sectors of the line, with the 9th RWF, 5th SWB and 9th Welsh of the 19th Division consolidating at Messines. The busiest of the Welsh units following the Battle of Messines appears to have been the 10th RWF, which had moved back into the Hindenburg Line, at Monchy on 12 June after two weeks at Arras. The battalion suffered a continual drain on its manpower: eleven men were killed on 14 June when 76 Brigade attacked the German positions facing them; six men on 15 June during a German counter-attack; fourteen on 16 June, when the battalion was shelled by the Germans; seven men died on 17 June during another failed attack; and two officers – Lieutenants David Ethelstone Davies and Leonard Patrick

Lieutenant David Ethelstone Davies, 10th RWF, of Dolgelly.

Vernon MC – and six men were killed on 18 June during heavy shelling of the battalion's positions.

Lieutenant David Ethelstone Davies was born on 11 April 1894, the son of Reverend John Davies and Edith Annie Davies of Llanelltyd Vicarage, Dolgellau, Merionethshire. He was educated at St John's School, Leatherhead, Llandovery and at Ystradmeurig and was about to begin theology at Lampeter College in preparation to enter the Ministry when war broke out. He was commissioned in the RWF on 3 June 1915 and promoted to lieutenant on 11 April 1916. He trained at Kinmel Park before joining the 10th RWF on the Somme. He was 23 years old when he was killed on 18 June 1917 and is buried in Feuchy Chapel British Cemetery, Wancourt.

Lieutenant Leonard Patrick Vernon, MC was born on 23 September 1894, the son of Captain William Henry and Elizabeth Vernon of Wrexham. He was educated at Grove Park School and was a bank clerk prior to joining the Manchester University OTC in 1913. At the outbreak of war he enlisted in the 20th (Public Schools) Battalion, Royal Fusiliers. He was commissioned in his father's regiment, the RWF, on 14 August 1915 and in March 1916 was posted to the 10th RWF. Vernon was awarded the MC for gallantry on the Somme in August 1916: 'For conspicuous gallantry during operations. Previous to a bombardment by us of an uncaptured portion of the enemy's trench he went around and warned back our men who were lying in shell holes near the enemy parapet.' (*London Gazette*, 20 October 1916.) He was 22 years old when he was killed while holding an advanced outpost on 18 June 1917. Vernon is buried in Feuchy Chapel British Cemetery, Wancourt.

Lieutenant Leonard Patrick Vernon MC, 10th RWF, of Wrexham.

The battalion was relieved at Monchy on the morning of 19 June, marched back to billets at Arras and spent the remainder of the month training. The 1st Monmouths were also in the Arras sector with the 46th (North Midland) Division and on 27 June lost an officer – Second Lieutenant Arthur Richards – and five men killed.

The 2nd SWB had withdrawn from the Monchy sector on 2 June 1917 and moved with the remainder of the 29th Division to Candas before moving to Atheux on 11 June. On 26 June the battalion entrained with the division for Poperinghe, arriving on the following day and taking up billets in some woods. The division, as we have already seen, relieved the 38th (Welsh) Division in the Canal Bank Sector in order to allow it to undergo its training for the forthcoming offensive.

On 2 July the 2nd SWB moved into the Canal Bank line for the first time, having already lost three men killed by shellfire and on 4 July lost an officer – Second Lieutenant John Howard Davies – and five men killed due to shelling throughout the day. Among the men killed was Private David Idwal James

Private David Idwal James (29194), 2nd SWB, of Llanelli.

(29194), the son of David and Mary Ann James of 19 Greenway Street, Llanelli. He was killed when a German shell hit a machine-gun pit that he was sharing with Privates Pitt and Morgan on 4 July. He was 20 years old and is buried at Bard Cottage Cemetery. His brother Brynmor had died just four months earlier.

On the same day the 6th SWB, the pioneer battalion to the 25th Division, was at work to the south of Ypres. The battalion suffered some casualties at Messines but had escaped the battle relatively lightly. On 4 July it was working in positions at Snipe and Toad trenches when the positions were shelled by the Germans. Eight men were killed, seven of whom are buried in Belgian Battery Corner Cemetery, while one man reached a CCS at Lijssenthoek alive, only to die during the afternoon.

On 10 July a son of the Welsh politician Sir Charles Leyshon Dillwyn-Venables-Llewellyn, 2nd Baronet, was killed while serving with the Coldstream Guards. Captain John Lister Dillwyn-Venables-Llewellyn was born on 20 March 1897, the eldest son of Sir Charles Leyshon Dillwyn-Venables-Llewellyn and Katharine Minna Venables of Llysdinam, Newbridge-on-Wye, Radnorshire. He was commissioned in the Coldstream Guards from the Royal Military College, Sandhurst on 13 January 1915. He was killed in action on 10 July 1917 while serving with the 3rd Battalion, Grenadier Guards. He was just 20 years old and is buried in Canada Farm Cemetery.

Further north the 1st Division moved to positions near Coxyde, where it began preparing to take part in Operation Hush, an offensive that was to be launched along the Flanders coast in conjunction with the offensive in the Ypres Salient. A Welshman from Dryslwyn, Gunner Sidney Perkins (124268) of 325 Siege Battery, Royal Garrison Artillery, wrote in his memoirs of the move to the coast:

Now we were moved north to the coast for the Yser attack on July 10th 1917. There was a coast road one dune from the beach. It was so very peaceful. With a second big dune to protect them, the fields were 'with verdure clad'. There were tales of Germans and Belgians fishing on their respective banks of the Yser. There were any number of massive and apparently safe dugouts left by the French and/or Belgians. These turned out to be terribly lousy so that a grain of sand became a louse when we thought that a louse was a grain of sand. I was given a tip for dealing with the nits in the seams of my trousers. For the only time in my life, I kept a cigarette going to burn these nits all down the seam. To my horror I found that I had an

The grave of Private John Ranger (13506), 1st SWB, at Coxyde Military Cemetery.

An aerial photograph of the sector of the canal at Boesinghe held by the Welsh Guards in July 1917. Note the battered state of the ground, even before the main battle.

array of holes down my trouser legs. The word got round and even the officers grinned at the sight.

Among the many Welshmen here attached to the 1st Division were the 1st SWB, 2nd Welsh and 6th Welsh. Within days of the move, on 13 July the 1st SWB lost four men killed by a German shell, all of whom are buried in Coxyde Military Cemetery. The battalion had three casualties over the preceding days; but this was the worst so far in this new sector.

Back at Ypres, the Guards Division, to the left of the 38th (Welsh) Division, had been listening to the Messines fighting while on parade, with a backdrop of music by the band of the Coldstream Guards! The Guards battalions also moved out of the line to prepare for their part in the opening assault and, like the 38th (Welsh) Division, trained on a scale model of the battle area in front of them. On 13 July the battalion was in bivouac on a crossroads by De Wippe Cabaret when the area was shelled by the Germans, killing three men and mortally wounding another, who died later that day. On 15 July the Welsh Guards took over the line in front of Boesinghe Château from near where they were to attack and were visited there by the Prince of Wales. Three more men were killed by shellfire while moving into position and another ten were wounded.

After an intensive period of training, which included carrying out forced marches from Tatinghem to Bléquin and then from Fiefs to Witternesse, the 38th (Welsh) Division began to make its way back to the Salient, first marching to billets near

Steenbecque on 16 July, then on to Hazebrouck, Proven, St. Sixtie and finally to G Camp near Poperinghe, when they moved back into their frontline positions.

While the Welsh troops due to take part in the opening of the Third Battle of Ypres were now in place and ready, back at Messines the 9th Welsh of the 19th Division suffered a bad day on 19 July. The battalion had moved into the line on the previous day to relieve the 9th Cheshires, who had been attacked by the Germans and driven from their positions at Junction Buildings. On 19 July two platoons of the 9th Welsh counter-attacked and drove the Germans back out of the position but were themselves counter-attacked, losing two officers – Second Lieutenants Victor Roberts and Stanley Francis Salmon – and thirteen men killed, ten men wounded and one missing.

Second Lieutenant Victor Roberts, 9th Welsh, from Llangefni. (Archives and Special Collections, Bangor University)

Second Lieutenant Victor Roberts was born on 24 May 1897, the son of Evan Morris and Anne Roberts of Metropolitan Bank House, Llangefni, Anglesey. He was educated at Llangefni and was studying at the University of Bangor when he enlisted in the army in January 1916. He had only recently joined the 9th Welsh and was killed while attempting to rescue Second Lieutenant Salmon, who was from Swansea. Roberts was 20 years old and

A row of mostly Welsh Regiment graves, exhumed from the Messines area and reburied in Voormezeele Enclosure No. 3 in October 1919.

was buried where he fell but in 1919 his body was exhumed and he was reburied in Voormezeele Enclosure No. 3, together with several others of the Welsh Regiment. His OC Major John Angel Gibbs wrote to his father:

Dear Mr. Roberts,
I regret to inform you that on the night of the 18th/19th inst. your son, Victor, while taking part in an attack by his Company is missing. He was last seen going towards another officer who had fallen, and nothing has been heard of him since. It is quite possible that Victor has been taken prisoner, in which case some little time will elapse before we get further news of him.

He was a great favourite with us all, and we are hoping for the best. During the action he behaved splendidly, and his action in going across to find out what happened to the other officer was especially gallant. Had he not done this he would most probably have returned safely to our lines. I shall not fail to inform you if we get any further information. I wish to express our deepest sympathy with you in your hour of trial, and remain,

Yours truly,
J.A. Gibbs, Major.

For the remainder of the month casualties continued on a daily basis for all the Welsh units at the front, interspersed with tragic events to mount such as the deaths of ten men and the wounding of eleven more of the 13th Welsh on 21 July when their positions were shelled by the Germans; but the forthcoming offensive would see the scale of casualties rising to a level not seen since the Battle of the Somme.

The scene was now set for one of the most notorious battles of the war: the Third Battle of Ypres, better known, simply, as Passchendaele.

Chapter 19

Disaster at Sea

W hile the war on the Western Front was still raging, life at sea for the Royal Navy was relatively peaceful. Since the stalemate of the Battle of Jutland the previous year, the Royal Navy had for the most part forced the German High Seas Fleet out of the North Sea. Many Welshmen were still serving at sea, a large number of them aboard the modern *St Vincent*-class dreadnought battleship HMS *Vanguard*, which was based at Scapa Flow.

Vanguard was assigned to the 4th Battle Cruiser Squadron at Jutland and had fired forty-two shells at the German light cruiser SMS *Wiesbaden*, helping to send her to the bottom. She had taken an active part in patrolling the North Sea during the ensuing months and her crew was regarded as well trained. During the morning of 9 July 1917 she was at anchor in Scapa Flow, with her crew on exercise, practising routines for abandoning ship in an emergency. The remainder of the day passed quietly, then, just before midnight, a catastrophic explosion inside the ship shattered the tranquillity of the night, tearing *Vanguard* apart and sending her to the bottom with the loss of more than 800 lives. A subsequent court of inquiry deemed that the explosion had probably been caused by an unnoticed stokehold fire heating cordite stored against an adjacent bulkhead in one of the two magazines that served the amidships gun turrets, P and Q.

Shipwright 1st Class Reginald George Thomas (344454), of Pembroke Dock, who was 31 years old when killed during the explosion of HMS Vanguard.

Among those lost were at least eighteen Welsh seamen, mostly of the Royal Naval Volunteer Reserve: David Bacon of Newport, John Henry Curtis of Rhymney, Herbert Dixon of Pembroke Dock, John Samuel Evans of Llwynhendy, Reginald Jenkins Evans of Llandyssul, George Raymond Gough of Abersychan, Gerard Younghusband Harrison of Burton, Pembs, William John Hopkins of Swansea, Edward Frank Hunter of Cathays, Daniel John Jones of Swansea, William Henry Long of Cardiff, Fred Nutt, Alfred Owen of Milford Haven, Frank Albert Poole of Cardiff, Wilfred Edward Stevens of Cardiff, Frank Ernest Tadman of Newport, Reginald George Thomas of Pembroke Dock and Owen Wynne Williams of Holyhead.

Able Seaman William John Hopkin (Z1240), of Fforestfach, Swansea. He was 23 years old when he was killed during the explosion of HMS Vanguard.

In terms of loss of life, the destruction of the *Vanguard* remains the most devastating accidental explosion in the history of Britain and one of the worst accidental losses of the Royal Navy.

In the Salonika theatre of operations, just a week after the loss of the *Vanguard*, a Welsh nurse with a strong maritime connection became the first Welsh female casualty of the disease-ridden campaign there. Florence Missouri Caton was born aboard her father's ship *Missouri* in 1876 and was brought up in the family home at 1 Bryn Draw Terrace, Wrexham. She trained as a nurse and volunteered to serve overseas with the Scottish Women's Hospital, sailing for the Mediterranean on 10 September 1915. She had spent a short period of time as a prisoner when the hospital where she worked was overrun by Austrian troops but had been released before embarking for the 4th Serbian Hospital in Salonika. Caton died there on 15 July 1917 following an operation for appendicitis; she is buried in Salonika (Lembet Road) Military Cemetery.

Conclusion

The first twenty-two months of the war had proved very costly for Wales, with at least 25,306 Welshmen and women and men of Welsh units having died up to 30 July 1917. The period between January 1916 and 30 July 1917, the day prior to the launching of the Third Battle of Ypres, had seen twice as many Welsh casualties as the preceding sixteen months of the war. The coming sixteen months of war would prove to be just as disastrous in terms of loss of life.

Breaking down the casualties into units, so far as I can calculate from the sources, the following Welsh servicemen and women fell in the period from the declaration of war until 30 July 1917, the eve of the Third Battle of Ypres:

Australian Forces	261
Belgian Forces (Belgians died and buried in Wales)	3
British Army	22,644
Royal Navy, RNR, RNVR and RM	1,098
British Air Services (RFC and RNAS)	110
Canadian Forces	429
Civilians (inc. Nursing staff)	49
French Forces	1
Indian Forces	19
Mercantile Marine	606
New Zealand Forces	51
South African Forces (and other African)	37

The battles of the Somme, Arras and Messines had taken a heavy toll on all the Welsh units that took part in them; however, the rapid expansion of the army had seen them relatively easily reinforced by fit and reasonably well-trained men. The war had ground on throughout the period leading up to the opening of the Third Battle of Ypres and had seen no real gains made by the allies or, indeed, by the Germans. The Western Front was still in a state of stalemate; however, new theatres of war had been opened up in Egypt, Palestine, Salonika and Mesopotamia.

The introduction of the Australians and South Africans into the Western Front theatre had helped add steel to the allied cause, and the two frontline Welsh divisions serving there were now battle hardened.

The Third Battle of Ypres would see the spilling of much more Welsh blood, while the remainder of the war until final victory and the Armistice on 11 November 1918 would stretch the allies to the limit. Welsh troops would continue to play an important role with their actions at Ypres and in the final offensives of 1918 would prove their mettle much as the earlier actions of 1914 had done, yet are now largely forgotten.

The continuing stories of the Welsh troops will be covered in the third and final volume of *Welsh at War, Through Mud to Victory: Third Ypres and the 1918 Offensives*. This final book will also cover the commemoration of the fallen in Wales, as well as casualty statistics and the fate of the Welsh units after the Armistice. All three volumes should be read in conjunction to follow the history of the Welsh at war during the Great War.

Bibliography

Anon, *A Short History of the 19th (Western) Division*

Adams, Bernard, *Nothing of Importance. A Record of Eight Months at the Front with a Welsh Battalion, October 1915 to June 1916*

Atkinson, Captain C.T., *History of the South Wales Borderers 1914–1918*

Blunden, Edmund, *Undertones of War*

Churchill Dunn, Dr James, DSO, MC, DCM, *The War the Infantry Knew*

Clayton, Charles Pritchard, *The Hungry One*

Depree, Major General H.D., *38th (Welsh) and 33rd Divisions in the Last Five Weeks of the Great War*

Dudley Ward, Major Charles Humble, *History of the Welsh Guards*

—, *History of the 53rd (Welsh) Division*

—, *Regimental Records of the Royal Welch Fusiliers, Vol III, 1914–1918. France and Flanders*

—, *Regimental Records of the Royal Welch Fusiliers, Vol IV, 1915–1918. Turkey – Bulgaria – Austria*

—, *The 74th (Yeomanry) Division in Syria and France*

Gaffney, Angela, *Aftermath: Remembering the Great War in Wales*

Gillon, Captain Stair, *Story of the 29th Division*

Graves, Robert, *Goodbye To All That*

Griffith, Wyn, *Up to Mametz*

Henshaw, Trevor, *The Sky Their Battlefield*

Hughes, Colin, *Mametz: Lloyd George's Welsh Army at the Battle of the Somme*

James, Brigadier E.A., *British Regiments 1914–1918*

Marden, Major General Sir Thomas O., *History of the Welch Regiment, Part Two, 1914–1918*

Munby, Lieutenant Colonel J.E., *History of the 38th (Welsh) Division*

Richards, Frank, DCM, MM, *Old Soldiers Never Die*

Putkowski, Julian and Sykes, Julian, *Shot at Dawn: Executions in World War One by Authority of the British Army Act*

Sassoon, Siegfried, *Memoires of a Fox-Hunting Man*

—, *Memoires of an Infantry Officer*

St Helier Evans, Lieutenant M., *Going Across: With the 9th Welsh in the Butterfly Division*

Various, *De Ruvigny's Roll of Honour*

Wyrall, Everard, *History of the 19th (Western) Division*

Battlefield Guides

Major and Mrs Holt's Battlefield Guide to Gallipoli
Major and Mrs Holt's Battlefield Guide to the Somme
Major and Mrs Holt's Battlefield Guide to the Western Front (North)
Major and Mrs Holt's Battlefield Guide to the Western Front (South)
Major and Mrs Holt's Battlefield Guide to Ypres

Primary Sources

Unit War Diaries (various), The National Archives, Series WO95
Welsh Newspaper Archives (various), The National Library of Wales,
Cymru1914.org

Newspapers and Other Periodicals

Aberdare Leader
Brecon and Radnor Express
Brecon County Times
Cambrian Daily Leader
Denbighshire Free Press
Glamorgan Gazette
London Gazette
Tenby and County News
The Welshman
Western Telegraph
Yr Adsain

Online Sources

Ancestry
Findmypast
National Archives

Index

Castlemartyr, Ireland, 235
Casualty Clearing Station, 43, 70, 99, 118, 159, 215
Caterpillar Wood, 99, 101–102, 104–105, 113, 120, 153
Caton, Florence Missouri (Nurse), 276
Cauchy-À-La-Tour, 97
Cavalry (Various), 12, 41–2, 44, 126, 140, 197, 200, 205, 208, 226
Cavalry Barracks, Ypres, 249
Cazalet, Edward (2nd Lt) Welsh Guards, 163
Cefneithin, 262
Cemaes, Anglesey, 114
Cemeteries,
  Abbeville Communal Cemetery Extension, 182, 233
  AIF Burial Ground, Flers, 186, 213
  Albert Communal Cemetery Extension, 125
  Amara War Cemetery, 205, 207
  Ancre British Cemetery, 183
  Auchel Communal Cemetery, 14
  Aveluy Communal Cemetery Extension, 95
  Bailleul Road East Cemetery, St. Laurent-Blangy, 255
  Bapaume Post Military Cemetery, Albert, 97
  Bard Cottage Cemetery, 221, 269, 271
  Bassonia Cemetery, 207
  Bécourt Military Cemetery, 95, 146
  Belgian Battery Corner Cemetery, 271
  Bernafay Wood British Cemetery, Montauban, 186
  Bois-Carré British Cemetery, Thélus, Pas-De-Calais, 231
  Boulogne Eastern Cemetery, 183
  Brandhoek Military Cemetery, 48, 49
  Bronfay Farm Military Cemetery, 188
  Bulls Road Cemetery, Flers, 179
  Cabaret-Rouge British Cemetery, Souchez, 57–8, 240
  Cairo War Memorial Cemetery, 44
  Cambrin Churchyard Extension, 14, 21
  Canada Farm Cemetery, 271
  Canadian Cemetery No. 2, Neuville-St. Vaast, 240
  Carnoy Military Cemetery, 109, 112
  Caterpillar Valley Cemetery, Longueval, 111, 118, 153, 159
  Châlons-En-Champagne Cimetiére De L'Est, 241
  Chocques Military Cemetery, 151
  Combles German Cemetery, 189
  Couin New British Cemetery, 218
  Coxyde Military Cemetery, 271–2
  Croonaert Chapel Cemetery, 261
  Dantzig Alley British Cemetery, Mametz, 83, 99, 115, 118
  Danygraig Cemetery, Swansea, 64
  Douchy-Les-Ayette British Cemetery, 220
  Dury Crucifix Cemetery, 240, 253
  Essex Farm Cemetery, 174
  Ferme-Olivier Cemetery, 213, 221, 230–1, 254, 256
  Feuchy Chapel British Cemetery, Wancourt, 243, 270
  Fifteen Ravine Cemetery, Villers-Plouich, 242
  Fins New British Cemetery, Sorel-Le-Grand, 242, 249
  Flatiron Copse Cemetery, 106, 114, 117–18, 120, 175
  Foncquevillers Military Cemetery, 74
  Fromelles (Pheasant Wood) Military Cemetery, 133
  Givenchy-En-Gohelle Canadian Cemetery, Souchez, 236
  Gordon Dump Cemetery, 146
  Grove Town Cemetery, Méaulte, 187
  Guards' Cemetery, Combles, 189, 219
  Guards Cemetery, Windy Corner, Cuinchy, 19–20
  Guards' Cemetery, Lesboeufs, 170
  Hamburg War Cemetery, 234
  Hamel Military Cemetery, Beaumont Hamel, 143
  Heilly Station Cemetery, Méricourt-L'Abbé, 92, 118, 125, 130
  Karasouli Military Cemetery, 194, 203
  Kilscoran Church of Ireland Churchyard, 182
  Kirkpatrick-Juxta Parish Churchyard, 214
  Klein-Vierstraat British Cemetery, 262
  Le Crotoy Communal Cemetery, 186
  Le Touret Military Cemetery, Richebourg-L'Avoué, 14
  Les Baraques Military Cemetery, Sangatte, 22
  Lijssenthoek Military Cemetery, 250, 271
  Lindenhoek Chalet Military Cemetery, 50
  Longueval Road Cemetery, 178

Jamieson, George Robert (Pte, 63668) 24th RWF, 237
Jarman, Harry Love (Capt) 7th SWB), 203
Jeffreys, William Stanley Goldsmith (Lt) 13th Welsh, 116
Jellicoe, Sir John (Adml), 61–3, 67, 246
Jenkins, Edward John (Pte, 63794) 24th RWF, 237
Jenkins, John Charles (2nd Lt) Welsh Guards, 220
Jennings, William David, MM (Cpl, 1595) 6th Welsh, 143
Jervis, Robert (Pte, 17869) 13th RWF, 13–14
Jesty, George (Pte, 2473) Welsh Guards, 169
Joffre, Joseph (Gen), 60, 202, 229
John Copse, Somme, 180, 183–4
John, Harold Thomas (2nd Lt) 8th Welsh, 205
John, James Henry (Rifleman, S/1027) 11th Rifle Brigade, 12
John, John James (Trooper, 4837) Pembroke Yeomanry, 38–9
John, Thomas (CSM, 23554) 16th Welsh, 106
John, Thomas Harold (2nd Lt) 8th Welsh, 205
John, Trevor (Seaman) Royal Navy, 66–7
Johns, Bernard Digby (Capt) 10th RWF, 16
Johnson, Harry Hall (Capt) 13th Welsh, 109
Johnson, Robert Inglelow Bradshaw (Lt Col) 8th Welsh, 30
Jones, Arthur Mervyn (Lt) Welsh Guards, 187
Jones, Basil Gordon Dawes, MC (Lt) 2nd Welsh, 180
Jones, Bryan John (Lt Col) 19th RWF, 59
Jones, Charles (Cpl, 35) Denbighshire Yeomanry, 39
Jones, Charles Godfrey (Maj) 11th Welsh, 194
Jones, Christopher (Pte, 2022) 6th Welsh, 143
Jones, Daniel John (Able Seaman, Z/177) Royal Naval Volunteer Reserve, 275
Jones, Daniel Thomas (2nd Lt) 1st RWF, 247
Jones, David (Capt) 10th Welsh, 116
Jones, David (Pte, 22579) 15th RWF, 122
Jones, David (Pte, 31421) 9th RWF, 182
Jones, Edward (Pte, 16775) 13th RWF, 100
Jones, Edward William (Pte, 29384) 19th RWF, 249
Jones, Edwin Tudor (Capt) 2nd RWF, 156
Jones, Ernest Kerrison (Capt) 9th RWF, 89–90
Jones, Evelyn Llewelyn Hustler (2nd Lt) 5th RWF, 227

Jones, Frank Aubrey, CMG, DSO (Lt Col) 4th SAEF, 124
Jones, George William (2nd Lt) 6th SWB, 52–3
Jones, Gilbert Evan Wyndham (Pte, 4530), 11th Battalion AIF, 146
Jones, Griffith David (Pte, 53638) 1st RWF, 230
Jones, Harold Vivian (Lt) 13th RWF, 115
Jones, Henry Myrddin (2nd Lt) 10th RWF, 184
Jones, Herbert Francis (2nd Lt) 10th Welsh, 116
Jones, Hugh (2nd Lt) 2nd RWF, 156
Jones, James (Pte, 20026) 15th Welsh, 116–17
Jones, James Ira Thomas (Capt) Royal Flying Corps, 233
Jones, James Mayberry (Pte, 26556) 2nd SWB, 143
Jones, John (Cpl, 20027) 15th Welsh, 116–17
Jones, John (Pte, 1880) 30th AIF, 135
Jones, John (Pte, 28428) 19th RWF, 238
Jones, John Thomas (Pte, 5893) 2/7th Warwicks, 133
Jones, John Wilfred (2nd Lt) 9th Welsh, 185
Jones, Owen Gwilym (2nd Lt) 7th RWF, 227
Jones, Raymond John, MB (2nd Lt) RAMC, 112
Jones, Reginald William Bamford (L.Cpl, 29519) 1st RWF, 155
Jones, Samuel (L.Cpl, 16623) 10th Welsh, 51
Jones, Stanley (Lt) 14th RWF, 216
Jones, Thomas (Pte, 14141) 5th SWB, 20
Jones, Thomas (Pte, 3273) 5th RWF, 198
Jones, Thomas Otto (Lt) 16th Welsh, 106
Jones, Vavasor (2nd Lt) 2nd SWB, 253–4
Jones, William (Cpl) 4th Welsh, 228
Jones, William (Sgt, 13664) 9th RWF, 91–2
Jordan, River and Valley, 222
Jutland (Battle of), 61–9, 275
Karoa, SS, 46
Karran, John Bowler (2nd Lt) 2nd SWB, 75–6
Kelk, Arthur Frederick Hastings, MC (2nd Lt) 14th Welsh, 220–1
Kelly, Edward Rupert (2nd Lt) 9th Welsh, 88
Kelsey-Fry, William (Capt) RAMC (Attached 2nd RWF), 155
Kemmel, 50–1
Kenfig Hill, 209
Khan Yunus, Egypt, 199
Khedive, 37
King Constantine (Greece), 33, 190
King Feisal, 42

Neath, 51, 63, 67, 92, 182, 184
Needle Trench, 169
Nekrews, David (Pte, 17367) 2nd RWF, 14
Nestor, HMS, 63
Neuve Chapelle, 20
Neuville-St. Vaast, 15, 52, 240
Neuvillette, 99
Neuville-Vitasse, 232
Neuvilly Trench, 232
Nevitt, Albert, MC (2nd Lt) 10th RWF, 50
New Quay, Ceredigion, 140, 215–16
New Zealand Expeditionary Force (NZEF), 8, 37, 44, 160, 197, 200, 226, 257, 262–3, 277
Newbridge-On-Wye, 57, 271
Newfoundland Park, 75, 77
Newfoundland Regiment, 77, 212
Newlyn, Walter Tessier (2nd Lt) 19th Welsh, 116
Newport, Monmouthshire, 21, 35, 74, 92, 143, 151, 161, 231, 238, 240, 242, 275
Newport, Pembrokeshire, 166
Newton, Vivian Frederick (2nd Lt) 1st RWF, 85
Newtown, Montgomery, 234
Nicholas, Thomas Price (Pte, 33673) 2nd Welsh, 150
Nicholls, Reginald Mortimer (Lt) 2nd Welsh, 130
Nightingale, William Bryant (2nd Lt) 2nd SWB, 240
Nile, River, 40–2
Nivelle Offensive, 229, 241
Nivelle, Robert (Gen), 202, 229–30
Nomad, HMS, 64
Noreuil, 234
Norfolk, 8, 38
Norfolk Regiment (Norfolks), 199, 208
North Staffordshire Regiment (North Staffs), 90–1, 259
Northampton, 8, 239
North Wales, SS, 182
Northcote, Ernest Percy (Pte, 3300) 6th Welsh, 143
Northcott, Jack (Cpl, 1997), 11th Battalion AIF, 146
Northop, Northop Hall, 198, 250
Norvell, Arthur William John (L.Cpl, 44571) 2nd SWB, 253
Nursery Sector, 11
Nutt, Fred (Musician, RMB/1605) Royal Navy, 275

O'Brien, Patrick (Cpl, 17337) 14th Welsh, 55
Officer Training Corps (OTC), 16, 215, 253, 270
O.G. Lines, 144, 146, 148, 153
Ogmore Vale, 143
Oil/Oilfields, 24, 25, 39
Olympic, SS, 203
O'Neil, Anthony (Pte, 15134) 1st SWB, 51
Onslaught, HMS, 65
Oosttaverne, Village/Wood, 257
Oppenheimer, Sir Bernard (Baronet), 97
Orchard, William Henry (Pte, 38191) 1st Welsh, 35
Orkneys, 69
Orme, Edward Leslie (Lt) 2nd RWF, 254
Ormsby, Harold Sydney (Capt) 14th RWF, 215
Osborn, Arthur Guy (Capt) 12th SWB, 249
Osborne-Jones, Noel (2nd Lt) 15th RWF, 52
Osmond, Richard (L.Cpl, 19345) 10th Welsh, 221
Ostend, 267
Oswestry, 203, 239
Overton, 216
Ovillers, 78–80, 88–9, 95, 102, 108, 127, 130, 145, 182
Owen, Alfred (Stoker, 2427S) Royal Navy, 275
Owen, Goronwy (Capt) 15th RWF, 51–2
Owen, John Morris (Capt) 2nd RWF, 14, 239
Owen, Thomas Oliver (Pte, 37787) 10th RWF, 218
Owens, Charles Percy (Maj) 2nd SWB, 237
Oxford University, 16, 27–8, 50, 89, 95, 97, 157, 179, 252, 264
Paddison, William Edward (Pte, 17741) 14th Welsh, 13
Padgett, William Reginald (2nd Lt) 10th Welsh, 54
Page, Henry (2nd Lt) 10th RWF, 139
Panteg, 161
Pargust, HMS, 265–6
Parker, William Arnott (Sgt, 291) Welsh Guards, 220
Parry, Alun (Pte, 8679) 4th RWF, 153
Parry, Joseph William (Pte, 5287) 2nd RWF, 14
Parry, Robert (2nd Lt) 7th RWF, 227
Passchendaele, 257, 274
Payne, Oswald John (Pte, 25457) 17th Welsh, 242
Peake Wood, 79, 148